T0340021

EAST ASIA
HISTORY, POLITICS, SOCIOLOGY, CULTURE

Edited by
Edward Beauchamp
University of Hawaii

A ROUTLEDGE SERIES

EAST ASIA: HISTORY, POLITICS, SOCIOLOGY, CULTURE

EDWARD BEAUCHAMP, General Editor

Liberal Rights and Political Culture

Envisioning Democracy in China

Zhenghuan Zhou

Routledge
New York & London

Published in 2005 by
Routledge
270 Madison Avenue
New York, NY 10016
www.routledge-ny.com

Published in Great Britain by
Routledge
2 Park Square
Milton Park, Abingdon
Oxon OX14 4RN
www.routledge.co.uk

Library of Congress Cataloging-in-Publication Data
  Zhou, Zhenghuan
    Liberal Rights and Political Culture: Envisioning Democracy in China

ISBN10: 0-415-97184-5 (hbk)
ISBN10: 0-415-88249-4 (pbk)

ISBN13: 978-0-415-97184-3 (hbk)
ISBN13: 978-0-415-88249-1 (pbk)

To Junling, Ian, and Noah

Contents

Preface and Acknowledgments

This book is based on my doctoral thesis, which was completed a little over four years ago. While portions of it, especially the last chapter, underwent major revision, I kept most of the chapters intact. This is largely because I am convinced now, as I was then, that the main arguments I have advanced in the study remain valid. My original intention was to rewrite the second chapter in a way that succinctly captures the key features of the political culture concept without delving too much into history. After rereading it, I decided to make only minor changes, as I realized that such a historical retrieval is rarely seen in existing literature and may be used for pedagogical purposes in undergraduate and graduate courses. Like perhaps most, if not all authors, I wish I had additional time to polish the final product that is to be presented to the reader till I am completely satisfied with it. This is of course unrealistic. We all have a series of deadlines to beat just as we are beating life's own deadline. Had I had a few extra months, I would have attempted a more substantive study of the idea of embedded rights, one that combines some of the enduring Confucian moral categories with the ideas and values underlying the liberal concept of rights. Seen from a different perspective, this sense of incompleteness is good because it gives us incentive to continue.

A word of explanation about notation is necessary since I have referenced a large number of sources in Chinese. First, unless indicated, all translations from Chinese into English are mine. I have given translated article and book titles only in endnotes for easy reference, but in the Bibliography I have listed article and book titles in *Pinyin* followed by translations in parentheses. Second, the names of authors are provided in the following way: Authors published in Chinese are quoted with their family names first and authors published in English are quoted with their family names last. There are those who write in English yet choose to have their family names listed first. I respect their choice and list their names the way they prefer. Third, the names of Chinese publishers are furnished only in *Pinyin* with no translation attached, but I have used their English names when and where they are available.

In researching for and writing the book, I have incurred tremendous debts to various individuals. I thank, first of all, my dissertation advisors: Dan Sabia, for his intellectual vigor and encouragement; William Kreml, for his insights and continued support; James Myers, for the research funding he provided for my field trip to China; Robert Angel, for his incisive comments on my dissertation; and Dean Kinzley, for his graciously serving on my dissertation committee.

I would like also to thank my editor at Routledge, Kimberly Guinta, for her patience and understanding.

A number of people provided generous support during my field trip in China. I greatly appreciate their help. I want to especially thank those who assisted me in the questionnaire survey process and those who made the interviews a much easier undertaking.

Finally, I thank my wife Junling whose integrity and unfailing love are an inexhaustible source of comfort and inspiration. Our children Ian and Noah have also cheered me on, not by what they do or say, but merely by being around. They have experienced just as much hardship and joy as I have through the entire process. To them this work is dedicated.

Chapter One
Introduction

This study, broadly speaking, is about political theory, political culture and democratic development in China. Its main concern is about how the three topics relate to one another, and about how this relationship may further our understanding of political theory in terms of both form and substance. It addresses the questions of how Western political theory, or certain parts of it, may be applied to provide guidance for democratic development in a non-Western political and cultural context, and of how this application may in turn help extend the limits of our conception of political theory. More specifically, it focuses on how the liberal concept of rights might fare in the Chinese political and cultural setting, and how this concept, viewed from a comparative perspective, might be able to offer a guiding hand in defining the nature and direction of democratic change in China.

There are two theses, one primary and the other secondary, that the study explores. The primary thesis is that the liberal concept of rights as a moral and political doctrine presuppposes and is grounded in a particular culture or shared way of relating. In China, where such a cultural grounding is radically lacking, the liberal notion of rights as we know it would be unlikely to provide a viable language for articulating visions of political change *vis-à-vis* democratization. The secondary thesis is that for a rights-based argument to bear on democratic change, a redescription of liberal rights is required. This redescription should take into account some of the most important characteristics that structure the Chinese politico-cultural tradition.

THE STATUS OF POLITICAL THEORY

The controversy over the nature and uses of political theory which was initiated more than four decades ago is widely known. While it should be clear by now that the case stacked by the behavioralists against political theory has been overstated and normative reflections on politics remain profoundly relevant to contemporary political analysis, the future path of political theory is once again uncertain. The traditional mode of theorizing, which carried the day up till the first half of the last century, has shown some weaknesses. In order to sustain vigorous growth, it must meet challenges from both inside and outside the field. Under the circumstances, there is a perceived need among political theorists to reappraise and renovate political theory.

In fact, the task of reappraising and renovating has been under way for some time now.[1] But except for a few notable cases in which synthetic efforts did broaden our understanding of some of the important theoretical issues and accordingly our conception of political theory,[2] reappraisal and renovation have seldom ventured beyond the familiar path set by the traditional mode of theorizing in terms of method as well as substance. It may be argued that this is not particularly unfortunate because political theory has its own logic, form and subject matter. To defend the identity of political theory solely on this ground, however, seems less than convincing, especially when we are confronted with an increasingly pluralistic world. This kind of regressive theorizing—regressive in the sense of staying within the confines of the much studied "canon"—is at least incomplete. One is tempted to say that it perhaps requires a progressive mode of thinking to return political theory to "its rightful role." This can be conceived as attempts to venture into the unfamiliar and unknown, whether it is new issue, new vocabulary, or new method, and these attempts may be a first step to the restructuring of a dynamic political theory.

The reconstruction of a dynamic political theory may be construed on two broad levels. The first is substantive and the second methodical. On the substantive level, political theory should and can reach beyond the much interpreted "canon," suspend received judgments on frequently written topics, and embrace rarely touched issues that are typically considered to lie beyond the purview of mainstream political theory. As the world becomes increasingly interdependent, moreover, there is perhaps another need to go across the borderline of Western political theory and delve into non-Western political traditions for additional sources and novel perspectives. In the past, non-Western political thought has remained largely a domain of international relations or comparative politics. Mainstream political theorists have had little incentive to explore it for various reasons. But even if we suppose—and here I risk assuming too much—that non-Western political thought were of little relevance to the West for addressing its urgent concerns, an adequate understanding of the former could better equip Western political theory to furnish a model or models of political change, as the language of human rights is attempting to do, for developing countries. This model-building is valuable because, among other things, it may help political theorists establish a special perspective from which to assess and hone their own arguments.[3]

On the methodical level, the way in which political theory has been studied is also in need of modification. Traditionally, political theory relies on interpretation as the basic method of inquiry. Although empirical observation was from the very beginning an integral part of political theorizing, it seems to have become less and less pertinent to normative thinking in the last few centuries. The introduction of the modern method of data-collecting and explanation has provided an additional pattern of thinking which may prove useful to political theorists. It is commonly acknowledged that being empirical does not mean being quantifiable. If ideas and values cannot be quantified because of their constitutive and meaning-laden nature, they certainly can be investigated in an empirical manner—empirical in the sense of being observable and intersubjectively verifiable. Empirical investigation is important insofar as it enables political theory to purge itself of assumptions having little bearing on political reality, to find out how the meaning of a given idea or value changes under different circumstances and over time, and to search for a pluralistic way of looking at things which helps us minimize the possibility of misjudgment.

Of course, these two levels of consideration do not exhaust the ways in which a dynamic political theory may be reconstructed. But they do constitute a metatheoretical starting point for this study. Put another way, this study is epistemologically predicated on the assumption that political theory should stretch its limits as far as possible to synthesize the unfamiliar and unknown, in terms of both substance and method. Only by doing so can it revitalize itself and recapture the crowning moment it enjoyed in the past. Built on this assumption, this study can be read as a modest attempt to experiment with such limits. It proceeds by reexamining one of the crucial notions in modern Western political thought, namely the liberal concept of rights. This reexamination will be conducted from a comparative perspective, with a view to applying it to a different political and cultural context.

RIGHTS AND LIBERAL DEMOCRACY

The importance of the notion of rights to liberal democracy and, for that matter, to Western politics in general is too fundamental to ignore. A brief review of modern political history, Anglo-American modern political history in particular, reveals a distinctive pattern of struggles for the individual's personal and political rights. This pattern has been well documented not only in the works of political theorists such as Hobbes, Locke, Rousseau, Paine, and Jefferson; it was also expressed through political actions such as those leading to the English Petition of Right and the American Bill of Rights. Contemporary political theorists and jurisprudents alike have observed that the notion of rights lies at the core of the Western political tradition.[4] To paraphrase d'Entreves, it may be said that the entire tradition of Western political thought is natural rights writ large.[5] Bentham's assertion that natural rights are "nonsense upon stilts" has never been the orthodox political tradition, particularly in England and the United States.[6] In both a chronological and an intellectual sense, later arguments for rights, including the United Nations' Universal Declaration of Human Rights and the two subsequent Covenants on rights, are all beneficiaries of this Western, largely Anglo-American, legacy.[7]

To say that the idea of rights as we know it today is largely an Anglo-American political heritage is to consider liberalism. It is generally agreed that liberalism has been a permanent structure of Western thought at least since the Reformation. But disagreements abound as to the character of liberalism. To be sure, as both defenders and critics have pointed out, pure liberalism has never actually occurred in history. One may be more justified in saying that it consists only of a set of principles and ideals which aim at creating a haven for the exercise of individual freedom.[8] If the nature of liberalism indeed lies in its fundamental concern with the individual's personal and political freedom—in the sense that she or he has an autonomous sphere of activity insulated from the interference of society and government—it is by no means clear what form or forms it takes in pursuit of that goal. There are as many types of liberalism as there are political theorists. Contemporary liberalism is just as colorful as its predecessors in the seventeenth and eighteenth centuries. We now have the liberalism of rights, of equality, of neutrality, of fear, of self-expression, and of humanism.[9]

Despite this blinding colorfulness, a commonality running through different understandings of liberalism is unmistakable. It is the notion of rights. The liberal concept of rights is so entrenched in universal terms that it is virtually impossible to talk about liberal politics without talking about individual rights. It should not come as a surprise, therefore, that this notion has become so deeply embedded in the language and practice of liberalism. Neither should it come as a surprise that, when democracy found its way into the modern era, it became an intimate partner in a seemingly perfect marriage which we come to call liberal democracy.

The alliance between liberalism and democracy is a historical, not logical, one. But it is so taken for granted that few seem to believe now that democracy could survive a day without individual rights. With possible exceptions, democracy is held, implicitly and explicitly, to be synonymous with a particular arrangement of rights in a political system. The extent to which that system is democratic is measured at least in part by its record for protecting and promoting individual rights.[10] Thus, Robert Dahl, a leading democratic theorist, develops seven institutional guarantees for democracy (or what he calls polyarchy) on the basis of his familiarity with Anglo-American liberal democracy. These guarantees are nothing more than a set of rights. It is these rights, according to Dahl, that define a given political system as being *actually,* not *nominally,* democratic.[11]

No doubt, the relationship between rights and democracy is a close and important one. This is particularly true of the modern age in which preoccupation with the idea of the individual has become a staple of social and political life in the West. But just like the contingent nature of the alliance between liberalism and democracy, the relationship between rights and democracy is historical rather than logical. Athenian democracy, for example, did not have an extensive list of rights at the disposal of its citizenry. In fact, as Socrates' trial shows, individual rights—if the term is appropriate here—were poorly protected. All this, however, is not meant to deny the central role of the rights-based argument in democratic development. Rather, it calls attention to the fact that the idea of rights is closely linked with the historical, cultural, and political context in which it has slowly and tortuously moved into our consciousness, vocabulary and practice. Without a clear understanding of this context, the liberal concept of rights may be of limited use in providing guidance for political change *vis-à-vis* democratization in a nonliberal setting. Of course the historicity of liberal rights does not necessarily preclude its universal validity. But if this presumed universal validity keeps meeting resistance in application, and if its legitimacy is enshrouded in controversy, it would be beneficial for us to pause and look for explanation and possible alternatives.

For the same reason, there must also be a clear understanding of the cultural context to which the liberal concept of rights is to be transplanted. A "culturally sensitive" approach to the question of political change in non-Western countries is needed on both moral and strategic grounds. Morally, respect for values different from one's own is, at least in principle, one of the basic virtues on which liberal society is founded. Strategically, respect for different values or different emphases on a particular set of values is more likely to win respect and hence open the door to dialogue.[12]

FRAMEWORK AND ARGUMENTS

This study contains six chapters. While the first chapter briefly identifies the rationale or what I call metatheoretical concerns behind my endeavor, the second seeks to retrieve and redefine one central concept of this study, namely political culture. Under the influence of the modern philosophy of language, conceptual analysis has taken on a critical role in political discourse.[13] This is not simply because, as Wittgenstein argues, the meaning of a concept involves rules, purposes, context, and interpretations thereof in the language game in which the concept is implicated. It is also because meaningful discourse can be achieved only by using and sharing concepts with delimited boundaries of meaning. Clarification and definition, thus, serve the twin purpose of unveiling the meaning of a concept as constitutive of our experience of social and political reality, and providing a moderate amount of order to the "prodigiously diverse" uses we make of our language.

The concept of political culture is believed to be a treacherous ground on which to tread. Some reject it as a useless explanatory tool, while others remain silent on its viability in the study of politics. Among those who embrace this concept, attempts to define it have so far met limited success. Part of the reason for this perhaps lies in the fact that each definition is tailored specifically to satisfy the requirements of a specific research methodology. I begin the chapter by providing a brief account of the impact of three major areas of study, namely political theory, cultural anthropology and political sociology, on the concept. Next, three influential conceptions of political culture will be delineated and evaluated. Finally, a modified alternative definition suggested by Chilton will be proposed and adopted.[14]

Political culture will be defined as *the shared way of relating among a group or groups of people pertaining particularly to the ordering of their collective affairs.* Two general comments need to be made here. First, this definition is chosen with a clear goal in mind. For example, one of the main premises of this study is that the liberal concept of rights as a moral and political doctrine is undergirded by important cultural groundings. The definition of political culture as the shared way of relating brings into focus what it is meant by cultural groundings, and this in turn enables us to see that behind the veil of its universal claim, the liberal concept of rights tacitly espouses a particular vision of a shared way of relating, namely one which privileges the individual. It is this shared way of relating that provides comfortable bedding for the legitimacy of liberal rights. But what makes this definition better than previous ones is not an *a priori* consideration of goals; rather, its superiority lies in its ability to repair the deficiencies of earlier conceptions and present itself as a more robust concept.

Secondly, political culture is at once a subordinate part of and a dominant influence over general culture. Hence it is difficult if not altogether impossible to draw a distinct line between the two. By adding "pertaining particularly to the ordering of their collective affairs," I emphasize the political quality of a particular shared way of relating on the one hand and include those seemingly nonpolitical factors which may help make sense of the political life of a people on the other.

The third chapter has three objectives. The first is to provide a general understanding of the concept of rights. This general understanding allows us to see that it requires more than conceptual clarity to appreciate the force of rights-based arguments. While a right may imply a claim that "others not interfere with what one wants to do or that others provide what wants to have done to one," as White argues, the issue with regard to the notion is not "purely conceptual."[15] There are different kinds of rights, and they may or may not imply a duty not to interfere or a duty to provide or a freedom to choose. There are different kinds of grounds on which a right is justified, violated, or otherwise annulled. "Whether or not something can be a ground of a right depends on how it is related to that of which it is a ground."[16] Thus, our understanding of a right, that is, of what it is for something to be a right, or what it is to have a right, or what gives one a right, must not merely deal with the concept itself. We must delve into "the characteristics either of him who has the right or of the circumstances antecedent to his possession of the right;" we must delve into "various moral, legal, institutional, conventional, etc. relationships in the complex system to which [the rights-holders] belong."[17]

A proper starting point to examine these characteristics, circumstances, and relationships is to take a close look at the evolutionary path of liberal rights. Before we can proceed, however, an important question warrants our attention. A general and seemingly neutral account of the concept of rights appears inevitably entangled with liberal values, whether the concern is with definition or with justification. Does this mean that all rights are liberal? If so, there seems no point in using the concept of liberal rights. The deep connection between the notion of rights and liberalism is often assumed without argument. This is partly because rights are one of the basic values of liberalism, and because the evolution of liberal thought may be understood in terms of the ascendancy of the idea of rights. Despite these considerations, it is nonetheless mistaken to assume that all rights are necessarily liberal rights. For, historically, the idea of rights antedates liberalism. The second objective of Chapter Three is to offer an account of the preliberal or what I tend to call nonliberal conception of rights. This account purports to show that the liberal notion of rights is a historically unique phenomenon that emerged only in the modern West. Thus, to argue about the liberal concept of rights is not to argue something inherent in and peculiar to liberalism, but to examine the ways in which rights are viewed and justified on the basis of liberal ideas and principles.

To sketch the evolutionary path of liberal rights and specifically to examine the ways in which rights are justified on liberal grounds is my third objective. To accomplish this goal, both classical and contemporary liberal thinkers will be discussed. Among classical liberal thinkers, Hobbes and Locke will be selected, because it is widely believed that their ideas helped set the stage for the emergence of modern liberalism. Among contemporary liberal thinkers, John Rawls will be the main focus, but the insights of other prominent rights theorists will also be occasionally considered. These considerations are intended to show that the liberal concept of rights as we know it now can be understood as "an ensemble of related doctrines, beliefs, and assumptions" about the nature of human beings, society and government.[18] Lying at the center of this ensemble is a particular conception of the individual as an ontologically irreducible, rational, and autonomous being in our moral and political universe. As such, the interests and happiness of the individual constitute the ultimate end of society and entitle him or her to certain liberties and privileges which society as a whole has a duty to protect and promote, even at the cost of overall social welfare.

Having examined the nature and meaning of the liberal concept of rights, I turn in Chapter Four to explore its important cultural groundings. One such grounding, namely individualism, merits special attention. This, of course, is not to say that there are no other groundings or other groundings are not important. The centrality of the idea of the individual to liberal rights and, for that matter, to the liberal doctrine as a whole, is readily observable in classical and contemporary liberal thought. Liberalism, in the first instance, is not about limited government, but about the individual—about his or her nature, values, and interests, and about his or her self-perceived relationship with other individuals and with society at large. In a sense, liberalism is a philosophy of the individual just as democracy is a philosophy of the common man.

But does this close relationship entail the claim that individualism provides an—perhaps the first—important cultural grounding? Clearly, to say that there is a causal link between the liberal conception of rights and individualism is one thing, and to say that the latter provides an important cultural grounding for the former is quite another. One may argue that the liberal notion of rights has been an impetus to the growth of individualism, not vice versa. Or one may safely assert that the two are mutually reinforcing. The question of causal links is a difficult one and requires an argument that goes far beyond the scope of this study. Suffice it to make three general comments here, and these comments may be used to justify the choice of individualism as cultural grounding. First, the rise of modern individualism historically antedates liberalism. As historians tell us, it is with the arrival of the Reformation, or even earlier with the Renaissance, that the idea of the individual began to make its presence felt.[19] Second, from an analytic point of view, liberalism clearly presupposes and is grounded in a particular conception of the individual. Third, individualism is much broader in scope than liberalism at least at its initial stage. While the former may be described as an all-embracing way of living, acting, and thinking which has penetrated virtually all facets of modern life, the latter is primarily a moral and political doctrine concerned with the relationship between the individual and the political order in which one finds oneself.

An additional caveat is also necessary. By cultural groundings, I do not mean prerequisites or preconditions without which certain events or situations would not have occurred. It is not my intention here to establish such a causal argument. This causal claim has never been established in any unequivocal sense. There are countless direct and indirect causes behind a given social and political phenomenon. Each is significant but each by itself does not explain the whole. Neither does the aggregation of all of them. The best one can do is to engage in a thought experiment in the Weberian ideal-typical sense, that is, to accentuate certain elements or points of view in order to come up with an analytic construct which, one hopes, may provide a useful frame of reference against which our knowledge and understanding of social and political reality could be meaningfully studied.[20]

Three sections compose Chapter Four. In the first section, an attempt will be made to clarify the concept of individualism. Coined in the nineteenth century, individualism was viewed as both a negative and a positive doctrine. On the negative side, it suggests, among other things, atomism, egoism, and anarchism; on the positive side, it is associated, at least insofar as the study of politics is concerned, with three main ideas, namely autonomy, equality, and self-development.[21] But it must be pointed out that individualism is not exclusively a political phenomenon. Contemporary writers tend to treat it as a cultural phenomenon. Some say that it is a "vast complex of interdependent factors,"[22] while others suggest that it is a belief system.[23] Still others consider it a form of modern ideology.[24]

This study suggests an alternative definition, realizing that each of these conceptions of individualism is to some extent unsatisfactory. If one is to treat individualism as a cultural phenomenon, one ought to adopt a definition on the basis of an adequate understanding of the concept of culture. Individualism thus will be described as a particular way of relating which gives preponderant weight to the human individual. It gives preponderant weight to the individual's consciousness as the arbiter of truth, to the individual's values as the basis of morality, and to the individual's interests and needs as the ultimate justification for social and political arrangements.

The second section offers a description of the roots of modern individualism. Although concerns with the individual or the self have existed in all societies and at all times, individualism as defined above is a peculiarly modern, Western phenomenon. I argue that the Reformation and Cartesianism contributed inestimably to its rise. The Protestant movement in the sixteenth century permanently changed the way the average individual related to God, to one another, and to society in general. If Martin Luther could be said to have initiated "the transference to the human individual and his subjective state of that absolute assurance in the divine promise which was formerly the privilege of the Church,"[25] John Calvin, through his doctrine of predestination, pressed even further that process in which the individual was increasingly turning inward in search of redemption.

In the same way the Reformation helped create a religious self, Cartesianism helped generate a metaphysical self. What in the beginning seemed to be an innocuous task for Descartes, that is, to come up with some reliable and certain rules for knowledge, turned out to be subversive. The celebrated principle of total doubt served as a catalyst that undermined the old foundations of knowledge and, by extension, of all social and political arrangements. The kind of philosophical individualism ushered in by the *cogito* assigns the individual and his or her mind a privileged and indeed first-order place in the entire universe. It infuses the individual with a strong and certain sense of self-sufficiency, autonomy and uniqueness. With the arrival of Cartesianism, Watt observes, "the pursuit of truth is conceived of as a wholly individual matter, logically independent of the tradition of past thought, and indeed as more likely to be arrived at by a departure from it."[26]

In the third section, a description will be given of the extent to which individualistic values and practices emerged and became entrenched in the West. For this purpose, early modern England and the United States will be chosen as illustrations. Although early modern England cannot be regarded unequivocally as an individualistic nation, it exhibited many signs of an individualistic culture in the making. The United States, on the other hand, has been deemed by many, and I think correctly so, as the embodiment of individualism *par excellence*. Two qualifications need to be made here.

First, the term "West" is ambiguous. Some may argue, and for good reason, that Europe and the United States are quite different in important respects. Collectivist sentiments in Germany, for example, are perhaps no less strong than the individualist ones.[27] While this point is well taken, there is reason to believe that individualism, at least since the Enlightenment, has become a powerful doctrine underlying social and political practice in major Western nations now led by the United States. Second, by saying that the United States is the embodiment of individualism, it is not meant that Americans do not cherish values of a nonindividualistic nature. But these values, as evidence has amply shown,[28] do not determine or strongly influence the conduct of the average American in the same predominant way as individualism does.

The fifth chapter will focus on the Chinese political and cultural tradition, especially as it pertains to the issue of rights. It will look into the ways in which its ordering of collective life differs from the Western experience. Furthermore, it attempts to unravel the nature of a political culture that at once provides groundings for and is perpetuated by this ordering of collective life. The primary goal of the chapter is to show that the groundwork laid by individualism for the emergence of the liberal concept of rights is radically lacking in the Chinese political and cultural tradition.

Four topics will be discussed in the chapter. First, efforts will be made to draw the boundaries of what can be reasonably called the Chinese politico-cultural tradition. The need to take on this task is warranted by the following consideration. It is sometimes maintained that there is no Chinese politico-cultural tradition, but only traditions. In so vast an area as the Chinese nation and so long a history as Chinese history, diversity is bound to flourish.[29] While this is undeniably true, enough evidence nonetheless seems to indicate that there has been a remarkable unity underlying the Chinese shared way of relating, particularly in respect to the government of social and political affairs. This is the pervasive force of Confucianism. Although various schools of thought such as Taoism and Legalism did have a significant role to play in shaping the Chinese politico-cultural tradition, it was Confucianism that has maintained its dominant and orthodox position as an ethical and political doctrine through the rise and fall of dynasties, especially after the Song dynasty in later medieval China.

An examination of the paradigmatic features that structure the Chinese politico-cultural tradition will be the second topic. The main focus will be on the structural features of Confucianism in its classical form. Despite the fact that Confucianism underwent great changes in the hands of neo-Confucianists in the Song and Ming dynasties, there is compelling reason to believe that it is ultimately the classical statements of Confucianism that have laid the vital foundation for the Chinese politico-cultural tradition as we know it now. What both classical and later Confucianism share is a set of core values, epitomized in the concept of *Li* (ritual) and functioning as a mechanism of control over social and political conduct. These values were originated in the rites, customs, and divining activities of a blood-based tribal society, prescribing and making enforceable the duties and obligations each member of the community was to live by. With the development of the idea of *Ren* (benevolence) by Confucius and his disciples, such duties and obligations were internalized to meet the exigencies of the time marked by social and political unrest. But internalization of this sort does not mean transformation of the individual into a moral being in the Kantian sense of being capable of rational self-determination.[30] As internalized *Li,* the concept of *Ren* signifies the individuation and self-imposition of hierarchically designed duties and obligations on the part of each member of society in a more austere manner. The concepts of *Li* and *Ren,* thus, formed a unified whole; they combined to reduce the individual to a mere role player in a hierarchy of duties and obligations. This conception of man and society has endured for more than two millennia, largely undisturbed by time. Until the turn of the century, the basic Chinese way or relating remained blood-based, hierarchical, and nonindividualistic.

Granted that the above account is acceptable, one may ask, in what concrete sense can we say that Confucianism has played an influential role in shaping the Chinese politico-cultural tradition? An answer to this question will be the third topic in the chapter.

Perhaps the best way to observe Confucian ideas and values at work is to examine the traditional Chinese family. The importance of the family to Confucianism and to Chinese society has been widely noted.[31] There are at least three reasons for this. First, the family was the most basic and the most intimate form of human association, and very likely the only one, that the individual ever knew throughout his or her life in premodern China. Second, it was also the most basic and effective unit of social control; its maintenance and stability directly affected the peace and continuity of the Chinese nation as a whole. Third, the family was a self-contained and self-sufficient political entity, with its own authority structures and laws. In the most genuine sense, traditional China has been an enlarged copy of the family. As one historian remarks, the names of administrative officials in successive dynasties were originally those of the clan chief's house keepers in charge of immolation, purse, kitchen, travel, security, and so on.[32]

An analysis of the traditional Chinese family will be conducted on two levels. On the first level, a historical account of the family—its nature, origin, and function—will be provided on the basis of recent scholarship on the subject.[33] Emphasis will be placed on the fact that Confucian ideas and values such as filial piety and fraternal affection furnished the most important foundation on which the family was built and maintained. On the second level, recent and near-recent anthropological studies will be used to provide a firsthand description of the central role the family as a concrete expression of Confucianism played in molding the conduct of Chinese.

The last section of the chapter is a descriptive account of contemporary Chinese political culture. This account will be based on recent empirical studies and, to a much lesser degree, on my own findings from a field trip in 1997. Its goal is to establish a point of comparison for studying cultural continuity and change and ultimately to provide supporting evidence for the thesis that the individualistic way of relating is lacking in China.

If Confucian familism provides a useful theoretical construct for understanding the Chinese politico-cultural tradition, political culture in contemporary China may be best described in terms of a quasi-familistic or, to use a native term, *guanxi* network. A quasi-familistic or *guanxi* culture is a way of relating which involves the cultivation and maintenance of a family-like network of personal ties. The primacy of personal ties and reciprocal obligation has furnished the important underpinnings for political life in today's China. The quasi-familistic character of contemporary Chinese political culture can be seen on two levels. On the elite level, as empirical studies have shown, the patterns of authority, the decision-making process, official recruitment, and the like are strongly influenced or constrained by quasi-familistic networks and values.[34] On the popular level, the ways in which individual Chinese think about and act in response to political affairs are also strongly influenced or constrained by network values and practices.[35]

In the sixth and concluding chapter, a summary argument will be presented about the liberal concept of rights, political culture, and the Chinese politico-cultural tradition. If it is tenable that the liberal concept of rights presupposes and indeed is grounded in an individualistic way of relating which emerged only after the Reformation in the modern West; and if it is also tenable that this individualistic cultural grounding is radically absent in China and instead a nonindividualistic and duty-sensitive way of relating was and still is dominant, what sensible conclusions could be drawn from all this? I suggest that the absence of an individualistic culture helps explain, at least in part, the gap between the moral appeal of liberal rights and the failure to take them seriously in the Chinese context. Consequently, I argue, a rights-based argument would likely be of limited success, as was the case in the past, in providing a language for articulating visions of political change vis-à-vis democratic development in China, at least over the short run.

However, this essentially negative conclusion appears to be of little use in building a viable model for democratic change. The important question facing us now is what constructive steps should be taken to ensure that liberal rights become a crucial part of the Chinese democratizing experience. To answer this question, I first briefly describe the main characteristics that go into the structuring of the Chinese rights discourse. This description will allow us not only to see historical continuity with regard to the question of rights, but also to highlight some of the pressing issues involved in building what is often referred to as a human rights regime. At least three key issues require our attention. The first is that the idea of (human) rights is often tied up with international power relations. The second deals with the selective use of the rights language in a way that prioritizes some rights at the expense of others. The third is a profound lack of moral grounding for the notion of rights accompanied by a purely instrumentalist justificatory scheme.

While all may agree on this characterization, there is no consensus over how we should go about tackling these issues. Some believe that liberal democracy is *the* solution, because only in liberal democracy can human rights and cultural diversity flourish.[36] Others argue that because liberalism is predicated on the assumption of self-interested and unsituated individuals, it is the source of moral conflict, not the solution.[37] Still others suggest that the Chinese political and cultural tradition may be able to provide sources of support for the idea of rights.[38] Oftentimes the debate is framed in a dichotomy between universalism and relativism. In my view, this dichotomy is misleading, not only because a purely relativist position, one that is construed by the universalist, is rarely if ever found in existing literature on human rights, but also because the universalist position itself is conceptually and philosophically problematic.[39]

This study offers an alternative approach to the rights-based argument for political reform in China. To the extent that an individualistic way of relating is radically missing in China, it will help us accomplish little to impose a liberal agenda without fundamentally changing the way the Chinese think about and manage political affairs. However, this is not to espouse the idea that one should wait for a rights-friendly culture to ripen so that it would provide comfortable bedding for democracy. In an era marked by a quest for the global community, an isolationist and bystander mentality will not get us very far. It seems to me that the best possible course of action for reconstructing a healthy rights discourse is to take a positive engagement approach that combines political activism with cultural sensitivity. We should actively engage a political regime in value dialogue and political innovation, while simultaneously fostering the conditions that are favorable to the development of a human rights regime.

As part of the requirement of a culturally sensitive engagement approach, a redescription of liberal rights is required, which would connect well with the nonindividualistic way of relating in China. This is based on the consideration that a redescribed notion of rights would likely appeal to a broad audience by utilizing familiar moral categories in the Chinese cultural tradition, thus making the rights-based argument bear effectively on democratic change. The core of this redescription consists in the idea of embedded rights. Embedded rights may be understood as a nonindividualistic conception of rights. They are nonindividualistic in the sense that they find their anchor not in a philosophical conception of the individual as a presocial and prepolitical being but rather in the understanding of the individual as a socially and culturally embedded being. Rights are embedded in the social and cultural life of a people and in the process of interaction between individual and society. They are not something the individual *qua* subject possesses inherently and transcendentally, but are to be seen as a way of adjusting social relations. Such adjustment is accomplished on the basis of a given standard or conception of justice in a given society and at a given time. This is of course not to deny that this given standard or conception may be deemed unjust in terms of the standards or conceptions in different societies and at different times. Nor is it to say that it should not be reformulated by every conceivable means as our moral ideal requires.

The nature of embedded rights may be described in the following terms. First, rights are to be viewed as embedded in the social interconnectedness of expectations and duties rather than as inhering in the individual presocially and prepolitically conceived. Second, they are to be treated as a way of adjusting human relations on the basis of a conception of justice rather than as things to be exclusively possessed. Finally, they should be regarded as a critical tool for creating a more humane and democratic vision of collective life rather than as a mere protective shield for individual self-interests.

The viability of the idea of embedded rights depends as much on an articulation of its nature as on a conception of justice. Absent a conception of justice as moral grounding, the idea of embedded rights would enjoy little legitimacy in the eyes of the Chinese public. In the past, the notion of rights was typically justified on the basis of imported concepts such as individual liberty. This kind of defense was ineffective and even counterproductive because the imported concepts themselves require justification. To ground the language of rights, familiar conceptual and moral categories such as the notion of self-cultivation and the notion of public welfare can and must be drawn from the duty-sensitive Chinese tradition. By renovating the traditional sources of value, and by acquiring an empirical understanding of what a just society should be in contemporary China, a conception of justice can be constructed to provide moral anchoring for the idea of embedded rights.

Thus conceived, the idea of embedded rights, I believe, can provide a viable language for articulating visions of political change. The kind of democracy that it is likely to promote, however, would not be a liberal model for reasons stated. In recent years, students of Chinese politics have proposed various models for the Chinese democratic project. For instance, Bell envisions a bicameral representative democracy in which members of the upper house are selected through examination.[40] Womack suggests that a party-state model of democracy in which the citizenry increases its control over official selection.[41] There is also the neo-constitutionalist argument that emphasizes the restructuring of the existing electoral system.[42] The model that the idea of embedded rights would support may be called a consultative one. It is consultative primarily in the sense that the views, interests, and expectations of the people should be consulted and incorporated into the national decision-making process. Consultation can take place through various channels and at various levels. In order for consultative democracy to work, two parallel developments are required. In one development, while some structural changes at the top, particularly within the monopolistic communist party are necessary, a strong central authority is to be maintained for coherent economic development as well as for social and political stability. In another development, grassroots political participation *vis-à-vis* village election should be strengthened and gradually extended to the county, prefect/municipal, and provincial level. Accompanying these developments there must be a firm policy of legal reform and a loosening of media control.

It must be noted that the idea of embedded rights is subject to criticisms. By defining rights in terms of duties and obligations, one may argue, we render the notion a toothless weapon for individuals to protect and promote their legitimate interests. By incorporating the elements of a nonrights-based cultural tradition, further, we cause the idea of rights to lose its moral force and restrict the already narrow range of free choices that the ordinary citizen enjoys. While these points are well taken, the idea of embedded rights can be defended as a transitional model, one which is used for a limited purpose and at a particular time. Future developments may well make it obsolete.

All said, one should remain clear-headed about the extent to which embedded rights and the consultative model of democracy are able to facilitate political change. Obviously, to make embedded rights work and to cultivate a participatory ethos in China involve more than theoretical exposition and model building. And given China's socio-economic and cultural constraints, many expect democratic transformation there to be a long and tortuous process. What one can do in one's capacity as a student of politics, in the mean time, is to observe, reflect, and recommend.

Chapter Two

Retrieving the Concept
of Political Culture

Like many other concepts in the study of politics, the concept of political culture has created as much controversy as consensus. Some reject it as a useful concept in explaining political phenomena, while others are skeptical of its value in providing an alternative conceptual tool for an increasingly rigorous political science. But many welcome it as a timely addition to the search for a better understanding of political life. This does not mean, however, that the concept is unidimensional. The variegated use we make of it may be partially responsible for this multiplicity of meaning: we see political culture in turn as subjective orientations, as traditional values and beliefs, and as political symbols. Such a state of affairs makes the selection of a particular understanding of this notion both difficult and necessary.

Before making this selection, this chapter seeks to offer a reassessment of the concept of political culture as it is currently used in the political science literature. This reassessment is warranted by three considerations. First, despite a few noticeable deficiencies in the current use of the concept, many still prefer a widely popular definition of political culture as subjective orientations rather than "reinvent the wheel."[1] This is understandable as an attempt to achieve consensus. But it would seem more rewarding intellectually to try to repair the deficiencies by providing a new account of the concept. Second, the interesting relationship between political culture and such concepts as democracy should give us another reason for critical reevaluation. A different understanding of political culture may shed light on how political culture and democracy are linked; it may also illuminate the extent to which this relationship helps shape the nature and direction of democratic development. Third, since concepts are temporally and spatially bound, a conceptual reanalysis of political culture may be able to provide some background knowledge, thus making comparative studies across time and cultures a more fulfilling experience.

THE CLASSICAL ROOTS

The study of political culture as it pertains to the establishing and maintaining of a polity is not new but goes back to the ancient Greeks. To be sure, the ancient Greeks never used the term "political culture" for political analysis, but their ideas about political constitution, social upbringing, and particularly the laws clearly reveal a pattern of understanding that is reminiscent of what we today may call the cultural approach to politics. Indeed the relationship between culture—here temporarily defined as a way of life—and politics is so close in their mind that it is often impossible to discuss them separately. For politics, after all, is about the way of life in the *polis*.

Perhaps the most important aspect of life in the *polis* is the rule of law. Demosthenes, a prominent Athenian lawyer, declares that "no man living will attribute the prosperity of Athens, her liberty, her popular government, to anything rather than to the laws."[2] Evidently law occupies a unique place in the *polis,* but for the Greeks it does not enjoy the same level of abstraction and differentiation as found in the modern conception. The Greek term *nomos,* like the French word *moeurs* that Montesquieu, Rousseau and Tocqueville would use much later, carries a rich connotation that goes far beyond the commonly translated meaning of law; it embraces custom, tradition, habit, manners, way of life, morals, and it is part and parcel of what is best known later as culture. Thus, the rule of law means more than anything else the customary or traditional way of doing things. It is the customs and traditions that govern the public and private life of the citizen as well as serve to legitimate legal and political authority.

The two legendary lawgivers Lycurgus and Solon are, in a broad sense, two reformers of political culture. When Xenophon spoke panegyrically of Lycurgus as the man who had brought fame and power to Sparta through constitutional innovation, he was at the same time explaining a series of cultural transformations which no modern legislation is capable of conceiving. These legal or more precisely cultural changes, ranging from child-bearing to slave policy and youth education, affected profoundly the public as well as the private life of the Spartans.[3]

But it would be incorrect to assume that performing a deed as monumental as Lycurgus,' a deed that was said to have brought a complete overhaul of the Spartan regime, must go against the entire cultural tradition. On the contrary; such an endeavor must be embedded in the culture of a people in order to succeed. The act of lawgiving, as Plato reminds us, is an act of choosing among existing customs and traditions those rules of conduct that are most agreeable to the community.[4] But a sense of continuity does not necessarily mean a lack of ingenuity. Like Lycurgus' constitutional reform which was grounded in a comparative study of the laws in Egypt and Asia, Solon's reform was rooted in a clear understanding of Athens. As Plutarch recounts, Solon knew only too well that Athens was a different city with different customs, traditions, morals, and even with a different temperament. This difference in cultural heritage required "fitting his laws to the state of things, and not making things to suit his laws."[5] A "cheerful" and "homely" people such as the Athenians did not need extravagance in, for instance, meal taking and mourning; neither did they need a harsh and rigid program as that of the Spartans for youth education.[6]

Plato, the most notable culturalist in antiquity, also provided a systematic account of the *nomos* that would serve as the cornerstone of political society. Nowhere can we observe a good combination of continuity and ingenuity more evidently than in his *Laws*. To Plato, while the laws are originated in cultural conventions, they have a higher and forward-looking purpose: they are aimed at achieving the good. In other words, custom and tradition do not merely govern social and political activities such as raising children, singing chorus, or honoring the gods; more importantly, they must cultivate good or virtuous individuals who are able to rule themselves.[7] This self-rule bears much resemblance to what social scientists now regard as the internalization of cultural norms. It also signals the advent of a culture of virtue. With the idea of the good, Plato elevated the relationship between culture and politics to a higher plane where human excellence, rather than mere habit, was to determine or at least condition the nature of cultural and political development.

It is true that Plato envisioned a culture of hierarchical virtues in which those with a higher order of virtues rule those on lower rungs of the moral ladder. But this does not diminish the value of his insight that personal qualities, rather than structural roles alone, would certainly be part of the inquiry about government. In a monarchy it is the personal qualities of one man that count, while in a democracy the psychological dispositions of the masses hold sway. Without the cultivation of proper virtues, monarchy can degenerate into tyranny and democracy into mob dictatorship. This concern with government *within* rather than government *without* clearly marks one of Plato's contributions to our understanding of the cultural underpinnings of politics.[8]

Aristotle entertained a similar view when he emphasized the connection between the best way of life and the best constitution. For Aristotle, the best way of life is a life in conformity with virtue and the best constitution a constitution characterized by its ability to promote the best way of life. While the best constitution is a necessary (though not sufficient) condition for obtaining the best way of life, the best way of life is the only form of living appropriate to the best constitution. The relationship between them is such that the end of political organization and that of individual action become identical. Here we see clearly Plato's influence. But unlike Plato, Aristotle did not prescribe a hierarchically structured moral life in which each class of citizens fulfills their naturally assigned functions. Like Plato, however, he recognized that the interconnectedness of culture and politics was founded on a moral vision; this moral vision deems virtue as the ultimate end of political as well as private life.[9]

Apparently, the ideal state and the cultural qualities that accord it are not Aristotle's only concern. His pluralistic, as opposed to Plato's unidimensional, conception of virtue seems to have made it substantively impossible to pinpoint a single most desirable quality of cultural life. A shift of emphasis from contemplation as the epitome of the best way of life in his *Ethics* to a combination of *vita activa* and *vita contempativa* in his *Politics* illustrates this point. The same fair-mindedness also enables him to perceive a need for a balanced account of the actual state. In keeping with the logic of a connection between the best way of life and the best constitution, Aristotle insisted that a certain type of regime must have as its cultural base a certain type of citizen character. "The democratic type of character creates and sustains democracy," he declares, whereas "the oligarchic type creates and sustains oligarchy."[10] It is also true of the best actual state, one which he called "polity" and which he created by striking a mean between oligarchy and democracy. This best actual state must have a type of citizen character that is appropriate to itself and functions as its cultural grounding. Aristotle found that the type of cultural quality most suitable to the best actual state rests with the middle class, because the middle class, unlike the "over-noble" and the "utterly ignoble" at the opposite poles, is moderate and "the most ready to listen to reason."[11]

A quick account of the classical writers on culture and politics seems to suggest at least two interesting conclusions. First, culture—if the term is understood as a depository of custom, tradition, habit, morals, citizen character or the dispositions of what Aristotle calls "civic body"—serves as an important underpinning of politics; second, the relationship between culture and politics must be guided by a higher moral purpose, and it is only on the basis of this higher moral purpose that cultural and political development can be meaningfully assessed.

MODERN POLITICAL THEORY AS A SOURCE

Montesquieu

Among modern political thinkers, few have done more than Montesquieu in regenerating the classical concern with the cultural foundations of government, law, and politics. Rousseau, Burke and later Tocqueville are exceptions, but their enormous debt to Montesquieu can never be over-emphasized. While other political philosophers in the tumultuous modern era were busy breaking away from the spells of goodness in politics or propounding natural law principles, it is Montesquieu who first drew attention to those questions about the interconnection of culture and politics which Plato and Aristotle had suggested. In a genealogical sense, *The Spirit of the Laws* may well be taken as a modern version of Plato's *Laws* and Aristotle's *Politics* combined.

To say, however, that Montesquieu is a close follower of the classical tradition in the study of culture and politics is not to dismiss his originality. Emile Durkheim believes that Montesquieu made a clean break with classical thought by reorienting social science from the contemplation of pure ideas to the study of actual social phenomena. Though Durkheim may have overstated the case of a burgeoning eighteenth-century sociology as intimated by *The Spirit of the Laws,* he is certainly correct in pointing out that Montesquieu's method of analysis portends well what would emerge as the social sciences.[12] But it is also beyond doubt that Montesquieu did use in analyzing governmental forms and the laws, customs, habits and manners that are supportive of them many of the categories and concepts as used by Plato and Aristotle. These resemblances are not superficial; they reflect, among other things, an unbroken chain of intellectual fascination with the relation of culture to politics.

In addition to the fact that he pioneered a new methodology for comparative legal and political studies, Montesquieu made at least three major contributions to our understanding of the relationship between culture and politics. First, he differentiated laws from mores and manners; he insisted that laws are legislated and "depend more on a particular institution" while mores and manners are "inspired," and they are that part of a nation's general spirit that laws cannot and do not want to establish.[13] This differentiation is of vital importance because it enables us to see clearly two distinctive spheres of social life which, though intimately linked, must be treated differently in order to maintain a relatively stable society. As Montesquieu realized, overlegislating or legislating each and every aspect of social life, especially morality, is an open invitation to tyranny. What properly belongs to the domain of culture ought to be left for the people, not the legislator or prince, to handle. For a political society to stay on its course, therefore, it is imperative to "reform by laws what is established by laws and change by manners what is established by manners."[14]

The separation of laws from mores and manners is important in yet another respect. This has to do with the question of viability. Montesquieu clearly understands that a free constitution does not necessarily entail a free people, and a change in a nation's government does not necessarily involve a change in that nation's social and cultural conditions which dispose it to a certain type of polity. The laws established as part of a constitution function only as a regulatory device for external actions; it is the mores, manners, and received practices forming the general spirit or way of life of a nation that provide underlying reasons for social and political conduct. Legal and political institutions alone can accomplish only a limited range of tasks and overstepping their capabilities is not merely "tyrannical" but also "useless."[15] This is why it is just as indispensable to examine how culture can affect political change as it is vital to know how structural reform can alter a nation's political landscape.

Montesquieu's second contribution to our conception of political culture lies in his idea of reciprocity between laws and culture. For Montesquieu, laws—if we understand the term as a set of structural principles of a political society[16]—are affected by cultural values and norms, and it is always salutary for the lawgiver, be it a legislative organ or a prince, to follow the mores so that the foundation, that is, the general spirit, of a nation remains undisturbed. But laws also have influence upon cultural values and norms; this influence must be accounted for in order for us to obtain a full appreciation of the problems and solutions with regard to government. This reciprocal relationship which Montesquieu suggests between the laws and the mores of a nation, between its governmental and institutional structures on the one hand, and its mores, manners, habits, and ways of relating on the other, captures the essence of a complex issue, and it continues to inform the debate between the structuralist and the culturalist today.

Thirdly, by offering an account of three *types* of government and their principles and laws in a seemingly objective manner, Montesquieu is said to have implicitly adopted a kind of moral relativism. There may be a grain of truth in this charge, but it does not mean that Montesquieu lacks moral vision. Ample evidence can be garnered to demonstrate that Montesquieu did have an acute moral sensibility when he condemned despotism as being corrupt by nature and when he exalted republican forms of government as champions of liberty. Perhaps the question that is of interest to us is not whether or not Montesquieu had a flair for relativism, but what kind of relativism he implicitly espoused and why his relativism is not pernicious but rather valuable in helping us better explain the triangular relationship among politics, culture and morality.

Montesquieu's relativism is a relativism with moral vision, although this vision may be a limited one. It comes rather close to what some contemporary writers call "bounded relativism."[17] Distinguished in some crucial aspects from crude relativism characterized by randomness and nihilism, Montesquieu's relativism anticipates the kind of pluralism that has become a hallmark of political discourse today. It tells us, among other things, that examining and evaluating existing types of government and the principles and laws that are congruent with them in terms of a singular standard will not be able to help us get at the true nature of things. Fatal are the consequences of a failure on our part to get at the true nature of things when we attempt to promulgate outlandish and misfitting laws, because such attempts may jeopardize the security, liberty and well-being of a people. Thus, good laws must be grounded in an adequate understanding of the mores, manners, and character of a people. But they should also be sensitive to those cultural facts that are repugnant to our basic moral sensibility. This second proposition, not systematically articulated but largely implied in *The Spirit of the Laws,* particularly in its treatment of slavery, is central to a theory of cultural and political change. It distances Montesquieu from the kind of cultural determinism that has been a basic component of crude relativism.[18]

Although Montesquieu's thinking has its own biases and limits, his differentiation of structural principles from cultural norms, his view of the reciprocal influence of culture and politics, and his morally bounded relativism can certainly provide a rich source for those who think about the concept of political culture to draw upon. These ideas can also furnish an intellectual context in which we are able to bring into focus later studies of the relationship between politics and culture.

Rousseau

In the intellectual context Montesquieu handed down to us, we can take a brief look at three other thinkers, namely Rousseau, Burke, and Tocqueville, to see how their understanding of the relationship between culture and politics contributes to the conception of political culture. As mentioned earlier, Rousseau's understanding of the relationship had been shaped by Montesquieu's idea that different political regimes have different customs and traditions as their distinctive bases of support, and this can be seen nowhere more clearly than in *The Social Contract*. There Rousseau echoed his French predecessor when he spoke about the most important type of law, namely the mores, customs, and opinions of a people. This law, he wrote, "is graven not on tablets of marble or brass, but on the hearts of the citizens" and forms the "immovable keystone" of political society.[19] But he went further than that, or perhaps we should say he took a different approach to the question. This difference suggests itself in his criticism of Montesquieu for failing to provide an adequate account of the ethical principles of law and government.[20] While Montesquieu was preoccupied with describing, in a factual manner and without ever coming to grips *fully* with the underlying moral issues of his description, the types of government and the cultural norms that undergird them, Rousseau combined his "principles of political right" with his cultural considerations to generate a unique conception of culture and politics, and this conception may well be deemed as an embryonic form of the concept of political culture as we use it today.

In writing up a reform plan for Poland, Rousseau made clear that the deeply rooted "tastes, customs, prejudices, and failings" of a people must be taken into account before anyone can embark on such an undertaking, namely to renovate the political constitution of a nation, because ignoring those cultural traits would result in a defective end product. But, as he quickly added, this is not to say that "things must be left as they are;" it only means that they should be handled with "extreme caution."[21] In *The Government of Poland*, as in *The Social Contract*, Rousseau began with the basic premise that human beings are both longing for and capable of freedom; it is the idea of freedom—not in the sense of the absence of restraint but in the sense of obeying self-prescribed laws—that propels the engine of human existence. When transplanted properly to or absorbed by a different cultural soil, this idea would bear a unique fruit which serves to distinguish in character one nation from another. It is the national character, writes Rousseau, that produces a sense of belonging and pride and helps cultivate civic virtue or patriotism in the citizen, thus keeping a nation's political constitution alive against both internal dissension and external aggression.

In a nation such as Poland, where despotism and serfdom are the only known ways of life, cultural tradition alone would have little chance to generate republican virtues; in a similar vein, a moral ideal which is blind to the cultural reality would appear alien and unappealing to its people, thus creating little incentive for them to engage in political action to change the status quo. The meshing of the two to yield a new political culture that would provide grounding for the would-be republic seems to Rousseau a proper way of thinking for the Poles to adopt.

The essence of this new political culture has been captured by Rousseau's inventive use of the classical notion of virtue. In the classical, especially the Platonic-Aristotelian, conception, this notion denotes in large measure an individual's functional excellence such as a soldier's courage or a statesman's prudence. Rousseau's conception, however, is more of an impersonal and egalitarian nature, carrying with it the accent of what Kant calls *sensus communis* and Hannah Arendt calls "the enlarged mentality."[22] Placed in the political context, the idea of virtue signifies for him a sense of duty and patriotism, the ability to judge and act in accordance with the true meaning of freedom, and the willingness to participate in and sacrifice for the general will of one's political community.[23] It is on the basis of civic virtue, Rousseau held, that a free and unified Polish republic could be constructed.

Burke

The remarkable similarity between Rousseau's idea of virtue and what today's students of political culture term as "civic culture" is another reason why Rousseau both as a culturalist and as a moral philosopher continues to fascinate us. As a moral philosopher, he gave radicalism a new meaning; as a culturalist, he went so far as to espouse the kind of gradualism that his conservative compatriot Montesquieu would be more than happy to embrace. This is borne out particularly by his substantive position on the issue of enfranchising the Polish serfs; there he suggested that liberty is a delicious but hard food for the Polish serfs to stomach and making them free is a "noble" but "hazardous" and prolonged undertaking.[24] A similar call for gradualism in the face of social and political change, ironically, is also found in Rousseau's arch-rival Edmund Burke across the English Channel. Rousseau and Burke are different in temperament, experience, interest, and even taste. Despite these differences, however, they do share some views in common, views that enable us to see some form of continuity in the study of culture and politics.[25]

Burke argued that a nation is not merely a territory of land mass; it is more importantly an embodiment of history, morals, and culture. It extends in time, stands for certain values, and enjoys a way of life that grows out of "the peculiar circumstances, occasions, tempers, dispositions, and moral, civil, and social habitudes of the people." It is an invention of ages and generations, "not a tumultuary and giddy choice;" it is in a nutshell "an idea of continuity" or tradition.[26] Burke saw tradition as providing a cultural milieu in which we live, work, and engage in politics; government as part of this tradition is not only not "a necessary evil" but rather a perfectible and valuable device that could be and has been actually used for the good of humanity. Thus, disrupting this naturally evolved order of things by "the most contemptible instruments" and "in the most ridiculous modes," namely by violence, is a monstrous act that Burke found both morally and emotionally impossible to reconcile with.

It must be noted that Burke's almost religious belief in the sanctity of cultural tradition does not mean that he denies the possibility of change; in fact, he admits that a nation "without the means of some change is without the means of its conservation."[27] But change in his view is not a radical break, as epitomized by the French Revolution, with existing social and political arrangements; such a clean split is neither possible nor desirable, because these arrangements embody the living reason of the past, imperfect as it may be, which saves us from error and brings us the benefit of an ordered collective life. What Burke envisioned about change instead is an amending process that must be "confined to the peccant part only," or "to the part which produced the necessary deviation," without threatening to dissolve the whole fabric of society.[28] In other words, change must be wrought within the boundaries set by tradition, by the values and practices that lay the groundwork for the proper functioning of government, and transgressing these boundaries are deemed by Burke as disruptive of the time-honored tradition and counterproductive to the purpose for which reform is instituted.

Burke's gradualism rests to a large extent on two considerations. First, he believed that political change takes place for the purpose of conservation, not destruction. There are certain good things in the cultural tradition of a nation which are essential to its constitution and thus should be diligently preserved. These good things put limits on political reform because the latter is designed to *perfect,* not *subvert,* and perfection takes time. This positive defense of cultural tradition against political radicalism as represented by the ideas and events on both sides of the English channel is most clearly shown in Burke's account of the historical development of the English constitutional order, particularly in his argument for the preservation of property and religion as the twin pillars of a free and benevolent society.[29]

Second, Burke contended that even if there exist certain practices or institutions which are morally unjustifiable in terms of the natural principle of justice, it may not be a good idea to end them abruptly for fear of more evils their abolition could cause. Whatever exists exists for a reason, whether this reason be utilitarian or otherwise; until such time as is suitable for its discontinuance, a time which cannot be decided in advance, particularly not in the name of "metaphysically true" but "morally and politically false" ideas, but by experience, we may be justified in keeping it for the moment, though in a restricted manner and with an eye to bringing it slowly to its demise. This, for example, is the position Burke took on slavery. A long opponent of the slave trade, Burke nonetheless was "fully convinced that the cause of humanity would be far more benefited by the continuance of the trade and servitude, regulated and reformed, than by the total destruction of both or either."[30] The conviction is based on a consideration of the simple reality that the slave trade was difficult to eliminate, regardless of the fact that it had been made illegal. Burke thus proposed a "gradual manumission of negroes" by taking concrete steps such as cutting off the supply of slaves and cultivating civilized minds that are capable of freedom.

Echoing the idea of his French teacher Montesquieu, Burke's gradualism reminds us of the limits that cultural tradition places on social and political change. It is true that overemphasizing the limits as he has done in the wake of the French Revolution may have a crippling effect on social and political reform, but he helps us see that ignoring them may be just as dangerous, particularly when reform is carried out in the name of abstract ideas such as the rights of man. Burke was well aware that cultural tradition can function as a countervailing force to the attractiveness and the disruptive potential of revolutionary ideas, and he insisted that political ideas and for that matter political institutions be viewed not in a simplistic way; rather, they should be understood in historical context and in the complexity of the relationships they have with the actual world. Only a few decades later, Tocqueville would begin his study of the idea of democracy on the basis of much the same assumption that democratic politics in America can be understood only by examining "the general equality of condition among the people" and by tracing its historical development in both the Old and the New World.

Tocqueville

Tocqueville has been often viewed as a derivative thinker following closely the steps of Montesquieu, Rousseau, and others.[31] What has been largely overlooked, however, is the fact that he is that crucial link between the crude sociological ideas in *The Spirit of the Laws* and contemporary political sociology from which the concept of political culture would benefit greatly. In this sense, to put him at the fountainhead of contemporary political sociology, at least from a substantive point of view, is not inappropriate. The biggest contribution which Tocqueville made to the conception of political culture and to the uses made of this concept in explaining political phenomena such as democracy and revolution is, in my view, not his attempt to make a connection between government and politics on the one hand and the socio-cultural conditions on the other as some critics tend to argue.[32]

This connection has been shown by many writers before him. What he had done most successfully is, rather, to make such a connection far more clear and compelling than ever before, and he did so by introducing for the first time a patterned or causal way of thinking about the relationship between culture and politics.

This patterned or causal way of thinking may be stated as this: The emergence of certain socio-cultural conditions will inevitably give rise to certain changes in the form of political rule. It should be pointed out that Tocqueville never stated this thesis explicitly, but even a casual reading of the most influential of his works will reveal that it is the fundamental structure of his thought. In the United States it was the equality of conditions, subjective and material, that paved the way for democratic politics. In France it was principally the incompatibility between the rising demand for equality and for the abolition of class barriers on the one side and the aristocracy's clinging to their privileges and power on the other side that led to the demise of the *ancien regime.*

Tocqueville admitted that tracing the important influence of customs, habits, attitudes, or in short culture on the political life of a people constitutes the central point of his inquiry, but he was also aware that this influence presents itself in a multifaceted way. Accordingly, no single cause can sufficiently account for the occurrence of any particular political phenomenon. Even if an exhaustive list of causes were enumerated, there would still remain the question whether the same social and cultural conditions that had led to the establishment of American democracy or the breakout of the French Revolution could produce the same results elsewhere. Tocqueville insisted that certain factors such as temperament and physical location are peculiar to a nation and its people and cannot be reproduced at will. These factors may or may not play a decisive role in determining outcomes, but they must nevertheless be taken into account in order to have an adequate understanding of such political phenomena as democracy and revolution and to forecast their future course of development in nations other than the place of their origin.[33]

In addition, Tocqueville tended to see this causal relationship not as unidirectional, but as reciprocal. If the emergence of social and cultural conditions gives rise to changes in political rule, a system of government also influences or molds customs, values and opinions. The democratic government in America, Tocqueville argued, plays an active role in shaping the customs, values, and opinions through its institutions and this kind of shaping can be observed in virtually every aspect of American society ranging from literary activity to family structure and economic transactions.[34]

It is certainly true that judged by today's standards, Tocqueville's causal analysis raises some difficulties. For example, it is not altogether clear whether the equality of conditions gives rise to democracy or the other way around. What one learns from Tocqueville's description is that the two social and political phenomena, namely the equality of conditions and democratic politics, exist contemporaneously in the New World. Nor is it sufficiently clear whether democratic institutions influence American society—its customs, manners and feelings—or the customs and manners existed prior to the advent of the democratic form of government. But despite these deficiencies, Tocqueville made a clear and compelling case for the special relationship between culture and politics by introducing causal analysis into the study of regime formation and by presenting social and cultural conditions as prerequisites for the establishment and maintenance of government. And in so doing, in examining in a conceptually lucid way "the whole moral and intellectual condition of a people," he transformed a hitherto nebulous idea that culture provides a base for politics into a worthwhile science of political culture. Viewed from this standpoint, he accomplished something beyond his modest claim of not seeking new truths but trying to show how facts already known are connected with his subject.[35]

THE BIRTH OF CULTURE AND CULTURAL SYSTEMS: ANTHROPOLOGICAL AND SOCIOLOGICAL INFLUENCE

Integrationism

The advent of anthropology in the nineteenth century as an intellectual inquiry into that part of humanity beyond the Western hemisphere brought the concept of culture to prominence. Indeed, in the sense of infusing new meanings into this old concept, anthropology practically reinvented the notion of culture. Previously, the term "culture" had been used to denote exclusively an aristocratic or upper class upbringing characterized by education, its refined social manners, and a taste for art and literature. This is the sense in which Aristotle and others used the concept. This usage found a clear expression particularly in Rousseau when culture was perceived by him as a corrupting force that destroyed a transparent and simple way of human living in modern society. But anthropologists look at culture in a drastically different light. For them, and later for many others, culture acquired a meaning that is broad in scope and inclusive in substance. It no longer refers exclusively to what is sometimes called "high culture," but represents the total way of living of a people—their ideas, customs, norms as well as those features that grow out of their interaction with the natural environment. In the words of Edward B. Tylor, one of the founders of anthropology, it is "that complex whole which includes knowledge, belief, art, morals, law, custom, and any other capabilities and habits acquired by man as a member of society."[36]

The Tylorean omnibus definition is important because it constitutes a starting point for what was to become a full-blown and colorful understanding of culture and because its influence would be felt far beyond the boundaries of anthropology. From this all-embracing conception of culture there sprung a host of other conceptions that would radically change our perception of "that complex whole."[37] In terms of their relation to the study of political culture, however, three conceptions call for special attention. The first is the idea of cultural integration, an idea closely associated with Franz Boas and his followers such as Ruth Benedict. Rejecting Tylor's grand scheme of a rational and universal evolution of culture from the primitive to the civilized, the Boasians see culture as consisting of a congeries of individual and irreducible traits; these traits are historically developed, local, and meaningful only in the context in which they are found, and they tend to diffuse over a geographical area and integrate or in Benedict's term configure toward a predominant motive to form a unique cultural entity.[38]

To the Boasians, the twin principles of diffusion and integration are characteristic of the historical development of cultural traits into a consistent and shared pattern of thought and action in a given cultural context. This process can be considered on two levels. On the macro level, though the traits of a culture take shape as a result of a series of historical accidents, they are not completely random. In the sense that they each go through a process of modification by which they are reshaped to fit the new cultural context, cultural traits are pregnant with meaning. It is meaning, be it the pursuit of social prestige or the glorification of one's family, that can provide a culture with unity and coherence that can account for the fact that a culture is not a simple aggregate of disconnected traits but an ordered whole. Cultural integration is achieved through the creation and maintenance of this whole which in turn enables us to distinguish one cultural pattern from another.

But cultural integration can be understood more concretely on a micro level. On this level, culture is viewed as an integrating force that shapes the individual's mind and behavior in a given society, and this integrating force manifests itself in the ideas, beliefs and practices that members of that society share in common. For the Boasians, culture is embodied in shared ideas, beliefs and practices acquired over an extended period of time and in a particular region, and human individuals are the bearers of culture in whom these ideas, beliefs and practices are represented and through whom they are transmitted from one generation to the next. The process of transmission and representation is more importantly also a process of regulation and control by which each and every individual as the bearer of a given culture is made to behave in a way consistent with the "unconscious canons of choice" within the culture.[39] Our understanding of cultural integration thus involves essentially an understanding of how cultural ideas, beliefs and practices disseminate and integrate, of how these ideas, beliefs and practices shape the mind and behavior of the individual.

Functionalism

While deemphasizing what anthropologists would later call the ecological factors, the Boasian interpretation of culture as, generally, a historical pattern of commonly shared ideas, beliefs and practices would have deep repercussions, as we shall see, in the formulation of the political culture concept. Exerting an equally important influence over the forms this concept would take in political analysis is a second, namely the functionalist, conception of culture. Functionalism has been successful in explaining cultural phenomena in the past, despite the fact that it has some flaws; for example, it has difficulty in accounting for social and cultural change and for the continued existence of dysfunctional traits in a cultural system. This success is due in part to the pioneering efforts of two anthropologists A.R. Radcliffe-Brown and Bronislaw Malinowski. As critics point out, Radcliffe-Brown and Malinowski had important disagreements over the nature and meaning of function in a cultural system, but they shared with each other, and with functionalists in general, a basic commitment to the view that a given socio-cultural phenomenon can be best understood only in terms of the function it performs in a larger system of which it is a part.[40]

The functionalist view has two essential components: system and function. Resonating with the idea of integration, it takes culture typically as an ordered whole. What distinguishes it from the Boasian conception, however, is that the whole is not considered to consist of a host of individual traits which are ordered around a major cultural motive; rather, it is conceived as a network of cultural elements including objects, activities, and rules (and to the list we may add a variety of other features such as customs, habits, ideas, beliefs, manners, and norms). These elements are related to one another and to the total way of life of a people such that they form a *system*. In this system each element has a role to play, and each is understood in terms of the role it plays in facilitating a deeper or larger purpose. In functionalist terms each element performs one or more functions in the larger system of which it is a part in order to make organized human life possible. Certainly not all functions are of equal weight in contributing to the maintenance of the whole system; some are more fundamental than others. Neither should they be thought of as a set of immutable relations linking the structural arrangements of a society to the actions and interactions of its people. But functions—be they the maintenance of social cohesion *a la* Radcliffe-Brown or the fulfillment of individual needs *a la* Malinowski—do allow us to make sense of the seemingly disparate cultural traits found in a socio-cultural system.[41]

The emphasis on system and function lies at the core of the functionalist's quest for an understanding of culture that is not merely descriptive and particularistic but generalizable across time and cultures. Certainly the notion of system is not the functionalist's invention; it can be attributed to Montesquieu.[42] Neither is the idea of function, an idea which is traceable genealogically to eighteenth-century utilitarianism.[43] But it is the functionalist who perhaps first brought these concepts to the fore by making them an explanatory tool specifically designed to capture the intricacy of a social and cultural entity. The most illuminating part of functionalism is that it allows us to see society and culture not only as an organization of individuals and activities but more importantly as a complex of relations, and to understand that the nature of these relations is such that an understanding of one element, one sphere of activity, or one subsystem, necessarily involves that of another and of the whole socio-cultural system. The interconnection of different elements, spheres of activity, or subsystems can be further explained by resorting to the function(s) each of them performs in and for this system. Thus, for example, a ceremonial ritual is to be viewed not as purely religious but as fulfilling certain political or social functions. As adequately described by Radcliffe-Brown, the idea of function signifies a set of relations; it is that dynamic link between part and whole and among various parts within the whole. The relationship between system and function, just like that between a living body and its blood vessels, is mutually dependent. Without function a system would be lifeless, and without system a function would be meaningless.

Symbolism

The integrationist and functionalist conceptions of culture have been the two dominant forces for organizing anthropological thought for decades. As such, they helped spawn a plurality of definitions of culture that are at once informative and confusing. This state of affairs did not go unchallenged, of course. Dissatisfied with many of the widely used yet ill-defined concepts of culture, Leslie A. White proposed a new concept based on his idea of symboling, and it was later represented in a number of anthropological studies including Clifford Geertz' *The Interpretation of Cultures* and Roy Wagner's *The Invention of Culture*. For convenience we may call this third conception of culture the symbolist one.

The symbolist conception of culture begins by arguing that symbols play a pivotal role in human life; among other things, they enable us to communicate effectively and make sense of an indifferent external world, help us cultivate standards and rules to live by, and preserve knowledge and experience for the continuity of our species. It is out of symbols that culture is born and through the use of symbols that culture is perpetuated. Symbols are so fundamental to human survival that they come to signify the essence of what it means to be human and form the very foundation upon which culture is built. The symbolist sees the ability to create and use symbols as a unique human quality. White calls this quality *symboling,* in the sense of "bestowing meaning upon a thing or an act, or grasping and appreciating meanings thus bestowed."[44] It is "the exercise of the symbolic faculty," White writes, that "brought a class of phenomena into existence that is . . . supra-biological and extra-somatic" and that "collectively we call *culture* (emphasis original)."[45]

The idea that culture builds upon symbols and symboling bears remarkable resemblance to what Boas describes as "the power of reasoning" that differentiates human culture from animal life. But White is careful not to embrace Boas' subjective interpretation in much the same way he objects to Radcliffe-Brown's impatient dismissal of culture as a mere abstraction. To him culture is as real and tangible as it is *sui generis*. Despite this, however, and despite the fact that he defines culture as "a class of things and events," a close examination of his emphasis on symbols and symboling seems to reveal a much less striking difference than he wants us to believe between his own idea and the idea he criticizes. As he has made clear, a thing or event is just that, a thing or event which has no significance or meaning to us; it becomes culturally relevant only when it is "symboled," turns into a "symbolate" and is interpreted in a particular (extrasomatic) context.[46] In other words, culture begins when things and events cease to be things and events *per se* and are conceived as symbols. Semantically, a symbol is not a thing or event, but a name or sign for something other than itself; it is a relation or association of signifier with signified, signifier with signifier. Such a relation or association is not in any sense obvious in things or events themselves, however, and becomes intelligible only when people impose meaning upon it and when they impose different meanings in different contexts. A symbol, thus, is best understood as a meaning or a set of meanings to be interpreted in context; as such, its existence is neither purely objective nor absolutely subjective. Viewed in this way, White's emphasis on symbols, on symboling and context, betrays a fundamental concern on his part with meaning, and with culture as a special category of meaning-laden phenomena.

This acute interest in meaning or more accurately in contextually defined meaning has found continued expression in Geertz and Wagner. Geertz, like White, interprets culture also in terms of symbols or systems of symbols, and in terms of meanings concealed and congealed in symbols. But he is able to transcend the debate on whether culture is material or nonmaterial, which by and large informs the way of thinking entertained by many of his predecessors including White, and focuses entirely and unequivocally on the concept of meaning. For Geertz, culture is "a historically transmitted pattern of meanings embodied in symbols" which needs to be interpreted and which can be understood only through such interpretation, only by delving into contextual details, not in terms of theories alone.[47] Situated at the center of this conception is the idea of meaning; vague as it may be, this idea carries a strong implication that we look beyond the symbolic, beyond what is obvious and ephemeral, to a deeper level where a more satisfactory explanation may be found for seemingly self-contradictory human behaviors. For Geertz, meaning is essentially given, at least insofar as any particular individual is concerned, and functions as a control mechanism to order and make sense of human experience which, if undirected, would be utterly ungovernable and chaotic.

Wagner shares many of Geertz's ideas, particularly the centrality of meaning to an adequate conception of culture, but he construes meaning in a slightly different way. For him, meaning is essentially *invented,* both in terms of the anthropologist's creativity in constructing his or her understanding of a culture and in terms of the creativity of the culture and its members in defining and extending the use of symbolic elements.[48] Wagner views culture as a dialectic process of symbolization that at once innovates upon and is controlled by conventional symbols and contexts. To know a culture is to understand its symbolic elements, and this in turn requires an understanding of meanings that are continually being created and recreated within all kinds of contexts and in opposition to these contexts. In the sense that it defines and narrows the possibilities of emerging meanings, context poses itself as the other, as an opposition; in the sense that it is an experiential environment in which symbolic elements relate to one another to generate new meanings, context becomes an integral part of meaning and meaning "a function of the ways in which we create and otherwise experience contexts."[49] The interpenetration of meaning and context to form a dialectic movement of complementarity and contradiction, of innovation and control in understanding culture as an unfolding experience is central to Wagner's idea of invention. Thus, culture can be regarded as a system of symbolic meanings that are in a constant process of being invented. But invention should not be considered as a mere act of imputing meanings to culture; it is also a transformative process in which the meanings we impute to culture in turn shape the way individuals think and act.

Durkheim

Although anthropology and sociology were considered a unified subject of inquiry rather than two separate fields of study in their formative years, they employed different concepts and ideas which would have important implications for the development of the two disciplines in the social sciences. For the anthropologist, it is essentially the concept of culture that provided a theoretical framework for studying human values, behaviors, and symbols; for the sociologist, it is the concept of society that played a central role in explaining the nature and functions of these values, behaviors, and symbols. The two concepts are often used interchangeably, and it is sometimes a matter of individual choice to use one instead of the other. Even if they are used distinctly as two separate notions, they often imply each other.[50] This is particularly evident in the writings of some of the early socio-anthropologists such as Radcliffe-Brown and Durkheim.

Among the key figures that helped shape modern sociology, Durkheim and Weber call for special attention. This is certainly not to say that no other intellectual figures exerted influence on sociological thought. But if we refer specifically to sociological impact on the conception of political culture, Durkheim and Weber remain unparalleled. A proper starting point for discussing Durkheim's influence on the conception of culture, perhaps, is his idea of the *conscience collective*. In an attempt to unravel the origins of an increasingly differentiated and individualistic society in the modern era, and to cope with the problem of order in such a society, Durkheim distinguishes between two types of social solidarity, mechanical and organic, which characterize two types of society, traditional and modern, respectively. Mechanical solidarity, which he also calls "solidarity by similarities" as opposed to "solidarity arising from the division of labor," is based on the total absence of individuality and on the individual's unqualified identification with his or her community. It is undergirded by a system of "beliefs and sentiments common to the average members of a society" or what Durkheim deems the *conscience collective*. In traditional society, this system of beliefs

and sentiments punished certain kinds of individual conduct with the undifferentiated sanction of society as a whole, but such undifferentiated sanction, according to Durkheim, did not persist in modern society due to social
differentiation, and the *conscience collective* took a turn toward an enlightened common consciousness based on the recognition and facilitation of the
individual's self-realization.[51]

It is worth noting that Durkheim's use of the French term *conscience
collective* is not without ambiguity. Its English translation "common consciousness" eclipses its moral connotation associated with the word "conscience." Talcott Parsons suggests that this connotation is more appropriate
to Durkheim's thought.[52] Paul Bohannan, however, goes further to argue
that there is still in it a "third and more important meaning" and this meaning, considered in conjunction with Durkheim's notion of collective representation, is one that would be best expressed by using the anthropological
concept of culture.[53] Bohannan's point is well taken insofar as the term *conscience collective* is taken to mean collectively shared representations of the
external world which unify the subject knower and the object, and culture
is regarded as "an analytic construct" involving such representations. But
there is a deeper and more dynamic sense in which Durkheim's conception
of culture can be grasped and this has to be understood in the context of
"representing."

Durkheim has been often credited with influencing a number of conceptions of culture, for example, as a control mechanism, as a *sui generis* reality, as superorganic, and as symbolic. To the extent that they capture one or
more substantive characteristics of the notion of culture, these views are
sound. But Durkheim's concern, as Bohannan correctly points out, seems
more epistemological than substantive. Bohannan, however, evidently mis-
construes the Durkheimian idea of collective representation, first, by viewing
representations as "communicable images or categories" in a mind (or, for
that matter, in an aggregate of minds) and, then, by reducing collective representation to "a concept or a category of thought held in sufficiently similar
form by many persons to allow effective communication."[54] He further adds
that here we are dealing with a *metaphor*, not a fact. This is by no means
Durkheim's intention. Durkheim said repeatedly that social facts must be
treated as "things," that collective representations "do not derive from [indi-
vidual minds] but from the association of minds," and that individual beliefs
and sentiments do not become social "except by combination under the action of the *sui generis* forces developed in association."[55] The idea of association is crucial here, as is the medium through which it is manifested, namely
social or collective action. Obviously "the association of minds" will not be

seen in any concrete and tangible way, but this does not imply that it is metaphorical. In the sense that it molds or otherwise conditions the individual's mind, it exists as a context; it is what may be called the context of representing. In this context, collective representation presents itself as *representing* which conjoins ideas, beliefs and sentiments, on the one hand, and practices and actions, on the other, in a single continuous process of contradiction, modification and becoming. It is through this movement that collective representation and the *conscience collective* are created and become known to us. Culture, insofar as it involves collective representation and the *conscience collective,* is embodied neither in ideas, beliefs, sentiments, or, in short, representations exclusively, nor in actions and practices alone; it exists only through the interaction between ideas and actions, beliefs and practices, only to the extent that and when such actions or practices occur. It exists, according to Durkheim, as a force in the context of representing.[56]

This construction of Durkheim's conception of culture, of collective representation and the *conscience collective,* as a process of becoming, as an interactive space between beliefs and practices, ideas and actions, may enable us to grasp in a more fruitful and tangible way an elusive concept in Durkheim's thought. Two important components of this concept need reemphasizing: First, the drawing together, combination, and accumulation of individual minds over time have produced the *conscience collective* which is collectively represented in various forms (for example, law, religion, morality, etc.); second, this combined state of mind to be best known as culture cannot exist except through collective action; it can be realized only when individuals act in their social capacities as "We" instead of "I," when ideas penetrate actions and actions embody ideas.

Weber

A similar action-oriented understanding of the concept of the social and the cultural which is so central to Durkheim can be found also in Weber's writings.[57] This is perhaps one of the instances of what Parsons saw as the convergence of two great sociological minds. But convergence entails difference, especially when we bear in mind the fact that Durkheim and Weber were working from different intellectual traditions, confronted different philosophical issues, and used different concepts and categories of analysis. For Durkheim, social action is an integral part of his conception of society as a collective entity and a *sui generis* reality which possesses an independent life of its own *vis-à-vis* its constituent individuals. By contrast, Weber is interested, strictly speaking, not in social action *per se* but in the *meaning* behind it and in the motivational forces that make it happen. For him, social action, only insofar as it enables us to secure meaning in an otherwise "meaning-less" world of multiplicity and infinity and only insofar as it serves as an in-strument to a meaningful end, falls within the legitimate purview of sociological investigation. This difference in emphasis between them—be-tween Durkheim's concern with knowledge of social reality and Weber's pre-occupation with the meaning of social action—may account for a different construction of the Weberian conception of the cultural.

Unlike Durkheim, Weber used the concept of culture in a quite explicit way, particularly in connection with his methodological inquiries. This fact, however, does not make it any easier to give an adequate account of what Weber meant by that notion and how he applied it to "the cultural sciences." As is known, the fragmented and broad nature of Weber's writings presents an obstacle to a systematic interpretation of his thought. Ralph Schroeder, in an attempt to provide such an interpretation, argues that there does exist in Weber a unified theme which can be used to structure otherwise diverse and seemingly disparate ideas in his works, and this theme is culture. While a detailed review of his three-pronged thematic treatment of Weber's central concern with the relationship between culture and social life is unnecessary, it is worth pointing out that Schroeder is certainly correct in calling atten-tion to the Weberian conception of culture as involving the role of ideas and beliefs in social change.[58] This is the understanding of some of the master interpreters of Weber, including Parsons, who took culture primarily as con-sisting of value orientations. But what Weber meant by "culture" includes a much wider range of phenomena, not merely values we cherish, but things we do not value; not merely ideas and beliefs, but artifacts as well so far as they acquire meaning in relation to human conduct. In this regard, Schroeder's view, like that of Parsons, is not entirely satisfactory.

By culture, Weber seems to refer sometimes to a whole civilization, sometimes to a set of attitudes and values, and sometimes to the ethos or *Geist* of a collectivity. The multifaceted meaning he implicitly or explicitly attributed to culture may reflect the influence of an intellectual tradition that includes Herder's idea of culture as both a universal and a relative phenom-enon. Weber's idea of the cultural as used to define "cultural sciences" is uni-versal in the sense that the human condition is the ultimate end of this kind of scientific inquiry, but Weber clearly had no intention of making any meta-physical claims as Herder had done in composing his philosophy of culture. What he was fundamentally concerned with is "meaning" behind the mul-tiplicity and infinity of empirical reality, and it is meaning which "the finite human mind" attaches to "a finite portion of this reality" that constitutes the core of what may be best described as culture. Empirical reality becomes *culture* to us, he wrote, because and insofar as it is perceived to have significance for us and can be related to our values and ideas.[59] Culture is sustained by meaning and meaning breathes life into culture; without meaning culture is nothing but mere physical sounds, movements, or things; with meaning these become cultural expressions, cultural events, or cultural symbols. In this sense, culture *is* meaning.

In Weber's scheme, meaning can be divided into two kinds: particular and ideal-typical. The former is "the actual existing meaning in a given concrete case of a particular actor" or "the average or approximate meaning attributable to a given plurality of actors," while the latter refers to "the theoretically conceived pure type of subjective meaning attributed to the hypothetical actor or actors in a given type of action."[60] The actual and particular meanings, which are useful in assisting us with details but which can never be completely known in their infinite variety, lie in the domain of historical inquiry. What the cultural sciences are ultimately concerned with is the pure or ideal type of meaning. Culture, insofar as it is the conceptual keystone of the cultural sciences and hinges on meaning, may be best understood in terms of its commensurability with ideal-typical meaning. It is ideal-typical, rather than particular, in the sense that it does not describe the actual and particular meaning in any concrete case, nor does it describe the average meaning induced from a number of particular cases, but rather is a pure form of reference against which concrete phenomena can be ordered and meaningfully investigated. It cannot be found correspondingly in reality, yet it can appear partially or in changed forms in reality. It does not attempt to generate laws or lawlike generalizations in terms of which multifarious concrete phenomena can be causally and universally explained, but rather aims to ferret out and interpret the significance of these phenomena in their unique configuration. Finally it is a rationally constructed type of meaning acquired through a process of selection, evaluation, and synthesis of certain essential elements of empirical reality and as such serves as a means to unveil "concrete cultural phenomena in their interdependence, their causal conditions and their *significance* (emphasis original)."[61]

Culture is ideal-typical as meaning is ideal-typical. We do not find culture as such in reality in the same way we do not find in religion asceticism as such, namely as a set of logically consistent doctrines, though it, like asceticism, *can* appear in reality, in empirically documented ideas, beliefs, symbols, artifacts, events and the like. Ideas, beliefs and symbols are in the strict sense not culture *per se;* they are merely ideas, beliefs and symbols which may or may not substantively go into the making of culture depending on the requirements of a given topic of investigation. Culture can be each and every one of these things, yet is none of them. The infinite particular meanings of culture make it virtually impossible to justify the superiority of one conception or description of culture over another except by "the one-sided accentuation" of certain points of view or elements of reality to form a rationally constructed conceptual scheme for specific explanatory purposes. Neither is it analytically useful to understand and explain diverse cultural phenomena by seeing culture as consisting of some sort of totality such as a self-contained system. Culture becomes intelligible to us only through the construction of an ideal type of meaning in relation to the interpretation of certain concrete cultural phenomena, and a particularistic or totalistic treatment of culture, whether to deem it as consisting of ideas and beliefs or as systems of value orientation, is quite misleading.

The ideal-typical conception of culture founded on the ideal type of meaning is perhaps one of Weber's most profound legacies. Unfortunately it has been largely overlooked, even by some of the most learned commentators on Weber. Talcott Parsons, for one, ignored this crucial insight in an attempt to build a three-dimensional comprehensive theory of action or orientation of action which embraces personality, culture and the social system. He created a near-exhaustive list of categories and subcategories under which myriad concrete phenomena, presumably, could be subsumed and in terms of which theoretical generalizations could be arrived at to provide a systematic and universally valid explanation of empirical reality. While doing so, he reduced culture to an all-encompassing system of cognitive beliefs, expressive symbols, and in particular ethical values which correspond in a general way to the *actual* motives or meanings controlling individual and social action.[62] This is by no means what Weber intended for the cultural sciences of which the sociology of culture is a part. What Weber was trying to say, if my reading is accurate, is that since particular meanings cannot be exhausted and any substantive approach to meaning is bound to be incomplete, it may be helpful to construct a rational scheme such as an ideal type and use it as a heuristic to "tease out" the cultural meaning of a historical phenomenon, to find out what it is that distinguishes it singularly from other meanings as plausible explanations of the same phenomenon. This is precisely the way in which Weber tried to understand and explain the significance of modern capitalism. He sought to illuminate its uniqueness in terms of the rationalization of conduct on the basis of the idea of calling and in contrast to other forms of wealth accumulation in the past and in other parts of the world.[63]

Some may argue, moreover, that Parsons' (and Schroeder's) "one-sided accentuation" of value orientation also constitutes an ideal type of culture. This is a mistaken view, primarily because it fails to take an account of the context in which Weber's one-sided accentuation takes place. For Parsons the conception of culture as value orientation aims at the generation of an all-encompassing theory, whereas for Weber it is embedded in the context of interpreting the meaning of a given cultural phenomenon (or, for that matter, a group of phenomena) in its concreteness and uniqueness. Culture as an ideal type exists only in relation to specific questions of meaning arising from the investigation of one or more aspects of concrete reality. Thus, it is misguided to treat it in a way that would lead or contribute to a general theory or part of such a general theory to be utilized to "cover" in a causally valid manner a whole range of cultural phenomena independently of specific questions of meaning under investigation.

RETRIEVING THE CONCEPT OF POLITICAL CULTURE

In "The Intellectual History of the Civic Culture Concept," Gabriel A. Almond conceded that the concept of political culture is steeped in the entire Western intellectual tradition beginning with ancient Greek thought.[64] This is no doubt true, particularly when we consider it as part of our enduring quest for an improved understanding of the relationship between politics and culture. But if we take a closer look, we would find roughly two major sources, as the foregoing discussion has attempted to show, upon which this concept is based. From classical and modern political thought it has drawn the concept of the political, and from modern anthropology and sociology it has taken that of the cultural. In a crude sense, the emergence of political culture can be seen as the result of a marriage between the political and the cultural, a marriage that was fully integrated in the life of the *polis* but began to crumble with the rise of the modern state.

The concept of political culture is an attempt to relate the political to the cultural. This attempt would not have been possible if it had not been for the increasingly critical role the concept of culture has come to play in the study of man and society. The concept of culture would not have assumed such a prominent place, as we have seen, without anthropology and sociology; it is anthropology and sociology that have provided many of the basic concepts and categories on which political culture draws. It bears noting that conceptions of political culture have not only made extensive use of these concepts and categories, but in some cases reproduced them. It is safe to say that political culture is to a considerable extent the concept of culture modified by the adjective "political." The close link between political culture and culture is borne out also by the fact that there is a persistent lack of homogeneity in the conception of political culture just as in that of culture, and that conceptions of political culture sometimes appear to be a close approximation, if not an exact copy, of conceptions of culture. In what follows, three conceptions of political culture will be chosen for description and evaluation, not merely because of this kind of approximation, but more importantly because of their wide acceptance in the study of politics. After that, an alternative understanding of political culture will be presented and defended.

The Individualist

The most popular conception of political culture may be tentatively called "individualist." Gabriel A. Almond has been often credited as the one who introduced and further developed it (in collaboration with Sidney Verba) in comparative politics, and it has since become virtually *the* concept of political culture to which no alternative seems to pose a serious challenge.[65] Political culture is defined by Almond and Verba as subjective orientations (or patterns of subjective orientations) to political objects among members of a society. These orientations can be categorized as cognitive, affective, and evaluative in terms of their character. Cognitive orientations refer to beliefs and knowledge, affective orientations refer to sentiments and attitudes, and evaluative orientations refer to moral judgments. Depending on the degree of differentiation of political roles and of policy input and output by these roles within a given political system, three types of political culture can be further classified. The parochial one is characterized by little or no differentiation of political roles and little or no control over policy input and output by the governed, the subject one by some degree of differentiation of political roles, yet little or no control over policy input by the governed, and the participant one by a high degree of differentiation of political roles and of policy input and output by the governed. Though the three types are analytically distinct, their empirical boundaries are by no means absolute; there exist borderline cases in which we may speak of parochial-subject, subject-participant or participant-parochial political culture.[66]

It is worth recalling that the individualist conception of political culture was proposed at a time when the so-called behavioral revolution was at its peak. The behavioralist cry for positive evidence rather than philosophical speculation, for systemic study rather than mere institutional and legal analyses, was accompanied by a similar concern with conceptual clarity. Such clarity was achievable, but often at a price. This is precisely the case with the individualist conception of political culture. By defining political culture narrowly as subjective orientations, Almond and Verba have considerably reduced the ambiguities surrounding this complex notion at least since Montesquieu. There emerges a clearly articulated concept, one which can provide not only a useful tool for communication so that we minimize the possibility of talking past each other, but also a much needed direction for the study of political systems. It points to the subjective aspect of such systems. Political culture, described by Almond and Verba as the political system "internalized in the cognitions, feelings, and evaluations" of the members of a given society,[67] is thus able to add a long neglected dimension to the dominant yet increasingly stifling external analyses of structures and institutions.

The pathbreaking work by Almond and Verba on political culture laid the groundwork for later studies, especially in respect to its conceptual clarity, simplicity and precision. But, as indicated above, clarity, simplicity and precision come at a price. Although Almond and Verba said explicitly that they had chosen only one among many possible conceptions of political culture, this preemptive remark did not prevent doubts from being raised about its adequacy. Notwithstanding its liberal bias, the individualist conception suffers from at least three deficiencies.[68] First, Almond and Verba's view of political culture is essentially a reductionist one. It is reductionist in the sense that it reduces a collective phenomenon to individualistic beliefs, feelings and value orientations. There is no denying that Almond and his collaborators also emphasize, especially in their later works, that these beliefs, feelings and value orientations are part of the political system as a whole and that they interact with other aspects of the same system and with each other.[69] But a close examination of their basic theoretical and methodological assumptions reveals a consistent tendency to treat political culture, in Lehman's words, as "merely the statistical aggregation of the intrapsychic orientations of the individual members of society."[70]

This reductionist view has several flaws. It is unnecessary to enumerate them here since they have been systematically exposed by critics at least as early as Durkheim. Suffice it to say that there are nonreducible collective entities and phenomena which can be properly understood only in terms of collective properties. To reduce these collective properties to individual traits would lead to the impoverishment of political discourse by rendering incomprehensible and meaningless many of the concepts we use to understand and explain our social and cultural world. This is of course not to deny that a collective entity or phenomenon is made up of individual components and the study of these components can provide us one perspective from which to examine received views and conclusions. It is untenable to say, however, that knowledge of a certain quantity of individual beliefs, feelings and value orientations will enable us to make valid inferences about a higher- or macro-level phenomenon called political culture, just as it is indefensible to suppose that the aggregation of neural cells can allow us to grasp the nature of human consciousness.

Second, Almond and Verba's conception of political culture is also an impressionistic one. It paints a political reality dotted with discrete individuals and their discrete perceptions. These individuals and perceptions are isolated and rootless, having been stripped of their historical contexts, social relations, and other unique circumstances that combined to make them what they are, to give shape to their beliefs, feelings and value orientations. It is hardly conceivable that such isolated and rootless individuals and perceptions have ever existed, and even if they did, it would still be difficult to see how they could furnish an adequate understanding of political reality given that the meaning of this reality is practically impossible to uncover without taking account of the social and historical context in which it is found. As historians remind us, it is not only the explicit words and acts of a political actor that can tell us something about his or her orientations; in many cases, the context in which words are spoken and acts performed, the formal or informal ways of speaking and acting, or even what has not been spoken or performed, can tell us more about the nature and meaning of these orientations.[71] The superficiality of the impressionistic view lies exactly in its failure to consider these factors as an integral part of political culture.

Third, to conceive political culture merely as political orientations is to obscure the fact that there may exist a gap between orientation and action. It is one of Almond and Verba's assumptions, for example, that one's sense of political competence would most likely lead to political action. As Carole Pateman duly noted, this is a false assumption.[72] Almond and Verba's own survey shows that there does exist a large gap in liberal democracies between one's feelings of political competence and actual participation in political activities. This divergence cannot be explained except by a proper account of a liberal culture that discourages participation in many spheres of life including the workplace and the family. Neither can it be understood exclusively in terms of the individual's own misperception, but also by delving into the political socialization process in liberal culture which tells ordinary men and women how the political system ought to work and what role they should play *qua* citizens. To the extent that this is true, we cannot afford to divorce orientation from action, belief from practice, in our appreciation of political culture. A conception of political culture which does so is a static one. It is static, not in the sense that individual orientations and beliefs are viewed as unchanging—in fact the authors of *The Civic Culture* have argued to the contrary—but in the sense that it fails to offer a dynamic understanding of political culture by ignoring how political actions and practices inform and shape political orientations and beliefs.

It is necessary to stress that this sketchy critique is not meant to do full justice to Almond and Verba's well articulated and popular concept of political culture. What it attempts to do is to point out that it is not unproblematic to use the concept as Almond and Verba and many others who follow them have used it. By recognizing and analyzing the weaknesses of this conception, we may be better able to make improvements upon this notion.

The Traditionalist

The second and traditionalist conception is marked essentially by two related characteristics: its tendency to be inclusive and its emphasis on history and tradition. The individualist definition has limited the utility of the political culture concept by reducing it to individualistic orientations. This limiting effect is felt particularly by those whose methodological preference is different from quantitative analysis. Facing this situation, some propose a conception of political culture which is inclusive in substance and rich in theoretical implications. Regardless of their specific concerns, they tend to emphasize the importance of history and tradition in providing the main sources for and in defining the loci of political culture.[73] Thus Lucian Pye is able to broaden the substantive scope of political culture by embracing "the traditions of a society, the spirit of its public institutions, the passions and the collective reasoning of its citizenry, and the style and operating codes of its leaders," and Archie Brown is able to do the same by emphasizing how the historical experience of a people and their traditional values and beliefs shape their political culture.[74]

This inclusiveness, with a special emphasis on history and tradition, is significant not only in a substantive sense but also in a theoretical sense. Substantively it provides a richer reserve of cultural traits than mere individual beliefs, feelings and values. Theoretically it directs the study of political culture away from the individualist approach conception to a different type of analysis. This type of analysis recognizes the possibility of discrepancies between individual subjective orientations and what exists independently of them as the ultimate politico-cultural reality; and while not denying that the former may to a certain extent reflect this reality, it gives primacy to the superorganic nature of political culture as a nonreducible collective phenomenon. This is clearly borne out by both Pye's and Brown's treatment of the subjective. Some may argue that Pye is of the same theoretical persuasion as are Almond and Verba, particularly in consideration of his explicit identification with the individualist conception. A close reading of his more substantive studies, however, reveals a similarity only in rhetoric. The "subjective realm of politics" which he likens to the political culture of a society cannot by any measure be pinned down exclusively at the individual level; in fact it takes on a supra-individual and collective nature, as manifested in his discussion of networking as one of the defining features of Chinese political culture and, most recently, of the two opposing Confucian and Taoist-Buddhist political cultures.[75]

Similarly, although Brown acknowledges his debt to the individualists for pioneering the use of the concept, there is no indication that "the subjective perception of history and politics" in his understanding and in the understanding of the authors under his editorship is confined to individual perceptions or, for that matter, to the aggregation of individual perceptions. The essays by Gray, White and others demonstrate that the political culture of a nation can be most fruitfully studied in terms of some of the general ideological, moral, and symbolic themes which go into the making of its unique cultural identity.[76] These themes are not dependent on the perceptions of any given individual for existence; they possess an independent existence of their own which endures far beyond the life span of individual men and women and as such are constitutive of what may be called collective subjectivity.

Despite its liberating effect, however, the traditionalist conception is subject to criticisms. A general criticism is that inclusiveness is both a strength and a weakness. While absorbing many of the merits other conceptions of political culture have to offer, the traditionalist also takes in many of their flaws; these flaws would tend to weaken the potential explanatory power of political culture as a concept. More specifically, as Chilton points out, Brown's approach conflates two different levels of analysis, namely the individual and the group.[77] This conflation can only result in conceptual confusion, rendering an otherwise useful concept ineffective. The same criticism can be leveled against Pye when he shifts freely between individual orientations and collective values in discussing political culture and when he defines political culture in terms of individual orientations but studies it in terms of collective traits. Such shifting is indicative of an attempt to bridge the gap between micro- and macro-political phenomena, that is, to make inferences about collective phenomena in terms of individualistic characteristics. From a substantive point of view, this may lead to some suggestive results in the study of political culture; but from a conceptual point of view, it creates just as much ambiguity as the Tylorean omnibus conception of culture has done in the past.

The traditionalist approach also has a tendency to shift between the past and the present without giving adequate account of cultural change. No doubt, history and tradition play a crucial role in shaping the political culture of a society, but it is problematic to make inferences about contemporary political culture solely on the basis of traditional values and practices. Such inferences can be misleading, because cultures change. Thus, for example, to obtain a proper understanding of contemporary Chinese political culture, it is not sufficient to merely give an account of Confucian values and beliefs, although such an account may provide a useful frame of reference. What is needed in this context is a description of the characteristics of political culture in contemporary China. This description helps us compare traditional with modern cultural values and practices. It also allows us to see the extent to which cultural change has taken place.

The Symbolist

The third conception of political culture has been clearly inspired by symbolic anthropology and has attracted little attention so far in political science. It is suggested by Lowell Dittmer. Dittmer argues that the political culture concept as developed by the individualist is inadequate because it is synthetically nondistinguishable from related concepts such as political psychology and political structure, on the one hand, and analytically unclear with regard to its characteristics, on the other. He proposes to redefine it as "a system of political symbols."[78] The new definition draws mainly upon two sources: political symbolism and political communication. From the former it takes the idea of symbol as something which has a degree of autonomy from either political psychology or political structure and as such can present itself as an independent empirical variable to be analyzed, whereas from the latter it takes the idea of meaning encoding and decoding. These two ideas are then synthesized in a semiological framework of signs, referents and signification to produce a symbolist conception of political culture.

According to Dittmer, three components make up political culture as a symbol system; they are pragmatics, semantics and syntactics. Pragmatics deals with the intention of the speaker and the reactions of the hearer, or more specifically with the relationship between the elite as speaker who manipulates symbols and the masses as hearer who responds to and interprets them. Semantics deals with the relationship between symbol and political reality to which it refers, and with how the core or original meaning of a symbol is extended through association, that is, through contiguity and resemblance, to illuminate experience. Syntactics deals with the internal logic and development of symbols in a symbol system; it focuses particularly on how symbolic themes are structured and how this structure reveals their meaning.[79]

By defining political culture as a system of political symbols and by placing the symbols in a semiological framework, Dittmer believes that he has provided a different perspective, one which enjoys several conceptual advantages over the popular individualist view. To isolate the symbol as the variable for analysis can help us steer clear of or bridge the gap between micro- and macro-politics. For although shared by individual human beings, symbols exist independently of them and can transmit meaning transpersonally. As such, they possess a certain degree of autonomy both from individual psychological traits and from political structural characteristics. Chilton sees further advantages in the symbolist conception; these advantages enable us not only to appreciate the uniqueness of each culture under investigation but also to see how "people's symbolically mediated understanding of the political world determines in part their political behavior."[80]

The symbolist view as articulated by Dittmer is a plausible alternative to the individualist position, but it has its own weaknesses. From an analytic point of view, two questions are worth raising. The first is about the nature of symbols and the second about the semiological view of symbolism. Nowhere is it clearly explained by Dittmer what a symbol is and how it is made "the empirical unit of analysis precisely." Is it a verbal utterance, a physical object, or a behavioral gesture like the boyish wink in Clifford Geertz's description? If it is all of these as Dittmer seems to entertain at one point (but not at others), does that mean then that we measure the regularity of winks and the relationship between winks and other symbolic gestures? This would be a futile task as it is a misleading one. To operationalize a symbol is to misunderstand its nature, for what makes something symbolic is meaning and meaning cannot be quantified.

This immediately leads to the semiological view of symbolism. Dan Sperber convinces us that the semiological understanding of symbols and symbolism is inadequate, primarily because it deems the symbolic process as a matter of decoding signs. Such decoding presupposes a given set of hidden meanings paired up to a given set of signs which are open to interpretation. Notwithstanding the fact that the idea of meaning itself is highly problematic, it is mistaken that the interpretation of symbolic meaning is obtainable by the exegetical commentary of a symbol. Exegesis, as Sperber shows, "does not constitute the interpretation of the symbol, but one of its extensions" which "must be itself symbolically interpreted."[81] If we recognize this in the symbol-meaning pair, and if we recognize further that the second is not simply an interpretation but a development of the first, it is conceivable that the first may as well be a development of the second. It is here that a semiological view of symbolism becomes problematic, as does a semiological view of political culture.

Political Culture as a Shared Way of Relating: An Alternative Conception

The problems and ambiguities in the symbolist, the traditionalist, and particularly the individualist conception of political culture have prompted a series of attempts to recircumscribe, reorient, or otherwise revise this notion. Kim advises that we use "political orientations" in lieu of "political culture," since the latter carries the baggage it inherits from cultural anthropology.[82] Lehman argues that political culture only "specifies the conditions under which more strategic correlations will exist in greater or lesser intensity" and "has only a 'modified' explanatory impact."[83] Tucker accepts the legitimate value of this concept, but disapproves of its current use in political science; he questions the premise that political culture, if it is to be useful at all, must explain something causally and espouses instead a cultural approach to politics, one which would provide a basis of understanding and stimulate analysis.[84]

More recently, Stephen Chilton has proposed nine criteria for defining the political culture concept:

1) *Supramembership* Political culture is not a mere aggregate of individual subjective orientations; rather, it manifests itself as a superorganic and collective phenomenon that transcends the particularistic existence of any given individual or an aggregate of individuals considered in isolation. It is characterized by "supramembership."

2) *Sharedness* Political culture must be capable of being shared in the sense that it provides "a common framework of mutual orientation." An arbitrary collection of people (e.g. travelers in the desert) with an equal distribution of characteristics (e.g. all thirsty) does not necessarily make a culture.

3) *Inequality* In defining political culture, one should also take into account the possibility that the levels of influence on political culture vary according to the political influence of individuals or classes of individuals. This difference in influence, say, between the elite and the populace, is instrumental in facilitating an adequate understanding of the scope and depth of political change.

4) *Behavioral Property* Political culture is not only a collection of abstract ideas and beliefs; it must be capable of being observed in social behaviors, that is, in the actual situations of relating to one another.

5) *Postbehavioral Property* Although political culture is observable in social behaviors, it should be distinguished from mere regularities of behavior. Behavioral regularities can be caused by factors other than culture. This distinction allows us to probe into embedded

cultural meanings and define culture by these meanings rather than by mere regularities.

6) *Unrestricted Applicability* The concept of political culture must be capable of being applied on different levels of social organization and across a broad range of societies. A narrow definition specially designed for a particular research purpose would limit the scope of the applicability of this concept.

7) *Nonreductionism* While a universally applicable concept is crucial for broadening the scope of cultural studies, attention should also be paid to "the uniqueness of any culture's approach to politics." Reducing diverse criteria to some lowest common denominator for cross-cultural studies are unsatisfactory, because they give insufficient attention to the richness and uniqueness of different cultures and to how such richness and uniqueness make one culture's approach to politics different from another.

8) *Comparability* A well-defined political culture concept must permit not only meaningful comparisons between cultures but also meaningful comparisons between different aspects of a single culture. Intracultural comparisons are as important as intercultural ones, because such comparisons allow us to see and understand the role the internal dynamics of a society play in effecting political change.

9) *Objective Testability* The concept of political culture must be capable of generating hypotheses that can be tested for validity in terms of some objective standards against empirical data. Such objective standards are currently lacking in the study of political culture.[85]

Chilton argues that a definition of political culture must meet these requirements and those which fail the test are not conceptually acceptable. Observing that no previous definition satisfies all nine criteria, he proposes a new one that does.

Chilton defines political culture as *the shared way of relating among a group or groups of people*. He adds two important points to the criteria listed above. First, sharedness signifies public commonness. Chilton deems his a bottom-up rather than a top-down approach. The latter supposes *a priori* some kind of collectivity and then tries to find out what are its common features, whereas the former stresses "the actual *use* of a way of relating" and insists that "a culture extends only so far as people choose the same way to relate to one another (original emphasis)."[86] Second, shared ways of relating are not fixed behavioral patterns but become known as "people engage in social situations by interpreting them." Such interpreting, in Chilton's view, ultimately involves moral reasoning, and moral reasoning has cognitive structure. It is cognitive structure that makes cross-cultural studies meaningful without passing judgment on cultural content.[87]

In a stimulating work, Michael Thompson and his co-authors have developed a substantive theory of culture on the basis of a similar understanding of the concept.[88] They view culture as a way of life which involves the combination of cultural biases (i.e. shared values and beliefs) and social relations (i.e. patterns of interpersonal relations). While social relations generate cultural biases, cultural biases in turn legitimize social relations. The relationship between the two is interdependent and mutually reinforcing, and the need for congruence between them constrains or otherwise impacts the viability of ways of life. Adopting a functionalist approach that takes "the consequences of some behavior or social arrangement" as "essential elements of the causes of that behavior,"[89] the authors have produced an account of how the viability of ways of life is sustained through the interaction between social relations and cultural biases, and how a cultural theory thus understood can provide a valid explanation for social and political change. Rejecting the dualism between hierarchy and individualism which characterizes the dominant mode of explanation in social science literature, they have proposed a pluralist model comprising a typology of five ways of life. These five ways of life, they contend, constitute the basic ways of relating found across a wide range of societies and cultures.

The concept of political culture as proposed by Chilton and expounded by Thompson and his collaborators provides a powerful alternative to those previously discussed. It enjoys a number of conceptual advantages. First, defining political culture as a shared way of relating allows us to correctly emphasize the superorganic and collective nature of culture. As Durkheim, White, and others have made clear, it is a mistake to conceive culture merely as an aggregate of individualistic orientations.[90] To be sure, political culture, or culture in general, may to a certain degree be reflected and embodied in individualistic orientations, but it is not defined by them. Rather, culture signifies something developed in association and shared among people, and something which has a meaningful existence of its own independent of the values, beliefs, and attitudes of individuals considered in isolation.

Second, a broadly defined concept of political culture also makes it possible to examine different cultural configurations, that is, different ways of relating, in a given society and across societies. Thompson and his collaborators argue, and I think convincingly, that a homogenized or dualistic conception of culture (e.g. hierarchy vs. individualism), which is characteristic of both the individualist and the traditionalist conception, is not satisfactory, because such a conception does not permit adequate attention to the diverse cultural forces found empirically in a society, nor to the shifting of these forces to create new cultural patterns.[91] A pluralist understanding of political culture allows us to study shared ways of relating not only in different social stratifications (e.g. elite and popular political culture), but also in the same stratification. This in turn helps us better understand the internal dynamics of a culture and the relationship between these cultural dynamics and political change.

Third, for the individualist, political culture is represented in individual value orientations; for the traditionalist, it is represented in a depository of traditional values and beliefs; and for the symbolist, it is represented in symbols and encoded signs. The idea of shared ways of relating insists that political culture is not only embodied in individual value orientations, traditional values and beliefs, and symbols and encoded signs; it is also expressed, as Durkheim has demonstrated, through social actions, through the actual situations of people relating to one another.[92] Political culture does not deal exclusively with individual perceptions, nor with past ideas and norms, nor with symbolic signs and language; it is also, if not more so, concerned with social, contemporary and nonsymbolic phenomena such as the Chinese Cultural Revolution. This allows us to have a dynamic rather than static view of the role that culture plays in shaping the politics of a society.

Fourth, as Thompson and his collaborators have correctly pointed out, the study of culture cannot be conducted in an institutional vacuum.[93] Cultural values and ideas typically have a historical trajectory and are attached to and indeed depend on institutional arrangements which result from historical development. Institutions provide the basis for an adequate understanding of cultural meaning. The Confucian value of filial piety, for example, is rooted in the institutional setting of the family; without an understanding of the traditional family and of the model of rule provided by it, filial piety as a political virtue makes little sense to us.

Fifth, the traditionalist studies political culture typically by emphasizing the uniqueness of each culture's approach to politics, while the individualist tends to design a set of universally applicable criteria for comparing the values and attitudes of different cultures. The concept of political culture thus defined has the double benefit of allowing general comparison on the basis of different ways of relating both across societies and within a single society and giving sufficient attention to the unique aspects of each culture. Thompson and his co-authors have suggested five ways of relating, arguing that these explain the unity in diversity of human experience.[94] This argument can also be used to tackle the problem of cultural relativism and moral relativism the former implies.

Sixth, conceiving political culture as a shared way of relating further opens the door to a variety of methodological studies. The traditionalist's account usually takes an interpretative approach, whereas the individualist's study often employs the survey and quantitative research method. Each provides a valuable perspective from which political culture can be effectively investigated, but each is not sufficient by itself to show the multidimensional character of the political culture of a society. The idea of shared ways of relating permits the possibility of broader perspectives by embracing not only the patterns of individual subjective orientations in contemporary cultures, but also traditional values and beliefs; not only the analysis of survey data, but also the analysis of historical documents and the ideas of past thinkers who have helped shape the cultural configurations of contemporary societies. Testing the validity of political culture as a theoretical tool should come from a plurality of methodologies, and this methodological pluralism is more likely to help us minimize the possibility of misjudgment.

It should be pointed out that the notion of political culture as proposed by Chilton and Thompson also raises some important questions. For example, Chilton uses the Piagetian idea of moral reasoning and its underlying cognitive structure to provide the basis for comparing politico-cultural developments. He argues that grounding politico-cultural development in the cognitive structures of moral reasoning allows one to evaluate "the developmental hierarchy of cultures" without passing judgment on "the moral worth of the culture."[95] This view is objectionable on several grounds. Perhaps the most significant one is the problem of shifting between micro- and macro-level analysis. Chilton's argument is built on the empirical findings of cognitive psychologists such as Piaget and Kohlberg, but, as Chilton notes, Kohlberg himself explicitly denies the applicability of his individual micro-level discovery to macro-level studies such as political and cultural development. Chilton defends his position by making a distinction between deontic judgments of moral obligation—the exclusive concern of his model of politico-cultural development—and aretaic judgments of moral worth. He further asserts that to judge the moral developmental stages of a culture is not to reproach that culture for its morally unacceptable practices. This defense is dubious. One may wonder if it is possible to judge the moral stages of a culture without judging what it is that makes it linger at a particular moral stage. In other words, determining which culture is at which moral stage presupposes judgment on the moral worth of that culture (i.e. advanced or backward, morally sophisticated or primitive, more human or less human). From an empirical point of view, moreover, a hierarchically construed structure of moral reasoning which postulates a linear development from lower to higher stages may not truly reflect the historical development of a culture; there is no lack of cases in which complex moral systems exist in traditional societies. Further, a hierarchically construed structure of moral reasoning has serious normative implications; it may, for example, lead to invidious comparison rather than meaningful cross-cultural studies.

Thompson and his collaborators construct their cultural theory on a functionalist approach. They argue that the deficiencies of functionalism can be repaired by taking a pluralist view of the way of relating in a society and by emphasizing the interactions among a plurality of ways of relating. While such a pluralist view provides a plausible explanation for the dynamics of social and cultural change, it remains to be answered how fundamentally incompatible and indeed conflicting ways of relating, instead of undermining one another, sustain a coherent and equilibrated social life. One may wonder whether there exists in a society a dominant way of relating which both functions as a unifying force and subjects other cultural forces to its influence.

Despite these weaknesses, however, the conception of political culture as a shared way of relating, in my view, provides a more useful conceptual tool than any of the three discussed above. For this reason, the study will adopt this conception. A shared way of relating may be described as a commonly shared framework of values, expectations and practices which guides and legitimizes social behavior. Three key features of it need special emphasis. First, shared ways of relating are socially constructed and perpetuated. They arise from a process of human interaction, congeal into recognized patterns of social relations, and are transmitted through socialization. As such, they take on the character of a superorganic and collective phenomenon. Although individual perceptions and beliefs may reflect collective values and practices, cultural values and practices have an independent life of their own and cannot be reduced to, nor defined by, the perceptions and beliefs of any given individual or an aggregate of such individuals.

Second, shared ways of relating are embodied in collective values and norms, but they are also expressed through social action, through people acting and interacting in concrete situations. A sacrificial ceremony, a parliamentary session, and a family gathering reveal perhaps as much about the cultural underpinnings of a society, if not more so, as an analysis of abstract ideas and beliefs.

Third, cultural values and norms must be understood in relation to the social institutions in which they operate. Social institutions are the established pattern or structure of social practices; they both support and set limits to the application of cultural values and norms. In this regard, they provide a necessary context for understanding the extent to which shared ways of relating are brought to bear on social life.

Chapter Three
Rights and the Liberal Concept of Rights

In *What's the Matter with Liberalism,* Ronald Beiner observes that "it is unmistakable that our contemporary political discourse is primarily conducted in the language of rights."[1] Though this remark is made in the context of criticizing liberalism or rather a certain brand of liberalism for its failure to bring the language of good to bear on issues of both theoretical and practical importance, it is nevertheless widely shared among those with whom Beiner disagrees. The fact that rights talk permeates our political life is corroborated in part by the statements made by leading political theorists in the last two or three decades and in part by the increasingly indispensable role rights have come to play in legal and political life. It is also borne out by an acute interest in seeing the idea spread to countries where a rights-based tradition is absent.

It is not surprising then that rights and rights-related ideas proliferate in this climate. While the traditional conception of rights continues to be relevant, there has arisen a plurality of new needs, interests, and ideals of which rights has become a convenient expression. We still talk about natural or inalienable rights; but to these are added rights that are analytically said to be general and specific, positive and moral, objective and subjective, formal and substantive. In terms of subject areas there are ethnic, cultural, animal, environmental, welfare, collective, democratic, and of course human rights, and from a historical perspective we have first-, second-, and third-generation rights. The list of substantive rights, such as the right to education, health, employment, leisure, paid holidays, peace and a clean environment, keeps extending and the end is not yet in sight.

The proliferation of rights and rights-related ideas has dramatically broadened our view of the notion as traditionally understood, but it also creates ambiguities, confusions, and in some cases even abuses. This accordingly forces us to reconsider rights. A quick review of the literature reveals that concerns with the notion of rights are typically concerns with the elucidation of its intrinsic and conceptual nature, and with its philosophical justification in relation to other moral and political ideas. While this line of inquiry is indispensable to a clear understanding of rights and their moral foundations, it stops short of a full appreciation of the complexity of the subject. Such complexity is manifested in the issues arising as a result of the ever-expanding boundaries of this notion and in the interaction of historical, cultural, and ideological forces that have shaped it. The question is often not about the justifiability of rights considered in general; few would now seriously dispute that it is morally objectionable to live a life in Nowheresville where there are no rights but only duties,[2] and for those who contend that the concept of rights is an exclusively Western construct and has limited application in other parts of the world, it is not the concept itself but the prioritization of certain types of rights that raises objection.[3] Rather, the question is about how to make sense of newly "discovered" rights while retaining the force of old ones, to account for competing theories of rights by uncovering their underlying assumptions, and to reconcile rights with other fundamental values and ideals. It is this latter question that will be the direct focus of this study.

With this focus in view, the chapter will try to provide an account of the liberal concept of rights. In the first section, the concept of rights will be briefly discussed. This discussion is designed primarily to show that a proper understanding of rights must go beyond mere conceptual analysis. Whether a claim, a liberty, a privilege, a power, an immunity, a choice or a benefit, a right becomes intelligible only when placed in its proper context, and this context includes a complex of human relations and assumptions about these relations. The second section seeks to describe the liberal concept of rights. The description of liberal rights is a difficult task because liberalism is a complex and changing idea. Some may ask whether there is such a thing as the liberal concept of rights or more bluntly whether there are in fact rights which liberalism, given its enormous adaptive capability, cannot assimilate into its vocabulary. Legitimate as these questions may be, it seems possible that a case can be made that liberalism in its variety is buttressed by some shared core values and no champions of liberalism, self-appointed or otherwise, are willing to turn away from them. It is these values that make the liberal concept of rights distinguishable from other views.

THE CONCEPT OF RIGHTS: TOWARD A PLURALIST UNDERSTANDING

Corporeality versus Incorporeality

The question "What is a right?" has long baffled political and legal thinkers. Is it corporeal or incorporeal? Is it a thing or nothing? Or, contradictory as it seems, is it an intangible "thing"? In ancient law where questions of rights began to emerge, a *ius* or right is taken to be something justice aims at; it is that just portion due between persons and is objectively discoverable.[4] In medieval law, as Pollock and Maitland tell us, a right, if it is "of a transferable nature" and has "a territorial ambit," "is thought of as a thing that is very like a piece of land."[5] The view that a right is a physical entity is perhaps rooted in a philosophical tradition in which a word must stand for its counterpart in the world as in the case of a tree or a river. But things would soon change at the turn of the modern era. With the transformation of the notion of *dominium* into *ius,* particularly in the hands of late medieval jurists and theologians alike, the scale is tipped toward deeming a right in a subjective sense as something which inheres in a person and over which he has sovereignty or total control.[6]

Among modern political and legal thinkers, a right is rarely if ever associated with a tangible thing. Grotius saw it as "a moral Quality annexed to the Person;" it is a liberty which permits us to act justly and according to reason and a power which enables us to demand what is due us.[7] Hobbes embraced this view but added a negative element to it, namely, one's liberty to abstain from action.[8] There is no explicit definition of a right to be found in Locke; considering the many uses he made of it, it is not unfair to say that Locke did not depart fundamentally from the meaning that Grotius and Hobbes had given the term.[9] Bentham, writing from a jurisprudential standpoint, regarded a right as a fictitious entity dependent on the legislator's will; it may be a privilege, a power, or a benefit from the discharge of a duty, but the request for its precise meaning cannot be met except by illustration in relation to situations in which questions of rights arise.[10] Following Bentham, later legal thinkers such as Austin, Hohfeld, and particularly Hart (though he later altered his earlier view) tended to emphasize the nonfactual and nondescriptive character of legal concepts such as rights. In their view, statements containing these concepts do not state any facts and instead are performative, operative, or ascriptive at least in their primary functions and in contradistinction to utterances of a nonlegal kind; thus they must be distinguished from statements made to ascertain the truth value of certain facts.[11]

More recently, White has challenged the essentially Benthamite premise from an epistemological perspective. He argues that statements containing legal concepts such as rights, like many others in ordinary language, can
be both non-denotative and fact-stating. Clearly "a right" does not denote
any entity, physical or otherwise, he contends, but this should not lead one
to conclude that "since 'A has a right' does not state those facts in virtue of
which it is true to say it, it, therefore, does not state a fact at all."[12] The mistake committed by Hart and the like is "their equation of fact with something in the *physical world* (original emphasis)." For "facts are not, and do
not have the characteristics of, any part of the world." They are not themselves items, like objects, events, situations, or states of affairs, that "exist in
time and space." "A factual statement," White says, "tells us how things are
in the world, no more and no less."[13]

This way of understanding the term "right" as both non-denotative
and fact-stating, which is predicated on a fundamentally different interpretation of fact as White has suggested, seems to have been an implicit assumption underlying many of the arguments about rights, particularly human
rights. On the one hand, few would deny that a right such as the right to free
speech or the right from fear does not have a counterpart in the world and
having it is not like having a car or a baseball cap; on the other hand, we are
often reluctant to say that sentences containing the notion of rights merely
express an evaluative judgment or a moral prescription about what we
should do and do not tell any truth about "something" we as human beings
naturally or inherently possess. The oscillation between "right" as fiction
and "right" as reality is very much a characteristic of political and legal discourse on rights. In legal usage, rights can hardly be conceived independently of legal rules which ascribe and give effect to them by imposing duties
on those against whom they are claimed. This makes the concept of rights a
seemingly artificial and imaginary product of the law. At the same time,
however, the bearer of a right is supposed to *possess* it; it is hers or mine or
yours in the sense of owning it as if it were a real thing. What the law does
is simply pass judgment on, or in Hart's words draw a conclusion about,
whether to affirm or to deny, but never to create, what already belongs to
the right-bearer. In political discourse, it is generally assumed, and rightly so,
that a right such as the right to liberty describes neither a physical entity nor
a psychological state, and having it is not equivalent to having an object or
having an idea. It cannot be seen, felt, pictured, or otherwise represented; it
does not exist in space and time. Nonetheless it is regarded as something
which is true and self-evident, as something which is objectively discoverable in human nature. It is in virtue of the moral qualities inherent in human

nature, considered also as true and self-evident, that we are said to hold, claim, and exercise it. It in fact *is* one of our moral qualities.

Definitions of a Right

The ambiguities surrounding the concept of rights, however, are not limited to those that result from the divide between corporeality and incorporeality, but are found in virtually all aspects of a right, in its subject, object, grounds as well as its relationship with correlative concepts. It must be stressed at this point that it is not my intention to claim any comprehensive treatment of any one of these issues. In fact, this entire section on the concept of rights can only focus on the issues dealing with the definition of a right, its grounds, and its relationship with correlative concepts. Even on these three dimensions, the discussion will be necessarily short and selective. For example, the correlatives of a right will be confined to duty rather than extended to include the Hohfeldian idea of no-right, liability and disability. This selection is based on the relatively noticeable role a given issue (such as the relationship between a right and its correlative duty) has played in contemporary political discourse. It does not mean, however, that less contested issues can and should be ignored. Some of these issues, for example, whether fetuses are bearers of rights, are becoming increasingly important to contemporary rights talk.[14]

Within the scope of its modern usage in an incorporeal sense, the concept of a right has a number of meanings not altogether apparent; it is insensitivity to the various meanings of a right that is believed to have caused confusion. Thus, Plamenatz begins his discussion on rights with a definition of a right as a power. "A right," he says, "is a power which a creature ought to possess, either because its exercise by him is itself good or else because it is a means to what is good, and in the exercise of which all rational beings ought to protect him."[15] This definition, which is clearly more than a definition for it also provides a basis of justification for such a power, has several difficulties. The most serious of these is the lack of a clear understanding of the term "power." Does it mean physical strength or mental capability? A handicapped person or a comatose patient may not have the physical strength or mental capability of a normal person, but he or she may certainly have rights. Conversely, if we understand by "power" might or authority, it is possible that someone or some entity may have no right to do or affect something yet this someone or entity may possess might or authority.

It is precisely for this reason that McCloskey rejects the notion that a right is a power. Having the right to drive a car is not the same as having the power to do so, he says, for I may be too ill to drive a car or too poor to buy one. Given that, "a right may exist and be possessed in the absence of the relevant capacity, rights are distinct from powers."[16] Neither is a right a claim against someone. A right is generally a right *to,* not *against,* except in specific cases. My right to live, for example, is not primarily one against others, and "the actual existence of other human beings is irrelevant to whether rights may or may not be possessed."[17] It is also true of the right to vote, which is not simply a claim against others but rather a right to act as one pleases within the definition of the law. For McCloskey, therefore, all rights are *entitlements,* entitlements which enable us to act as we choose, or refrain from action, or receive positive assistance where and when needed in accordance with certain rules and standards, and which, if denied, would provide grounds for making demands or claims on others.

Despite McCloskey's objections, however, some, for instance Joel Feinberg, insist that a right is a claim or a valid claim. Although his reasons for such insistence are not particularly illuminating, Feinberg is correct in pointing out that McCloskey is wrong in assuming that all claims are claims *against* rather than *to* and all rights are rights *to* rather than *against.* He sees no paradox in saying that rights are essentially held against others, whether *in personam,* that is, against specific persons, or *in rem,* that is, against hundreds of millions of what Bentham called "unassignable individuals." Rights so conceived, according to him, have two dimensions, as suggested by the prepositions "to" and "against," and they "seem to merge *entitlements to* do, have, omit, or be something with *claims against* others to act or refrain from acting in certain ways."[18]

The idea of merging hints at the complex nature of a right which Feinberg's otherwise narrow definition—narrow in the sense that it "hardly applies to moral rights"—would obscure. The complex nature of a right was noted some time ago by Hohfeld. Hohfeld distinguishes four different conceptions of a right as involved in legal reasoning and seeks to elucidate them in terms of their correlative and opposite concepts. A right, according to him, may in a given case be understood as a privilege, a power, an immunity, or a right in the strictest sense, namely a claim, and the indiscriminate use of a right or a claim to cover all legal relations has led to "a confusion or blurring of ideas." Thus different legal relations should be separately represented by different terms accurately expressing them rather than lumped together under a single protean word "right."[19] Hohfeld defines the four terms in this way:

> A right is one's affirmative claim against another, and a privilege is one's freedom from the right or claim of another. Similarly, a power is one's affirmative "control" over a given legal relation as against another;

whereas an immunity is one's freedom from the legal power or "control" of another as regards some legal relation.[20]

No doubt, Hohfeld's conceptual analysis is very important; among other things, it provides a plausible solution to the misuse and abuse of the notion of rights by applying distinct terms. But does this mean our understanding of rights is clearer? Not necessarily. It seems that the search for synonyms in definition is often circular and further definitions and synonyms are required. Such circularity is characteristic of Hohfeld's conception of a privilege, a term which can be conceived in turn as a liberty, a franchise, an advantage, a benefit, or an immunity. To avoid the pitfall of offering definitions *ad infinitum,* we may have to look elsewhere rather than focus on conceptual matters alone; we may have to locate a right in the context of social relations which it purports to regulate and in the principles and theories which it presupposes and is embedded in.

A Right and Its Correlative Duty: Two Theories of Rights

Fully aware of the futility of defining the concept of a right in terms of synonymous words, Hart resorts to a theory of rights for elucidation. He argues, following Bentham's advice, that a right cannot be meaningfully investigated unless we put it in a statement in which it appears, as in "A has a right to X," and study it in conjunction with various elements which are logically involved in such a statement. Thus, in explaining "A has a legal right to X," we should take into account: 1) there exists a legal system which the above statement presupposes, 2) under a rule or rules of the system some other person B is held under a duty to do or abstain from some action, and 3) B's obligation to perform the corresponding duty is made by law to depend on the choice of A who is said to have the right or the choice of some person authorized to act on his behalf.[21] Hart believes that though what he deals with here is a claim-right, his "choice theory" can be applied with equal validity to the other senses of a right identified by Hohfeld. It can be applied in either a negative or an affirmative sense; negatively, "there is no law to interfere if the individual chooses to do or abstain from some action (liberty), or retain his legal position unchanged (immunity);" affirmatively, "the law gives legal effect to the choice of an individual that some other person shall do or shall abstain from some action [claim] or that the legal position of some other person shall be altered [power]."[22]

It is worth noting that Hart's choice theory of rights has been discussed in legal contexts, but it has obvious implications for political morality, given that there is an intimate connection between legal and moral rights. Hart himself does not hesitate to use it in the elucidation of moral rights. He argues that, if individual freedom is a fundamental and equal right of man *qua* man, it will provide moral justification for interfering, by the *choice* of one individual, with the freedom of another individual and for resisting another's interference with his or her own freedom of action.[23] According to this argument, the statement that X has a right is distinguished by three important features. First, it implies that the agent is capable of rational choice; second, for a choice to be meaningful there must be a range of options available to him or her; and third, for every right there must exist a correlative duty and it is solely up to the right-bearer to decide whether to release the duty-bearer from performing or refraining from certain action. As we shall see later, these features in the choice theory are subject to objection.

The choice theory is often contrasted with the benefit theory in the understanding of rights. Bentham is said to have originated the benefit theory. According to him, to say that one person, A, has a right is to say that A stands to benefit from another person B's discharge of a duty. This statement can be more fully appreciated by attaching three further observations. First, it must be understood in the context of Bentham's total denial of natural or moral rights and of his insistence that these rights are imaginary in nature, absurd in logic, and pernicious in morals. For him, rights are created by the law, and by the law alone; there are "no rights without law, contrary to the law, and anterior to the law."[24] Second, Bentham argues that it is in the nature of the law to command or prohibit certain acts. A law that does so thus creates a duty or obligation. A duty or obligation is a fictitious entity created out of the combination of two real entities, namely an act and a law. A right is a secondary fictitious entity resulting from the imposition of a duty or obligation. In Bentham's view, it is impossible for the law to create a right, that is, to confer a benefit, without at the same time imposing a duty. Third, duties can be divided into extra-regarding and self-regarding ones; there are rights corresponding to the former but none to the latter. Thus, while for every right there must be a corresponding duty, it is not necessary that for every duty there must be a corresponding right.

The benefit theory as Bentham framed it is deficient in several major aspects, as critics have pointed out. Hart, for one, thinks that to be an intended beneficiary of a duty is neither a sufficient nor a necessary condition for the existence of a legal right.[25] Defenders of the theory such as David Lyons and Joseph Raz, however, remain unconvinced and continue to argue in favor of the theory, albeit in a more subtle way. Unsatisfied with Hart's reading of Bentham, Lyons suggests a qualified version of the benefit theory which he believes to be truer to Bentham's spirit. Three qualifications can be summed up as follows. First, the beneficiary of an obligation is not merely one who stands to benefit actually or directly from the performance of such an obligation, but one for whom a good is assured; second, the agent has an interest in such a good; and third, an obligation that requires or prohibits certain action is designed to serve, promote, or secure this interest of the agent, regardless of this good or benefit being strictly guaranteed to him or her.[26] Following this line of reasoning, Raz goes further to argue that rights are simply grounds of duties in others. To say that X has a right, he contends, is to say that "an aspect of X's well-being (his interest) is a sufficient reason for holding some other person (s) to be under a duty."[27] This is a more plausible theory than either Bentham's unqualified or Lyons' qualified version. But, again, as we shall see, the advantages it enjoys over them are not enough to insulate it from objections.

Grounds of a Right

Theories of rights that aim at the elucidation of the concept of a right often implicitly espouse a particular view of the ground on which a right can be justified. This is true of almost all the rights theorists mentioned above. The sheer variety of justifications offered by both legal and moral philosophers, all of which seem plausible to a greater or lesser degree and in one or another theoretical context but never fully so and under all circumstances, makes it impossible to pin down any single one as the ultimate ground of a right. This pluralism is perhaps reflected more clearly in discussions on moral rights than in those on legal rights. Legal rights are said with less ambiguity to be grounded in the law and in the legal interests that the law promotes and protects. But it is not so obvious with moral rights or certain legal rights imbued with moral force. Alan Gewirth has distinguished and rejected five types of ground on which moral rights can be justified: self-evident truth, institutional rules, interests, intrinsic worth or dignity, and social contract.[28] White also described and evaluated more than half a dozen proposals for the grounds of rights; among these are good, need, duty, choice, claim, rules, title and righteousness.[29] In the following, three general arguments will be presented for illustration because these arguments play an important role in political discourse, and because they encompass a large number of individual justificatory concerns.

The most commonly defended idea on which rights are said to be grounded is one that emphasizes the intrinsic and moral worth of the individual *qua* person. This idea begins, arguably, with Kant but its origins are traceable to earlier thinkers in the medieval and early modern periods. It finds its more forceful expression in the Kantian maxim that each and every individual be treated as an end rather than merely a means, and has been well assimilated into and in fact has become a staple of the liberal tradition. According to this view, each human being is a moral person, irreplaceable, self-owning, and capable of free action. To respect his or her moral worth is nothing less than to respect these properties intrinsic to the value of one's very being. Whichever course of life one chooses for oneself is ultimately one's own decision; others ought not to interfere with one's freedom without legitimate reason and ought to assist or provide for one in cases in which one lacks the ability or resources to exercise such freedom. The only justification for interference, to take one widely shared position, is to prevent harm to others. Rights, thus, are regarded as a fundamental guarantee, and a manifestation, of the individual's moral autonomy and dignity.

This justification for the existence of rights is embraced by a broad range of thinkers. These thinkers of course may disagree with one another on certain issues, but their differences are ones in emphasis, not in essence. Thus it is not surprising that we should find among them a fundamental and unwavering commitment to the idea that human creatures are by nature free and equally so, and as such they deserve to be treated with respect and dignity. It is this intrinsic moral worth of human beings that provides the ultimate basis for making free choices, being treated equally, claiming what is one's due, being entitled to have and enjoy certain things, or engaging in autonomous action.[30]

The second general defense is centered around a quasi-utilitarian or what Raz calls humanist argument for human well-being. To say that it is quasi-utilitarian is to admit two things. First, pure utilitarianism is at heart hostile to the idea of rights. The view as advanced by Mill, Hare, Scanlon and the like can and does accommodate the idea of rights, and as such it can no longer be regarded as a strictly utilitarian argument, at least on one level on which individual rights are judged not solely in virtue of the consequences they incur, but also in terms of their own logic and structure in our moral thinking, of their relationship with other equally important moral concepts.[31] Second, this position is shared more or less by some writers who are not professed utilitarians but who recognize the instrumental role that rights play in promoting human welfare.[32]

The quasi-utilitarian or humanist basis of rights can be described roughly as follows. Lying at the core of the mainstream rights theory, it argues, is an exclusive and intuitionist concern with the individual and his or her inherent dignity. This is not only an impoverishment of moral discourse, but also a misconstrual of the ground on which rights can be founded. Rights are grounded not in such a formal, intuitive, and presocial notion as

dignity, or freedom, or equality, but in human well-being and in the interests, needs, and goods that are constitutive of it.[33] Unlike pure utilitarianism
which considers the general welfare in undifferentiated terms, the idea of
well-being here includes both the individual and the collective dimension.
While the ultimate end of rights is to facilitate the moral, intellectual and
material development of the individual as a human person and as a member
of the human race, collective goods such as a tolerant society are values indispensable and intrinsic to such development. Thus conceived, rights are
nothing more than a means to the advancement of humanity, individually
and collectively.

The third type of justification is contractarian in nature and its most
outspoken contemporary advocate is Rawls. To be sure, Rawls' primary
concern is the idea of justice, not that of rights, but he links the two ideas
in such a way that a theory of rights can be reasonably constructed out of
the two principles he has advanced for a just society.[34] According to Rawls,
what can justify the claim that X has certain basic moral rights is neither
the inherent quality/qualities of X (though it seems clear that the assumption of such quality or qualities is present in constructing "the initial situation") nor some teleological argument for human flourishing. Rather, rights
are created and held as a result of deliberation and agreement among individuals or groups of individuals in the hypothetical original position of
equality, rationality and uncertainty, and they are the requirement of the
principles of justice arrived at through such deliberation and agreement. In
other words, rights can be said to be grounded in a contract agreed to unan-
imously by all interested parties or their representatives in the hypothetical
original position, and in the principles of justice reached through such a
contract which lay the foundation for and are built into the basic structure
of a just society.[35]

Rawls' justificatory scheme may be called a sequential one. The two
principles which are chosen behind a veil of ignorance in the initial situation
can each be deemed as a general right, and they are arranged in a lexical
order that requires the first to be fully satisfied before the second can be considered. The first is a general right to "the most extensive total system of
equal basic liberties compatible with a similar system of liberty for all," and
the second a general right to equality of opportunity and fair treatment in
the social and economic sphere.[36] From these two general rights flow a set
of basic rights, be they civil, political, socio-economic, which are institutionalized and built into the basic structure of society; and these basic rights then
provide groundings for secondary and nonbasic rights which may arise
under special circumstances.

Toward a Pluralist Understanding of Rights

If there is one benefit this brief survey can yield, it would appear to be the insight that the nature of rights is such that we gain little in understanding by focusing solely on conceptual matters. This is clear from the fact that attempts to capture the full significance of a right from a definitional standpoint do not meet with much success. A right may be a claim, an entitlement, a privilege, an immunity, or a power, as Hohfeld and others have demonstrated, but that it is any one of them does not depend on different concepts of a right. Rather it depends on the different circumstances under which questions of rights arise and on the different social relationships which rights purport to govern. One's right to property, for example, may be best understood as a privilege in the case of uninterfered enjoyment, a power in the case of transfer or alienation, an immunity in the case of eminent domain or easement, or a claim in the case of just compensation. It is thus incorrect to assume that a right always implies a power, or an entitlement, or a claim and so on. In this respect, Hart's warning that we look beyond mere definition to the specific conditions under which a right is claimed and to the characteristic role it plays in drawing certain conclusions about human relations is valid.

Interestingly, however, Hart seems to have forgotten his own warning when he attempts to explain the concept of rights in terms of his overarching choice theory. Such a theory stipulates that "A has a right" can be framed in the form of a choice that some other person B is under a duty to do or to abstain from doing. No doubt, there are many advantages associated with the choice theory; it does tell us, among other things, one vitally important aspect of rights which the competing benefit theory is incapable of conveying, namely the kind of control a right-holder has over his or her action. But it is not true to hold that a right always involves a choice of this sort, as shown in the case of the rights of fetuses, the mentally deficient, or animals. Neither is it tenable to say that such a choice always implies a duty or obligation of someone other than the right-holder to do or not to interfere. To take Hart's own example,[37] my right to look over the garden fence at my neighbor does not entail his duty or obligation to be looked at or to refrain from building a wall in-between to interfere with my view. It may be argued that he has a duty or obligation not to jump over the fence and give me a beating, but this proves precisely that we should not talk about a general duty or obligation to do or not to interfere; rather we have to specify the conditions under which a particular kind of duty or obligation is said to be binding on him.

What has been said about the choice theory can be applied also to the benefit theory. There is no denying that sometimes a right may be better conceived as a benefit and its holder the (intended) beneficiary of a duty or obligation. However, this does not hold true in all cases. The problem of the third-party beneficiary is a case in point. Contemporary benefit theorists such as Raz also argue that rights are grounds of duties in others. Again, this is only partially correct because there are clearly cases in which the questions of rights figure prominently while those of duties do not arise. My right to enjoy a Van Gogh paining exhibited in a privately owned museum open to the public, for example, does not justify barring the museum from interfering with my enjoyment by selling the painting. Such justification must go beyond the mere correlativity of rights and duties and delve into the private property relations defined by the law which determines the nature of rights and duties in a given society. Similarly, to use a frequently used example, my right to be fed is not a ground for holding any philanthropist under a duty or obligation to feed me, and in order to make it such a ground, we must have a legal or moral system which stipulates that it is wrong, legally or morally, for men of wealth not to perform charitable deeds of this kind.

All this is not to deny, of course, that the correlativity thesis that for every right there is a corresponding duty constitutes a major step forward from the impasse to which various attempts at the definition of a right lead us, and contributes substantially to our understanding of the concept. It merely points out the limits of such a thesis and the theories in which it is embedded. Similar limits are also found in arguments about the grounds of rights. As critics have shown, to ground rights in an intuitive idea such as the intrinsic moral worth of the individual *qua* person is question-begging. Notwithstanding the fact that there are conflicting intuitions (and hence the denial of such intrinsic moral worth because human beings are capable of evil), the use of intuition, recommendation, self-evidence, or stipulation in order to ground rights distracts us from arguing about "substantive moral issues."[38] More importantly, to assert on the basis of a vague notion such as dignity that individuals have fundamental moral rights, say, to autonomy or to equal respect and to regard these rights as presocial, prepolitical and pre-institutional is not only to commit the individualistic fallacy in moral thinking, but also to invoke a non sequitur and groundless first principle.

It is equally indefensible to ground rights solely in the individual's interests, needs, or goods, even if such interests, needs, or goods are said to be of ultimate or intrinsic value to his or her well-being. For one thing, it is extremely difficult to determine the meaning of ultimate or intrinsic value; my interest in a Van Gogh painting may be of ultimate or intrinsic value to my well-being because it increases the options of a worthwhile life for me, but others may not have such an interest or may not regard it as fundamental.

In addition, simply because something is in one's interest, or need, or for one's good does not necessarily give him or her a right, that is, justify holding some other person under a duty or obligation. Nor is it persuasive that the interest, need, or good itself rather than what someone is interested in or in need of or benefits from provides either a sufficient or a necessary ground of his rights.[39]

The Rawlsian contractarian basis of rights also poses certain difficulties. Gewirth charges that it is circular in reasoning, in the sense that a general equal right to liberty is concluded only by postulating a universal right to equality as its premise.[40] Perhaps a more serious challenge to the Rawlsian argument, insofar as it is viewed as giving a justificatory answer to the grounds of rights, can be presented along the following lines. In addition to the indeterminacy and arbitrariness of how much to know or not to know in the original position, which would have direct bearing on what is to be agreed upon subsequently, rational and self-interested individuals in such a position have no good reason to choose either the Rawlsian two principles or the lexical order in which they are to be satisfied. On the one hand, they would not necessarily choose the second principle that inequalities are to be arranged to the greatest benefit of the least advantaged. For this is a conservative strategy that "maximizes the minimum pay-off," and rational choosers may look at the average, not just the minimum, and then "pick a set of principles which would lead to a high average level of well-being" depending on "their taste for gambling."[41] On the other hand, they would not necessarily choose the priority of liberty over equality in order to play safe in the face of future uncertainties. They may, for instance, prioritize absolute equality considering certain facts of life such as old age, infirmities, or sheer unluckiness, for this would insure that they be provided for when and if these situations arise.

With these limits in mind, it seems impossible for us to avoid the conclusion that no single definition, theory, or formula of justification in itself can provide a conception of rights sufficient to capture the complexity and subtlety of this notion. A right may in a given case be defined as a power, a claim or an entitlement. It may imply or entail a duty or obligation that one perform or refrain from certain acts. It may be grounded in individual dignity, well-being, agreement, or in rule, principle, policy, licence, deed, antecedent behavior and characteristics of the right-holder. There are different kinds of rights, and these differences are not differences in the concept of a right, but related to the different areas in which the question of a right is raised. There are different contexts in which rights are asserted and different sources from which they are derived, and these differences cannot be settled beforehand by conceptual analysis. All this suggests that an adequate understanding of rights requires discrimination and careful argument. It requires an assessment of "various moral, legal, institutional, conventional, etc. relationships in the complex systems to which [rightholders] belong."[42] A pluralist understanding, which is not simply an attempt to dodge the question of incommensurability of theoretical views but is attentive to the complexity and subtlety of the concept of rights, particularly to the different contexts and sources from which it springs, seems an enlightened choice under the circumstances.

THE LIBERAL CONCEPT OF RIGHTS

The Possibility of Nonliberal Rights

It has become a noticeable characteristic of contemporary political discourse that rights are taken to be a largely liberal trademark. Critics of liberalism rarely if ever invoke the language of right; instead they tend to emphasize other important values such as the idea of good in opposition to the idea of right. Defenders of liberalism, on the other hand, hold firmly to their long and carefully guarded position that individual rights provide the ultimate basis for and play a central role in moral and political debate. Even a general and seemingly neutral account of the concept of rights such as the one presented above appears unavoidably entangled with liberal values, whether the concern is with definition or with justification. This seems to make the proposal of a liberal concept of rights look rather redundant. Since it is impossible to talk about rights intelligently without at the same time invoking liberal values, one may ask, what is the point of using such a concept? Aren't all rights liberal in this regard? What do we mean by the liberal concept of right? Does it imply that there are also nonliberal rights? If it could indeed be said that there are, what would be the key characteristics which distinguish liberal from nonliberal rights?

Perhaps a proper starting point to explore these questions and, ultimately, to understand the liberal concept of rights is to consider the possibility of nonliberal rights which this concept implies. As is well known, there exists an intimate connection between rights and liberalism; not only are rights one of the most basic values of liberalism, but it is not impossible to argue that the evolution of liberal thought may be understood in terms of the ascendancy of the idea of rights. This having been said, it is nonetheless wrong to assume that all rights are necessarily liberal rights. For though the idea of rights or natural rights was utilized by liberal thinkers as a weapon to battle political, social, and religious oppression, particularly in the formative years of liberalism, and to defend an ascending liberal order afterwards, it was not their invention. Arguments of liberalism are preceded in time by arguments of rights in both political and legal thought, and there is reason to say that the connection between rights and liberalism is a historical rather than logical one. Thus, to argue about the liberal concept of rights is not to argue about something inherent in and peculiar to liberalism, but to describe and examine the ways in which rights are viewed and justified on the basis of liberal ideas and principles.

By the same token, to argue about nonliberal rights is to argue about how rights are viewed and justified on the basis of nonliberal assumptions about the individual, society and government. It must be noted at this point that a construction of nonliberal rights cannot be carried too far for at least two reasons. First, if the notion of right—right in the singular, not plural—could be identified at all as one of the concerns in both ancient and medieval thought, it played no central, systematic, and clearly defined role there as it did in the modern liberal thought. This is further compounded by the fact that the idea of right is often implied in and dependent on the more familiar notions of good, justice, and law, as the Greek *dikaiosyne* and the Latin *ius* indicate. Thus to talk about right as if it were immediately revealed to us is vulnerable to the charge of anachronism. Second, the nonliberal nature of right can only be construed in relative terms—relative to the philosophical outlook of ancient and medieval thought in general. For many of its elements, considered in isolation, would not only pass for liberal values, but have in fact been incorporated into the liberal doctrine.

In *Natural Right and History,* Leo Strauss offers an account of the preliberal or what he calls the classical conception of natural right. He argues that the classical, as opposed to the modern, idea of natural right is inseparably connected to the idea of a good life, and with human excellence toward which it is the natural end of man to strive. According to the classical thinkers, particularly Plato and Aristotle, a good life is one which aims at the good, the virtuous, or the just, and human excellence is manifested and culminates in the achievement of these. The quest for natural right is simply a quest for the good, the virtuous, or the just, and for human excellence.

But the good life or human excellence cannot be achieved by the individual in isolation; it can only be pursued and realized in a communal setting or in the *polis*. For, as the classical thinkers see it, man is by nature a social being or in Aristotle's words "a political animal;" his nature is such that he cannot live and live well except with others in society. In this connection, the idea of natural right presupposes a particular conception of the relationship between the individual and his or her community; it also presupposes a set of virtues that both inform and govern this relationship. Of all the virtues which are constitutive of the good life or human excellence, none can be cultivated and make sense independently of the society of which the individual is a member. Insofar as they must be viewed and nurtured in relation to others, all virtues are in a broad sense social. And these include the social virtue *par excellence,* namely justice or right.

It is also part of the conception of natural right that the good life or human excellence can be achieved not in any society but in a society that is most conducive to and compatible with such an end. This in turn requires the designing and establishing of the best social and political arrangements or the best regime. To be sure, the classical thinkers disagree on what constitutes the best regime, just as they disagree on what constitutes the good life. But there is one thing they all seem to agree on; that is, they believe that the best regime, desirable as it may be, is extremely difficult if possible at all to realize. What mortals can practically accomplish, as Plato and Aristotle have done in *The Laws* and *The Politics* respectively, is to approximate the ideal or utopia by constructing the best *actual* regime, one which is ruled by law. The best actual regime is just in the sense that being just is defined by obedience to the law and the law is an expression of justice. Further, the classical thinkers also seem to believe that different people or different classes of people are equipped with unequal capacities for justice, and thus the question of what is just or right must be answered by taking into account such inequalities. Plato's answer is simple: The wise should rule the unwise, although all classes of citizens should have some role in ruling. A plausible answer offered by Aristotle and later followed by Cicero is to have a mixed regime in which different classes of people strike a balance among one another.[43]

The classical understanding of natural right, in more than one important respect, provides a model for thinking about *jus* or right that retained its force well into the late Middle Ages. This is the model according to which the idea of natural right is defined in terms of the pursuit of the good or the just. Such pursuit necessarily involves identifying with one's community and with its laws, and it is this identification that gives meaning and justification to right. Thus the Roman jurists and later Aquinas were able to talk about right as a cultivated disposition to render to each his due according to the law.[44] This is not to say, of course, that the classical teachings are in any sense impervious to time and change. On the contrary, with the decline of the small-scale and closely knit political society, namely the *polis,* and with the rise of the vast and fragmented Roman Empire, some of the ideas, for example, that of human excellence, which structure classical thought gradually lost their appeal. In their place there arose a set of new ideas and beliefs in keeping with the emergence of new social and political conditions. The idea of man's natural-born equality was a case in point, as was the belief that perfect justice is possible only in God's kingdom. But, with the possible exception of the egalitarian argument that was also found in Stoic thought, these additions, modifications, or shifts in emphasis did not in any fundamental way alter the central assumptions underlying the classical nonliberal conception of right.

In recent years, Richard Tuck, Brian Tierney and others have done much to enlighten us about the origins of natural rights theories. Although they disagree on the designation of the earliest proponents of natural rights, the choice of particular literary texts, or the translation of certain Latin terms, these historians seem to share the view that the modern liberal notion of rights as a neutral sphere of personal liberty, a zone of autonomy, or an area of licit power, has its roots in medieval thought. They find in the writings of Ockham, Gerson, or even earlier thinkers such as the Decretists a clear indication of the subjective sense of right, one which foreshadowed the ideas of natural rights theorists in the sixteenth and seventeenth centuries. They argue that this use of right in the subjective sense sees right as *facultas, potestas,* or *dominium* which belongs to the individual, as an inherent moral quality which resides in the individual; that it differs in a fundamental way from the objective sense of right in classical thought which deems right as something objectively discoverable and interpersonal, as the object of justice which involves a nonindividualist conception of the good and the just, and as the just portion due between persons; that it comes closest to, if not identical with, what contemporary political and legal thinkers call a kind of control or sovereignty over one's moral person. Although most of them are careful not to invoke the charge of anachronism, they are convinced nevertheless that there is a clear intellectual continuity between medieval and modern natural rights theorists, and this continuity is extremely useful in understanding the evolution of the concept of rights in the liberal tradition.[45]

The cogency with which Tuck, Tierney, and others have argued their case is impressive, but this should not lead us to conclude that a full-fledged liberal theory of natural rights is evident in medieval thought. Two caveats are in order. First, we should not lose sight of the fact that the term "right" was used in the objective as well as the subjective sense in medieval texts, as Tierney is well aware; and in some cases, as in that of Aquinas, it was used almost exclusively in the objective sense following the classical tradition.[46] Second and more importantly, to the extent that there were close affinities between medieval and modern theories of rights, we should not lose sight of the different social and political orders in which rights were propounded and defended. This second point is all the more crucial to our understanding of nonliberal rights.

Medieval discourse on rights belongs to a different world of thought from that of "possessive individualism" which C.B. Macpherson believes to have characterized the natural rights theories of sixteenth and seventeenth thinkers such as Hobbes and Locke. It is undergirded by a different set of assumptions and beliefs about the individual, society and government. These assumptions and beliefs draw heavily upon the classical notions of good, justice, law and community on the one hand, and manifest their unique attributes in harmony with the medieval theocratic-political order, on the other. Walter Ullmann describes them succinctly in terms of two related themes, namely, "the overriding importance of law" and "the organiological conception of society."[47] He continues:

> What mattered was . . . not the individual, but society, the corpus of all individuals. In the high Middle Ages, thinking in the public field concerned itself with the whole, with society. But law at all times and in all societies addresses itself to the generality, to the multitude and, by definition, sets aside the individual. . . . [T]he medieval emphasis on the collectivist phenomenon of the law successfully prevented the emergence of a thesis concerning such rights which the individual had apart from the law and before the law was given. The theme of the law as the soul of the body (public and politic) was, in other words, explicable by the overriding importance attached to society and by the negligible role which the individual played in it.[48]

This is not to deny that the individual *qua* subject did have rights or certain kinds of rights as defined by law throughout the Middle Ages; such rights had been held as a matter of custom and tradition since time immemorial and set down in the *Corpus Iuris Civilis* of Justinian.[49] The point is rather that the individual and his rights are accorded little significance, and rights did not become a central force shaping the nature and direction of politics in medieval times as it did in the modern era. Whatever rights the individual had or might have, as Ullmann and others remind us, must be viewed in close relation to, rather than as an independent criterion for evaluating, the assumptions and beliefs that were constitutive of the theocratic-political order. At least two ideas figure prominently in the conception of rights in this context. First, rights are defined by and identical with law; conversely, no rights exist independently of and prior to law. But the meaning of law is subject, *at least in theory*, to the restraints imposed by two related principles, namely *princeps legibus solutus est* (the prince is not bound by the law) and *est pro ratione voluntas* (his will is held to be reason). In the words of one legal historian, "Whereas '*princeps legibus solutus est*' described the prerogative of the prince to promulgate, abrogate, or derogate law, '*pro ratione voluntas*' placed the prince's will at the center of the legislative process. Law was derived from his will and his will alone."[50] What pleases the prince has the force of law, as another legal doctrine states, thus it is not surprising that rights should be viewed as something coming down in a descending order from the divinely sanctioned princely authority. They are conferred on the individual *qua* subject "as a matter of royal grace, of royal concession." "The essential point of the concession thesis is," Ullmann writes, "that whatever rights a subject has, he has as the effluence of the king's good will, of the king's own grace, which was a favor and which the subjects could not claim as a right. One has no right to claim a good deed, to claim a favor."[51]

Second, the conception of the individual's rights is conditioned by the common good which it is the purpose of government and law to protect and promote. This can be understood both in a negative and in a positive sense. Negatively, rights can be and in fact were violated, infringed upon, or overridden in the name of the common good. Given that the prince's will and the common good are identified with each other, and that the individual is absorbed into the body corporate of the kingdom and entrusted to the tutelage of those who are selected by divinity to take care of the community, the idea of rights could not play a large role in providing the kind of protection for the individual as it has done in modern times. The dispossessing of the heretics and of their descendants, even if unborn, which Ullmann points out, is one good example.[52] Positively, rights are not contemplated from the standpoint of the individual in isolation from his community, but derived from "reflection on the right ordering of human relationships" in it.[53] They can be justified only on the basis of this right ordering; they signify an adjustment of the relationship between individual and society, and between individuals themselves, a disposition to give to each his due (however much the term "due" is devoid of content), and a determination to do the right thing in conformity with justice and the rule of law. Natural right is thus "a kind of *habititas* by which man is able to discern between good and evil."[54] Granted that *ius* or right was increasingly used in the subjective sense as a faculty or power by jurists in the late Middle Ages, it is still one in accordance with right reason. Right reason resides in each one of us, and ultimately in God, and as such, it always inclines us toward the good of the community as a whole. Even in the late scholastic thought of the fourteenth and fifteenth centuries, where the conception of rights as liberty or control clearly took hold, we learn that the individual's right of liberty was not seen as taking precedence over, but rather as depending upon or at least being closely tied to, the liberty of the political society in which one lives.[55]

In contrast to the liberal notion of rights, the classical and medieval conception of right has three important features. First, the term "right' in the classical and medieval context does not connote individualized and individualizable qualities or "things," as the liberal one does; nor does it suggest that we each *possess* these qualities or "things" naturally—naturally in the sense that the individual is endowed with them at birth or that he or she owns them prior to society and social action. Rather, it is extrapersonal and objective; it is something which, given human nature, people can achieve only through participation in the common life of the community. Thus the presocial and prepolitical individual does not exist for this nonliberal notion of right. This immediately leads to the second feature, that is, that right is embedded in the conception of the good life or the common good. Such life or good is marked by a mutually dependent relationship between the individual and his or her community and by a nonindividually conceived end to which all individual members of a political society are bound. Third, since an ultimate end, whether it is the perfection of human nature or the realization of God's kingdom on Earth, is envisioned, and since individuals each are naturally endowed with unequal capacities for this end, egalitarianism plays no part in the conception of right. Although the idea of natural equality began to appear in the writings of the Stoics and was often postulated in medieval thought, yet merits set individuals apart in a hierarchically structured order. In both the classical and the medieval context, therefore, the meritocratic principle, namely from each according to his capacity and to each according to his merit, seems more applicable.

Classical Liberal Rights

The nonliberal conception of rights encountered in classical and medieval thought provides a useful frame of reference for considering the historical uniqueness of the liberal concept of rights. As mentioned earlier, since the idea of rights existed long before the advent of liberalism, understanding liberal rights requires that we examine the ways in which the notion of rights is justified on the basis of liberal assumptions and beliefs about the individual, society, and government. As mentioned also at the beginning of the chapter, describing liberal rights is a difficult task because liberalism is a vast and constantly changing doctrine. Thus it may be helpful to divide this task into two parts. The first part seeks to offer an account of the conception of rights in the classical liberal tradition, and this will be done by examining two political thinkers, namely Hobbes and Locke. The second part will focus on the way in which the idea of rights is defended by some of the most prominent political theorists today. This two-part consideration should enable us to get a sense of continuity without losing sight of some of the important differences between classical and contemporary liberal theory.

Like other intellectual forces, classical or traditional liberalism as a body of doctrine is not the making of one man, one age, or one locality; rather it has grown out of a multitude of minds living in different times and places. Thus, to choose certain political thinkers—in this case, Hobbes and Locke—as best representing the classical liberal tradition requires a word of explanation. The status of Hobbes as one of the founders of liberal tradition has been a subject of debate for more than half a century beginning, arguably, with Taylor and climaxing in Warrender and Macpherson.[56] But while it is questionable whether his theories of political obligation and ideal government could be deemed as part of the liberal doctrine, it seems less disputable that many of the premises, particularly those regarding the individual and his rights in the state of nature, from which Hobbes deduced his conclusions, would fit squarely into the liberal tradition. It is these premises, not his conclusions, which establish Hobbes' place in the history of liberal thought.[57] In contrast, Locke seems to have posed fewer problems for critics. Despite recent attempts to cast him primarily as a natural law thinker who recognizes the primacy of duties or obligations over rights, of the common good over the individual's self-interest, there is evidence that Locke's thought, especially of his more mature years, played a pivotal role in shaping the rights-based liberal tradition.[58] Perhaps a more appropriate way to read Locke is to recognize the transitional character of his political theory which involves a shift from the traditional natural-law discourse to an argument for individual rights in a rapidly changing political world.[59] All this having been said, it still needs to be kept in mind that what is intended here is not a historical study of the development of liberal thought; rather the aim is to disclose the core values underlying the liberal concept of rights.

The study of Hobbes has long been characterized by controversies. This is in large measure because his political philosophy contains a rich variety of ideas and these ideas can be elicited and developed to yield radically different readings. The traditional reading sees Hobbes essentially, but not without variations, as a radical individualist, a psychological egoist, or a utilitarian rationalist.[60] The antitraditional reading takes the opposite view, regarding him as a natural law deontologist.[61] An eclectic reading concedes the Hobbesian individualist and rationalist premises, yet denies that no moral rules can be generated from them to serve as the basis of obligation. According to one critic, it is rational for individuals to be moral.[62] And an institutional-structural reading interprets Hobbes' political theory in the context of containing elite ambitions for power, rendering the individual and his rights politically irrelevant.[63] Given these diverse and conflicting accounts of Hobbes' thought, to argue that there is a unified liberal theory of rights in Hobbes seems problematic. Such a theory, like those which tend to see him homogeneously as a champion of, say, divine politics or market individualism, can only be built at the cost of evidence to the contrary.[64] Moreover, while the idea of rights clearly plays a role in Hobbes' political thought, it is not the centerpiece of his enterprise. Thus, there exists a second danger of trying single-mindedly to prove one's case by ignoring his central contention that obedience is the cornerstone of any stable and prosperous political society. It bears remembering therefore that a construction of Hobbes as a rights theorist must be viewed in connection with these two qualifications.

Hobbes' conception of rights begins with an account of natural right. Natural right, he says, "is the Liberty each man hath, to use his own power, as he will himselfe, for the preservation of his own Nature; that is to say, of his own life; and consequently, of doing any thing, which in his own Judgement, and Reason, hee shall conceive to be the aptest means thereunto."[65] This definition, it seems to me, bears the influence of the late medieval and early modern use of right in the subjective sense as *potentas, facultas,* or *dominium,* although ambiguities also exist with regard to such influence.[66] Hobbes is innovative in at least three respects. First, he sees natural right not merely as a power that nature implants in the individual, but more importantly as the natural condition of man as totally free and equally so. This equal freedom is conceived as "the absence of externall Impediments" or more precisely as the absence of restraints, interferences, and obligations. Hobbesian natural right, thus, is a combination of two hitherto separate elements, namely a naturally endowed power or faculty and a natural condition of unlimited freedom. Fundamentally, it is what contemporary writers would call a negative conception of right. As we shall see, this view of the individual's natural rights has deep implications for the liberal concept of rights. Second, for Hobbes, reason is no longer oriented toward a teleological and objectively discoverable good or common good; rather it is individually and subjectively owned by each individual for the sole purpose of self-preservation. In this sense, there is no *right* reason, one which underlies the classical and medieval doctrine about man, society and government, but only instrumental reason which each individual uses to his own advantage in the state of nature. Third, unlike medieval theologians and jurists alike who tend to view right as grounded in and derived from law, Hobbes denies such a close connection by pitting right against law. For him, right "consisteth in liberty to do, or to forbeare; Whereas Law, determineth, and bindeth to one of them; so that Law, and Right, differ as much, as Obligation, and Liberty; which in one and the same matter are inconsistent."[67]

Hobbes clearly intends the right of nature to be a ubiquitous, unqualified, and general right; from it there can be inferred numerous specific and derivative rights which enable everyone to lay claims to everything, "even to one anothers body." This natural condition of absolute freedom or license, according to Hobbes, is a condition of war of all against all; it is characterized by a never-ending struggle for wealth, honor, and power which it is the destiny of human beings to pursue and which contribute to human felicity. But the condition of war causes unhappiness in the sense of lack of security and constant fear of untimely death. In such warring circumstances, it seems to Hobbes, the only way to survive is for individuals to give up or transfer their natural right and institute, via an irrevocable contract, a common power called the sovereign to arbitrate over their affairs. It must be noted, however, that by giving up or transferring the individual's natural right Hobbes does not mean a total loss of freedom, which would amount to slavery. He does not believe that the right to defend one's life under an oppressive government is among the rights to be alienated.[68] Whatever the individual gives up or transfers are only those rights which, if retained, would jeopardize peace and security, thus defeating the purpose for which political society is instituted.

The institution of political society creates for Hobbes two main categories of rights which belong in two distinctive domains, namely public and private. Public rights or what may be called political rights are in the exclusive possession of the sovereign, be it one man or an assembly of men, and they cover all three fundamentally important areas of government, namely legislative, executive, and judicial. Given the peculiar nature of the contract which Hobbes envisions, the sovereign does not have to be responsive to his subjects, and whatever he does and the means by which he does it are solely his own judgment, provided that his action abides by the laws of nature, aiming at common peace and security. The rights held by the sovereign may thus be understood in the Hohfeldian sense as powers and privileges, but not claims, with the correlative liabilities and no-rights of the subjects. This asymmetry and the related denial of the right of the contracting parties to nullify and renew a contract lie at the center of Hobbesian political absolutism. It would be for later liberal thinkers such as Locke to reject this absolutist conclusion while retaining the consent premise and to redesign a political contract by insisting on, among other things, the citizen's right to resist the sovereign who abuses his power.

Although Hobbes believes that the rights of the sovereign as a public person can never be challenged, yet such rights are neither boundless nor capricious. Hobbes imposes two constraints on them, one practical and the other normative. Practically it is not only impossible but unnecessary for the sovereign to control every aspect of the subject's life, and normatively the sovereign must act in accordance with the laws of nature. These constraints provide a distinct perspective from which to view the transitional and quasi-liberal nature of Hobbes' theory. For Hobbes, the sovereign's rights are con-fined, at least in principle, to the public domain, but beyond it, and where the law is silent, there remains a great deal of latitude for the individual to act or not to act. This may be called the sphere of private dealings. In this private sphere, one can pursue whatever one perceives to be good, a good which is distinctively one's own and which others should not interfere with. The individual has a broad range of rights going from economic, legal, civil to religious; these rights entitle one to enjoy one's property, choose one's place of living, pursue one's trade of life, or engage in other activities entirely at one's own discretion and free from restraints and interferences. One even has the right to sue the sovereign in the latter's *private,* though not *public,* capacity if and when there arise disputes between one and the sovereign over, say, private property, service, and debt.[69] It is true that whatever pri-vate rights an individual holds are subject to the sovereign's review; it is also true that the sovereign answers to no particular individual or, for that mat-ter, group of individuals for his conduct. This, however, should not lead one to conclude that the idea of individual rights has no important role in the Hobbesian vision of an obligation-dominated political society. The private rights which Hobbes prescribes for the individual may not be novel, partic-ularly when we bear in mind the common law rights which Englishmen en-joyed, but to draw on the basis of these rights a private sphere in which individuals act according to their own judgment and have control over their own actions and defend it, if necessary, by invoking the most fundamental right of all, namely the right of self-preservation, even at one's own peril, is no mean achievement on Hobbes' part. It is precisely this distinction be-tween, and the subsequent rebalancing of, private rights and public obliga-tions that would later become a weapon in the hands of liberal rights theorists to shield the individual from the power of the state.

Hobbes' theory of rights—his postulation of human beings' natural state of freedom and equality, his conception of the individual as a self-in-terested and competitive rights-bearer, his negative definition of right as the absence of restraint, his pluralist understanding of good, his contractarian view of the relationship between the individual and the state, between individuals, and his drawing of a private sphere of autonomous or semi-autonomous action—sets the preliminary stage for the emerging liberal argument for individual rights. It is partially in this intellectual milieu that we find his compatriot Locke. As is well known, Locke's intellectual apprenticeship was spent in a climate of anti-Hobbism. But a careful reading of his early writings reveals that he covertly endorsed many of Hobbes' views; for example, he opposed Edward Bagshaw's plea for individual conscience and liberty in favor of the wide and supreme power of the civil magistrate in "indifferent" matters with regard to religious practice.[70] Although for some reasons—his association with the liberal Earl of Shaftsbury among them—he altered his early views and went on to reject Hobbes' absolutist conclusions in his later works, this did not preclude him from accepting at least some of the Hobbesian premises from which he deduced his own doctrines concerning "the true original, extent, and end of civil government."[71] In fact, his argument about the foundation and purpose of government is predicated on these premises in a spirit that is evocative of Hobbes.

To say this, however, is not to restate the Straussian position that Locke is not a believer in natural law, but fundamentally a Hobbist whose attempt to situate man, rather than the will of God, in the center of our moral world prioritizes the individual's natural rights over his natural duties or obligations.[72] The untenableness of such a position lies in its failure to account for the importance of the notion of natural law which appeared in Locke's early writings and continued to be of relevance in his later ones.[73] But neither is it entirely convincing to limit oneself to a predominantly natural law duty-based reading of Locke, particularly with respect to his political doctrines.[74] Tully justifies this line of interpretation by saying that the seventeenth-century natural law language is a basic, if not the only, intellectual medium through which Locke articulated his theory of property and that it constitutes the proper context in which a proper understanding of this theory can be obtained.[75] This position is, however, unconvincing, since the natural rights language was clearly also available to Locke, as Tully himself is fully aware. An even more vexing problem is that such a duty-based reading reduces to redundancy and meaninglessness Locke's extensive use of the language of rights. If rights were to be explained solely in terms of duties or obligations, for example, the active sense of self-ownership and self-control contained in the Lockean notion of property would be lost. Further, to use Locke's early *Essays on the Law of Nature,* a work which he never intended for publication, as a basis for a coherent reading of his later writings is unsatisfactory, for it ignores precisely those differences in time, purpose, and audience which give credibility to a proper contextual understanding of his thought.

More recently, a more balanced view has been suggested by A. John Simmons. Simmons argues that Locke is not a 'Hobbes in disguise," nor does he take rights to be "mere shadows of duties under the law." In fact, the idea of natural law and the idea of individual rights are both at play in Locke's political thought, and there is no obvious incoherence involved in combining the two elements. He sketches two pictures to illustrate his point. In the first picture, God is "at the center of all moral relations" and whatever rights we have, if any, are not claim-rights but mere third-party benefits of duties owed to God; and in the second, God is still "central" as creator and lawgiver, but He also endows us with rationality and purposiveness, and it is the rationality and purposiveness that enable us to see our individual moral worth, to define our moral relations in terms of the rights we hold and the duties we perform, and ultimately to fulfill God's plan for mankind as a whole.[76] Simmons holds that Locke shifts between the two descriptions in a way that reveals the transitional character of his political theory. And he continues:

> "His emphasis on God's ownership of and interest in humankind as a whole points to the importance of the common good and to the collectivist, communitarian aspects of Locke's thought (the irresistible teleological pull of natural law theory). His emphasis on the natural equality, freedom, and purposiveness of persons points to the sanctity of each person's life and plans and to the individualist, libertarian aspects of his thought. But his Kantian and rule-consequentialist arguments constitute a way of pulling the two lines together in what really amounts to a pluralist moral theory."[77]

Simmons' well-reasoned middle-ground stance provides an attractive theoretical framework for discussing Locke's conception of rights. It recognizes the theological natural-law foundation of Locke's thought, while allowing for a genuinely independent consideration of the central role the idea of rights plays in his understanding of man, society and government. This, however, does not mean that there is no ambiguity involved in the relationship between natural law and natural right, a relationship which directly affects the reading of Locke as a rights theorist. It is not always clear whether the latter is derived from the former with no independent status of its own, or the former functions merely as a restraining mechanism on the latter whose existence is justified by an entirely different purpose. In his *Essays on the Law of Nature*, while not denying the consistency between natural law and natural right, Locke nevertheless keeps them distinct.

Natural "right is grounded in the fact that we have the free use of a thing," he says, "whereas [natural] law is what enjoins or forbids the doing of a thing."[78] What he emphasizes in this definition and in the passages that follow it is that natural law functions as commands or prohibitions that we do or refrain from doing; in other words, it creates duties or obligations. This distinction between natural right and natural law, however, is blurred in his *Two Treatises of Government*. There we find that natural law not only creates duties or obligations but also rights. It is perhaps this blurring that has prompted some critics to deem rights as mere shadows of duties or obligations in Locke's thought.

To make sense of such equivocation and to assign the notion of rights the independent status it justly deserves, it may be useful to distinguish in Locke two realms of discourse which, though inseparably linked with each other, nevertheless are governed by different assumptions and concepts. In the first and theological realm in which the subject is the relationship between God the creator and man the created, no language of rights is possible; what man can have are duties only, duties which are owed to God and embodied in natural law. In the second and secular realm, however, in which the focus is on the relationship between man and man, both the language of rights and that of duties are employed. By assigning both rights and duties rather than duties only, Locke is able to affirm the active rational capacity of man to discern and execute God's plan for humanity, an act which a passive follower of duty simply could not accomplish. Thus, when Locke talks about one's duty to preserve oneself, he should be understood as stating both a duty and a right, depending on which issue he is addressing. When self-preservation is answerable to God, it is no doubt a duty; but when self-preservation is discussed in the context of the human community, it would be more appropriately understood as a right to be held against those who attempt to subject others to their arbitrary will and power. This point about the difference in context will become clearer as the theological argument retreats into the background and political questions are brought to the fore in the *Second Treatise*. It is there that rights talk begins to assume an increasingly important, if not larger, place, although the law of nature always imposes constraints on it.

Locke does not begin his conception of rights, as does Hobbes, with a clear definition of a right in his *Two Treatises*. The one definition which is available to us is in his *Essays on the Law of Nature* where, as quoted above, he takes a right to consist in "the free use of a thing." It bears close resemblance to the definition employed by Hobbes and which regards a right primarily as a liberty to order one's action without being subject to another's power and control. As we shall see, this signification of a right or what may be called a liberty-right in the Hohfeldian sense is clearly intended by Locke for at least some of the individual's rights in the state of nature. But it is not the only meaning he gives to the concept, and there are other kinds of rights, such as a child's right to be nourished and educated and a needy person's right to be fed and clothed, which cannot be fitted into this category. Considering the various contexts in which Locke uses the term, one may find three senses of a right corresponding roughly to the Hohfeldian liberty-right (self-preservation), power-right (the execution of natural law), and finally claim-right (charity). It must be kept in mind, however, that each of these senses is not fixed in Locke's usage and can be used interchangeably depending on the context in which it is used. For example, the right of self-preservation may be a liberty when one thinks about means to preserve oneself and a claim when one's survival is jeopardized by another's commission or omission.

In developing his political theory, Locke postulates three fundamental and first-order rights that each individual is believed to possess equally in the state of nature, namely, the right of self-preservation, of "perfect freedom" or "uncontroleable liberty," and of property. He justifies them on the theological ground that God created men, that they are his property and workmanship, "sent into the World by his order and about his business."[79] While He wills and grants these rights to human creatures, God also imposes restrictions on their exercise through the principles of natural law or what Locke calls "the decree of the divine will." It is at this juncture that Locke parts company with his predecessor Hobbes. Hobbes' bleak assumptions about human nature and his anthropocentric position leave him no room for the interposition of a friendly notion of natural law between self-preservation and social cooperation; for him, a war of all against all *is* the law of nature. Locke from the very beginning entertains a fundamentally different understanding of such law and provides it with an oversight power to rectify or at least constrain all the vices, such as partiality, passion, violence and slavery, to which man is susceptible. Thus, a right to preserve oneself is limited by a duty not to "harm another in his Life, Health, Liberty, or Possessions," but rather "to preserve the rest of Mankind" when and if this is not in conflict with one's own survival; a right to one's natural liberty is curbed by another duty not to attempt to "get another Man into his Absolute Power;" and a right to property is restrained by still another duty to leave as much and as good for others.[80]

The three natural rights which Locke believes the individual to be endowed with by virtue of the self-evident fact that each person is born a free, equal, and rational being lie at the center of his theory of rights and, for that matter, of his political theory as a whole. Two structural features of these rights need to be emphasized here, because they inform the very manner in which the liberal conception of rights would proceed in the centuries to come. First, the relationship among the three natural rights is conceived in such a way that they come to imply one another and form a conceptual whole which Locke terms property. Though first on Locke's list, the right to life cannot be viewed independently of the other two rights, and vice versa. A life that is devoid of the liberty to "follow my own Will in all things," to order my actions and dispose of my possessions and my person as I think fit, without being subject to the arbitrary will and power of others, would be unacceptable. Liberty, says Locke, "is so necessary to, and closely joyned with a Man's Preservation, that he cannot part with it, but by what forfeits his Preservation and Life together," and as such, it is the "Foundation of all the rest."[81]

Just as liberty is essential to self-preservation, so is property narrowly understood as material possessions. Insofar as it provides the means of support and comfort for an individual's existence, property is an outward extension of life. To take the means whereby I live, as Shakespeare has Shylock say in *The Merchant of Venice,* is to take my life. But insofar as it also connotes a sense of *dominium,* property has for Locke a larger and deeper meaning than a mere right in things. This meaning may provide a clue to the debate over whether the right to property is of an exclusive or an inclusive nature.[82] If property is understood primarily as lands and goods, it is clearly an inclusive right, particularly when we bear in mind the argument advanced by Locke against Filmer in the *First Treatise.* If, however, property is understood as property in one's person and in one's labor, it cannot be taken as a right common to and claimable by all, but rather as a private and exclusive domain that one has total control over and cannot alienate without forfeiting one's life and liberty altogether. This second sense, it seems to me, is what Locke means by property when he subsumes life, liberty, and property under it and when he argues that the chief end of government is the preservation of property. It signifies for him not merely a material condition for self-preservation, but a moral claim to a sphere of autonomous action in which individuals can choose their course of life without being subject to "the inconstant, uncertain, unknown, Arbitrary Will of another Man." In this connection, it is identical with life and liberty.[83]

Second, the three natural rights provide both the source from which an extended list of rights can be derived and the ground on which they can be justified. Thus, from the right to life there flow the right of children to nourishment and education, the right of parents to have control over their children before the latter reach maturity, and the right of the poor and the needy to take from and be provided for by those in plenty. On the basis of the right of freedom in the state of nature, we can defend the right to execute natural law and punish its offender and the right of the injured to take reparation from the injurer; we can also defend the right to contract, to engage in religious, civil, and economic activities, the right to have those "innocent delights," and the right to do or forbear "where the Rule prescribes not." With the right to property in order, we can secure and justify the right to appropriate, own, exchange, enjoy, inherit, and alienate lands and goods.[84]

In the Lockean scheme, all natural rights, whether fundamental or derivative, are *private* rights, although they are held and exercised in the context of a natural community. They are private not because God grants the world to Adam's private possession, a view which Locke clearly rejects, but rather because they are those rights which an individual possesses *prior to* the establishment of political society. The prototype of a private right is the right to property, either narrowly or broadly understood.[85] It is in this fundamental respect that private rights are distinguished from public or political ones. Upon entering political society for want of an indifferent and common judge and for fear of "the Invasion of others," one must give up, or transform the nature of, some of the private and prepolitical rights one possesses in the state of nature. One must give up, for example, the right to "punish the Offender, and be the Executioner of the Law of Nature" and accordingly the right to take reparation from the criminal who has victimized him; one must transform the nature of property rights in a way that is consistent with the regulations and laws of the commonwealth of which one is now a member.[86] But there are certain natural rights, particularly the right to life, which the individual cannot abandon or alienate without defeating the purpose for which he or she voluntarily contracts with other like-minded individuals to institute a government, and these rights no authority can take away without putting the individual back in a state of war. It is these inalienable rights that provide a private zone of autonomy, enabling the individual to act according to his or her own will and have sovereignty over his or her person and possessions within the bounds of the law of society, even in times of war and conquest.[87]

By contrast, rights in the public or political domain are quite different in nature, origin and purpose. Locke stipulates a host of political rights while constructing what he perceives to be a legitimate political order; these include, but are not restricted to, the right to be represented fairly and equally in the supreme legislative body, the right to appoint and remove its members, and ultimately the right to resist and reconstitute the government.[88] Here, again, he is opposed to Hobbes. For Hobbes, political rights are in the possession of the sovereign and do not provide remedies for the individual in cases of the abuse of political power. One certainly can invoke the right of self-preservation to defend oneself against the sovereign, but only at one's own peril. For Locke, however, political rights are precisely those remedies to which the individual can have recourse in abusive situations; or, better, they serve as a buffer zone which insulates the individual from the power of the state. The Lockean conception of political rights may be characterized along these lines. First, unlike natural rights, political rights are artificially contrived and second-order rights derived from the act of consent on the individual's part to form a political compact. Second, unlike natural rights again, they are not constitutive of the autonomy of the individual as a person, but conceived merely as a pragmatic tool for creating conditions for such autonomy; in this regard, they are valuable in an instrumental rather than intrinsic sense. Third, to the extent that political power is limited, rights in the political arena are limited in both scope and purpose; they are intended solely to circumscribe the exercise of political power and provide institutional protection for the individual in the enjoyment of his preexisting rights, and beyond this, they have no important role to play.

By distinguishing between first-order and second-order rights, and by advancing an instrumentalist understanding of the nature, origin and purpose of political rights, Locke helped usher in a conception of rights that, in one critic's words, "formed the armature of modern liberal ideology."[89] This conception is predicated on an assumption of the individual as ontologically distinct, private, autonomous, and self-interested. It privileges first-order private rights and the individual's private interests, particularly property interests, which these rights are designed to protect and promote, and relegates public rights to a position divorced from and external to the individual's autonomy and well-being. It also inaugurates the notion of a useful yet limited public sphere and the attendant view of political society and political obligation as based on a prepolitical, presocial and rights-informed contract.

The Lockean idea of rights has had strong impact on the liberal conception of rights and on the liberal doctrine as a whole. It has helped set a pattern of rights thinking which liberal political thinkers in successive generations after Locke would follow, improve, enhance and sanctify. This is certainly not to say that liberal rights as envisioned by Locke and his like have gone unchallenged. On the contrary, the liberal notion of rights was from the very beginning subject to intense criticisms from within as well as from outside the liberal persuasion.[90] These criticisms have prompted liberal rights thinkers to reformulate or adjust their theory. But whatever reformulations and adjustments, the core values and beliefs underlying the liberal argument for rights, as we shall see in the next section, have remained remarkably stable, and they provide the basis, in terms of both rhetoric and substance, for the argument of contemporary liberal rights theorists.

Contemporary Liberal Rights

Nearly four decades ago, in a spirit that was clearly reminiscent of Locke, Friedrich A. Hayek presented an eloquent case for individual liberty.[91] The central argument on which Hayek's case depended may be stated as follows. Freedom, that condition of humanity in which individuals can order their action according to their own plans and decisions without being subject to the arbitrary and coercive power of others, is the mainspring of civilization and progress; as such, it must be secured. The best and time-tested way to secure it is by drawing a protected private sphere of activity in the form of rights against the most formidable coercive force of all, namely the state; since no political society can exist without some form of coercion, the primary task of "a regime of freedom" then consists in minimizing such coercion and its harmful effects in a way that is most conducive to the maximizing of the fundamental value of individual or personal liberty.

The appeal of Hayek's argument rests to a considerable extent on its conscious use of and identification with the classical liberal doctrine. But it is not a simple restatement of a Lockean position on natural liberty and natural rights; rather, it is a narrow reformulation of that position which provides no adequate account of its philosophical foundations. Neither does it give sufficient attention to problems of justice *vis-à-vis* rights which loom large in contemporary society. In fact, on several issues, particularly on those which deal with distributive justice, it carries to the extreme and impoverishes that position by making assertions which would make even a Locke wince at the thought. At least two characteristics distinguish it from the classical view. First, Hayek does not believe that there exists such a thing as the state of nature in which humans enjoy perfect and equal liberty. For him, the state of freedom is a product of history rather than a hypothetical Archimedean point on which a liberal theory of government can be constructed; it is "an artifact of civilization" which has been obtained through trial and error and "did not arise from design."[92] And since liberty is not originally given to us at birth by our Creator, it can be justified only on grounds other than those based on natural law and the will of God. The grounds on which Hayek defends freedom and rights that surround it are essentially consequentialist ones. The answer he gives to the question of why freedom is good and desirable is predicated on the perceived utility of freedom and rights in allowing each and every individual sufficient space to pursue his own ends in a creative way, and it is this free and creative use of one's talent and energy that leads to the growth of civilization and progress.[93]

Second, by prioritizing individual liberty and individual rights over all other values as *the* foundational principle on which political society is based, and by justifying it in consequentialist terms, Hayek preempts fruitful and intelligent discussions on the issue of equality, an issue which has come to be regarded as one of the twin pillars of liberalism. He argues that social and economic inequality resulting from the exercise of individual liberty and individual rights is not an unfortunate but rather a requisite feature of a free society. This view is not exactly the one endorsed by Locke. In the *Second Treatise,* Locke provided a possible description of the origin of unequal possessions. Although his discussions about the appropriation of property narrowly understood may lead one to conclude that inequality in material possessions is justified, he did not *explicitly* encourage the view that material equality is detrimental to the welfare of society as a whole. Hayek carries the Lockean argument for property rights to its logical extreme, regarding any redistribution of wealth that is aimed at reducing socio-economic inequality as harmful and unjust, because it necessarily involves coercion by government and thus violates the individual's rights. The only kind of equality he believes to be possible without destroying liberty is equality before the general rules of law. The achievement of such equality does not only *not* require our efforts to minimize material inequality, say, by means of "a deliberately chosen pattern of distribution;" in fact, it would create greater material inequality. While "the state must use coercion for other reasons," Hayek writes, "the desire of making people more alike in their condition cannot be accepted in a free society as a justification for further and discriminatory coercion."[94]

Hayek's argument constitutes a proper starting point for considering the liberal conception of rights in contemporary political theory because it speaks to two important questions with which liberalism must cope in order to maintain its appeal. The first question is epistemological and concerns the foundation of liberalism. Hayek's answer is not untypical of a secularized liberal stance which has been widely shared at least since J.S. Mill. Rather than rest the idea of freedom on the divine will as Locke did, it grounds individual liberty and individual rights on "utility in the largest sense," that is, on "the permanent interests of man as a progressive being."[95] The second question is substantive and concerns those vitally important values which are constitutive of a desirable human society and which liberals cannot ignore. With respect to this issue, Hayek's view has come to signify for many a "pure" liberal position in the replacement or revision of which various models of liberalism have been sought. The two questions are closely related yet separable; discussion of one may or may not involve discussion of the other. But it is undeniable that answers to the question of foundation will certainly shed light on the substantive issues such as justice and equality which go into the structuring of liberalism.

In contemporary political thought, no work can be said to have accomplished more than John Rawls' *A Theory of Justice* in offering a comprehensive and principled liberal response to both of these questions. Rawls answers the first question by the idea of a contracting original position in which free and rational individuals agree behind a veil of ignorance to the principles of justice for the basic structure of their society, and the second question by the difference principle that inequalities are to be arranged to the benefit of the least advantaged in society. By integrating these two answers in a coherent theoretical framework, Rawls' work has produced an argument that is not merely philosophically and logically plausible, but also satisfies, or at least makes an honest attempt to satisfy, the moral aspirations of our own age. For this reason, it is widely hailed by both defenders and critics as the paradigm of contemporary liberal thought.

A Theory of Justice is paradigmatic, however, not in the Kuhnian sense of a break with the paradigm that precedes it; on the contrary, it revives a long and well-articulated liberal tradition in a way that breathes new life into it. It is paradigmatic in the sense that it helps define both the scope and the content of political debate today not by creating something entirely new, but by reordering familiar ideas and concepts in an inventive way. This inventive reordering connects the present to the past. Not surprisingly, we find the notion of rights included and indeed figuring prominently in this reservoir of familiar ideas and concepts.

Clearly the Rawlsian theory is not a theory of rights *per se;* it deals with a larger argument, namely justice. But the idea of rights plays such a fundamental role in it that it cannot be defended in any meaningful way without an adequate account of this idea. We may recall that a general right to basic liberties is not only built into the principles of justice but also given priority over the difference principle. Though it would be unfair to Rawls' theory to read it simply as a rights-based moral argument, it may not be inappropriate to see it as exhibiting certain essential characteristics of or being keenly informed by the conception of rights which is found prevalent in the writings of contemporary liberal thinkers.[96] Rawls makes many implicit and explicit assumptions about rights in his principal work and elsewhere, and he does so with no systematic reference to any theory of rights. Despite this, and despite also that ambiguities and questions abound with regard to the language of rights in his discussion of justice, it is possible to construct a reasonable account of the Rawlsian position on the nature, purpose, and grounds of rights on the basis of his scattered comments. Indeed, some insist that such an account is not only possible but indispensable to an adequate understanding of Rawls. A rights-based approach, it is believed, would shed new light on his theory and even revolve some of the difficult problems accompanying it.[97] Tempting as it may be, this approach raises some questions. Chief among these is that a rights-centered reading of Rawlsian theory would limit a broad appreciation of that theory. Perhaps a more suitable way to consider the Rawlsian conception of rights is to view it as embedded in rather than imposing a structure over his theory of justice.

Like many other contemporary rights theorists, Rawls begins by advancing a widely shared liberal belief that each individual *qua* moral person "possesses an inviolability founded on justice that even the welfare of society as a whole cannot override."[98] He believes that the biggest threat to this intuitive conviction of ours comes from utilitarianism, an ethical doctrine which in its classical form takes the greatest happiness of the greatest number as the ultimate basis for answering all moral questions. The utilitarian doctrine, Rawls argues, is hostile to the idea of individual rights and liberties in that it allows greater social and economic advantages to be achieved for many at the expense of the interests of a few. To defend this idea requires not only a refutation of the utilitarian doctrine, but more importantly a principled alternative to it in the sense of the Kantian categorical imperative. Hence the principles of right and justice which Rawls thinks all would accept as self-prescribed rules for governing the basic structure of their society in a hypothetical and fair choice situation called the original position. While a full review of Rawls' arguments leading to these principles is beyond my immediate purpose here, it is necessary to call attention to a few key issues that are essential to an appropriate understanding of his conception of rights.

Rawls presents the original position as a contractual situation in which "rational individuals with certain ends and related to each other in certain ways are to choose among various courses of action in view of their knowledge of the circumstances."[99] It is not an ordinary contract; rather, it is restricted by a peculiar set of circumstances artificially designed for the purpose of achieving a permanently binding moral agreement. But it is a contract nonetheless. As a contract, it presupposes a number of things that the contractees must be presumed to have fully understood; these include, but are not limited to, the fact that two or more individuals are involved, the mental competence of these individuals, the voluntary nature of the contract, the absence of duress and fraud, and the prospect of enforcement in

case of nonperformance. These elements are very much part of a contract—
a point which Durkheim made forcefully in *The Division of Labor in Society*
nearly a century ago. The Rawlsian original position presupposes all of them
plus a few more of its own.

Perhaps the most fundamental of all the presuppositions built into the
original position, one which lies at the fountainhead of the liberal conception of rights, is the ontological primacy of the individual. The primacy thesis views the individual as a rational, autonomous, and irreducible being in
our moral and political universe. As such, the individual comes first in the
order of things. The individual manifests himself or herself as the ultimate
end, never merely as a means, and it is with respect to this end that he or she
comes to be regarded as the bearer of rights. Rawls apparently has this in
mind when he argues, following Kant, that the original position provides a
special vantage point from which individuals *qua* noumenal selves choose
the principles of their action as the most adequate possible expression of
their nature as free and equal rational beings. And he continues:

> "The description of the original position interprets the point of view of
> noumenal selves, of what it means to be a free and equal rational being.
> Our nature as such beings is displayed when we act from the principles
> we would choose when this nature is reflected in the conditions deter-
> mining the choice. Thus men exhibit their freedom, their independence
> from the contingencies of nature and society, by acting in ways they
> would acknowledge in the original position."[100]

However, this should not be perceived as a Hobbesian egoistic conception of the individual. In fact, Rawls is emphatic that his view of the contracting individual is not egoistic, for egoism would lead to a situation of
no-agreement, defeating the purpose for which the original position is stipulated. But neither does Rawls say that individuals are altruistic. Although
social cooperation, in Rawls' view, is a decisive natural feature of human beings, Rawlsian individuals are essentially self-interested and seek social cooperation primarily to advance their self-interests.[101] It is neither that
individuals are stripped of social attachments like those in Nozick's invisi-
ble-hand conception of the minimal state, nor that such attachments are essential to defining their very nature as moral agents which we find in
Sandel's vision of an intersubjective and embodied self.[102] Individuals are
not devoid of ends in pursuit of which they are thought to be engaged in the
deliberation of the principles of justice, but they do not regard these ends as
part of who they are and how they function in a particular society at a particular time and place. They are not anti-social creatures, but society exists,

rather than as an end itself or an integral part of that end, only as a means to an end chosen by individuals in their capacity as rational and free moral beings; that is, it exists *for,* not *through* or *in* each of them. In short, the key Rawlsian assumption about individuals is that they are self-interested, though not selfish, beings.

When the individual is conceived in such an *a priori* way—a conception which one may trace back to Descartes—that he or she assumes the center stage in the drama of human life, it should come as no surprise that the idea of rights would be brought into play in the Rawlsian theory of justice. For it is no other idea but this one that would ensure to the fullest possible extent the self-interest and well-being of the individual. A conception of the ontological primacy of the individual *vis-à-vis* society seems to lead naturally to a conception of justice in which rights play a pivotal role; it is not that social cooperation is unimportant, but that it is only secondary to the interests and expectations of the self thus understood.

This helps explain why Rawls frames his first principle of justice in terms of a general and equal right to basic liberties. Not only so; it is assigned a priority over the division of advantages from social cooperation. Rawls sometimes refers to these liberties as rights, and they include such civil and political liberties or rights as freedom of speech and liberty of conscience which we find standard in a liberal democracy. Conceptually they may well be called liberty-rights in the Hohfeldian sense. But liberty-rights are not the only kind Rawls has in mind, and there are also claims, permissions, and expectations which we may appropriately place under the rubric of rights. Insofar as they are founded on the first principle of justice and built into the basic structure of society, however, these are first-order and the most basic rights. As such, they are given a moral status not unlike that of natural rights found in the classical liberal doctrine: they are absolute, inalienable, and expressive of the individual *qua* moral person. In a revealing passage that is worth quoting at length, Rawls writes:

> [The concept of natural rights] explains why it is appropriate to call by this name the rights that justice protects. These claims depend solely on certain natural attributes the presence of which can be ascertained by natural reason pursuing common sense methods of inquiry. The existence of these attributes and the claims based upon them is established independently from social conventions and legal norms. The propriety of the term "natural" is that it suggests the contrast between the rights identified by the theory of justice and the rights defined by law and custom. But more than this, the concept of natural rights includes the idea that these rights are assigned in the first instance to persons, and that they are given a special weight. Claims easily overridden for other values

are not natural rights. Now the rights protected by the first principle have both of these features in view of the priority rules. Thus justice as fairness has the characteristic marks of a natural rights theory.[103]

The reformulation of traditional natural rights as grounded in the first principle of justice which each individual would agree to in an initial contractual situation is a salient characteristic of Rawls' theory of rights. It bears close resemblance to positions most forcefully defended by a number of liberal thinkers as diverse as Hart, Dworkin, and Nozick, notwithstanding their crucial differences. In their view, as in Rawls,' rights are a special moral category which recognizes the inviolability and independence of the individual *qua* person. They are side constraints (*a la* Nozick) or trumps (*a la* Dworkin) that accord people protection from disadvantages incurred in the name of overall social good.[104] They function as a form of control that other persons or the community as a whole act or refrain from action in ways compatible with that inviolability and independence, and provide, in Hart's words, "a moral justification for limiting the freedom of another person and for determining how he should act."[105] They define those areas of action which one has sovereignty over and which others have a corresponding duty or obligation not to interfere with. One must respect them even if their exercise offends one's own sense of what constitutes a good life. In the sense that they are "not subject to political bargaining and to the calculus of social interests," rights are absolute; the only reason they may be circumscribed is for the sake of protecting similar rights from being violated, and no moral grounds other than this can justify limiting the exercise of rights and adjudicating conflicting rights claims.[106]

Clearly, Rawls intends his first principle to be a general and equal right, and this right in turn guarantees the basic rights which go into the structuring of a well-ordered society. But it is far from clear that his second principle, which consists of two parts, namely the difference principle and fair equality of opportunity, can also be deemed as a fundamental right in consistency with the first principle. It is at this juncture that some of the ambiguities begin to surface in the Rawlsian conception of rights. Rawls does not explicitly use the concept of a right to describe the second principle; in fact, it would seem incomprehensible for him to do so, for that would undermine his argument for the rule of priority and equal rights. It would seem absurd to argue that some rights are worthier than others on the scale of justice. In a situation in which two rights claims conflict, one claim is defeated not because it is less worthy but because circumstances in support of it are weak and thus do not call for a ruling in its favor. But some critics take a different view on this. Martin argues that the difference principle and fair equality of opportunity can and should be regarded as basic rights on a par with the first-principle rights, and that only this way of understanding could give the Rawlsian theory the kind of solid grounding it strives for.[107] Though Martin's argument has some merit, it is not without difficulties of its own. Suffice it to say for our purpose that given the lexical order in which the two principles of justice are arranged, it is difficult if not altogether impossible to defend the difference principle as a basic right. Rawls is unclear on this, and this ambiguity, in my view, represents a tension in liberal theory between a commitment to civil and political liberties and, ordinarily, an unwillingness to recognize basic economic well-being as a fundamental right.[108]

In Rawls' design, the two principles of justice, once chosen in the original position, would assign rights and duties and determine the appropriate division of social benefits, and these rights, duties, and benefits, accordingly, would be institutionalized through a properly constructed mechanism called a constitution. To the extent that rights as secured by the first-principle go into the framing of such a mechanism, they become institutional rights. But they are institutional rights not in the ordinary sense of being created by and grounded in an existing institution; rather it is the other way around. Established by the first principle, they exist prior to basic institutions, and as such, their justification does not rest on institutional grounds. The Rawlsian justificatory scheme may be considered a sequential one. In this scheme, nonbasic rights depend on basic rights which in turn depend on a general and equal right as specified by the first principle. But what is the basis of the first principle? Rawls' answer to this question may be sought by looking at two related ideas: One is the contractual original position as a formal device and the other a substantive argument about the moral person.

The original position is contemplated by Rawls as a formal device; formal in the sense that it provides a mere condition of fairness for choices to be made and no considerations about the position would play a substantive part in making those choices. Whether this is true remains open to debate. But granted that it is true, can the original position be said to provide a ground for justifying the choice of the principles of justice? Rawls is inclined to deny this,[109] and some critics agree with him. Kukathas and Pettit argue that what the idea of an original position tries to accomplish is simply to construct a strategic point from which the principles of justice are to be evaluated, and that it does not serve as a ground on which a particular arrangement will be chosen as just.[110] Such a view rests on a perceived need to separate the condition of fairness from the principles to be agreed to in that condition in order to bring about a conception of justice as fairness. But as many have pointed out, arguments leading to that separation are not entirely convincing.[111] Even if we allow that these arguments are acceptable, there is still a formal sense in which it may be said that the contractual nature of the original position provides a ground for justifying the choice of the principles of justice.

That the original position provides a *formal* ground for justifying the choice of the principles of justice may be understood in terms of the contract metaphor Rawls uses to describe that position. In traditional natural rights theory, the fact that we as human beings are bearers of natural rights is based on nature or the divine will; it is nature or the divine will that endows us with these rights. In the Rawlsian conception, however, the fact that we have rights such as those stipulated by the first principle of justice is predicated on a hypothetical contract. We come to be regarded as bearers of certain rights in the first instance because, suspending any substantive considerations for reasons of fairness, we contract in an initial situation of uncertainty that we'd better have them and have them built into the basic structure of our society. A contract is a promise, and a promise is a *prima facie* ground for saying that we shall act in certain ways or shall be entitled to certain things. Regardless of what is contracted or promised, of whether or not it is just, the act of contracting or promising itself has a moral force that is binding on the parties involved because of its voluntary and rational nature. As such, it constitutes a separate, albeit formal, reason for accepting what is contracted or promised, even if one realizes later on that one's interests are not advanced but rather disadvantaged by it.[112] It is in this sense that the original position may be said to provide a justification for the Rawlsian first principle and the basic rights it secures. What the substance of this particular principle is founded upon is a different matter and requires a substantive argument.

This immediately leads to the second idea. Viewing the contractual original position as a formal ground of justification does not mean that it is sufficient as such for justifying the choice of the principles of justice. The fact that certain basic rights are contracted for in the original position by representative citizens can only be viewed as a *prima facie* reason for accepting them as morally binding. There is, however, a deeper and substantive reason for saying that we as human creatures possess certain basic rights, and this reason is rooted in the idea of the moral person.

Rawls argues that the individual *qua* moral person is distinguished by two features. The first is that one is capable of having a conception of the good, and the second is that one is capable of a sense of justice. Expressed in more concrete terms, these two capacities are signified by a rational plan of life and a regulative desire to act upon certain principles of justice. It is clear that a deciphering of this conception of the moral person involves an understanding of the good and the sense of justice. Rawls' arguments about them are complex, covering a number of difficult issues ranging from a thin theory of the good, deliberative rationality, to the development of moral sentiments. Suffice it to note for expository purposes that when looked at closely, the Rawlsian conception of the moral person is essentially Kantian, and at its core is the Kantian idea of rational self-determination.

Rawls assumes, as does Kant, that being rational is a natural and defining feature of being human. He interprets rationality sometimes in purely instrumental terms as the most efficient means to a given end, but at other times he uses this notion in such a way that it is pregnant with important moral claims. Two such claims need to be emphasized here. One is that the assumption that a person is a rational being provides the basis for saying that we are equal. This is not to claim that all individuals are in equal possession of some substantive quality or skill such as intellect; rather, it merely points to a general yet fundamental property which human beings equally possess in contrast to nonhuman beings. It is in this sense that we are said to be equally rational. The other is that rationality, in the Kantian interpretation, is fused with a strong sense of autonomy. To be rational is to be capable of prescribing for ourselves certain rules of action and to be able to act upon them accordingly. To act in a way that conforms to what is prescribed by reason is to act autonomously and self-determinatively. These two claims are clearly incorporated into the Rawlsian understanding of the moral nature of human beings as rational choosers.

In Rawl's view, as in Kant's, morality is a matter of rational choice or self-determination, and moral principles are those which it is in the rational interest of individuals to choose and apply for governing their action. A moral person, thus, is one who is capable of choosing and applying such principles. For Kant, rational individuals are capable of forming a kingdom of ends, legislating for it, and governing themselves in terms of the self-legislated moral laws in interaction with each other. In Rawls' theory, individuals in the original position are described as being capable of acting in the same way. They are capable of conceiving a rational life plan on the basis of some general goods which they all recognize regardless of their specific interests, of choosing certain principles of right and justice on the basis of their sense of justice, and of acting upon these self-chosen principles in relating to one another. In doing so, they express their nature as free and equal rational beings; that is, they manifest themselves as moral persons. "Thus," Rawls says, "a moral person is a subject with ends he has chosen, and his fundamental preference is for conditions that enable him to frame a mode of life that expresses his nature as a free and equal rational being as fully as circumstances permit."[113] Although the idea of the moral person may not be an *explicit* component of Rawls' design of the original position, it is unmistakably an *implicit* assumption which goes to the heart of his "considered judgments" and which informs, and indeed provides a base for, his theory of rights.

It is precisely on the basis of the idea of the moral person that the individual is owed equal and basic rights. Individuals are bearers of rights not only because rights guarantee the integrity and well-being of personhood thus understood, but also because they are best expressive of their moral nature as free and equal rational beings. The Rawlsian first-principle right finds its substantive grounding in this conception of the moral person. To be sure, justifying the first-principle right and other basic rights that it secures on this ground is not without problems. Some argue that Rawls' reasoning is circular. Rawls reads into the original position many of the liberal assumptions and beliefs and then uses that position as a vantage point to argue for the principles of justice which he believes would be chosen with certain restrictions attached. He calls this reflective equilibrium. This claim need not concern us here. What needs to be pointed out is that Rawls' ground of justification for the first-principle right is a position that contemporary liberal rights theorists, including even some who criticize Rawls, would ordinarily accept. This position, in some fundamental respects, bears resemblance to the natural rights theory we find well-articulated in classical liberal thinkers such as Locke. It is in this regard that one may be justified in arguing that the liberal conception of rights has maintained remarkable continuity since it became an influential political doctrine in the seventeenth and eighteenth centuries. It must be quickly added, however, that to say this is not to endorse the view of a unified liberal tradition embodied in "a single unit idea." It seems beneficial to regard the liberal conception of rights as "an internally complex set of evolving doctrines, theories, beliefs and assumptions."[114] The aim of comparing the classical and the contemporary liberal view of individual rights, thus, is not so much to find some family resemblance *per se* between the two, but to identify the enduring core values and beliefs underlying both views regardless of their differences.

Chapter Four
Individualism as Cultural Grounding

From its birth in the sixteenth and seventeenth centuries to the present, the liberal concept of rights underwent a long and dramatic path of growth and triumph. In the course of this evolution, it also went through many changes. The language of natural law, for example, which was so fundamental to Hobbes and Locke, no longer plays such a theoretically and morally persuasive role. Even the term "natural rights" itself seems to have fallen into disuse; only rarely do we see it surface in political discourse, and when it does, it conveys to us a largely different set of connotations. Perhaps for this reason, many prefer the concept *human* or *moral rights*. Having said this, however, it should be noted that these changes have not in any fundamental sense altered the core values, beliefs, and assumptions underlying liberal rights. We cannot but notice, if the preceding description of this concept is plausible, that certain basic assumptions and beliefs remain more or less intact, and that there is a remarkable continuity between the old and the new notion of rights in regard to these basic assumptions and beliefs.

Such continuity is most illuminatingly and most consistently revealed in an intriguing idea called the human individual. The centrality of the individual to liberal rights, or for that matter, to the liberal doctrine as a whole is readily observable in classical and contemporary liberal thought. This should not surprise us, for liberalism is, in the first instance, not about limited government, but about the individual—about the individual's nature, value, interests, and about the individual's self-perceived relationship with others and with society at large. Whatever else it may involve, liberalism first and foremost involves a conception of the individual; indeed, it presupposes and is grounded in this conception. The liberal notion of rights and that set of values and beliefs which is often described under the rubric of individualism are closely related. Such close relationship is not exhausted in the common expression "individual rights." The connection goes deeper. As Lukes has suggested, the basic components of individualism go directly to the heart of liberalism.[1] And if we take a close look at the values and practices that define individualism, we cannot fail to see that they are equally fundamental to the defining of the nature, purpose, and ground of liberal rights.

But does this entail the claim that individualism provides a *cultural* grounding for the liberal conception of rights? To establish that there is a conceptual link between individualism and liberalism is one thing, and to say that the former provides a cultural grounding for the latter is quite another. Two general comments need to be made here. In the first place, individualism should not be considered only as a cluster of ideas and beliefs; it also involves or is embodied in individualistic practices and behaviors. This understanding of individualism as a cultural phenomenon, as a shared way of relating, is in keeping with the definition of culture outlined in Chapter Two. While examining a conceptual link between the liberal notion of rights and individualism is important to the thesis of this study, I want also to explore the possibility of a historical relationship between them as manifested in actual events, situations, and patterns of social relations. This historical relationship is equally indispensable to our understanding of the extent to which the liberal concept of rights may be applied to a different political and cultural setting.

In the second place, the question of whether there is a causal link between individualism and liberalism is a difficult one and requires an argument that goes far beyond the purpose of this study. Fortunately, there are chartered routes to follow with respect to it. Following Weber's suggestions, I tend to view cultural grounding in terms of a rationally constructed scheme of understanding. This scheme of understanding is derived on the basis of "the one-sided accentuation" of certain points of view or elements of reality and designed for specific explanatory purposes.[2] The reasons for viewing individualism as providing an important cultural grounding for the emergence of liberal rights have been given in the introductory chapter. It may bear repeating them briefly here.

First, the rise of modern individualism historically antedates liberalism. As historians tell us, it is with the arrival of the Reformation, or perhaps even earlier with the Renaissance, that the individual began to experience emancipation from medieval corporatism, from its control over virtually every aspect of the individual's life, particularly religious and political life.[3] Second, from an analytic standpoint, liberalism presupposes and is predicated on a particular conception of the individual. It is a philosophy of the individual just as democracy is a philosophy of the common man. Third, individualism is much broader in scope than liberalism at least at its initial stage. While the former may be described as an all-embracing way of living, acting, and thinking which sweeps and penetrates virtually all facets of modern life, the latter is primarily a moral and political doctrine concerned with the relationship between the individual and the political order.

It is largely on the basis of these reasons that one may be justified in hypothesizing that individualism provides broad cultural bedding for the liberal notion of rights. An additional caveat is in order. By taking the individualistic way of relating as a crucial cultural grounding for liberal rights, I do not mean to exclude or disregard the role that other factors, particularly economic factors, played in shaping liberalism. As Marx reminded us, the rise of industrial capitalism has in a fundamental sense changed the way in which the individual was perceived in relation to his or her self-identity, labor, and community as a whole.[4] From a historical point of view, as Tocqueville recounted, economic activities have contributed enormously to the ascendancy of liberal values and practices such as self-sufficiency and self-ownership, particularly in the United States.[5]

With these comments in mind, we are in a position to explore the individualistic cultural grounding of liberal rights. There are three sections in this chapter. The first section is an attempt to determine the meaning of individualism, while the second section seeks to uncover its roots. The third section will be presented as a description of the extent to which individualistic values and practices emerged and became entrenched in the West. For this purpose, early modern England and the United States will be chosen for illustration. While the former may be seen as providing an example of an emerging individualistic culture, the latter is, in the eyes of many, the embodiment of individualism *par excellence*.

THE MEANING OF INDIVIDUALISM

In a famous study, Max Weber observed that "[t]he expression individualism includes the most heterogeneous things imaginable" and that historians use this concept in an *ad hoc* fashion "as a label for any epoch of history they please."[6] This remark was made well over half a century ago, but it still rings true today. Even a cursory look at the way this concept is being used in the social sciences appears to confirm that it indeed becomes a catch-all label for characterizing whatever it is that deals, often favorably, with the nature and value of the individual. An approach, argument, or inclination is described as individualistic because it concentrates on individual values, beliefs and wants. One often feels puzzled at phrases such as individualistic political theory, individualistic morality, and individualistic psychology. In anthropology, a form of understanding which was pioneered by Malinowski and which stresses the study of the individual's drives and needs in a culture is said to be individualistic in nature. But Malinowski is equally concerned, if not more so, with cultural integration or patterns.[7] In sociology, Durkheim is widely credited for having dismantled the myths of individualism and engendered a new way of thinking about society and social phenomena. As some argue, however, an individualistic reading of him is not only possible but beneficial.[8] In the study of political theory, liberal political theory is often criticized for its individualistic bias, for prioritizing the individual's self-interests over the well-being of community. But this claim requires qualification. For one thing, not all liberal theories fit the description. For example, communitarian or perfectionist liberals, while emphasizing the importance of individual values and interests, are opposed to the idea of individualism insofar as it fosters atomism. Moreover, it is not clear what kinds of individualism liberal theory is said to endorse. Endorsing moral individualism does not necessarily involve endorsing economic individualism; sharing the view of a Rawls or a Raz does not entail sharing the view of a Hayek or a Nozick; and recognizing individual rights does not have to lead to a rejection of group or minority rights.[9]

This suggests that individualism is complex in meaning and a simplistic and undifferentiated use of this term can be misleading. To avoid confusion and ambiguity, some writers distinguish types of individualism by adding adjectives to it, and by narrowing down its meaning by drawing attention to a particular subject area or discipline. Thus Lukes classifies individualism in terms of religion, ethics, politics, economics, and methodology, and Shanahan in terms of political thought, epistemology, and art and literature.[10] No doubt, this kind of differentiation can be helpful for some purposes, but it comes at a price. Arranging individualism into separate categories creates a situation in which intellectual discourse becomes highly cumbersome because concepts are multiplied and unmanageable. More importantly, it gives the impression that the new categories are logically distinct and denote independent meanings with little or no need for cross reference or reciprocity to determine what they signify. Further, even if such categorization is valuable, we are still no closer than when we started toward an understanding of individualism as a generic concept. We may be in a better position to assess religious individualism, for example, as a shift of moral and spiritual responsibility from the church to the individual believer, but we are not sure that this understanding can be extended to moral or political individualism.

This lack of clarity may be dealt with by placing the concept of individualism in historical perspective. A historical account is useful in two ways. First, it can provide an understanding of the variety of connotations associated with this idea; for example, it can help us understand how the concept of individualism has developed from a largely parochial concept— parochial in the sense that it had both a limited purpose and scope—to a universal idea (or ideal) with broader implications. Second, it can provide a frame of reference for determining which connotation or cluster of connotations is most relevant to this study.

Although its sources stretch far back in time to classical antiquity, the term individualism appears to be essentially a nineteenth-century semantic phenomenon.[11] Hobbes and Locke may be called "possessive individualists," but they themselves did not make use of this term in any self-conscious way as did, say, Tocqueville and Hobhouse. Swart explains that in its nineteenth-century usage, individualism used to designate at least three clusters of meaning. First, it conveys a sense of egalitarianism as manifested in the rights of man. This sense is closely linked to political liberalism and has its roots in the French Revolution. Second, it suggests the economically self-made man under the auspices of the utilitarian doctrine of free market and laissez faire. Third, it was seen as a romantic sentiment which glorifies a cult of individuality and exalts such individual qualities as creativity and self-reliance.[12] Notably, what Swart portrays for us is largely a positive picture of individualism, one which we would better appreciate from a liberal point of view. However, a different set of meanings would likely emerge if one shifts away from the liberal position to a conservative or socialist one. Only then would one realize that the term "individualism" is not only imbued with basically negative values, but also viewed as the most corrupting force in society.

In both the conservative and the socialist view, individualism is synonymous with social atomism, political anarchism, and economic egoism. Closely following the steps of Edmund Burke, Tocqueville saw individualism as one of the most powerful forces likely to breed social isolation and threaten the fabric of modern life. It draws the individual away from public life into "a little circle of his own," fosters a sense of loneliness, and encourages dependence and conformism in judgment. Comparing selfishness with individualism, Tocqueville noted that the former is "a passionate and exaggerated love of self" and "originates in blind instinct," whereas the latter is "a mature and calm feeling," "proceeds from erroneous judgment" and "disposes each member of the community to sever himself from the mass of his fellows." He concluded:

> Selfishness blights the germ of all virtue; individualism, at first, only saps the virtues of public life; but in the long run it attacks and destroys all others and is at length absorbed in downright selfishness.[13]

And this view is echoed in the socialist critique of individualism. As Lukes points out, the socialist typically contrasts individualism with such values as harmony, cooperation, and community. While socialism is identified with these values and with an ideal social and political order, individualism embodies the economic doctrine of laissez faire and along with it rapacious capitalism and social disintegration. "The principle of individualism," Louis Blanc remarked, "is that which, taking man out of society, makes him sole judge of what surrounds him and of himself, gives him a heightened sense of his rights without showing him his duties, abandons him to his own powers, and, for the whole of government, proclaims *laissez-faire.*"[14]

The criticisms advanced by the conservative and the socialist formed the main backdrop of the voices against individualism in the nineteenth century. But, interestingly, many liberals who are deemed champions of the individual's cause also have reservations about this notion. J. S. Mill, for one, entertained distrust, to say the least, for individualism as the principle on which human life is to be founded. While defending individuality as a main ingredient of social progress, he also believed that such a principle, according to which each is for himself and against all the rest, is antithetical to the idea of social progress. It is the notion of the advancement of society as a whole, not only the propertied class, but also the poor, the dispossessed and the underrepresented, that led some liberals to attempt to design a new brand of individualism in a way that is sensitive to the socialist argument. Agreeing with Mill on the basic principle of individual liberty, Hobhouse set before him the task of renovating classical individualism which he believed to be closely associated with laissez faire theory. The result is individualism with socialist characteristics. The core of "socialist individualism," as Hobhouse viewed it, rests on the idea of self-development and along with it an organic conception of the relationship between individual and society. It not only emphasizes the compatibility between legitimate social control and the individual's personal liberty, but sees such control as prerequisite to "the harmonious growth" of all members of community as a whole. "The foundation of liberty," Hobhouse claimed, "is the idea of growth." To the extent that it is consistent with this end, liberty "becomes not so much a right of the individual as a necessity of society. It rests not on the claim of A to be let alone by B, but on the duty of B to treat A as a rational being."[15]

Hobhouse's idea of self-development, which drew considerably upon modern liberal thinkers such as Mill and T. H. Green, should not be seen as a parochial reaction to the negative conceptions of individualism prevalent in the nineteenth-century intellectual climate. Rather, it suggests a deeper and broader concern with the individual as the center of moral, political, and economic life, a concern which had been growing since the Reformation. It synthesizes two seemingly incompatible philosophical positions, namely the classical liberal doctrine of individual liberty and the socialist principle of collective welfare, into a coherent whole, providing a far more persuasive grounding for liberalism than previously construed. Insofar as it presupposes all the key elements which go into the defining of individualism, and insofar as it foreshadows much of the debate about this notion in the century to come, it may be regarded as the consummation of an evolving idea in modern liberal thought.

The debate which was carried on between liberals and conservatives/socialists through much of the last century has shaped our understanding of individualism both in scope and in substance. Whether the issue is moral individualism, economic individualism, or democratic individualism, we are indebted to those who thought and wrote about individualism a hundred years earlier. They not only coined the term but also made self-conscious efforts to elucidate and shape its meaning. As a result of their efforts and, from a larger perspective, as a result of the gradual ascendancy of liberalism as both a political and an economic doctrine, the concept of individualism has been transformed into a broad and predominantly positive principle. As a positive principle, it is constituted by three basic ideas, namely autonomy, equality, and self-development.[16] As a quick glance at contemporary political discourse reveals, it is these ideas that largely determine the way in which both critics and defenders of individualism make use of the concept.[17]

This sketchy account should not lead one to conclude that individualism is largely a political idea originated in the nineteenth century. As mentioned earlier, the term may have been coined in the nineteenth century, but its intellectual roots go much further back in time. The emergence of a concept is not an overnight event; it takes a long period of gestation. In *Toward a Genealogy of Individualism,* Shanahan argues that the idea of individualism can be traced all the way back to the ancient world. Taking a psychological approach to the question of the self which he believes individualism presupposes, he is able to show that in the process of representing the physical world as dominated by images of gods (in Greek mythology) or God (in Hebrew religion), the ancients developed a way of self-referring which laid the foundation for what was to emerge as the self-conscious mind of the subject individual.[18] Early Christianity modified this primitive self in ways, Shanahan says, that led to the emergence of a transcendent self. The new self is marked by its inborn capacity for moral self-sufficiency, for distinguishing between good and evil, and ultimately for choosing God. If it can be said that the Greek period "represents the virtual emergence of the human self-concept," the Christian era "represents the evolution of the self-concept into a vessel of moral and spiritual . . . self-creation."[19]

Dumont makes a similar point when he traces the genesis of modern individualism to the early Christian tradition. Using a conceptual category called the outworldly individual, he is able to describe how the individual "as a value, as a creation *ex nihilo*" emerges in Western culture. The early Christian individual, Dumont suggests, sees himself or herself as one who exists only in relation to God; as such, he or she may be deemed the outworldly individual analogous to a hermit or a world renouncer in ancient India. This conception ended with the Reformation when the individual began to live *in* the world. With the Calvinist view of God as Will who predetermines the elect and the condemned, the individual, instead of "taking refuge from this imperfect world" in a spiritual one, must now "work for God's glory in the world, and faithfulness to this task will be the mark and the only proof of election."[20]

A second point is that individualism is not exclusively a political phenomenon. While examining it in the political context is warranted for certain purposes, it should not be forgotten that the concept of individualism has a broader and richer meaning. For example, Waldo Emerson and Henry Thoreau developed individualistic ideas and beliefs which may be better described under the rubric of transcendental individualism. While sharing certain basic epistemological assumptions with political individualism, transcendental individualism is distinguished by its conception of the individual as a unique gift of nature and by its emphasis on the individual's ability to transcend his or her physical existence through an internalization of nature. This is of course not to deny that the three basic ideas discussed above are essential to our understanding of the notion. What needs to be stressed is that a broad perspective is needed if individualism is to be understood as providing a broad *cultural* basis for the emergence of liberal rights.

This broad perspective can be obtained by treating individualism as a widespread cultural phenomenon, and by taking different forms of individualism as expressions of an individualistic way of relating in different spheres of social life. It seems clear from the studies of Swart, Lukes, Dumont and Shanahan, moreover, that although various types of individualism each have their own cluster of meanings that may or may not overlap, they share with one another certain key ideas, beliefs and assumptions. This kind of sharing provides the basis for understanding individualism as a generic concept.

That individualism is a broad cultural phenomenon has been widely recognized. Thus, in studying the individualistic motif behind the literary genre of the novel, Watt says that "from the Renaissance onwards, there was a growing tendency for individual experience to replace collective tradition as the ultimate arbiter of reality; and this transition would seem to constitute an important part of the general cultural background of the rise of the novel."[21] Writing from a comparative anthropological standpoint, Dumont also recognizes individualism as a modern configuration of value peculiar to Western culture.[22] However, disagreements abound as to what values, beliefs, or assumptions should be construed as definitive of the notion of individualism. Watt's definition is not untypical. He describes it as a "vast complex of interdependent factors" and adds that it "posits a whole society mainly governed by the idea of every individual's intrinsic independence both from other individuals and from that multifarious allegiance to past modes of thought and action denoted by the word 'tradition.' . . ."[23] In the strict sense, this is not so much a definition as an exposition of individualism. It is pregnant with ideas: the individual *vis-à-vis* society as a whole, intrinsic value, moral independence, the relationship between individuals, and cultural tradition, and these ideas extend rather than define the concept.

Having perhaps realized the complexity involved in the definition of individualism, Morris seeks to simplify the matter and focus on the psychological experience of human beings *qua* individuals. He characterizes individualism as "the sense of a clear distinction between my being and that of other people."[24] This psychological sense of distinctness between beings is useful to the extent that it speaks to an important dimension of modern individualism—-namely the self-consciousness of one's uniqueness. But it is too narrow a definition to warrant broad application.

More recently, Dumont suggests that we take individualism as a form of modern ideology. Modern ideology is individualistic in the sense that it valorizes the individual as "the independent, autonomous and thus (essentially) nonsocial *moral* being (original emphasis)."[25] No doubt, Dumont's definition has several advantages over Watt's and Morris'. The most noticeable of these is that Dumont's definition allows us to probe the configuration of ideas and values underlying modern individualism, especially in contrast to nonmodern ideas and values. But it also has at least one serious deficiency. By focusing exclusively on ideology, Dumont precludes from consideration many nonideological facets of individualism which are as much an important part of Western culture as their ideological counterpart.

Although disagreeing with Dumont that a distinctively political and institutional perspective is an adequate approach, Shanahan nevertheless opts for a definition of individualism not unlike that suggested by Dumont. Individualism, he says, is "that system of beliefs in which the individual is not only given direct status and value but becomes the final arbiter of truth."[26] What distinguishes him from Dumont is the way in which "that system of beliefs" is investigated. Shanahan wants to approach the concept of individualism from "the individual's perspective," emphasizing the individual's psychological self—an idea which is indebted to Morris' sense of distinctness. This approach also raises certain difficulties. To see individualistic culture purely from the standpoint of the individual's psychological self is subject to similar criticisms as against an individualistic conception of political culture. As a shared way of relating, individualism manifests itself as a superorganic and collective phenomenon; as such, it should not be defined solely in terms of individual perspectives or, for that matter, an aggregate of individual perspectives, although such perspectives may to a certain degree reflect individualistic culture.

A definition of individualism as a cultural phenomenon hinges on a definition of culture. The definitions suggested by Shanahan and others are unsatisfactory, because a clear understanding of the concept of culture is missing in them. In the second chapter of this study, a definition of culture was proposed and its superiority over alternative definitions defended. Culture is a shared way of relating among a group or groups of people. Following this conception of culture, we may define individualism more adequately as providing both a broad perspective and a delimited focus. Individualism thus signifies *a particular way of relating which gives preponderant weight in all spheres of life to the human individual vis-à-vis the social milieu*. It gives preponderant weight to the individual's mind or consciousness as the arbiter of truth; to his or her value as the basis of morality; and to his or her needs, interests, and purposes, however conceived, as the ultimate justification for social and political arrangements.

THE SOURCES OF MODERN INDIVIDUALISM

A common view among students of the Western cultural tradition is that individualism is a distinctly modern phenomenon. Most would agree that it gains prominence in the wake of the Reformation. This is certainly not to suggest that there is a clear-cut division between a given modern cultural form such as individualism and the entire two-thousand-year tradition preceding it. No such division is possible. As Dumont, Shanahan, and others remind us, the roots of individualistic culture are deep. Having acknowledged this, however, we should not be led to the other extreme view that there is absolutely nothing novel about modern individualism. To be sure, concerns about the individual, about his or her status, value, and interest, can be said to have existed in all societies and in all ages; Dumont's world renouncer is a good example. But only in the modern era is the individual given such enormous weight. Here a word of testimony from one of the most renowned medievalists offers us a chance to see what the modern individual is by way of contrast with what he or she was.

In the high Middle Ages, Ullmann argues, society was viewed as one organic and indivisible whole. In this whole, the individual played an "infinitesimally small" part. In one's religious capacity, one was a member of the Church participating in *Corpus Christi;* and in one's political capacity, one was a subject belonging to the corporate body politic. The individual had no rights and no equality of standing in the public sphere, but rather "was placed *under* the tutelage of those who had been selected by divinity." Whatever value one had *qua* individual was all too easily "sacrificed at the altar of the public good." This was shown by collective punishments such as the interdict of a locality or the amercements of towns and villages and by confiscation of the personal property not only of those who were accused of heresy but of their unborn offsprings. It was not the individual, but the well-being of community as a whole that mattered. Individuals, Ullmann concludes, were absorbed by society and individuality was absent.[27]

As a general observation, Ullmann's words are valid. One can also say the same about the claim that the Reformation was the key event which precipitated the rise of modern individualism. Some historians, however, disagree. Taking issue with Weber and others who see the Reformation as the driving force behind economic and social individualism, Macfarlane argues that at least in the case of England, individualistic impulses were strongly felt long before the arrival of Protestantism and can be traced far back in time to the Middle Ages or even earlier. "In fact," he writes,

> within the recorded period covered by our documents, it is not possible to find a time when an Englishman did not stand alone. Symbolized and shaped by his ego-centred kinship system, he stood in the centre of his world. This means that it is no longer possible to 'explain' the origins of English individualism in terms of either Protestantism, . . . or the other factors suggested by [Marx, Weber, and Tawney]. Individualism, however defined, predates sixteenth-century changes and can be said to shape them all.[28]

Macfarlane's thesis is both challenging and important. Resolving these difficult theoretical issues is beyond the capability and the purpose of this study. Suffice it here to make two general comments with respect to Macfarlane's findings. First, Macfarlane's thesis about the uniqueness of English individualism, valid as it may be, does not necessarily prove that Weber and others are completely wrong; it only limits the applicability of their theory. Second, the materials Macfarlane presents as evidence are highly selective; they are not only restricted to a certain social stratum, but also are narrow in subject matter: the overwhelming majority of records concern only land dealings. To conclude on the basis of these that English individualism is both unique and old is problematic. His thesis is inconclusive at best since he fails to take account of how and the extent to which individuals related to one another and to society at large when the Church had such a powerful impact on the conduct of the average subject. In property management, lower-class Englishmen may have enjoyed relatively more freedom than their counterpart on the Continent, but such freedom at best illustrates one possible source upon which modern individualism has drawn. It is hardly a clear indication of an influential cultural trend in full swing. Historically, this trend emerged and gained momentum only in the wake of two epoch-making events, namely the Reformation and the advent of Cartesianism. These laid the foundation for the emergence of modern individualism and produced individualist thinkers such as Hobbes, Locke, Kant, Jefferson, and Mill.

It needs to be reemphasized that modern individualism is a product of multiple forces. These include not only philosophical and religious forces, but also changes in economics, technology, politics, and demographics, as the historian Christopher Hill has aptly described in his historical study of early modern England.[29] An account of these changes, particularly the impact of capitalism on modern individualism, is undoubtedly important, but for reasons not difficult to understand, this study will focus on the two major intellectual forces.

Descartes

Descartes is often hailed, and deservedly so, as the founder of modern philosophy. His presence can be felt, directly or indirectly, in virtually all aspects of modern intellectual life, particularly in epistemology. In tracing the Cartesian lineages in various disciplines, David Weissman makes the following assessment. "Many notions that shape our thinking," he says, "originated in or passed through Rene Descartes. We are forever saying that he is the step beyond late medieval times into the modern era; but this estimate minimizes the range and impact of his views."[30] Such a view is echoed in the evaluation of Descartes' influence on political thought. Though he "did not write a politics," William Bluhm remarks, Descartes' thought "encapsulated in his cogito contains the seed from which the lineage of individualist liberal political theory has sprung . . ."[31] Perhaps even this is too modest an appraisal. According to Charles Taylor, Cartesianism has in the most fundamental sense determined the entire way in which we have come to think about ourselves *qua* individuals and relate to the world around us today.[32]

What is it exactly that makes Descartes a formidable thinker and his thought a cornerstone of modern individualism? Descartes begins by taking upon himself what appears to be a rather innocuous task: he wants some reliable rules for the attainment of knowledge. But this deceptively simple proposal, as we shall see, has subversive consequences. What triggered his search for reliable rules or methods of knowledge, according to his account, is the sheer diversity of opinions on issues ranging from philosophy to mere fashion and the concomitant lack of ways of ascertaining their truth. Dissatisfied with the speculative nature of knowledge claims taught in the "Schools," he finds in mathematics a model of "certain and simple rules," rules which enable him to say with absolute certainty that A is demonstrably true while B is not.

The two rules Descartes provides as "the most certain routes to knowledge" are intuition and deduction. In his understanding, intuitive knowledge is neither "the fluctuating testimony of the senses" nor "the blundering constructions of imagination;" rather it is "the undoubting conception of an unclouded and attentive mind, and springs from the light of reason alone." Deductive knowledge, by contrast, consists in a process of inferring necessary truths "from true and known principles by the continuous and uninterrupted action of a mind."[33] While either can itself lead to valid knowledge claims, it is often the combination of the two methods that provides the kind of certainty with which we are able to distinguish truth from falsehood, particularly in cases in which complex ideas are involved. The mental operation Descartes offers is a chain of reasoning which starts from the most simple to the most complex. He claims that "there are but few pure and simple essences;" these essences are known to us either through our experiences or through the light of reason which God planted in us. They are "primary and existing *per se*" and independent of any other facts. The secret of his method, he tells us, consists in, first, assembling these simple, self-evident and absolutely certain truths, then proceeding step by step "to inquire whether any others can be deduced from these, and again any others from these conclusions and so on, in order."[34]

In his first published work *Discourse on the Method,* Descartes summarizes his argument for "the true method" in terms of four criteria. First, he is "to avoid precipitation and prejudice in judgments" and "to accept nothing as true" which he does not clearly and distinctly recognize to be so, that is, which there is no reason for him to doubt. Second, he would tackle any given difficult problem by dividing it into as many parts as possible and as required by clarity and distinctness. Third, investigation is to be conducted in a sequential order in which he would proceed from the simplest to the most complex objects. Fourth, efforts must be taken to ensure as thorough and comprehensive an examination as possible, so that nothing has been omitted.[35] These criteria, in Descartes' view, constitute the right direction for the mind to follow in pursuit of knowledge. He maintains that what he has done in devising this new method is no more than an act of "exercising my reason in all things." Reason being a gift granted to us equally by God and "the only thing that constitutes us men and distinguishes us from the brutes," it would be ungodly to content ourselves with merely accepting others' opinions without using this faculty for obtaining the knowledge of the truth. Though "it was most expedient to bring my conduct into harmony with the ideas of those with whom I should have to live," he says, "we should never allow ourselves to be persuaded excepting by the evidence of our Reason."[36]

Armed with reason and the four criteria it has generated, Descartes goes on to examine and define what was to become the central issue for metaphysics and epistemology in the centuries that followed. The devising of a rational method has for him a definite purpose: to apply it strictly and without exception to all knowledge claims, including even our idea of God. It is precisely through this application that the full significance of Cartesian epistemology is revealed. In Descartes' view, anything that aspires to the status of true knowledge must go through the microscopic scrutiny of reason and meet the test of clarity and distinctness. To accomplish this, as we may recall from the first of the four criteria, one starts out with the celebrated principle of doubt. It is worth noting here that this principle is not intended to apply to "the conduct of our life," because our actions are subject to certain restraints such as time limits and "we are frequently obliged to follow opinions which are merely probable." Rather, it is doubt in the metaphysical sense, "only when we are engaged in contemplating the truth."[37] The utility of such a general and fundamental doubt "about all things," in Descartes' view, is that it "delivers us from every kind of prejudice, and sets out for us a very simple way by which the mind may detach from the senses; and finally it makes it impossible for us ever to doubt those things which we have once discovered to be true."[38]

The Cartesian doubt is not a doubt in the ordinary sense of being merely suspicious. It is a denial that anything has ever existed, and a negation that reduces the entire creation to nothingness. It is a process of purging ourselves of inherited ideas and beliefs, which promises total freedom for the intellect. What it aims to create is a metaphysical state of nature, an

Archimedean point of absolute certainty on which knowledge can stand. In a soliloquy-like style, Descartes offers us the following scenario:

> I suppose, then, that all the things that I see are false; I persuade myself that nothing has ever existed of all that my fallacious memory represents to me. I consider that I possess no senses; I imagine that body, figure, extension, movement and place are but the fictions of my mind.[39]

Not only so. He also supposes that God is not "the fountain of truth" but "some evil genius" bent on deceiving him; and that this genius deludes him into believing that what he sees, hears, touches, and smells are true, while in fact they are nothing but illusions and dreams.

What eventually emerges from this radical skepticism is indeed impossible to doubt, just as Descartes has indicated. It is the indubitable fact that for all the things he doubts and dismisses as the fictions of his mind, the doubter cannot deny his own being. The moment he doubts the existence of each and every thing including that of his own, he immediately affirms that he exists. Paradoxical as it may be, the very act of doubting and self-doubting is precisely a self-affirming process. In order to doubt, the doubter must necessarily exist even if he assumes that nothing else has ever existed. And, further, even if he supposes that God were indeed such an evil genius, deceiving him on such a grand scale and making him believe what he senses was in fact true, there must not be any doubt about the fact that he exists. For the very act of deceiving presupposes the deceived. To be deceived is to exist. Descartes writes:

> But there is some deceiver or other, very powerful and very cunning, who ever employs his ingenuity in deceiving me. Then without doubt I exist also if he deceives me, and let him deceive me as much as he will, he can never cause me to be nothing so long as I think that I am something. So that after having reflected well and carefully examined all things, we must come to the definite conclusion that this proposition: I am, I exist, is necessarily true each time that I pronounce it, or that I mentally conceive it.[40]

For Descartes, knowledge of one's own existence is the very first knowledge that one obtains with absolute certainty. But this knowledge does not depend on one's identity as a physical body, because the existence of such a body is also doubted. Perhaps the most compelling reason for not relying on it as the ultimate basis for saying that I exist is the self-sufficiency of the doubting "I" in sustaining first knowledge. There is simply no need for knowing that my body exists—and such knowledge is difficult to have anyway, in Descartes' view, without a conscious self—before I can prove my own existence. Doubt alone can provide that fundamental knowledge, and does so in an indubitably clear and distinct way. The doubting "I" is independent of and separable from my physical body which, as Descartes tells us, has a totally different nature and is governed by mechanistic laws of motion and extension. So long as I doubt, I exist. But who am I? A thing that thinks. To doubt is for Descartes to think, and to think is necessarily to be. The doubting self is nothing else but a thing that thinks. It is a thinking substance, that is, a mind. Hence the most celebrated Cartesian aphorism: *Cogito ergo sum;* I think, therefore I am.

The Cartesian mind is the first and most certain of all knowledge that one is able to secure by mere self-reflection. It exists as a self-contained, self-perpetuated, and self-sufficient whole, with its own contents or objects and generating certainty for itself. "I find here," Descartes says, "that thought is an attribute that belongs to me; it alone cannot be separated from me. I am, I exist, that is certain."[41] The immediacy and transparency with which the mind sees itself makes it possible for the Cartesian to move in an unmediated way from consciousness to existence. The mind is separable and separated from the body and, for that matter, from all material reality; in fact it acquires an independent reality of its own. This is certainly not to deny that Descartes holds that the mind and the body interact with each other, the crossover point being the pineal gland, and form a whole in what we perceive to be a thinking (or toothaching) human being. None the less they are distinctly separate substances, sharing no common ground. The point is rather that in the beginning, there is the mind, individuated and autonomous. It is from there that one can proceed to contemplate other things such as our idea of God.

It must be pointed out that this account of the Cartesian mind is incomplete. It ignores the ambiguities and problems that have occupied scholarly attention for many years. The problem of the "Cartesian circle" is a good example. Descartes holds that the mind knows itself before it knows anything else, including the idea of God, but he also thinks that the mind's self-knowledge rests on the metaphysical claim that God is not deceiving us, but rather is the guarantor of clear and distinct ideas, including that of the self. It has been suggested that we can break the circle by distinguishing existence from essence, knowledge from being.[42] Peter Markie argues that Descartes' claim to certainty about one's own existence is not without ambiguity. The path from thought to existence is not an intuitive and self-evident truth as Descartes says it is, but involves a syllogistic inference which he repeatedly denies.[43]

Notwithstanding its ambiguities and problems, however, Cartesianism has exerted a profound impact on the modern conception of individual identity. It would not be much of an exaggeration to say, when we bear in mind those who helped shape the intellectual and cultural landscape of the modern West, that Cartesianism has permanently changed the way we think about ourselves and relate to one another as individuals. The kind of philosophical individualism ushered in by the *cogito* assigns the individual mind a privileged and first-order place in the entire universe, and this in turn, by implication, makes the idea of God seem precarious and arbitrary. It also infuses the individual with a sense of self-sufficiency, autonomy, and uniqueness. Reviewing the sources of modern thought, whether it is the Humean concern with sense perception or the Kantian concern with moral self-legislation, one cannot but notice that it is individual self-perception and self-determination that constitute the defining features of individual identity. In discussing how individual self-consciousness provides a crucial underpinning for the emergence of the novel, Watt observes that with Cartesianism, "the pursuit of truth is conceived of as a wholly individual matter, logically independent of the tradition of past thought, and indeed as more likely to be arrived at by a departure from it."[44] When each individual is regarded as an independent center of consciousness and each mind an arbiter of the truth, the groundwork is laid for a society composed of distinct individual minds, each deciding separately on its own what is right and true. If there is sociality at all, as Weissman points out, it exists, as in the Kantian case, merely as a formality, "one mediated by each thinker's determination to do nothing that every other thinker could not also do."[45]

In a critique of Cartesian epistemology, Taylor makes perhaps one of the most insightful comments about Descartes' influence on the formation of individualism in modern social and political thought. Clearly, his view is not meant to be an exhaustive analysis of the Cartesian self; neither is it free from objections.[46] But it offers a well articulated perspective from which to consider the close relationship between Cartesianism and individualism. The Cartesian self, Taylor argues, is characterized essentially by three distinct features:

> The first is the picture of the subject as ideally disengaged . . . as free and rational to the extent that he has fully distinguished himself from the natural and social worlds, so that his identity is no longer to be defined in terms of what lies outside him in these worlds. The second . . . is a punctual view of the self, ideally ready as free and rational to treat these worlds—and even some of the features of his own character—instrumentally, as subject to change and reorganizing in order the better to secure

the welfare of himself and others. The third is the social consequence of the first two: an atomistic construal of society as constituted by, or ultimately to be explained in terms of, individual purposes.[47]

Calvin

Nearly a century before Descartes wrote his first work *Rules for the Direction of the Mind,* the Reformation had begun. The advent of Cartesianism was at least in part indebted to the religious movement in the sense that the Reformation had broken the all-pervasive spiritual and institutional control of the Church and set free the creative energy of the individual mind.[48] The fact that Descartes could contemplate and publish largely free from harassment in an intellectual atmosphere to which Dutch Reformed Protestants contributed considerably is confirmation of this indebtedness.[49] This is of course not to suggest that the Reformation did little more than create a situation of volatility and uncertainty in which radical ideas such as the Cartesian self could ferment and emerge. It is itself a vital cultural event which resulted in a radical change in thought and conduct more penetrating and more broad-reaching than Cartesianism of itself could ever have dreamed of producing. The Reformation not only precedes Cartesianism in time but also had a wider and more popular appeal than the latter.

The Reformation is often associated with two individuals. The reason for highlighting Calvin instead of Luther is based largely on consideration of brevity, and both will in any case be discussed in the pages that follow. Though it has been long held that Calvin surpasses Luther in important respects, the centrality of the latter to the Reformation cannot be overestimated. In fact, some hold that Luther is unparalleled as a religious reformer as Descartes is as an epistemological reformer.[50] This is not only because Luther single-handedly initiated the protest, but also because his theology provided the hotbed on which Calvinism was to develop.

Luther's role in shaping modern individualism lies in the fact that he engendered a process in which the individual believer was increasingly able to turn inward in search of the source and ground of Christianity. From this standpoint, it can be said that Luther helped create a religious self in the way Descartes did a metaphysical self. But Luther's revolt against the Catholic establishment was not aimed at creating a brand-new religion; rather it was a revolt from within. In other words, it was an attempt to reform and revitalize an existing body of religious doctrine which had become, in his view, corrupt. Thus, it seems appropriate to briefly review what this existing body of religious doctrine was and what Luther revolted against.

In one of the most illuminating studies of the Christian Church, Ernst Troeltsch argues that by the time Luther began writing his rebellious tracts and sermons, medieval Christianity had evolved to a point where the idea of Christian society came to be embodied in Catholicism. Catholicism embraced a particular conception of the Church and with it a particular conception of God, man, and the world. The Catholic views the Church as a universal institution, hierarchically structured or graded in terms of holiness and possessing "a *depositum* of absolute truths" and "the sacramental miraculous power of grace and redemption."[51] In harmony with this view is the idea of God as the absolute divine being, remote, infinite, and mysterious; as such, He is accessible, if at all, only through the mediation of a hierarchical and sacramental institution, that is, the Church. The indirectness and artificiality with which God's grace is imparted made the individual believer depend on that institution. As members of the Church, individuals meet with grace in varying degrees on the basis of their good works, merits, and positions in the hierarchy. The secular world with its institutions and values was conceived of as a natural stage in the divine creation which has as its ultimate end an ideal, perfect, and supernatural state of being; it is the stage of the fallen man as signified by the idea of sin, and only the miraculous power of grace can purify secular institutions and values and use them as the basis for building a higher structure of authority and perfection.

It is well known that the Catholic emphasis on the Church as the intermediary between God and man, between grace and sin, led to many abuses. It is in large measure for rectifying these abuses that Luther was embarked on a crusade against the Catholic establishment. But rectification is not merely a practical matter to be accomplished by eliminating certain institutional practices; it is more importantly a theological one, affecting the core assumptions of the Church, particularly the idea of institutional mediation in the individual's pursuit of grace and redemption. Luther's rejection of Catholicism may be characterized by a radically different understanding of the idea of grace, one which is Pauline and Augustinian in nature. For this reason, Luther's ideas and Protestantism in general are often regarded as the restoration of the Pauline and Augustinian doctrine of grace. But, as Troeltsch points out, Lutheranism is not a mere "reemphasis;" rather, it infuses the idea of grace with a new meaning. According to the new conception,

> grace is no longer a mystical miraculous substance, to be imparted through the sacraments, but a Divine temper of faith, conviction, spirit, knowledge, and trust which is to be appropriated; in the Gospel and in the Love and Spirit of Christ towards mankind it can be discerned as the loving will of God which brings with it the forgiveness of sins.[52]

Troeltsch argues that this gives rise to an altogether different understanding of religion as a whole. It reduces religion to an object of faith alone, faith in a God who is embodied in Christ and perceived as a loving and gracious Will. It encourages a direct and inward communion with God free from the mediation of a hierarchy, of sacraments and indulgences. It "leads to the doctrine of the priesthood of all believers . . . to the renewal of the primitive Christian independence and autonomy of the knowledge of God affected by 'the Spirits.'"[53] If there is mediation at all, it is that of the Word or Scriptures, and through the ministry and preaching of the Word, the message of Christ, man lays the foundation for salvation.

Perhaps a more important implication of Luther's view is what Troeltsch calls the emergence of "a pure spiritual ethic." If the essence of a Christian life consists in nothing but "a right attitude of faith and trust towards God in the Word," the burden of responsibility then shifts from the Church to the individual's conscience. As a result of this shift, the mediating institution with its ecclesiastic law and authority collapses, and good works and merits are no longer important, because the only thing that matters is the individual's self-proclaimed faith or, in Troeltsch words, "a spirit of whole-hearted conviction."[54] This spirit as expressed succinctly in the idea of "justification by faith alone" is truly a liberating one; it signifies what Maritain, one of the most prominent Catholic scholars of his century, calls "the transference to the human individual and his subjective state of that absolute assurance in the divine promise which was formerly the privilege of the Church."[55] In this sense, as Maritain argues in a critical spirit of his own, Luther pioneered the spiritual principle of modern individualism with his emphasis on individual withdrawal into a subjective state and on grace as a matter of "the simple exterior favor of God."

It is in Luther's theology of grace that his conceptions of God, man, and the world finds a solid grounding. While to elaborate on them goes beyond our purpose here, it is necessary to point out that basically they are the antithesis of Catholicism. This is not to deny that despite its position on religious freedom, Lutheranism holds in common with the Catholic doctrine a number of important assumptions. The commonality between them is clearly shown, for example, by Luther's stress on the universality of the Church, though its meaning is not based on the hierarchical and sacramental impartation of grace but on the Word and on the inward and personal experience of the individual believer. It is this commonality that gives Luther's ideas such broad influence; without it, as Troeltsch says, "Luther would have been merely the founder of a new sect."[56] Perhaps also because of this commonality, Luther's reform took on a partial character, leaving many questions unanswered. Especially troubling is the question of where the protest leads to in terms of organization and discipline. What Luther did in this regard was simply to profess personal faith with the assurance of blessedness flowing from the forgiveness of sins, while leaving problems of organization to the local congregations and ultimately to the power of the secular state.[57] It is not until the rise of Calvinism that the task of creating a new organized religion in replacement of the Catholic establishment was to be fulfilled.

If we follow Maritain's assessment that Luther "makes the science of divine things revolve around human corruption," we are likely to find in Calvin a complete shift of the center from the blessedness of man to the glory of God. This shift signifies one of the most important contrasts between the two reformers. To be sure, Calvinism builds upon Lutheranism. As Troeltsch tells us once again, the core of the Calvinist teachings is "of Lutheran origin," and Luther's fundamental doctrines of justification and sanctification are adopted without qualification by Calvin. Calvin not only regarded Luther as a great reformer of the Christian Church, but also "laid great stress upon his agreement with Luther and upon his personal relations with him."[58] But this close affinity between them should not obscure the fact that they have remarkable dissimilarities, and some of them boil down not merely to differences in emphasis, but to fundamentally different conceptions of God and the Christian life.

It has been customary to view the idea of predestination as one of the most notable features of Calvinism. This is certainly correct. But few seem to understand that it is logically traceable to the central point of the Lutheran and even earlier the Pauline doctrine of grace. What distinguishes Calvin from his master is not the idea of predestination *per se,* but the idea of God lurking behind it. Calvin's conception of grace does not rest, as does Luther's, on a humanly and personally construed faith; no such human element is allowed in Calvin. Rather, faith is given by God "out of His freewill and choice" and as "an absolute miracle." So are salvation and damnation in which the individual has no part to play whatsoever. "In entire and arbitrary freedom," Troeltsch says, God "lays down the law for Himself; and this law is the law of His own glory which is served both by the gratitude of the undeserved bliss of the elect and by the misery of the merited despair of the damned." Thus, the elect are "a symbol of His mercy" and the damned "a symbol of His wrath."[59] For Calvin, God manifests Himself as absolute and majestic will, a will which is exclusively concerned with itself. Luther also conceives God as will, but that will is a loving and gracious one, responding to the fallen condition of man the same way a forgiving father treats his lost son. Their essential difference lies between "the self-centred personal salvation of the creature and the universality of the Divine Will of Love" on the one hand and "the Glory of God" and "the duality of His counsel of election and of reprobation" on the other.[60]

At first glance, as Dumont points out, the Calvinist conception of God as self-glorifying Will and its view of man's total impotence in face of salvation or damnation seems to be "a limitation rather than a development of individualism."[61] Troeltsch thinks that the individualism contained in Calvinism differs from that found in Lutheranism; it is a particular kind of individualism, one which is founded on not only "a crushing sense of sin" and "a pessimistic condemnation of the world," but "the certainty of election" and "the sense of responsibility and of the obligation to render personal service under the Lordship of Christ."[62] Dumont disagrees with Troeltsch, arguing that Calvinist individualism is not so much a special type as an intensification of the individualism inaugurated by Lutheranism. Such intensification, in Dumont's view, involves the individual's active participation in "contributing to the implementation of [God's] designs."[63] While the Lutheran individual awaits God's grace passively, rejoicing at the knowledge of being forgiven for his sin as represented in the sacrifice and sufferings of Christ, the Calvinist individual must positively "work for God's glory in the world" and take up the task of sanctifying the world as an expression of God's absolute and majestic will. This positive attitude toward work, toward worldly activities, as Weber and others have famously argued, would prove extremely productive in wealth accumulation and in economic development in general. It produced an individualism not only of pure faith but of active participation as well. This is what Dumont means by intensification.

But this way of understanding individualism also poses special problems for the logic of Calvinism, a point to which neither Dumont nor Troeltsch paid adequate attention. The basic question of why Calvin emphasized active participation in worldly activities and along with it a sense of self-discipline in action, given his idea of predestination and his radical renunciation of the world, is by and large enigmatic. Troeltsch attributes this peculiar aspect of Calvinism, explicitly or implicitly, to the Genevan's inborn temper for methodical and systematic reasoning, his capacity for organization and action, and his love of discipline and order. It is also closely connected to Calvin's fundamental purpose of building a Protestant Church or a holy community, a goal which Luther stimulated yet never intended to pursue in practice. Troeltsch relates that,

> [Calvin] finds it impossible to deny the world in theory and enjoy it in practice. This lack of system is contrary to his reflective and logical mind. He cannot leave the world alone in all its horror and comfort himself with the thought of a 'finished salvation.' That kind of Quietism is totally opposed to his impulse towards activity, and the idea of a 'finished salvation' is opposed to his orientation towards the aim of a salvation which is yet to be attained. . . . In view . . . of his Protestant estimate of the secular life, and of his ideal of a Holy community summed up in the form of a State Church, *he can only overcome the world by at the same time recognizing the value of its life* (emphasis added).[64]

This apparent paradox of renouncing the world by accepting it is one of the most intriguing features of Calvinism. Coupled with an instrumentalist conception of man as the means to God's ultimate purpose, it led to the unusual combination of "cool utilitarianism" with "an other-worldly aim" and of a strong drive for action with a total lack of interest in its results. Troeltsch recognizes this paradox. What it poses for Calvinism is the problem of motivation. If election or damnation is predetermined by the arbitrary and self-glorifying will of God, and if no matter what one does and how well one does it, one can only pray in the dark that one would be put on the list of the elect, why does one have to work actively at all? What is the real drive behind and ultimately justifying the Calvinist's active involvement with worldly activities? Calvin's successors such as Theordore Beza tried to solve the problem by emphasizing good works as outward signs of election. This is plausible enough. It does provide a coherent explanation of the connection between the idea of predestination and active participation in worldly activities. It is the line of argument which Weber advanced in explaining the link between Calvinist asceticism and capitalism.[65] But the question that needs to be answered is whether this constitutes what Dumont terms as intensified individualism.

To the extent that the idea of good works encourages the individual to pursue a course of life which would elevate him to the class of the elect, to the spiritual aristocracy, active participation does give an impression of intensified individualism. Troeltsch notes that from Beza onward, there were indeed periods of time in which individual believers, under the influence of the idea of good works, were driven to intense pursuit of independent achievement. But independent achievement seems to be more an expression than an intensification of the Lutheran individualism of a purely spiritual kind. It implies that personal faith and piety alone was not sufficient and one must now do something to deserve God's grace. There is, however, a somewhat different way to approach the intensification argument. It goes something like this. By conceiving God as absolute and majestic Will and man as a creature of utter insignificance and impotence, Calvin created a God who was remote, inscrutable, and wholly alienated from man. If the Catholic Church embraced a God who could only be perceived through sacraments and indulgences, and if Luther invented a God who could be felt and trusted through personal experience, Calvin envisioned a God who had nothing to do with man. Such alienation threw man into an abyss of lovelessness, insecurity and isolation. This is what Weber describes as a sense of "unprecedented inner loneliness."[66] With no automatic favor from God, and with the holy community still beyond reach and maybe never within reach, the experience of being an individual was truly solitary. This loneliness pushed further the inward-turning process started by Luther. It created a situation in which the burden of moral and spiritual judgment fell solely on the individual believer. Without recourse to anything else but one's own conscience and effort, salvation became a wholly individual matter both in belief and in action.

This is primarily the way in which Troeltsch, Weber, and others understood the motivating force behind the Calvinist's positive involvement in worldly affairs while caring little for its results. Considered from this standpoint, intensified individualism is based not on Dumont's outgoing and activity-oriented attitude, but on a further inward-turning process which was carried to its logical conclusion, and on a view of man and the world at large as utterly lacking intrinsic meaning.

It needs to be emphasized here that such a construal of Calvinist individualism should be placed in the context of the Calvinist doctrine as a whole. Though individualism can be seen as one of its major developments, Calvinism, even at its early stage, contains many and even conflicting strands of ideas. For example, Calvin's idea of fellowship, his stress on a minority of the elect to exercise rule and authority, and his subjection of individual purposes and interests to a common ideal can be construed as, if not completely hostile to, at least incompatible with, his individualism. Troeltsch is right when he reminds us that we should not confuse Calvinist individualism with modern individualistic ideas. But neither should we conclude, as a result of this consideration, that Calvinism provides no significant grounding for the emergence of modern individualism. A quick glance at the idea of Christian liberty for which Dutch Protestants and English Puritans fought in the century following the Reformation will testify to the claim that it does. The individualistic ideas which we find constitutive of the core values of "the age of individualism" in the seventeenth and eighteenth centuries can all be traced in one way or another to the two epoch-making events.

INDIVIDUALISM IN PRACTICE

From the Reformation onward, the valorizing of the individual gathered momentum. At first, this was manifested in cries for individual conscience and personal faith, but it was also strongly felt in other spheres of life. In this sense, the Protestant movement not only set the stage for religious freedom; it also ushered in changes that undermined the existing social and political arrangements and created a favorable environment for social, political, and particularly economic freedom. It must be stressed, however, that this is not to suggest that an individualistic culture emerged suddenly after the Reformation in the modern West. Nor is it to suggest that the advent of new ideas and beliefs, whether religious or epistemological, was by itself sufficient to produce changes in the actual way in which people related to one another. Although the Reformation was clearly a watershed event, it was not the only force that had contributed to the rise of individualism as a broad cultural phenomenon. As historians have reminded us, the ascendancy of individualistic values and practices was a long, and at times bloody, process in which social, economic, political, and legal factors played a role just as vital as that played by religion. During the two hundred fifty years between the Reformation and the Industrial Revolution in England, for example, dramatic changes had taken place as a result of the expansion of trade, enclosure, demographic migration and urbanization, peasant revolts, civil war and revolution, and the rise of commercial and industrial capitalism. It is the combination of these changes that gradually altered the way in which ordinary people related to one another.[67]

Nor was the impact of the Reformation always direct. Beyond religious life, Protestantism influenced the formation of an individualistic way of relating often in indirect and partial ways. The emergence and flourishing of humanist grammar schools is a good example. According to one historian, the traditional form of education had a clerical vocational bias and "was geared first and foremost to the needs of the Church;" by contrast, the humanist grammar school which rose rapidly after the Reformation and appealed to the English Protestants stressed the study of classical language and literature in both Latin and Greek. It "had no specific vocational bent, but had a relevance to all callings, secular as well as clerical."[68] As such, it contributed immensely to the increase in the level of literacy and the consequent increase in political awareness and activism among the middle class Englishmen.[69]

Before a description takes place of the entrenchment of individualistic values and practices in the United States, it seems necessary to give a brief account of the individualistic way of relating in its formative years from the Reformation to the Enlightenment. This account, I believe, will lend support to the thesis of this study that individualism provided a broad cultural bedding for the rise and prevalence of liberal rights. For this purpose, England has been chosen as an illustration, not only because England was leading Europe in social, political, economic, and legal developments at the time, but also because it played an indispensable role in shaping the politics and culture in the United States.

England in the post-Reformation era cannot be described unequivocally as a predominantly individualistic nation. The sixteenth- and seventeenth-century England which social historians have delineated for us is largely a society in transition. In this society, order existed side by side with disorder, and old values and practices intermingled with new ones.[70] In English towns, for example, while the rising powers and interests of merchants, craftsmen, yeomanry, and better-off husbandmen threatened the traditional social and political arrangements such as hereditary powers, the new elite also felt the need for a civic order that was reminiscent of the patriarchal and harmony-inducing society it had undermined.[71] A similar blending of old and new has been also found in the coal industry where an emerging capitalist culture was strongly constrained by traditional values and customs such as the cult of gentility and kinship loyalty.[72] From a historical standpoint, thus, it is problematic to describe post-Reformation English society in terms of "possessive individualism," although this term may be of great theoretical importance to our understanding of the evolution of liberal thought.

To say this, however, is not to suggest that signs of an individualistic culture in the making were entirely absent. On the contrary, these signs were emerging slowly but unmistakably. Since R.H. Tawney's day, the historical study of socio-economic and political development in early modern England has been surrounded by controversy. Some adopt an essentially Marxist theoretical framework that embeds social and political change in the rise of agrarian capitalism, while others approach the issue from a pluralist perspective which involves the central role played by the landed aristocracy as well as a diversity of economic and social forces outside it.[73] Whatever their theoretical approaches, these social historians all agree that fundamental changes were occurring in post-Reformation English society and these changes had an important economic dimension. The rapid development of trade and industry within the period of one hundred years between the mid-sixteenth century and the English Revolution had seriously eroded the traditional agrarian community and engendered a novel kind of society. This new society, though filled with ambiguities and uncertainties, began to exhibit some of the key elements of an individualistic way of relating.

One of the important aspects of social life which was greatly affected by a rising market economy is the family. The medieval English aristocratic family, like its counterpart in continental Europe, was perpetuated along patrilineal lines, although bilateral (i.e. patrilineal-matrilineal) kinship relationships also existed to ensure political allies and property.[74] Structured by patriarchal principles and practices, it dominated social and political life at both the national and the local level. By the time of the English Revolution, however, such dominance was seriously eroded as a result of the growing economic power of the gentry, merchants, and artisans, and of the inability of the aristocratic family to generate enough wealth to satisfy its lavish life style. With this erosion came the diminishing role of the patriarchal language in maintaining social and political order.[75]

While the aristocratic family was declining in power and prestige, the lower-class family in English towns and villages was also subject to the pressures of social and economic change. The rise of a market economy produced a noticeable change in gender relations within the family. In towns and pasture or clothing districts, local authorities dealt with an increasing number of rebellious (e.g. husband beating or cuckolding) women by resorting to public shaming rituals. The defiant behaviors of these women may signal the decline of the patriarchal familial order; they may also indicate that taking larger responsibilities in running the household business as wives were accustomed to do in pasture or clothmaking districts gave women "a greater sense of independence."[76] Further, the erosion of the traditional family can also be seen in yet another respect. By the turn of the fifteenth century, in at least one region, the educational role of the gentry and rural middle-class family was gradually replaced by the humanist grammar school, and family traditions and skills became largely irrelevant to the task of preparing children for their future callings. As a result, family cohesion was weakened.[77]

The breakdown of the traditional community and the emergence of new patterns of social cooperation are another sign of the changing cultural landscape. The medieval rural community was bound tightly to the land. The rapid growth of wool trade and subsequently the growing need for more pasture for grazing gave rise to the brutal act of enclosure. The bitter joke of Sir Thomas More that sheep eat men turned out to be a truer description than he realized of the reality in the English countryside at the time.[78] As the concentration of land in the hands of a few accelerated, and as more and more peasants were evicted or bought out of their land, a community based on the land could no longer be sustained. The late fifteenth and early sixteenth century had witnessed an increasing population of rogues, vagabonds, and beggars roaming the countryside and flooding into towns and the city of London. These "masterless men," together with an itinerant trading population of peddlers, carters, badgers, and merchant middlemen, contributed to a sense of rootlessness and, ironically, a sense of freedom as well, and paved the way for an emerging individualistic social order.[79]

In regions where commercial and industrial capitalism was fast growing, the traditional emphasis on community harmony and deference to hierarchy was gradually replaced by a new style of social cooperation. In the coal industry, for example, the bond of loyalty and mutual obligation between lord and subject disappeared; in its stead rose an impersonal and contractual tie between moneyed interests and wage laborers. While labor was considered a commodity to be sold and bought, its price varying with seasonal demands, coal-owners were typically separated from the community in which colliers lived and worked and had no interest in its development. They were "essentially employers, not masters, their remoteness from the [pitmen] increasing as the size of collieries grew."[80] In commercial ventures, merchants, particularly in London, began to band together on a voluntary basis for business, charity, and local improvement. During the eighteenth century, such voluntary associations became an influential force in both national and local politics. Regarded as one of the "public bodies," they played an important role in relieving the poor, building schools, and establishing hospitals.[81] In a genealogical sense, they may be said to have provided the model for voluntary associations that decades later Tocqueville found so crucial to the constitution of American society.

A more revealing sign of an emerging individualistic culture can be found in changing property relations. Property narrowly understood as land has long been taken by Englishmen as one of the twin pillars—the other being liberty—of the ancient constitution.[82] In medieval England, land was held by individuals rather than by wider groups such as the family or lineage and fully alienable. This is largely the basis of Macfarlane's argument about premodern English individualism.[83] As critics have pointed out, however, Macfarlane's claim is flawed in several respects.[84] For example, Lawrence Stone argues that Macfarlane "totally ignores the close communal control, through the manorial court, of almost every aspect of the use of property. Such courts could tell people when, where, and what to sow or reap."[85] Stone's view has been corroborated by many social historians including Macfarlane himself. The chief difference between the traditional and the emerging conception of private property in land, according to one social historian, involves a distinction between the use of land for production and the use of land for profit. Under the feudal tenure system, "the ownership of land was always burdened and hedged with a great variety of obligations to other persons."[86]

But such obligations apparently lost much of their appeal when by the late sixteenth century land became a lucrative commodity to be sold and bought freely on the market. The result was the widespread use of land at the discretion of the individual with no regard for the "customary rules prescribing the methods of cultivation."[87] The enclosing landlords, yeoman farmers, and better-off husbandmen used their landholdings for high rents and for profitable crops such as tabacco and sheep. Although these practices might have existed at an earlier time, they did not seem to constitute a clear threat to the feudal tenure system. But their subversive force was clearly felt by the time of the Civil War with the ascendancy of propertied interests, whether landed, commercial or industrial, in the Parliament.[88]

Accompanying the changing property relations in rural communities was an expansion of the form of property. This expansion occurred evidently as a result of the rise of commercial and industrial capitalism. In addition to land or real estate, there emerged other forms of property such as stocks, merchandise and machinery. There was even property in ideas, a new phenomenon which caused much controversy in the eighteenth century.[89] These new kinds of property carried an even stronger individualistic possessive tone than landed property; they were considered exclusively the individual's personal wealth and possessions, and their use and alienation were considered exclusively an individual matter and subject to no customs and obligations as land to some extent continued to be subject to long after the abolition of feudal tenures in 1641.[90]

If there was prior to the Civil War a burgeoning awareness that self-interest and economic freedom provided "the basis of human society," the transition from medieval corporatism to economic individualism was largely complete by the end of the eighteenth century.[91] After the Revolution, English society was sharply divided along property lines into the propertied and the propertyless. The century between 1689 and 1789 had witnessed the dominance of propertied interests in both public and private life. This dominance was manifested, for example, in the landed and personal property qualifications for MPs, JPs, and other public office holders such as commissioners of peace and taxation, and in a widespread tendency to "view the rights of individuals in terms of their property and public affairs as an expression of propertied interests."[92] Property, whether it was land or commercial, was widely perceived to have given the propertied Englishman the kind of material and political independence and freedom that the propertyless class did not possess. It embodied and indeed often took priority, in practice if not in theory, over the value of individual liberty. In view of this, one may be justified in arguing that private property relations had provided the economic basis for and defined an emerging individualistic culture in early modern England.

It must be stressed that the rise and entrenchment of individualistic values and practices in the modern West was a gradual and sometimes painful process, and different nations each had their own trajectory of development which may not be identical with that of England. This is even true of the United States where the English influence was strongly present in virtually all aspects of life. But as a general trend, the ascendancy of individualism as a cultural phenomenon was unmistakable.

Perhaps nowhere can one observe this ascendancy more clearly than in the United States, for the United States is in the eyes of many the embodiment of individualism *par excellence*. It has been known at least since Tocqueville's day that individualism is a central American value. While the republic was founded upon the values and beliefs that go to the heart of modern individualism, the absence of a historical tradition, the vastness of uncultivated and rich land, and ultimately a divinely ordained sense of mission, combined to foster a strong and unique form of individualistic culture that is unparalleled in any other nation in the world. To read American history—from the Puritan settlers in pursuit of religious liberty to the revolutionary war that led to political independence, from the lonesome frontierman chasing his "manifest destiny" to the economically self-made capitalist—is to watch individualism grow. To observe the ordinary lives of ordinary men and women in America is to see individualism in action.

Of the important studies of the ordinary lives of ordinary Americans, two works stand out in offering a most perceptive look at the individualistic way of relating in the United States. Though written a century and a half apart, *Democracy in America* and *Habits of the Heart* demonstrate a remarkable similarity, not in terms of method and style, but in terms of substantive conclusions.[93] It goes without saying that dramatic changes have taken place between the two studies. Small town expands into big metropolis; family shop is replaced by transnational corporation; and face-to-face contact gives over to telecommunication. But if we look beneath these variegated and dazzling phenomena, we will find that the individualistic values and practices by which the average American lives remain remarkably enduring.

The manifestations of individualism in American life may be organized in terms of two main categories, namely private and public. This is the approach which Bellah and his collaborators have taken. Tocqueville, on the other hand, did not have such an explicit structure in mind, although a similar idea could be extracted from his account. It also needs to be pointed out that Tocqueville's usage of the term individualism was influenced by the nineteenth-century intellectual climate. This is clear from his description of the way in which the Americans combated individualism. But he did not, as did many of his contemporaries, treat individualism entirely as a negative concept. He saw it as "a novel expression" and indicative of "a novel idea." For him, individualism is distinct from egoism or selfishness, though if unchecked it may well evolve into egoistic or selfish obsession. It signifies what he describes as "a mature and calm feeling."[94] The words "mature" and "calm" here warrant special attention, for they speak to one of the defining features of individualism as we know it today. They imply that individualism is not an ephemeral and flitting passion, directed at a particular thing at a particular time and place; rather, it connotes a sense of identification with one's own values, interests, and needs. It is based on an understanding of the self and of the fundamental role this self plays in both private and public life.

Tocqueville surveyed a large number of private areas of life ranging from intellectual and artistic pursuits to religion, family, and gender relations. To an acute observer like him, the fact that individualistic ideas and sentiments permeated the new world was impossible to miss. Perhaps to say that individualism dominated the private life of ordinary citizens in America is tautological, for the very idea of privacy, of an independent and autonomous personal sphere of life, is precisely an avid expression of individualism. Tocqueville's findings about this private sphere of life may be summed up by the celebrated maxim that everyone is the best and sole judge of his own private interest and welfare. The "private judgment of each man" is paramount not merely with respect to his utilitarian interests; it is also paramount in the profound epistemological sense of being the subject knower and the ultimate judge of truth. In discussing what he called "the philosophical method of the Americans," Tocqueville made these remarks:

> To evade the bondage of system and habit, of family maxims, class opinions, and, in some degree, of national prejudices; to accept tradition only as a means of information, and existing facts only as a lesson to be used in doing otherwise and doing better; *to seek the reason of things for oneself, and in oneself alone;* to tend to results without being bound to means, and to strike through the form to the substance—such are the principal characteristics of what I shall call the philosophical method of the Americans. But if I go further and seek among these characteristics the principal one, which includes almost all the rest, I discover that *in most of the operations of the mind each American appeals only to the individual effort of his own understanding* (emphasis added).[95]

If this is an accurate assessment, it may well be taken as a description of a Luther or a Descartes or both. Indeed, Tocqueville noted that Descartes was "least studied," but "best applied" in America. He went further to assert that the Americans' understanding of the self, of its rational ability to judge for itself, was not culled from philosophical books, but cultivated through practice. This may sound too sweeping. But if we examine closely what Tocqueville said about the cultural forces impacting all of Europe since the Reformation, we can safely infer that America's deep appreciation of the self is not so much an argument for innateness as an unconscious process of cultural acquisition.

This epistemological outlook, as an acquired cultural trait, provided the foundation for each individual's private judgment in virtually all areas of personal life. Consider two areas, religion and family. Tocqueville's comment on how religion played a vital role in American life is widely known; he reminded us that "religion gave birth to Anglo-American society."[96] Less widely known, however, is his observation that the Americans followed their religion from the principle of self-interest. By self-interest, he did not mean selfishness; instead, he meant a form of enlightened self-interest which was capable of making certain sacrifices for the good of the community as a whole. It was also a form of self-interest which was capable of reconciling worldly pursuits with heavenly rewards, materialism with salvation. In Tocqueville's view, religion was conceived by the Americans not only as a wholly personal matter of belief; it was also closely related to, and indeed provided justification for, one's desire to achieve as much as possible in this world.[97] This clearly anticipates the thesis advanced by Weber and others about the connection between the Calvinist work ethic and the rise of economic individualism in the modern West.

Tocqueville considered the family another area of personal life in which the Americans showed a strong sense of individualism. He observed that in the medieval and aristocratic sense of the word, the family did not exist in America. While this can be seen as part of a general trend involving the breakdown of paternal authority and the rising tide of egalitarianism, it carries some distinctly American characteristics. A young adult's claim for independence and freedom was not accompanied by animosity or "moral violence" on the part of father and son. Rather, it was based on a mutual recognition that such claim was due the latter as a matter of right. The desire to be independent and free, to be master of one's own thought and conduct, and the willingness to accept such independence and self-mastery, were all driven by the same individualist principle of autonomy and self-reliance. Whereas the father "foresees the limits of his authority long beforehand," "the son looks forward to the exact period at which he will be his own master, and he enters upon his freedom without precipitation and without effort, *as a possession which is his own and which no one seeks to wrest from him* (emphasis added)."[98] A similar practice was also found among other members of the family, according to Tocqueville. The family bond was forged not on the basis of ascribed ranks and privileges within the family; it was founded on the fact of living together as equal and independent persons, and on mutual respect for such equality and independence.

When Tocqueville turned his attention from private to public life in America, his observations were equally revealing. Tocqueville's description of a private life governed by individualistic values and principles might leave one wondering how a public life was at all possible. If individuals were concerned only with their private interests and made decisions on the basis of their private judgments, organized collective life was sure to appear unimportant. This is perhaps one of the ill effects of individualism Tocqueville mentioned in his work. He argued that while encouraging the cultivation of positive values such as autonomy, self-reliance and self-sufficiency, individualism seemed to have left little room for public life. But he did not deny that Americans did have a public life and a unique one as well. Whatever mixed feelings he entertained about individualism, he found in America a rather extraordinary and inspiring public life grounded in individualist principles and ideas.

The one notion which holds the key to an understanding of life in the public domain in the United States is voluntary association. The idea of voluntary association may be used in two senses. In a narrow sense, it refers to professional or civic groups which make up what is often called civil society and which form an intermediate buffer zone between the individual and government. This is the sense in which Tocqueville is commonly said to have used the concept. But voluntary association can be broadly understood as extending to all levels of organized political life, including the national community as a whole. This usage is also found in Tocqueville, particularly in his account of the voluntary nature of local community. It is in this broad sense that voluntary association may be said to provide the key to understanding the individualistic nature of public life in America.

Tocqueville's description of the local community is familiar to the contemporary reader. He saw the township as the most basic form of voluntary association, and it was on the townships that counties, states, and finally the union were built. But the township was important not only in a structural sense; it was vital also because it was the most direct expression of popular sovereignty and political freedom. It offered an opportunity for each individual to take a direct and equal part in sharing political power, practice the art of self-government, cooperate in managing collective affairs, learn and enjoy one's rights, and fulfill one's duties. In other words, the township was a public way of life. It is worth bearing in mind, however, that this way of life encouraged and required individual participation by voluntary choice, as the notion of voluntary association amply suggests to us. Public life in the township signified a voluntary act of individuals coming together in order to do things which none could do alone. The voluntary nature of township life involves at least three implicit claims. First, public life is a matter of individual choice; second, such choice has been made on the basis of one's rational self-interest, free from coercion; third, it is a choice that can be undone, undone in the sense that one can exit as one sees fit. Though not arranged in such a neat fashion, these claims are clearly present in Tocqueville's account. They provide some of the most important underlying assumptions for the form of public life embodied in the American system of townships. It is a form of public life individualistic at heart.

What Tocqueville discovered about American culture has been reproduced with remarkable resemblance a century and a half later in *Habits of the Heart*. Taking their cue from Tocqueville, Bellah and his collaborators set out to observe in a more intimate way how individualism informs and shapes both private and public life in America. They wanted to know specifically the extent to which the middle-class American lives and works by the individualist principles and values which give American culture its distinctive quality. The results of their investigation are summarized in these words:

> Individualism lies at the very core of American culture. . . . We believe in the dignity, indeed the sacredness of the individual. Anything that would violate our right to think for ourselves, judge for ourselves, make our own decisions, live our lives as we see fit, is not only morally wrong, it is sacrilegious. Our highest and noblest aspirations, not only for ourselves, but for those we care about, for our society and for the world, are closely linked to our individualism.[99]

But, as the authors immediately point out, while individualism has given rise to America's highest and noblest aspirations, it is also responsible for "some of our deepest problems." Their goal is not to abandon individualism, for that would mean to abandon the fundamental American identity. Rather, the aim is to find a way to reconstruct a coherent moral life which would preserve the positive values contained in individualism while eliminating or at least circumscribing its ill effects.

Like Tocqueville, Bellah and his co-authors offered two perspectives; one looks at the individual in his or her private capacity as a person and the other in his or her public capacity as a citizen. In the private sphere, individualism manifests itself most strikingly. Though the time has changed, the same principles of autonomy, self-reliance, and self-sufficiency which inspired admiration in Tocqueville remain strong moral forces guiding personal conduct with respect to the family, religion, and work. Bellah and his co-authors symbolically describe the young American's declaration of independence as "leaving home." Ironically, for many Americans, it is precisely within the family that the spirit of self-reliance and autonomy has been cultivated. The act of leaving home is in large part not a hostile rebellion. Rather, it signifies a positive act of living one's own life, making one's own decision, and thinking, judging and taking responsibility for oneself.[100]

A similar claim for independent and autonomous choice can be heard concerning the objects of belief. If we recall Tocqueville's account of how Christian religion played a fundamental role in American life and how a plurality of religious sects or denominations provided the dynamics for American society, we may be surprised to find a somewhat different situation today. Now religious belief has become a predominantly personal and in many cases educated choice which may or may not have anything to do with the church. It is educated by a liberalized pluralist understanding of religion in particular and world culture in general. Like the act of leaving home, leaving church throws individualism into high relief. It signals a relaxed sense of duty and a concomitant heightened sense of rights. It represents a profound sense of being alone, as one of the interviewees so eloquently put it; of taking responsibility for none but oneself, not even including one's nonage offsprings; and of having one's destiny totally under control both in the negative sense of helplessness and in the positive sense of self-sufficiency. It also suggests knowledge of the lack of objective criteria for moral conduct and, in place of these, drawing on one's own preferences so long as one's conduct does not pose harm to others.[101]

This understanding of the self as the "arbitrary center of volition" and as the ultimate source of one's interests, wants, responsibilities, and values also lies at the core of the work ethic. The idea of work or calling is relevant to the extent that it helps define one's identity; as is often said, what one does defines what one is. But it is largely stripped of moral connotations. Rather than denote a moral relationship which relates the calling of each individual to his or her community, work has come to be viewed as "a segmental, self-interested activity." It has become essentially a source of material rewards and personal satisfaction and a way of both making a living and making oneself worthwhile. Hence the single-minded pursuit of career advancement, and along with it, financial gain, in terms of which

success is measured. This is the basic component of what Bellah and his collaborators called utilitarian individualism, a form of individualism that
takes certain human interests and needs as given and sees work as a
medium through which individuals maximize their self-interest relative to
these ends.[102]

In the public sphere, individualism also makes a strong appearance.
While Tocqueville's observations on the voluntary nature of public life in
America are still fundamentally relevant, there are a few peculiarly contemporary tinges of color added to it. As Bellah and his collaborators aptly note,
the United States is often conceived of as "a nation of joiners." This conception gives the idea of public life an individualistic accent by making it depend
on the willingness and self-interest of each volunteer to participate or "get
involved," to use a common expression. This is true of both the national and
the local community. On the national level, the electoral process, particularly the principle of one person one vote, is one of the clear illustrations of
the individualistic biases in public life. On the local level, however, things
seem much less individualistically oriented. Indeed, people in some communities still maintain a strong attachment to their small communities and
communal values are very much a part of their life as is the idea of individual rights and dignity. But on closer examination, public life there is constrained by individualistic values and beliefs. Several such constraints may
be described as follows.

First, the idea of community is defined by individual self-interests. In
the eyes of one of the town fathers Bellah and his co-authors interviewed,
the good of the community is "defined in terms of the long-range ability of
individuals each to get what they have paid for, no more and no less." Thus,
"[o]ne's contribution to the community—in time and taxes—is not thought
of as a duty but as a voluntary investment."[103] Second, with the individual's
self-interest as the basis of the idea of a community, getting involved in community affairs and in politics begins only when one's private sanctuary is
threatened. This is characteristic of the so-called "concerned citizen." For
the concerned citizen, there is no lack of community involvement, and such
involvement is always a positive educating experience. But the fundamental
problem remains. When the community is seen as an aggregate of self-interested individuals, its existence hinges upon a perceived need to protect or
promote these self-interests, and failing such protection or promotion, it has
no legitimacy. Third, in cases of conflicting claims on either an intercommu-
nal or an intracommunal level, instead of engaging in dialogue and deliberation to find a common ground, an individualistic approach tends toward a
mediating and value-neutral broker. A language is unavailable that would

both recognize the differences among people and see them as parts of a larger community. Finally, the view that the public sphere is an arena for adjudicating various interests leads to a conception of justice as "a fair chance to get what one wants."[104]

In describing the essential features of American individualism, Bellah and his collaborators found that it bears a remarkable resemblance to "therapy." They conclude that American culture is therapeutic in the sense that the same underlying assumptions which provide the philosophical basis for therapeutic practice also lie at the foundation of American individualism. While they applied the metaphor only to the private sphere, it seems appropriate to apply it also to the public sphere. At least four characteristics of therapeutic individualism deserve special attention. First, the interests, needs, and values of each person are taken as given; they are defined individually and prior to coming to therapeutic sessions, that is, presocially. Second, therapeutic sessions are designed to alleviate the stress and pain of a particular individual, and no social and moral commitment is necessary on the part of either the therapist or the patient. In fact, the former should keep a neutral stance and avoid imposing his personal values on the patient. Third, the relationship between the therapist and the patient is strictly contractual; whatever else it is, it is also a form of economic transaction. What one gets is what one pays for. Fourth, seeing the therapist is entirely one's own choice and depends on whether doing so is in one's best interest. One can begin and quit at any given time. There may be a few rules of the game, but no interpersonal bonding is necessary. Whatever temporary bonding there is, it is not an integral part of one's life and identity.

As a metaphor, therapy aptly captures the essence of contemporary individualism in America. It "reminds us how closely these therapeutic interpersonal virtues resemble the long-standing social virtues of modern liberalism." It is these social virtues that provide the basis for "an individualistic and egalitarian society," a society which assigns enormous weight to "each person's rights and liberties, held in balance by contractual negotiation and reciprocal exchange."[105] While Bellah and his collaborators clearly have a moral vision in mind in addressing the issue of individualism, we need not agree with their moral vision to see how individualism has played a dominant role in shaping American society. If Tocqueville's legacy is to have offered a balanced understanding of how individualism contributed to the formation of a cultural tradition in its early stage, the authors of *Habits of the Heart* have done much in taking that understanding a step further and furnishing a forceful account of its current condition.

Chapter Five
Confucianism and the Making of Chinese Politico-Cultural Tradition

If, as the previous chapters have sought to show, the liberal concept of rights presupposes and indeed is grounded in an individualistic way of relating, and if this way of relating emerged in the wake of the Reformation in the modern West, then what are the prospects for applying it to a different political and cultural context where such a way of relating is radically missing? How would it fare there? What, if anything, could be done if it should indeed fare poorly? In China, the notion of rights was introduced one hundred years ago, but it had and still has enormous difficulty in getting absorbed into the consciousness and practice of ordinary people. Many reasons have been given for this. Some argue that there has been a gross lack of commitment on the part of the political elite in promoting and institutionalizing rights practice. Others delve into modern Chinese history for insights and perspectives, stressing the historical circumstances under which the idea of rights failed to take root and thrive. Still others blame the Marxist ideology or Maoism for continued disregard for and violation of individual rights. While these claims all have some plausibility, they are not entirely satisfactory. For they provide an explanation that itself needs to be explained. The political elite's lack of commitment, for example, is something that itself needs to be accounted for. An alternative cultural perspective, it seems to me, may allow us to gain a deeper and more fruitful understanding of the issue.

It is on the basis of this premise that a description of the Chinese politico-cultural tradition will proceed in this chapter. In what sense(s) can one be justified in saying that the Chinese politico-cultural tradition is different from the one in which liberal rights are embedded? What exactly is the Chinese politico-cultural tradition? What are its basic features? Answers to these questions will provide the groundwork for arguing that, because the individualistic way of relating is radically missing, the liberal concept of rights is not likely to play a significant role in promoting democratic change in China.

The chapter contains four sections. The first deals with the boundary question of what it is that can be properly said to be the Chinese politico-cultural tradition. Reasons will be given for holding the view that Confucianism has been the dominating cultural force ever since the Han dynasty ruler Wu Di declared it the supreme principle of government and moral conduct when he came to power in 140 BC. The second section reviews the core features of Confucianism, with special attention given to some of the widely debated issues in Confucian scholarship. The third section offers an account of how Confucianism helped to define and shape the nature and structure of the most fundamental aspect of socio-cultural life in dynastic China, namely the family, and of how the family in turn helped to furnish a model of political rule and create a duty-sensitive and nonindividualistic political culture. Based on recent empirical studies and, to a much lesser degree, on my own findings from a field trip to one of the provinces in northern China, the fourth section surveys contemporary Chinese political culture. This survey is necessary because it enables us to compare the past with the present and determine the extent to which the traditional shared way of relating has changed in contemporary China.

THE BOUNDARIES

The term "Chinese culture" has been used in a variety of intellectual disciplines. But its meaning is not always clearly defined. Given so vast a geographical area as China, and given so long a history as the Chinese history, talking about Chinese culture as if it were a unified whole is sure to invite criticism. The simple fact that there are more than fifty ethnic minority groups living in that vast land should give one reason to pause. In recent decades, the resurgence of localism and the effort to reclaim ethnic identity have made the issue especially conspicuous, and there is a growing concern among cultural historians about the ill effects of an undifferentiated use of the concept. In particular, they are worried about the fact that equating Chinese culture with Confucian culture may lead to a distorted view of a culture that has long been characterized by diversity and inclusiveness. Tan Qixiang, one of the most outspoken cultural historians on the issue, points out that Chinese culture has both geographical and temporal differences and that to speak about it in universal terms is misleading. Whereas geographical differences manifest themselves in ethnic regions, temporal differences are seen in different historical periods. For those who claim that

Confucianism is the ultimate expression of Chinese culture, Tan argues, there is a potential danger of misrepresentation. The Tibetans and Mongolians, for example, have never shared Confucian culture with the dominant Han ethnic majority; instead, their identity is informed by a special form of Buddhism. From a temporal point of view, each historical epoch was distinguished by a different cultural trend the source of which can be traced back to the various schools of thought in the ages of Spring and Autumn and the Warring States. Even if Confucianism was a dominating influence, as in the Song and Ming dynasties, it was a reinvented version that incorporated important elements of Taoism and Buddhism. Thus, Tan concludes,

> The Chinese culture has been evolving with time, and each historical period is quite different from another in terms of cultural traits. It cannot be supposed therefore that there has been an immutable and timeless culture with Confucianism as its core or hallmark for thousands of years. . . . Confucianism has never been the only ruling principle of any given age.[1]

Tan's point is well taken. Apart from the fact that a large variety of ethnic groups live in the so-called periphery areas and each have their distinctive cultural identity, even within the central part of China where Chinese civilization is said to have originated, there are a number of cultural blocs each of which enjoys to a greater or lesser degree its own customs and traditions.[2] The roots of these customs and traditions can be traced to a five-hundred-year period of dramatic change prior to the establishment of the first dynasty, the Qin dynasty. It is commonly recognized that the pre-Qin era, which was marked by an extraordinary outpouring of political ideas and experiments, sowed the seeds of cultural diversity one witnesses today.

Insofar as recorded history is concerned, there were three clan-based kingdoms, namely Xia, Shang, Zhou, in the pre-Qin era. The Zhou kingdom, the last of the three, was divided into the Western and the Eastern because its capital was relocated from the Western to the Eastern part of central China. Toward the end of Western Zhou, the central government's authority was greatly weakened due to the ever-increasing power of its vassal states. The rulers or lords of these vassal states, originally the blood relatives of the Zhou clan, began to claim their independent authorities after a few generations of self-rule. The rise of small and independent states led to the disintegration of the Zhou kingdom. It also created a vacuum in which an unprecedented release of intellectual energy gave rise to the flourishing of moral and political thought. A multitude of schools of learning emerged in an attempt to provide both theoretical justifications and policy recommendations for the rule of rising feudal lords. Among various schools of thought, three would come to play a vitally important role in shaping the Chinese political cultural tradition. These are Taoism, Legalism, and Confucianism.[3] While a detailed account of the three doctrines is not at all necessary here, it may be useful to take a brief look at some of their main ideas, as this will help us understand the role they each played in the development of Chinese culture.

The central idea of Taoism is nonaction (*Wu Wei*). Paradoxical as it may be, the principle of nonaction is, according to the founder of Taoism Lao Tzu, the ultimate guiding principle of all forms of human action. It is also the only path to *Tao* (or Way). The concept of *Tao* is one of the most difficult notions in Lao Tzu. It defies definition. In fact, Lao Tzu said explicitly that if *Tao* could be explicated, it would not be the real Tao. But a close reading of his *Tao Te Ching* (or Book of *Tao*) reveals that it not only suggests a way of living, doing, and thinking; it also hints at the presence of an ontological being which exists independently of human understanding and provides a constant and reliable guide for human action. What is remarkable about *Tao*, however, is not that it can only be known through human intuition; rather, it must be lived to be known, and to achieve it, one must practice it. It is only in doing it that Tao can be intuited. But, for Lao Tzu, doing should be governed by the principle of nonaction. Nonaction is not literally doing nothing; it signifies a way of doing in accordance with *Tao*. It is a natural way of doing, a pursuit of harmony with Heaven and Earth and with all living creatures, and an awareness of the necessity to follow the inner logic of things without imposing human will and desire on them.

The principle of nonaction has tremendous implications for the art of government and for politics in general. Lao Tzu's ideal society is a small, face-to-face community in which people live a natural, conflict-free, and self-sufficient life. Two main features are characteristic of nonaction politics in this context. First, the ruler should place the least possible social and economic burden on the ruled; second, the ruled should be purged of knowledge and desire so that they remain ignorant yet satisfied.[4] The following passage perhaps best illustrates Lao Tzu's political philosophy. A wise ruler or sage, says Lao Tzu, would rule his people this way:

> He empties their minds, and fills their bellies; he weakens their ambitions, and strengthens their bodies. He strives always to keep the people ignorant of knowledge and desire, and to keep the wise from interfering. By doing nothing that interferes with anything, he leaves nothing ungoverned.[5]

To the extent that nonaction aims to minimize political action as much as possible, Taoism is an attempt to retreat into a nonpolitical, if not antipolitical, world. In contrast, Legalism entertains a very different and indeed opposite view. Rooted in political reforms of the day, it was a materialist and policy-oriented philosophy. Lying at the core of Legalist thought are three notions, namely power, statecraft, and penal code (*Fa*). Unlike Taoism, Legalism sanctions an extensive use of power by the ruler for effective government. For the Legalist, all power must concentrate exclusively in one person, that is, the sovereign. It is only by centralizing and consolidating political power in the hands of the sovereign and in him alone that stability and prosperity can be achieved. Separation of powers frequently leads to internal turmoil and bloodshed. In addition to advocating the absolute power of the sovereign, the Legalist thinkers also emphasize statecraft, particularly when dealing with the relationship between the ruler and his ranking officials. But statecraft has a delimited meaning here. It does not necessarily indicate the practical art of ruling, though there are traces of that connotation in it. For the most part, it refers to an artful and cunning scheme designed to boost the majestic and powerful image of the sovereign. Such image boosting is accomplished often by downplaying the role of his ranking officials and manipulating disagreements or conflicts among them.

The third key component of Legalism is its stress on the establishment of a penal code. This is what made the Legalists most famous. The purpose of having a penal code is twofold. First, it rewards talents and merits rather than ascribed statuses and ranks. Second, it punishes bad deeds regardless of whether or not the accused is of an aristocratic origin. But it must be noted that the Legalist's argument that the law should be applied universally and equally is not an unqualified argument. The sovereign is not subject to the rule of law. He is the maker of the law and has the absolute legal authority in adjudication. It is in this sense that he is above the law.[6] The supremacy of the sovereign is distinguished from the position occupied by his subject officials. "The sovereign and his subjects do not follow the same principle," says Han Fei, the great synthesizer of Legalist thought. It is also compared to the oneness of *Tao*. Like *Tao*, the supreme authority lies exclusively with the sovereign and sharing it would lead to the demise of the state.[7]

While Taoism espouses the view of nonaction with respect to government and Legalism maintains a positive and indeed aggressive attitude toward political power, Confucianism is distinguished, at least in its early stage, by an understanding of man, society and politics that has little in common with either of the two. It is an understanding that is centered on humanity rather than on Nature *a la* Lao Tzu or on law *a la* the Legalists. To

be sure, the concept of *Tao* (Way) and that of *Fa* (Law) can both be found
in Confucius, but they receive a treatment entirely different from the one
found in Taoism and Legalism respectively. Instead, it is two other concepts,
namely *Li* (Rituals) and *Ren* (Benevolence), which become the cornerstone
of Confucianism. The fundamental point of departure for Confucius was to
return to, or more accurately to revitalize, a moral and political tradition
which was inaugurated by the wise rulers in the three earlier kingdoms but
began to decline at the end of the Western Zhou kingdom. In particular,
Confucius wanted to salvage or reinstitute the idea of *Li* in an age that witnessed the breakdown of ethical standards. He devoted his entire life to the
task of editing, commenting on and teaching the rituals and conventions of
the past. In his view, the saintly king Zhou Gong created for his people and
their posterity a magnificent body of ethical rules and institutional arrangements encapsulated in *Li,* and this legacy would provide the foundation for
a good and prosperous society just as it had done for the Zhou kingdom.

But Confucius went further. Realizing that as a set of external standards, *Li* had quite limited effects on conduct, he renovated the idea of *Ren*
as a way of internalizing moral imperatives. Just as legal rules must be enforced in order to fulfill their intended purpose, external check is required
for meeting the standards as specified by *Li*. Absent such check, *Li* is nothing but a collection of empty phrases. Confucius saw this occur in the conduct of feudal lords. It was precisely the lack of a higher power to restrain
them that led to the abuse of institutional arrangements. With the reestab-
lishment of *Ren,* however, this situation would, in Confucius' mind,
change. For the idea of *Ren* rests on a self-conscious effort of the ruler and
indeed human beings in general to act in accordance with an ethical code
they themselves believe to be good and beneficial. Through the transforming power of *Ren, Li* becomes a set of self-imposed duties or obligations
which each member of society, including the sovereign, willingly accepts
and lives by. Thus, as the Confucianist says, a gentleman must watch his
conduct even when he is alone.

The idea of *Ren* is central to the Confucianist conception of government and politics. For the Confucianist, good politics is benevolent politics,
and benevolent politics can be realized only by cultivating personal virtues
on the ruler's part. It is in personal virtues that political virtues find their
grounding. With rectitude, one is able to transcend one's selfish interests and
care for the good of society as a whole; with compassion, one is able to understand the people's pains and sufferings and make policy decisions to alleviate them. Personal virtues are thus regarded as the very basis for legitimate
rule in all spheres of life and at all levels, whether it is managing the family,

running the state, or governing everything under the heaven. Interestingly, from an etymological perspective, the word "politics" in Chinese signifies an act of making things straight or upright. Perhaps this could offer us, albeit intuitively, a glimpse of what it means to govern.

This brief account shows that the three schools of thought each have fundamentally different ideas and concerns about the nature of man, society and government. This diversity of ideas and concerns constitutes the sources of the Chinese politico-cultural tradition. But given the influential role each has played in shaping this tradition, one may ask, how can it be said that a commonality exists, with Confucianism at its core? This commonality even a cultural pluralist like Tan Qixiang does not deny. An answer to this question may be sought by taking a look at the fate of each school after the death of its founders.

The most reputable student of Taoism after Lao Tzu is Zhuang Zi. While clearly sharing with his master predecessor the central idea of *Tao* as the ultimate way of living, Zhuang Zi tends to cover the notion with a veil of mysticism. This mystical element carries him even further away from the real world and politics and enables him to experience the ineffableness and freedom of Nature. He regards political power as a source of evil, attacks Confucian ideas such as benevolence, filial piety and loyalty as unnatural, and detests fame and wealth. His mystical experience with Nature leads him to espouse agnosticism. The story which he told about his dream of a butterfly—or, as he said, perhaps the butterfly dreamed of Zhuang Zi—is most revealing about his agnostic attitude. The kind of Taoism he handed down in the form of mysticism and agnosticism had enormous impact on Chinese poetry and painting, particularly from the Wei and Jin historical periods onward. The same Taoism also provided intellectual and moral justifications for holding a negative or even hostile attitude toward government and politics.

By contrast, Legalism fared much more smoothly in the world of politics, at least in the short run. As mentioned previously, Legalist thought was rooted in the practical affairs of the time, and as such, it had great success with those who sought hegemony in the era of the Warring States. The practical strategies as suggested by the Legalist Shang Yang led the State of Qin from a mediocre power to the strongest state among its rivals. With the aid of Han Fei and his classmate Li Si, the Qin ruler finally completed his conquest and created the first unified empire in Chinese history. It has been recorded that the first emperor Qin Shi Huang held Han Fei in high esteem and once threatened to seize him by violence from his home country Han if the ruler of Han refused to hand him over. Ironically, however, the Qin Empire which was built on the Legalist vision and method did not last very long. Fifteen years after its founding, it was overthrown by rebellious peasants. For this, according to Confucian historians, the Legalists should take a large part of the blame. From that time on, Legalism as a political doctrine never regained the popularity it had enjoyed with Qin Shi Huang, although elements of the Legalist teaching passed on and were absorbed into the Confucian ideology.

The fate of Confucianism was not particularly glamorous in its early years. After Confucius, Confucianism branched out into eight denominations. By the time Mencius began to develop his thought on the basis of the idea of *Ren,* it became one of the widely circulated ethical doctrines. But for some reason it did not enjoy much success with the rulers of various states. The Legalists such as Han Fei disliked it, because they believed it misrepresented human nature and was too idealistic to be of any practical use. Mencius was tenacious in trying to persuade various state rulers to adopt his philosophy and to no avail. It was not until the Han dynasty, the second in Chinese history that things began to change. Not long after emperor Wu Di came to power in 140 B.C., he adopted a policy suggested by one of the Confucian scholars Dong Zhongshu, a policy which banned all other schools of thought and established Confucianism as the orthodox moral and political doctrine. He also created the official title of Five Classics Scholar, and the five classics were the Confucian texts of *Shi* (Book of Poetry), *Shu* (Book of History), *Li* (Book of Rituals), *I-Ching* (Book of Change), and *Chun Qiu* (Spring and Autumn Annals). This effort to unify thought, which was functionally in keeping with the need to maintain a unified empire, transformed Confucianism from one particular ethical view to the dominant ruling ideology governing all aspects of social and political life. A further development of this dominance occurred when the Song dynasty Confucian scholar Zhu Xi selected and edited the *Four Books* as the mandatory reading materials for all candidates taking the civil service examination. From that time on, up till the turn of this century, the orthodox position of Confucianism in the Chinese politico-cultural tradition had never been seriously challenged.

A final note is in order. By claiming that Confucianism constitutes the mainstream of the Chinese politico-cultural tradition, I do not mean that it resembles anything like an immutable and closed system. On the contrary, it has been changing ever since it became one of the eminent schools of thought in the pre-Qin era. It has never been an airtight whole which excludes outside ideas from penetrating it. Rather, one of the salient characteristics of Confucianism is precisely its ability to borrow and absorb, although it clearly has a set of ideas and values that remain relatively stable through the vicissitudes of time. Even in its formative days, Confucianism already borrowed and absorbed elements of both Taoism and Legalism, just as the Taoists and Legalists borrowed and absorbed Confucian ideas and each other's ideas as well. The most evident example of this is found in the writings of the great Confucianist synthesizer Xun Zi. Ironically, Xun Zi taught Han Fei, one of the most outspoken critics of Confucianism. Contemporary students of Confucianism tend to see Confucius' teaching as indicative of primitive Confucianism.[8] Its later-day version, especially the one found in the Song dynasty, is believed to be radically different from the central ideas in primitive Confucianism. While this is plausible, there are good reasons for arguing that the fundamental aspects of Confucianism, particularly with regard to the question of government and politics, have undergone little substantive change even in the hands of neo-Confucianists. It is also true that, though the rulers of dynastic China venerated Confucius, they did not always follow his teachings in the practice of government. Instead, they used a combination of Legalist, Taoist and Confucianist ideas, and which idea emerged relatively strong at a particular time depended on the liking and disliking of the autocratic ruler. But, to the extent that it was treated as the official ruling ideology one dynasty after another, Confucianism had produced an impact on Chinese society and culture which is unparalleled throughout Chinese history. It is largely in this sense that Confucianism is commonly regarded as the crystallization of the Chinese politico-cultural tradition.

THE STRUCTURE

It has been often noted that Confucianism is for the most part an ethical doctrine. It focuses on practical reason and adopts a human-centered approach to moral and political questions. It rarely deals with abstract and metaphysical ideas, but always has as its fundamental concern the ethical standards governing the relationship between the individual and the family, between the individual and society, and between individuals themselves. While the point is well taken, it needs to be stressed also that this human-centered outlook is undergirded by a particular conception of human beings, one which had its roots in an earlier clan-based society. It is true that Confucius was able to transcend that society in several important respects; for example, he distanced himself from one of the central concerns of the previous ages, namely the role of gods and spirits in human life.[9] But for the most part Confucius was a conservative thinker, albeit a highly innovative one, in the strict sense of the word. He wanted to conserve a nearly lost tradition, one which in his view had laid the very foundation of his own society. In this regard, it is not satisfactory merely to say that the vestiges of the clan-based society lingered on in Confucius' thought. The point is rather that the ideas, beliefs, and institutional arrangements of that society were well integrated into Confucianism.

The historical tradition which Confucius sought so enthusiastically to preserve was founded on a clan-based and blood-related society. This society was created through war and conquest. It was organized on the basis of a set of hierarchical rules defining the scope of authority, social classes and individual roles. At the top of the social and political hierarchy was the sovereign ruler or the son of heaven as he was called. The ruler had in his sole possession all the land, and people living on this land were all seen as his subjects.[10] He divided the land and leased it to his blood relatives who were lords in their own jurisdiction, and these lords in turn each subleased it to lower ranking aristocrats. The process went on through still lower ranking aristocrats until the land was finally in the hands of the tiller, that is, the common people. This system of land division tied each individual, whether of an aristocratic or a common origin, closely to, and indeed made him totally dependent on, the social and political hierarchy.[11] In keeping with these institutional arrangements, there was a system of clan rules or *Li* (rituals) which helped define the kind of role individual members were expected to play in society. This system of clan rules or *Li* was believed to have been composed by Zhou Gong, one of the most prominent rulers in the Zhou kingdom. For this reason it was often referred to as the rules of Zhou or *Zhou Li*. At least three features are characteristic of the Zhou clan society.

First, ancestor worship was one of the most important aspects of clan life. In fact, the word "clan" in Chinese originally means place of worship and sacrifice. The function of ancestor worship was twofold. It helped both to legitimate clan authorities in the name of the sacredness of ancestry and to create a common bond holding the blood-based community together. "Ancestry is the basis of the clan," says Xun Zi.[12] Second, clan rules were rigid and meticulous, ranging from funeral wear to ways of greeting to succession of the throne and of course ancestor worship. These rules evolved and congealed into a set of basic ethical principles which could be applied ubiquitously to all areas of social and political life. The logical development of clan rules into basic ethical principles may be illustrated in the following way. If one cares for one's blood relatives, one must also be capable of respecting one's ancestors and clan. This will generate love for one's community, which in turn creates just laws, peace, wealth, and finally happiness.[13] Third, political rule was deemed as a divinely sanctioned mission. In order to fulfill this mission, the ruler should rule by virtue and in accordance with the standards of *Li;* he should use punishment carefully and sparingly. The highest virtue was for him to protect and nourish the people. Heaven created the ruler for the people rather than the people for him.[14]

The Zhou clan society lasted for several hundred years before it began to disintegrate. In its stead there arose the increasingly strong vassal lords in pursuit of their hegemonic ambitions. The result was a period of chaos. The era of Spring and Autumn (770–476 B.C.) in which Confucius lived witnessed a large number of instances of regicide and patricide. The clan rules as encapsulated in the notion of *Li* broke down. When, for example, Confucius saw eight rows of pantomimes in the courtyard of the Ji family, he was furious, because this behavior grossly violated the traditional rule according to which eight rows of pantomimes were reserved only for the son of heaven, not a family like the Ji.[15] It was in response to the breakdown of *Li* and ultimately for restoring a legitimate moral and political order that Confucius took on himself the task of reviving and renovating the clan-based tradition.

One of the conceptual tools which Confucius used for accomplishing this task was the concept of *Li*. From a semantic perspective, the word "Li" in Chinese denotes a container used for sacrificial purposes. It is a symbol which connects the heaven, ancestry, and community together in an unbroken chain of meaning. The importance of the rules and standards as congealed into the idea of *Li* lies not only in the fact that they regulate personal and social conduct; they are vital also because they help maintain the hierarchical structure of society and legitimate political authority. The Confucianist's explanation of the origin of *Li* typically emphasized that it was the wise kings of the past, Zhou Gong in particular, who created the existing set of rules and standards assigning duties and obligations to each member of society. Xun Zi offered a plausible theory of its origin on the basis of his understanding of the depraved nature of man.

> Men are born with desires. If these desires are not met, men cannot but pursue their satisfaction. Unrestrained pursuit only leads to conflict, and conflict to chaos, which in turn gives rise to destitution. The wise kings hated chaos, so they instituted the rules of decorum and righteousness, dividing men into different ranks and classes and enabling them to satisfy their desires and pursuits according to these ranks and classes.[16]

This view of the origin of *Li* was not uniformly shared by all Confucian thinkers. Mencius, for one, held that the rules of *Li* originated in the goodness of humanity, in particular in the feeling of modesty and congeniality.[17] But when it comes to the function of the rules of *Li,* few seem to disagree that they are fundamentally important in maintaining the social and political order and cultivating personality. Confucius saw them as providing the basis for being a good person. "Without knowing the rules of *Li*," he says, "it is unfit for one to live in society."[18] In a similar vein, Xun Zi regarded the idea of *Li* as the guiding principle of politics and government.[19] Perhaps the most thorough understanding of the function of *Li* is found in the *Book of Rituals:*

> The rules of *Li* function to discriminate between close and remote social relations, clear doubts and questions about propriety, ascertain the identity and difference of family origins, and determine the rightness and wrongness of action. . . . Without the rules of *Li,* it is not possible to cultivate *Tao,* virtue, benevolence, and righteousness; nor to carry on education and rectify improper practices; nor to pass judgments in conflicts and litigations; nor to differentiate the sovereign from his officials, superiors from inferiors, father from son, and older brother from younger brother; nor to define the standing of officials in front of the sovereign, lead the army, appoint officials, and enforce the law in a solemn way; and nor to pray and sacrifice to the ghosts and spirits earnestly and honestly.[20]

The rules of *Li* acquired a paramount status not unlike that of a modern-day constitution. In fact, they furnished a code of conduct which governs public as well as private life. In this regard, the concept of *Li* should not be seen merely as an ethical category; it is more importantly a social and political category.[21] Indeed, it is a total way of life. For this reason, Confucius warned his disciples that if something was not permitted by *Li,* no one ought to listen to, look at, talk about, or touch it.[22]

This way of life may be placed in fuller and clearer perspective when one examines the minute details of the contents of *Li*. The fastidiousness and comprehensiveness with which the rules and standards were prescribed under the rubric of *Li* were remarkable; one cannot help but marvel at both the ingenuity and the rigidity of the ancient Chinese. These rules and standards governed every utterance and every move of the individual; they specified how one should walk, speak, eat, drink, smile, cry, and even have sexual intercourse; they regulated who should enter the door first, sit in a given seat, and drive a five-horse-pulled carriage; and they dictated also how people should get married, sacrifice to ancestry, and commence wine-drinking and other festivals. Xun Zi summed all this up in the following way. The idea of *Li,* he said, was to show deference to those in higher social positions, to be filial and obedient to those in old age, to love and care for the young, and to be charitable to those of an inferior class.[23] As historians inform us, the meticulously detailed rules as specified by *Li* have provided structural principles for the administrative system of successive dynasties.[24] But it seems to me that far more important is the enormous and long-term impact they have had on the individual's personal and social life, and on the way he or she lived, acted, and thought. No matter what his or her origin was, aristocratic or common, the individual was tightly bound by the rules, duties and imperatives of *Li* to his or her role in society.

The centrality of the concept of *Li* to Confucius and, for that matter, to the entire Chinese politico-cultural tradition has been widely recognized, but it is not the only concept that structures Confucian thought. There is another important notion, namely *Ren* (benevolence), which Confucius used extensively and his disciples, particularly Mencius, regarded as the foundational principle of Confucianism. Like *Li*, the concept of *Ren* was not Confucius' invention, but he reformulated and enriched it in such a way that it came to embody the very essence of Confucianism in the eyes of many.[25] Unlike *Li*, however, it was extremely elusive in meaning. In the *Analects*, Confucius gave different answers to the question of what *Ren* was in different contexts and to different people, and even to the same person the answer was different each time. Sometimes the concept referred to certain moral qualities or virtues such as kindness, honesty, and diligence; other times it signified a universal love for humankind; and still other times it implied a sense of conformity with the rules of *Li* on both a personal and a political level. Li Zehou has identified four basic characteristics of *Ren*: blood-based relations, psychological requirement, humanism, and cultivation of personality.[26]

In the first place, ambiguous as it may be, *Ren* is not a substanceless notion. Rather, it has as its immediate object the idea of *Li*. For Confucius, as for later-day Confucianists, the essence of *Ren* was to restrain one's own desires and conform to the rules and standards as specified by *Li*.[27] It is thus not surprising that Confucius regarded filial piety as the basis of *Ren*.[28] As has been noted, these rules and standards are rooted in a blood-based clan society, and they govern the way in which members of that society relate to one another personally *and* politically. It is in this sense that the idea of *Ren* can be said to be grounded in blood-based relations.

Secondly, though the idea of *Ren* is manifested in and realized through the acting out of the idea of *Li*, it is not identical with the latter. What distinguishes the two is the fact that *Ren* has an important psychological component. While *Li* presents itself as a set of external rules and prescriptions, *Ren* is characterized by a process of internalization of such rules and prescriptions and by a psychological "fit" between one's own desires and needs, on the one hand, and the ethical requirements of society, on the other. It emphasizes the inner dimension of human life, one which, in Confucius' view, fundamentally separates humanity from the animal world. This emphasis in turn allows the idea of *Ren* to acquire a quasi-religious status.

Thirdly, *Ren* is also undergirded by a strong sense of humanism. When asked by one of his disciples what *Ren* was, Confucius answered that "it is to love man."[29] This general love should not, however, be equated with the Mohist's altruistic and unqualified love of all regardless of social rank and position. Neither should it be treated as a transcendent and metaphysical idea as found in the Song and Ming dynasty neo-Confucianists. Instead, it should be understood in the context of a slow yet steady movement away from a gods-and-spirits-dominated to a human-centered world. It should also be understood against the background of an awakening of humanity against inhuman practices of the time such as massive war killings and companion burial.

Fourthly, *Ren* emphasizes the cultivation of personal virtues, and such cultivation requires the individual's own efforts. For the Confucianist, personal virtues provide the basis for an ordered moral and political life. A good person is someone equipped with *Ren;* and only a person equipped with *Ren* can successfully manage the family, run the state, and govern everything under the heaven. Thus, cultivating virtuous personality becomes the ultimate goal for anyone who wants to live a good life. Indeed, it becomes one's responsibility to fulfill whatever the idea of *Ren* dictates. "Man of virtue and determination will not seek to live by damaging *Ren;*" says Confucius, "rather, he will sacrifice his life to preserve *Ren*."[30] This sense of responsibility is evident in many of Confucius' teachings on *Ren*.

Li's analysis of *Ren*, I believe, provides a valuable framework for understanding this elusive notion. However, it also raises some important questions. At least two such questions deserve special attention because they have direct bearing on the central argument of this study about the nature of the Chinese politico-cultural tradition. The first question is concerned with the relationship between the idea of *Ren* and that of *Li*, and the second with the implications the cultivation of personality has for the conception of the self.

The close relationship between the idea of *Ren* and that of *Li* has been widely recognized by students of Confucianism. It is not difficult to see that the four basic features of *Ren* which Li Zehou has outlined above are connected with *Li* in such a way that it is impossible to talk about one without talking about the other. As Li has argued, for example, the rules and standards as specified by *Li* form the basis of *Ren*. However, while not hesitating to recognize the important role both notions play in Confucius' moral and political thought, many critics, including Li, tend to assign priority to

Ren and relegate *Li* to a subordinate place. They tend to view *Ren* and *Li* as graded or ranked, with the former in a higher order of importance than the latter. They argue that it is *Ren,* rather than *Li* or the unity of them, that constitutes the core of Confucianism.[31] This, I believe, is an inadequate view, because it seriously undermines our understanding of the concept of *Li* in shaping the Chinese politico-cultural tradition. Rather than arrange *Ren* and *Li* in a hierarchical order, it seems more appropriate to see them as signifying a dialectic relationship of complementarity and interdependence. They presuppose and imply each other, and form a unified whole. By taking this dialectic view, we can obtain a more balanced understanding of the idea of *Ren* as it pertains to the making of the Chinese politico-cultural tradition. The idea of *Ren* has never been an independent and transcendental standard which guides personal and political conduct, but has always been in close contact with the idea of *Li.* It is not some abstract moral ideal which constitutes the ultimate criterion for evaluating the performance of the ruler and the ruled, but rather is deeply rooted in and expressed by the concrete rules and standards of society. It is first and foremost an ethical doctrine which stipulates the duties and obligations required of each member of society.

Two levels of application of the idea of *Ren* will help clarify this point. On the political level, the idea of *Ren* is translated into an argument for benevolent politics. Although many strands of thought go into the composition of this argument, its basic tenet may be described as "rule by virtue." Benevolence as a political virtue emerged earlier in the Zhou kingdom,[32] but it was Confucius and later Mencius who made it the centerpiece of Confucian moral and political thought. While the Legalist assigned enormous weight to the use of penal law and the Taoist to naturalism and nonaction, Confucius maintained that the ruler's personal virtue laid the foundation for good government. "He who rules by virtue may be compared to the north polar star;" he says, "it is well situated in its place with all the stars looking up to it."[33] It is worth noting that the very word "politics," according to Confucius, denotes correctness. A virtuous ruler sets a virtuous example for the ruled to follow, and a virtuous people would self-consciously and willingly obey and act by the rules and standards of society. Consequently, there is no need for law and punishment to enforce those rules and standards. True obedience comes only from the heart, not from threat and force.[34] The Confucian political ideal which captured the imagination of generations of rulers in dynastic China, thus, begins with cultivation of virtuous personality; and with virtuous personality in place, all—managing the family, running the state, and governing everything under the heaven—will follow automatically.[35]

But virtue is not an abstract and contentless concept. In Confucius' view, virtuous conduct clearly presupposes a set of criteria. To be virtuous is to act by or conform to certain preexisting rules and standards of conduct, and the rules and standards with which Confucius and his disciples were concerned, as has been discussed, are firmly grounded in the idea of *Li*. To rule benevolently, thus, is simply to extend *Li* into the practice of government. It is the duty of the ruler to rule as it is the duty of the ruled to obey, and the ruler should conduct himself in a way that is proper to his autocratic position as the ruled should function properly in their capacity as filial subjects.[36] In a nutshell, to act properly is in the fundamental sense to fulfill the duties and obligations prescribed by one's ascribed role in a hierarchically structured and clan-based society.

On the personal level, the idea of *Ren* is best understood as an internalized and self-imposed code of conduct. It manifests itself in interpersonal requirements and social obligations. It may be of interest to note that the word "*Ren*" stands for two people closely related. This suggests in part why Confucius and later Mencius defined it as affection or love. For Confucius, *Ren* is composed of five personal virtues: respectfulness, generosity, sincerity, diligence, and kindness. The cultivation of the five virtues will enable one to sail smoothly through life. "Respectfulness will not be returned with disrespect; generosity will earn the support of many people; sincerity will win others' trust; diligence will help one accomplish much; and kindness will enable one to employ others' service."[37] But these virtues are not vague or general requirements as they appear to be at first; like benevolence, they are firmly based on the rules and standards of *Li*. To be respectful, for example, is to act in accordance with certain behavioral requirements as specified by *Li*. These requirements, as mentioned earlier, were handed down from a blood-based clan society and meticulously recorded in the *Book of Rituals*. Without knowledge of the rules of *Li*, Confucius remarked, respectfulness would become laboriousness, prudence timidity, bravery unruliness, and candor rudeness.[38]

This consideration makes it clear that the notions of *Ren* and *Li* are interdependent and mutually reinforcing. They should not be seen as independent of each other or structurally graded, with the former in a higher order of importance than the latter. Rather, they are interlinked and form a complete whole, and an adequate understanding of the idea of *Ren* cannot be rendered without at the same time invoking the idea of *Li*. In both Confucius' and Mencius' words, filial piety and fraternal affection, which are considered as a part of *Li*, provide the basis for *Ren*.[39] While *Li* is an external expression of *Ren*, *Ren* is an internalized form of *Li*. To achieve *Ren*, therefore, one must go through this process of internalization; merely knowing or posting the rules *Li* is not enough. The breakdown of these rules which Confucius witnessed in his own time confirms this point. It is not that violators were unaware of the existence and even the value of *Li,* but that they did not take it into their heart. One must therefore cultivate it constantly and self-consciously, and absorb it into one's personality, into one's very being. In this sense, internalization is self-cultivation; it is a way of individualizing and imposing upon oneself the rules and duties of *Li.*

This immediately leads to the second question, namely the cultivation of personality. The idea of personality cultivation is crucial to the Confucianist *Renism* (for lack of a better word to describe the study and thought of *Ren*). It devolves ethical duties and responsibilities completely on the individual by encouraging self-awareness and self-scrutiny. Ultimately, what it aims at achieving is a perfect or ideal personality, one which is commensurable with the moral requirements prescribed by the notion of *Ren*. In cases where the pursuit of this goal demands that one sacrifice one's worldly interest or even one's life, one ought to be prepared to do so. This aspect of Confucianism has provided the source for a pattern of heroism and idealism throughout Chinese history, particularly in times of national crisis. It has also led many to conclude that the idea of self-cultivation signifies the emergence of a self-conscious claim for the individual's independence and autonomy.[40] Indeed, some even go so far as to assert that Confucianism, or certain parts of it, are logically connected to modern democratic thought and bear a close affinity with the Western liberal tradition.[41]

This view, I believe, is overstated. It is true that Confucianism in both the classical and the new form registered important concerns about the individual. The question is whether such concerns in fact amount to individualism and liberalism. Some think they do. Wm. Theodore de Bary, for one, argues that the ideas of learning for one's self, self-development, and self-discipline found in the writings of neo-Confucianists in the Song and Ming dynasties as well as in Confucius' own teachings closely resemble those that are constitutive of the individualism we have seen in the modern West. He maintains that the institution of locally run schools and community compact under the auspices of the Song neo-Confucianist Zhu Xi and others signifies a liberal democratic tradition that is consistent with the one found in Western liberal democracies.[42] There are several problems with this argument. Two of them are worthy of close attention. First, the evidence de Bary has garnered in support of his thesis is dubious. Take for example community compact. De Bary describes it as "the establishment of stable self-regulating local communities through the leadership of an educated moral elite that encouraged self-discipline, mutual respect and assistance, voluntary efforts, and joint rituals to provide for the needs of the community as a whole."[43] This description is a bit misleading, because it fails to consider a number of crucial elements, such as the kinship family and the dominant role of local elites, which helped in a fundamental way define the nature of community compact.[44] Even if one accepts de Bary's account as valid, one may still find it problematic to treat the features of the compact as constitutive of a liberal democratic tradition—unless, of course, one is willing to engage in concept stretching.

Secondly, to say that some ideas contained in Confucianism may be extracted and further developed into a coherent doctrine of individualism is different from saying that they are manifestly constitutive of it. To obtain a plausible account of individualism, it is not enough to study isolated philosophical ideas. One must also take into consideration the larger context in which these ideas are embedded. This context covers a broad range of issues, such as the nature and basis of government, the moral and political status of the individual in society, and particularly the purpose, institutional processes and substantive rules of self-cultivation. In the absence of these considerations, any talk about "Confucian individualism" is bound to be radically incomplete, if not entirely mistaken.

If one takes a close look at this larger context, one cannot help but be struck by the fact that the cultivation of perfect or ideal personality has never been pursued independently of a particular conception of the individual, society and government, of the basic social institutions such as the family, and of the rules and duties as specified by the idea of *Li*. There has always been a social or political or familial meaning attached to it or underlying it. In other words, self-cultivation has never been a wholly individual matter in the sense in which, say, Luther proclaimed the priesthood of all believers, Descartes asserted the idea of a thinking substance, and Kant devised his rational and self-sufficient moral legislator. Presumably for this reason, Yu Yingshi, one of the most reputable cultural historians writing today, is careful not to conflate individualism and personalism, although he also assumes that self-cultivation is an indication of the Confucian emphasis on the inner value of the individual. While the former is a uniquely Western notion and may not be a very useful tool for unraveling the nature of the Chinese cultural tradition, the latter term is in his view more appropriate for describing the Confucianist pursuit of an ideal type of personality.[45]

As I have argued, cultivation of the ideal personality in Confucianism presupposes a detailed set of rules and standards. What it seeks to develop is not an ontologically distinct and autonomous and morally self-sufficient being. Rather, it takes as its fundamental concern the proper role which each duty-bound and self-denying individual should play in a hierarchically structured society. In the strictest sense, the idea of the individual does not exist in the Confucianist moral and political context. A person is in the first instance a role-player in the interconnectedness of social rules and responsibilities. An abstract and natural man who possesses presocial and prepolitical rights in the Hobbesian and Lockean sense has never been a possibility for the Confucian, for such a person, in the view of Confucius and later Mencius, would be no different from a beast.

The twin notions of *Ren* and *Li* have provided the basic conceptual framework in which a nonindividualistic politico-cultural tradition was to flourish. According to this tradition, the essence of the individual is not defined by some universally derived and inherent human qualities that are believed to exist independently of social relations. Rather, it is defined by how one individual relates to another in his or her ethical role as a member of society, and by how each individual fulfills the duties and responsibilities attached to such role. While *Li* prescribes the substantive rules and standards for personal and political conduct, *Ren* requires each person to internalize them in a continual process of self-cultivation. The dialectic relationship between *Li* and *Ren* has provided the dynamics for the development of the Chinese politico-cultural tradition.

THE PRACTICE

Despite the fact that it never ceased to evolve and change, Confucianism as an ethical and political doctrine has maintained remarkable stability and continuity for more than two millennia. The twin pillars on which such stability and continuity rest are the notions of *Li* and *Ren*. It is these two notions that have played an enormously influential role in shaping the Chinese politico-cultural tradition. Within the framework of this tradition, the individual is typically and in the first instance considered a constitutive part of a larger and hierarchically structured entity, be it the family, the village, or the nation as a whole. From the time of birth, each person is woven into an intricate web of social relations and expected to perform certain duties and responsibilities that are believed to be naturally bound up with his or her place in these relations. Each person is encouraged to strive for personal and social prominence, but such prominence is thought of as a way of bringing status and glory to his or her family, clan, or village; it also creates an obligation on the individual's part to assume moral leadership, and to inculcate and reinforce those rules and values which have guided him or her to success. It is in this sense that we may be permitted to say that an individualistic way of relating is radically missing in the Chinese politico-cultural context.

This description is no mere theoretical conjecture; it has been strongly supported by a variety of empirical studies in various social science disciplines. An anthropological study half a century ago, for example, documented in stunning detail how Confucian values informed and governed the family and clan life of a small town in a remote province in southwestern China.[46] The work done by a sociologist in the Yangtze River valley a decade earlier produced an identical account of village life.[47] These studies have provided a vivid picture of what it means to be an individual living in the Confucianist moral and political order. A close reading of them also suggests that the best way to observe Confucianism at work is to study the family—to examine how it is perceived, structured, and managed.

The importance of the family to Chinese society—here the term "family" is defined broadly to include both a single household and its extended form, namely the clan—has been well known. Yu Yingshi argues that any theory of the Chinese cultural tradition must take into account two basic elements; one is the individual and the other is the family (*Jia*). He observes that larger collective entities such as the clan, the nation, and the universe are mere expansions of the family; and town organizations, religious bodies and secret societies are no exceptions.[48] The vital role the family has played in molding the Chinese mentality can be seen in at least three respects. First of all, the family is the most natural and the most basic form of human association, and in all likelihood the only one, that the Chinese individual ever knows throughout his or her life, particularly in premodern times. It provides emotional, educational, and moral as well as material support. Secondly, the family is also the most basic unit, and the most effective form, of social control; its maintenance and stability directly affect the peace and continuity of the nation. For this reason, nearly all dynastic rulers from the Han dynasty onward paid close attention to the strengthening of the family through the dissemination of Confucian teachings, especially those about filial piety and fraternal affection, through the issuing of imperial edicts or injunctions, and ultimately through the use of force.[49] Thirdly, from a political standpoint, the family as a self-contained and self-sufficient entity is a small kingdom in its own right, with its own authority structures and laws. In fact, the Zhou kingdom which preceded the first Chinese empire Qin by more than half a millennium was no more than a large family. This model of political rule on the basis of family blood ties has been duplicated, at least insofar as the imperial power was concerned, one dynasty after another until the turn of this century. It may be of interest to note that the names of administrative officials, especially those of the prime minister, in successive dynasties were originally those of the clan leader's house keepers in charge of immolation, treasury, kitchen, transportation, security and so forth.[50] For these reasons, traditional China is often considered an enlarged copy of the family. The family, thus, provides the most appropriate institutional setting for discussing Confucianism and the Chinese politico-cultural tradition.

While it is fairly safe to say that we cannot have an adequate understanding of the Chinese politico-cultural tradition without an adequate understanding of the family, it remains to be seen whether and to what extent Confucian values dominated or at least influenced the way individuals conducted themselves in the family. In other words, we need to know how the family represented and applied the twin ideas of Confucianism, namely *Li* and *Ren*. Evidence regarding these issues can be gleaned from two types of analysis based on recent scholarship on the Chinese family; one is historical and the other anthropological. The historical analysis focuses on the nature, origin and function of the family in medieval China, specifically in the Song and Ming dynasties. This period is said to have created the traditional family form as we know it up till the middle of this last century. The anthropological study offers a real-life description of the actual working of the family through participant observation, interviews and content analyses. It also gives confirmation to the findings of the historian.

In perhaps the most thorough historical study of the family in dynastic China to date, Xu Yangjie points out that the family has undergone roughly three forms throughout Chinese history. The first was the clan family system in the pre-Qin ages. Extant records show that the Western Zhou kingdom had a well-designed and comprehensive system of clan rules. In terms of the structure of political power alone, this system devised a complicated yet strictly observed scheme of dividing political power on the basis of the blood-based relations and of the closeness or remoteness of such relations. The Zhou kingdom can be conceived, thus, as a giant family containing layers and layers of vertically and horizontally interlinked medium and small families.[51] This system began to fall apart in the era of Spring and Autumn but lingered on well into the Han dynasty.[52] The second was the patrician family system which flourished between the late Eastern Han and the Tang dynasty in the early medieval period. Its main feature was that a powerful landowner incorporated through political and economic means into a manorial estate a large number of small households who shared (though with exceptions) the same family name. The family members leased land from the patrician, but did not have to contribute income tax to the national treasury because they were not listed in the national registrar. In a sense, they were privately owned indentured tenants with no personal freedom.[53]

The third form of the family began to emerge in the middle of the medieval period. It would become the model for the next millennium. To distinguish it from the clan system, we may call it the kinship family system. The kinship family, though differing in several important ways from the previous two, was also undergirded by the same blood ties and the same set of values. It has at least four notable features. First, there was a common male ancestor to worship and a place to conduct such worship; second, a multigenerational family made up of a number of single households sharing the same surname lived together, typically with a patriarch as the head; third, each family was a self-sufficient economic unit with its own land, and several such units formed a village; and fourth, each family had a genealogical book in which the family's glorious past was recorded; and the book also contained a set of rules to regulate the conduct of family members. The genealogical book was handed down from one generation to next, and family rules were enforced within the family independently, but with the sanctions, of imperial laws.[54]

Although the forms of the family changed over time, yet their underlying values and norms remained remarkably stable. This stability can be attributed in part to their promulgation and enforcement by dynastic rulers. But it is also due in part to the Confucianists' efforts to inculcate and disseminate these values and norms for the consolidation of the family. This is precisely what the neo-Confucianists did in an attempt to rejuvenate Confucianism. As Yu Dunkang forcefully argues, the neo-Confucianists may disagree with the Buddhists, the Taoists, or the Mohists, and they may disagree with early Confucianists and with each other on important philosophical issues, but when it comes to filial piety and fraternal affection, to the hierarchical structure and rules of the family, and to the conception of the family as the cornerstone of society, they expressed surprisingly little disagreement with the other intellectual persuasions. What is more remarkable, they furnished no innovative idea whatsoever of their own on this issue. Neo-Confucianists such as Zhang Zai, Cheng Hao, Cheng Yi, Zhu Xi and Lu Jiuyuan all gave overwhelming emphasis to the idea of filial piety and other rules and duties specified by *Li* as the basis of a good society.[55] Some, Zhu Xi for one, not only compiled the rules and norms specifically for the reconstruction or consolidation of the family, but also had a detailed working manual for how to administer sacrifice, maintain the temple, use the family land, and run other day-to-day rituals. It was largely on the model designed by Zhu Xi that kinship families would be built in the three dynasties to come.[56]

The kinship family as handed down from the Song dynasty, like the two types that had preceded it, was an ensemble of hierarchically structured relations. It had two forms of its own; one was the big family with multi-generational members living together and the other a collection of single-household families bound by a common male ancestor. Despite their superficial differences, the structures and values underlying the two were virtually the same. Within the hierarchy of the kinship family, authority was typically invested in a patriarch; in the father or grandfather if it was a large family and in a male leader if it was the collective form. The patriarch held enormous powers, just as a father did in a natural family, over family members; these powers covered a wide range of affairs from large decisions such as ancestral worship, distribution of land and punishment of deviant behavior to small matters such as the naming of a newborn. It should be noted that the patriarch who ruled the kinship family in its collective form was in a formal sense elected on the basis of virtue, age, wealth, and talent; he could also be appointed by the incumbent leader. But we should be careful not to conflate such election with its modern meaning, for not only was there not the kind of process that is often associated with the election we know now, but once "elected," the patriarch would wield his power as he saw fit and without restraint. In reality, the patriarchal position was usually held by wealthy landowners or the literati, and the average peasant had no chance to be "elected."[57]

Essentially three elements served as a binding force to hold the kinship family together: the temple of ancestor worship, the genealogical book, and the family land. While the land physically bound the family to one place by providing the material means of living for its members, the temple and the book functioned in a symbolic way to enhance the blood-based relations, creating a common bond among members and justifying the carrying out of the family rules of punishment and reward. It cannot be overemphasized that the temple played a vitally important role in kinship life. It was regarded as the center of the family; it housed the protective spirit of the ancestor, symbolized kinship solidarity, and served as a pulpit for preaching virtues and rules. It was also used as a court of law for enforcing family rules.[58] But, in the first instance, the temple was a place for ancestor worship.

Ancestor worship was the most fundamental of all activities in kinship family life. It was a quasi-religious phenomenon in that it did not have a systematic belief in a universally recognized God. It was particularistic, practical, and this-worldly. Insofar as recorded history is concerned, the institution of ancestor worship can be traced to Western Zhou more than two and half millennia ago. Since its inception, it has had an extraordinarily powerful grip on the Chinese mind, thanks in large measure to the Confucian teachings. Based on a field study in a southwestern Chinese town called West Town, Hsu's work has offered one of the most illuminating accounts of how ancestor worship became the basic organizing principle for kinship family life. A similar, though less thorough, account has been found in Fei's field work in a southeastern Chinese village. There Fei has found that the duty which the living owed to their dead ancestors was manifold, ranging from propagation of posterity to submission to parental authority to the maintaining of the integrity of the family land. In a recent study of country life in a northern region, a group of social scientists have discovered that though its religious character was not as apparent as was the case with West Town, ancestor worship was a widespread and critical component of peasant life.[59] Even today, after decades of campaigns to uproot it under the Communist reign, ancestor worship remains alive and well.[60]

The purposes of ancestor worship were mainly three. First, it reminded family members that the spirit of the ancestor lived on, guiding and protecting each of his offspring and spurring them on to accomplish great deeds for the glorification of the family. Second, it served as a symbolic force around which the entire family would rally and unite; it did so by inducing a strong sense of blood-related commonality and sharedness. Third, it was designed to educate the young in virtuous conduct such as filial piety and fraternal affection and prepare them for assuming their role in adult life.[61] Ancestor worship was not merely a sacrificial, socializing, and educational event, however; it was also an important occasion to remind kinsmen of the hierarchically structured power relations, of the difference between virtuous and punishable behavior, and of the duties and responsibilities assigned to each position in the family hierarchy. If the general goal of ancestor worship was to strive for and maintain the unity of the family, as Hsu aptly puts it, such unity was achieved "not so much by a better adjustment of the many personalities involved as by a gradual inculcation in the individual of his or her place in the kinship hierarchy."[62]

The reading and revision of the genealogical book was also an important part of kinship family life. The book contained not only the origin, lineage, number of people, ownership of land, and past honors of the family, but also a set of rules by which the family was governed. These rules are of special interest here because they reveal how the Confucian values penetrated the life of the average individual and dictated the way in which he or she was to conduct himself or herself in and outside the kinship family. The emphasis on blood-based relations and on the idea of the family is itself an implicit indication of the impact of Confucianism. But the family rules endorse Confucian values in such an explicit way that one cannot but be led to conclude that such influence was not only present but immensely powerful.

In analyzing the rules of the family, Liu points out that the ethical values underlying them were not composed of Confucian teachings alone, for they also embraced Taoist and Buddhist teachings as well as the imperial laws and the social customs of the day. But the Confucian classics were clearly a predominant presence in the construction of kinship rules. The most important of all the ancient Confucian classics cited by the kinship family rules was, not surprisingly, the *Book of Rituals*. Where other classics were quoted, Liu notes, emphasis was placed on the idea of *Li* and on those aspects of Confucianism which were associated with the concept of filial piety and fraternal affection.[63] The first virtue which the individual should acquire was in every single case "to render filial piety to your parents." This was the case with the Six Injunctions issued by the founder of Ming dynasty and also the case with the Thirteen Injunctions issued by Kang Xi, emperor of Qing dynasty, in 1670.[64] If we turn to West Town or Eastern Hebei Province, we find that filial piety was the most basic of all the virtues to be cultivated within the kinship family regardless of one's social status.[65]

It may be useful to reacquaint ourselves here with the fundamental role which the notion of filial piety has played in Confucianist moral and political thought. Hu Shi, one of the most respected intellectual voices on ancient Chinese thought last century (and incidentally a student of John Dewey), argues that filial piety was not so much a crucial concept for Confucius as for his disciples. He suggests that while the essence of Confucius' thought may be captured by the concept of *Ren,* his disciples, particularly Zeng Zi, abandoned it for the notion of filial piety and took the latter as the centerpiece of Confucianism. As a consequence, the value of the individual as embedded in the conception of *Ren* was largely lost.[66] Hu Shi is correct in pointing out the gradual ascendance of the notion of filial piety, but he is incorrect in assuming that this idea is not as essential to Confucius as is the concept of *Ren.* It is even more inadequate for him not to call attention to the close connection between the concept of filial piety and that of *Ren.* For Confucius, the basis of *Ren* is precisely filial piety.[67] What his disciples did was merely to elaborate on the spirit of a doctrine firmly entrenched in Confucius' thought.

In all the Confucian classics that deal with the issue of ethics and politics and, as mentioned earlier, in the writings of prominent neo-Confucianists, the notion of filial piety clearly occupies a much larger place than Hu Shi has suggested.[68] It is true that the term "filial piety" appears only nineteen times in the *Analects;* in contrast, the concept of *Ren* appears more than one hundred times. But this should not obscure the facts that 1) Confucius interpreted *Ren* in terms of filial piety; 2) filial piety was often implied in discussing the relationship between father and son, the sovereign and his subjects; and 3) some other concepts such as loyalty should be seen as an extension of this notion. In a strict sense, filial piety is merely one category under *Li,* but because of its enormous practical implications for the maintenance of social stability, it gradually became the most influential concept in Chinese family life. The meaning of being filial is multi-layered, depending on the relationship involved; but at its core is a strong emphasis on submission to authority, parental, kinship or imperial. Such submission was based not on the persuasiveness of moral truths or the consideration of utilitarian interests, but merely on the position or sex into which one was born in the family. In other words, it was unconditional and total submission. The most basic of all filial behaviors in the family was the son's submission to the father; on the basis of this were built the wife's submission to the husband, kinsmen's submission to the patriarch, young people's submission to the elderly, the inferior's submission to the superior, and finally the subjects' submission to the sovereign ruler.[69]

With filial piety comes unconditional and total submission, and with submission there ensues a stable moral and political order. Confucius saw this clearly: "It is rare that those who are filial to their parents and have fraternal affection for their older brothers are predisposed to offend their superiors; and none of those who do not offend their superiors is seen to have caused unrest."[70] For this reason, it was in the acute interest of both family patriarchs and imperial rulers to promote and protect the practice of filial piety. In the *Book of Filial Piety,* it was said that "there are three thousand offenses under the five criminal categories, but the biggest of all crimes is disregard for filial piety."[71] As the biggest crime, disregard for filial piety was punished most severely; death by beheading was listed in the penal code as early as the Qin dynasty. After the Sui dynasty, it was deemed one of the most egregious evils beyond imperial pardon.[72]

Caught in the web of blood-based relationships and in the power hierarchy, the individual was anything but an independent and autonomous person. Each individual was born a father, a son, a wife, a husband, a kinsman, and a subject, and each was expected to fulfill the set of duties and responsibilities relative to any of these ascribed positions. No one should have secrets, privacy, opinion, will, career, or even life independent of the family, and there was absolutely nothing which could be considered the individual's own business. Self-cultivation served to maintain harmonious relations in the family and in society at large, and the individual's competition for social prominence was aimed at the glorification of one's ancestors. A person was in the strictest sense not an individual human being, but "part of the infinite continuum of the lineage."[73] He or she was an infinitesimally small cog accidentally placed in the giant and complex machine called tradition, and dependent on other cogs and ultimately on the entire machine for survival and meaning. This tradition, backed by the power of the state, in turn perpetuated in the individual a strong sense of his or her place in the family hierarchy; it inculcated in the individual a fatalistic sense of belonging to his or her blood-based social environment; and it also created a submissive personality which was incapable of dealing with a public life beyond the family. Here, once again, the anthropologist's findings are pertinent:

> The individual encounters comparatively little insecurity in life, but neither is he encouraged to make any plans of his own. He does not have to grope for his future, but he is also not equipped to meet new situations. He will certainly possess no means for seriously challenging the existing scheme of things. If and when the existing scheme of things has broken down, he will merely try to build up a new series of schemes in strict accord with the forms and principles defined and delimited by the recognized authority. Within the framework of tradition the individual behaves and works with the greatest of ease; outside the framework the individual is at a loss and puzzled at every turn. . . . Within the framework the individual is fortunate, lucky, and secure; outside, he becomes unfortunate, suffers, and is miserable and insecure. Since the individual has been trained to depend upon this framework for his every movement, it is obvious that only the eccentric will even dream of trying to question or improve it.[74]

Through the institution of the family, Confucianism as a complex ethical and political doctrine was able to penetrate the lives of ordinary people in traditional China. It has molded the Chinese individual into a duty-sensitive and relation-dependent person. Such a person is as far removed as imaginable from the conception of the individual as an independent truth seeker, a self-determining moral agent and a bearer of natural rights. It is primarily in this sense that one may be justified in saying that the Chinese politico-cultural tradition is nonindividualistic. It is worth noting also that the family should not be seen merely as an instrument for training the followers of the Confucian moral and political doctrine; it is the very embodiment of that doctrine. As mentioned earlier, the family has in the past provided not only the fundamental form of human association which functioned to meet the private needs of the Chinese as a people, but also a viable model of political rule. Beyond the family, there has been literally no political or public life. In this regard, family culture is the essence of political culture. Thus, Confucian familism, with its emphasis on hierarchically structured human relations and on the values and beliefs that are perceived to be naturally embedded in these relations, can be said to constitute the core of the shared way of relating with respect to the ordering of collective affairs in premodern China.

QUASI-FAMILISM AND CONTEMPORARY POLITICAL CULTURE

For nearly two millennia, particularly since the medieval Song dynasty, Confucianism had been the dominant ideology in traditional China. As such, it played the most crucial role in shaping the mentality and conduct of the Chinese, both individually and as a collectivity. The primary institution that helped implement and consolidate the Confucian ideology, as we have noted, was the family. In the course of implementing and consolidating this ideology, the family as a political and economic as well as a social institution laid the cultural foundation for traditional Chinese society. This in part explains why anti-traditionalists in the May Fourth Movement at the turn of this century saw the family as the source of social and political evils and launched a vociferous cultural crusade against it. A similar crusade to dismantle the family and emancipate the individual from its repression later also became an important intellectual force that propelled the communist revolution.

If Confucian familism provides a paradigm for understanding the Chinese politico-cultural tradition, can the same paradigm be used to describe contemporary Chinese political culture? An answer to this question involves, in essence, consideration of the issue of cultural continuity and change. Although a clean break with the past as envisioned by Mao Zedong and others like him is unlikely to happen, the historical changes that have taken place since the demise of dynastic rule nevertheless render Confucian familism a problematic if not entirely obsolete theoretical model for the study of Chinese culture. An alternative conceptual framework, thus, is needed which would both capture the sense of continuity and account for change. In the last few decades, studies of contemporary Chinese political culture have typically been concerned with identifying and evaluating any number of salient yet largely disparate cultural traits, regardless of their differences in methodology.[75] These studies have clearly increased our knowledge of the many substantive features of Chinese political culture, but they have not been able to develop a coherent theoretical model which would integrate and make better sense of a diversity of cultural phenomena. As a consequence, what they have conveyed to the reader is often a fragmented and puzzling picture of a cultural landscape. Compounding this problem, moreover, is the fact that many of the studies make free inferences about contemporary political culture on the basis of China's Confucian past. They assume that there is a strong continuity between then and now, and believe that this continuity would allow one to explain today's social and political problems in terms of the tradition.[76] The result is often a reiteration of Confucianism with no adequate account of cultural change.

Though theoretical paradigms for understanding contemporary Chinese political culture are lacking, attempts have been made to locate key cultural values for analyzing the social and political behavior of the Chinese. Lucian Pye argues that the concept of patron-client relationship plays a central role in understanding the vitality of the Chinese political system.[77] Li Yiyuan suggests that the Chinese traditional concern with harmony and balance is crucial to explaining many of the industrial and commercial behaviors in contemporary Chinese societies.[78] Huang Guoguang and Ambrose Y.C. King call attention to some of the widely shared concepts, such as *Renqing* (personal obligation and affection), *Mianzi* (face), and *guanxi* (personal network), and stress their theoretical importance to the study of culture and society in contemporary China.[79] These considerations all point to a shared way of relating which shares with the basic values and practices of Confucian familism, yet also shows a few distinctly modern characteristics.

More than half a century ago, Fei Xiaotong, the founder of Chinese sociology, proposed a theoretical framework, *chaxugeju* (the differential and hierarchical categorization of social relationships), for understanding the cultural foundations of traditional Chinese society. According to Fei's translators, this kind of categorization has four main features. First, it presupposes multiple linkages of a hierarchically differentiated self with others, and these linkages form interpersonal ties or networks known as *guanxi*. The prototypical network in traditional China is the kinship family. Second, each tie is a specific category of human relationship the maintenance of which requires the reciprocal fulfillment of particularistic norms and obligations. Third, network membership is essentially ascribed rather than subscribed, although networks themselves have no explicit boundaries. Fourth, morality in such a network-based society is situation-dependent; that is, what is moral depends not on abstract and universally applicable principles, but on the situation and on the specific categories of social relationships in which the actor is involved.[80]

Fei's is a theory of traditional Chinese culture and society, but it is still of relevance today. This relevance has been shown by many other studies on contemporary Chinese culture, including those done by Pye, Li, Huang, and King mentioned above. What Fei could not foresee at the time are the historical changes that have resulted from the political and socio-economic reorganization of Chinese society after the communist takeover in 1949. These changes have in important ways reshaped the cultural configurations in contemporary China. The most important of all the changes, it seems to me, is the abolition of the traditional family. With the family transformed from a basic political and economic institution into an essentially reproductive unit closely controlled by the state, individual Chinese have been thrust into a cultural twilight zone between a public life that is entirely alien to them and a familiar shared way of relating that is vanishing.[81] Such cultural dislocation has created a situation in which traditional habits blend with modern practices to yield a peculiar form of political and cultural life. This form of political and cultural life, I propose, can be called a quasi-familistic one.

As a theoretical construct for understanding contemporary Chinese political culture, quasi-familism bears resemblance to Fei's theory of multiple linkages and reciprocal obligations. But it differs from the latter in one crucial respect, that is, that it does not gives cultural primacy to the family. As has been noted, the family as traditionally understood formally ceases to exist and can no longer provide the cultural basis for political rule after the founding of the People's Republic. This, however, is not to say that the values and practices underlying the traditional family have totally disappeared. On the contrary, many of them continue to govern or influence the way individual Chinese think and act. The concept of quasi-familism, I believe, comes close to capturing this continuity while at the same time remaining sensitive to cultural change.

A quasi-familistic culture may be characterized as a shared way of relating which involves the cultivation and maintenance of a family-like network of personal relationships. Of its important features, four need to be emphasized here in view of their impact on the political life of the Chinese. First of all, the underlying principle of quasi-familism is the primacy of personal ties. These ties are predominantly of a nonfamily nature, though family relationships still constitute a significant part of them. This is especially true in urban areas in contemporary China where there is neither the economic basis nor the physical space for the existence and reproduction of extended families. A multiplicity of personal ties give rise to a network, and the network weaves together separate individual lives into an intricate cultural web of mutual dependence, indebtedness, and obligations.

Second, quasi-familistic networks have no organizational structures, no clearly defined boundaries, and no publicly announced rules to follow. They are completely informal. Entry into networks is voluntary and requires no formal procedure. One can forge a network bond depending on one's own needs and desires and at one's own risk. One can also get involved in different or even opposing networks, as long as one is skillful enough to manage the tensions between them. Being a relative, classmate, colleague, neighbor, sharing the same place of birth, interest, profession, or simply doing someone a favor can all provide a base for network building. Moreover, networks can be cultivated vertically and horizontally, and there are no rigid lines dividing their practitioners into hierarchically ranked social classes.

This kind of informality makes quasi-familistic networks virtually invisible to those outside them. As a consequence of this lack of transparency, social relationships become subtle, intractable, and difficult to handle in the sense that intentions and sentiments are not always expressed openly and a great deal of guesswork is involved. No one knows exactly what connections another may have, and it would thus be imprudent and even dangerous to openly express differences with someone, for these differences may offend not only this particular person but his or her entire network of friends. This situation is particularly evident in the realm of politics where knowing the right person may launch one's political career but creating opponents means the end of it.

Third, network building is a person-to-person undertaking and requires no threshold of eligibility for practicing it. As such, it is accessible to anyone who wants to connect. The idea of being well connected to others beyond the family, particularly to those who hold political power, had been an important feature of traditional Chinese society. The idea has acquired added importance today, as the family by itself can no longer provide for one's basic needs and one must cultivate good personal ties to accomplish virtually anything in a state-controlled and often unfriendly social environment. Thus it comes as no surprise that personal networks have become so pervasive a social and cultural phenomenon in contemporary China. They can be found operating in all spheres of life and at all levels of society; they govern or constrain political action, economic dealings, legal adjudication, as well as routine social interaction. One of the most serious consequences of this is that the line between the private and the public has been completely blurred. The intermingling of the private and the public in turn creates a situation in which personal preferences, convictions, differences, affections, obligations, and the like strongly impact, albeit in disguised forms, policy decisions, official recruitment, authority structures, the administering of justice, and public discourse.

Fourth, the ethical imperative that helps sustain quasi-familistic networks is the notion of reciprocal obligations. Central to this notion is a strong emphasis on personal indebtedness and a concomitant emphasis on the de-centering or de-valuing of the self. With this emphasis comes a view of the individual, not as an independent and autonomous human being, but as a congealed network relationship. The moral worth of such an individual, thus, lies not so much in his or her presupposed intrinsic qualities, whatever those qualities might be, as in the sustaining of personal relationships and the repayment of personal debts. It is the interrelatedness and mutual dependence, not the pre-existing "I" and the values and beliefs that undergird it, that define the individual's self-identity.

It should be pointed out, however, that reciprocity is not predicated on universally applicable moral principles; rather, it is conditioned by a particularistic and result-oriented conception of moral conduct. According to this conception, whether an act is morally right or wrong depends on its relation to a particular circumstance in which it occurs and/or to a specific result which it purports to achieve. In other words, moral conduct is subject to the test of whether it satisfies the particularistic requirements for the mutual strengthening of personal ties, and not judged in accordance with a set of preconceived abstract rules. This is not to say that widely accepted moral values do not have any effect on the individual's behavior; in fact, they do, at least in theory, set the parameter within which one acts. But when it is one's personal ties that are at stake, rules may be bent and laws violated insofar as this does not constitute grave danger to one's well-being.

To the extent that it shares all the above mentioned characteristics, contemporary Chinese political culture may be regarded as quasi-familistic. In the following, a description of this culture will be provided. This description will be based on recent empirical studies and, to a much less degree, on my own findings from a field trip.[82] The quasi-familistic underpinnings of Chinese political life can be discussed on two levels, namely the elite and the popular. The elite political culture can be illustrated by considering the ways the political elite—by which is meant primarily the top echelon of political leadership—conducts itself in matters of government. These matters include, but are not restricted to, the process of decision making, patterns of authority, official recruitment, and the relation between the governing and the governed. The popular political culture can be illustrated similarly by considering the ways ordinary people think about and act in response to political affairs.

The Elite Political Culture

In contemporary China, political authority has long been enshrouded in mystery. Policy decisions are made behind closed doors, the personal lives of high-level officials are top secrets, and the average individual has no opportunity to participate in government—except in a rebellious and self-destructive way as epitomized by the Cultural Revolution. This way of conducting politics has its traditional roots; it rests, among other things, on a deepseated belief in the sacrosanct nature of political authority and in the categorical differentiation between the ruler and the ruled. Like their dynastic counterparts, communist rulers have in the past done much in perpetuating what Pye calls the "mystique of leadership."[83] At the core of this mystique is an idolization of the charismatic personalities, real and imagined, of political leaders and of their often exaggerated role in shaping national destiny. The result is that politics begins to revolve around personalities. As this happens, political authority becomes indistinguishable from personal authority.

That personal authority takes precedence over institutional mechanisms can be seen in the era of both Mao and Deng. In a historical study of modern Chinese revolutions, Fairbank observes that Mao Zedong's personal leadership became "the object of a cult of veneration" soon after the Communist victory and gave him a culturally sanctioned and unparalleled privilege to do whatever he willed. This privilege enabled Mao to engineer a succession of political campaigns on the basis of his personal visions and concerns. And it reached its peak in the Cultural Revolution when a large number of top-echelon political leaders were fatally persecuted and purged at his command without any due process whatsoever.[84] In recent years, no one has revealed more than Dr. Li Zhishui, Mao's personal physician, about the extent of Mao's personal authority, and about how his personal preferences, convictions, and even whims impacted so profoundly and extensively on virtually all facets of the Chinese national life. In his memoir, Li chronicled a series of major events involving the making of domestic and foreign policies, change in bureaucratic structures, cadre recruitment, public discourse, and the like. In all these events, according to Li, it was Mao's personal will that prevailed over the institutional authority of the so-called "collective leadership."[85]

A similar attitude toward personal authority also characterizes Deng Xiaoping's rise to power and his subsequent efforts to carry out economic and political reform. Deng's maneuver to topple Mao's hand-picked successor Hua Guofeng is a textbook case of how political authority in China builds on the basis of personal ties and networks. Of the four types of power bases on which Deng relied, namely personal, credential, institutional, and territorial, it was predominantly his personal ties in the military, the Party, and the administration that shored up the required support for his emergence as the political patriarch in post-Mao China.[86] As the chief architect of reform policies, moreover, Deng was acutely aware of the necessity of personal authority to carry out and insure the success of his goals. Without such authority and a network of supporters it both generates and depends on, reform would never have been possible. But with it, he was able to retire from his official positions completely yet still exercise control over the national agenda from behind the scenes. "In this respect," as one critic remarks, "Deng was heir to Mao's political legacy."[87]

The centrality of personal authority reflects a fundamentally important dimension of the elite political culture in contemporary China. An understanding of this dimension can provide a useful clue to understanding other basic politico-cultural values and practices that govern or constrain the elite's behavior. For example, top leaders divide up political power into various carefully guarded zones of personal authority, and key policy decisions are often negotiated and made through an informal process of communication (i.e. circulation of personal opinions written on the margins of drafted documents or memoranda) between them before they are sent to the Politburo for formal discussion. This, however, should not be interpreted as implying that formal institutions confer no real authority whatsoever and thus are insignificant in the study of decision-making processes. As some have pointed out, in the last two decades, bureaucratic institutions have begun to assume an increasingly large role in the designing and implementation of economic policies.[88] But granting that a pluralistic tendency is on the rise in certain areas of policy making, there is ample evidence to show that the two types of authority, namely personal and institutional, are hierarchically ranked, and that the personal continues to have an overriding power over the institutional, particularly on key issues.[89]

A common practice among the political elite is attachment to personal authority, not to formal institutions. It is among the first lessons for any official to learn that institutions are created, run, altered, and abolished by people. In contemporary China, it is frequently the case that many of the institutional arrangements are established or eliminated depending on the needs of the political elite at a particular time. Even if one supposes that impersonal offices remain in place for a longer period of time than their individual occupants, it is the latter rather than the former that ultimately determine one's promotion or demotion in the hierarchy of authority. No less important is the fact that personal attachment creates a quasi-familistic sense of belonging and trust. It cultivates emotional bonds that transcend and outlast the political and the institutional. Deng's triumphant return to power clearly proves this. How personal ties are formed is a complex question, but one thing is certain, that is, that once formed, they work reciprocally to provide both the power bases for key political actors and a safe haven for their supporters. This reciprocal relationship between a political patriarch and his followers is sometimes referred to as political patronage.

Personal authority produces political patronage, and patronage breeds political factions. It has been noted that factional strife is an enduring feature of Chinese politics.[90] In dynastic China, battles for the adoption of major policies were often fought in court along factional lines. The communist revolution from its inception was plagued by factionalism. Even during the heydays of Mao's dictatorship, factional politics never stopped. The fatal persecution of Liu Shaoqi, president of the People's Republic, and the purge of Deng Xiaoping during the Cultural Revolution, are the most egregious examples of factional politics. Apparently, the existence of political factions is not a phenomenon peculiar to the Chinese; the Federalists, for example, were deeply concerned with the divisive force of political factions. What is unique in the Chinese situation, however, is the fact that political factions are built essentially around the axis of personal authority and on the basis of a close-knit network of personal ties. This is certainly not to say that other factors, in particular political ideology, plays no significant role in the formation and cementing of factions. That the two main factions in the reform era, one led by the conservative economist Chen Yun and the other by Deng have been apparently built on ideological differences is a case in point.[91] But one should not lose sight of the fact that in the Chinese political and cultural context, the ideological and the personal tend to mix together and can hardly be separated. Because philosophical, political, or moral convictions are not something with a transcendental and independent status but are rather the concrete expressions of a particular person, ideological differences are often regarded as personal differences. In this sense, factional politics can be said to be based primarily on personal ties and networks.

Closely associated with patronage is another commonly shared value, namely, personal loyalty. In contrast to the imperative of winning the approval of the electorate in democratic politics, as Hamrin and Zhao put it, the imperative for any practitioner in the Chinese political system is to remain loyal to his or her patron and the patron's faction.[92] Loyalty as a political virtue is highly regarded and outweighs most other virtues. Why it enjoys such importance may be explained in part by the closed nature of Chinese politics. In a political system like the Chinese, policy and personnel change decisions are made behind closed doors, and loyalty is an effective way both to prevent information from leaking out to the opposing faction and to guarantee sufficient support for these decisions. The meaning of loyalty comprises three components. First, one must follow one's patron absolutely on all important issues, even if this may at times contradict one's own value system. Second, in cases where sacrifices are to be made to protect the powerful status of one's patron, one must be willing to do so. Third, undivided allegiance to one's patron is required. This requirement, however, is often ignored in reality because one has to cultivate different relationships in order to survive. As the traditional saying advises, a cunning hare must have three holes in the ground to avoid being trapped.

It is worth mentioning that the emphasis on loyalty affects the culture of officialdom in various ways. It is a widespread behavioral pattern, for example, that one avoid differences, not to mention confrontations, with one's superior at all costs. Such avoidance creates a semblance of conformity, which further enhances the sense of patriarchal power. It also causes communication from subordinates to superiors to be evasive if not untruthful. Since the important thing is to cultivate good personal ties with one's patron, moreover, official accountability tends to go upward to a higher level of authority rather than to ordinary people.[93]

In sum, the elite political culture in contemporary China can be understood essentially in terms of four clusters of values and practices. These are 1) the priority of personal and patriarchal authority, 2) patronage and the cultivation of personal ties, 3) factionalism, and 4) the imperative of loyalty. The impact of these deeply entrenched patterns can be felt across a broad spectrum of official behaviors from the top down to the county.[94] Local variations notwithstanding, the style of ruling, the patterns of authority, the process of decision making, and the basis of cadre recruitment at each level of government are remarkably similar. This similarity certainly has much to do with the reorganization of Chinese social and political life according to the Leninist principles after the communist takeover, but it also has much to do with the Chinese political and cultural tradition which has provided comfortable bedding for these values and practices to reproduce themselves, albeit in slightly changed forms.

The Popular Political Culture

Participation in self-government is one of the paradigmatic features of democratic politics. How citizens participate, whether it is to elect officials or to organize interests, not only defines the nature of a given political system, but also reflects the values, attitudes, and practices that provide the cultural underpinnings for such a system.

While political participation in Western democracies occurs typically in institutionalized forms, in contemporary China it involves mass mobilization and large-scale campaigns. In some cases, it is consumed by political violence in such a way that it comes dangerously close to peasant rebellions which bedeviled dynastic China.[95] The difference between the two types of participation can tell us something about the difference between the two types of political system. In the Chinese political system, it has been argued, there is a lack of institutionalized interest groups and opposition parties independent of the state, and this lack contributes in large measure to the underdevelopment of autonomous channels *vis-à-vis* the dictatorship of a single political party for well-ordered and meaningful political activities. While the point is well taken, however, why institutionalized forms of participation are lacking in the first place is a question that requires further thinking. As this study has been arguing all along, a cultural approach can shed light on this question.

One such approach has been offered by Fei Xiaotong.[96] Fei uses a straw/ripple metaphor to describe the difference between the Chinese and the Western cultural experience. He argues that Western society is structured in a way that resembles the collection of individual rice straws into small bundles, and these are then organized into large bundles and eventually stack together to form a haystack. In contrast, Chinese society is like a network of circular ripples on the surface of a lake when a rock is thrown into it; everyone is a circle and all circles are interrelated with no clear boundaries. What the metaphor suggests to us is a shared way of relating which many today call *guanxi*. As I have explained above, *guanxi* may be best understood as a quasi-familistic network of personal ties, and it is sustained by an ensemble of values, attitudes, habits, and practices. Traditionally, the kinship family embodies the interrelatedness of personal ties. In the modern era, with the disintegration of the kinship family, there has been a widespread trend in society to construct and use quasi-familistic *guanxi* networks. A *guanxi* network, thus, is the family constructed on non-blood ties and without kinship structures. The constraint it places on political participation is manifested in the fact that it makes autonomous organizations entirely expendable by promoting a personalistic form of political participation. In doing so, it eliminates the possibility of a buffer zone which may be used to shield the individual against state power and opens the door to the manipulation by autocrats of the masses to get involved in large-scale political movements.

The ways individual Chinese think about and act in response to political affairs are strongly constrained and shaped by personal ties and the quasi-familistic networks. This view accords with the conclusion reached by a large number of empirical studies. For example, a recent survey study has found that citizen participation in Beijing takes different forms, varying from filing grievances through formal organizations such as the trade union to writing to newspaper editors to lobbying colleagues and neighbors. But a common thread running through these political activities is the fact that people tend to mobilize personal resources or use personal channels for articulating their interests or seeking remedies for wrongs done to them.[97] Another study based on extensive fieldwork has also shown that *guanxi* is a multi-dimensional cultural phenomenon which involves ethical values, affective elements, material exchanges, and tactics, and dominates the ways the Chinese conduct themselves politically, socially and economically. A salient feature of the art of *guanxi,* as the author puts it, is that "one gets one's way not by observing formal and bureaucratic regulations or by going through proper channels, but by creatively seeking out unofficial routes, detours, and shortcuts to get around the officially recognized ways of doing things."[98]

As a basic framework for understanding and coping with social and political life in present-day China, *guanxi* finds concrete expression in a variety of value orientations, attitudes, habits, and practices. In a comparative analysis of interest representation in China and Vietnam, Yeonsik Jeong concludes that in China, the clientelistic or personal networks of individual leaders in a given organization are the dominant channels through which the interests of the organization and its members are voiced and satisfied. This has been the case with both the state-controlled trade union and relatively independent local business associations. In contrast, the mode of interest representation in Vietnam increasingly becomes an openly contested and group-oriented process, and this process creates favorable conditions for the emergence of an independent civil society *vis-à-vis* the state.[99] In recent years, local People's Congresses, particularly at the provincial level, have become a central agency for handling people's complaints about injustices done to them. When asked about how the average citizen can get his or her complaint through, one journalist said that one must have personal ties, direct or indirect, with congressional officials or staff members in order for one's grievances to be heard.[100] Speaking from his own involvement in a lawsuit, another journalist observed that winning a case depends not so much on the merit of the case, or even on money, as on the relationship between the lawyer and the judge.[101] Again, in a group interview, several municipal People's Congress representatives commented that purchasing official positions at the township or county level may not come as a surprise nowadays, but getting a high-level appointment in the municipal or provincial government with money alone is nearly impossible. One must have a high-profile network.[102]

A *guanxi* network is cemented by personal affections and exchanges; and personal affections and exchanges are one of the main sources of political nepotism. According to the chairman of one township congressional committee, political nepotism in the sense of allotting power positions to relatives and protégés is not uncommon at the village level of government. One of the most flagrant cases in his experience is that the position of party secretary in one village has been circulating among family members and relatives.[103] It should be pointed out that cadre recruitment is not in every instance the result of political nepotism; other criteria are also relevant. A survey study of cultural change which was conducted in the Shanghai region in the late 1980s shows that, although an overwhelming majority of those surveyed still perceive *guanxi* networks and personal ties to be important, there is a rising tendency, especially in metropolitan areas, to view technical competence rather than personal connections as the most desirable leadership qualification.[104] This is clearly an indication of value reorientation occurring today in China, but it should not blind one to the fact that *guanxi* continues to play a decisive role in shaping the way individuals cope with social and political reality. In a questionnaire survey I conducted of congressional representatives in one county, respondents were given a hypothetical situation in which two candidates were nominated for one of the county deputy mayors; one candidate was a relative but not talented and the other was talented but not a relative. When asked whom they would vote for in an election, 41.3% said their relative, 38.7% said the talented, and 20% said that they were unsure.[105]

A quasi-familistic network of personal ties is a nonexcludable good everyone has a chance to enjoy, but this nonexcludability should not be interpreted as a kind of publicness in the sense of being openly and equally applicable to all. In fact, network building is essentially a particularistic, discriminative and closed practice. It tends to draw a dividing line between a tightly knit circle of relatives and friends and the rest of the world that is unknown, unreliable and potentially harmful. In doing so, it creates an attitude of indifference, distrust or even hostility toward anyone outside the network and impedes the idea of a publicly shared sphere of life. The *guanxi* mentality goes like this: If someone is not one of us, he or she is by definition one of the other side. This explains in part why there is an extremely low level of interpersonal and public trust among the Chinese.[106] It is also responsible for or associated with other cultural sentiments and habits such as noncooperation and intolerance.[107] In an office interview, for example, one township deputy mayor remarked that village election is a good thing, but villagers are just not ready for it yet. When asked why, he said that the "moral quality (*suzhi*)" of the voter is not advanced enough to make election work. "True, more than half of the total votes win the election," he added, "let's say 60%. But, remember, there are still 40% who did not vote for you, and they will make trouble for you. Consequently, you will have a very tough time doing your job."[108] In reality, the percentage of trouble makers are probably much less than what the mayor projected, but they are a formidable influence on a large number of so-called *shunmin* (obedient subjects) who are generally unwilling to participate openly in political activities and thus take a noncooperative position against whatever is not in their immediate interest.[109]

Like noncooperation, intolerance is another embedded feature of the *guanxi* culture. The survey study conducted by Nathan and Shi has found that the level of tolerance with respect to political views is considerably lower in China than elsewhere. Perhaps more interesting is the fact that education which is widely considered a positive influence on tolerance does not in the Chinese case contribute much to the reduction of intolerance.[110] A similar conclusion has been suggested by Chu and Ju's survey findings. If we take the protection of minority rights as one of the important indicators of political tolerance, an overwhelming majority of Chu and Ju's respondents can be interpreted as being intolerant when they are found generally reluctant to defend the individual and his or her interests *vis-à-vis* collective welfare.[111]

Such reluctance reflects not only a politico-cultural tradition that tolerates no deviance from established value and belief patterns, but also one that tends to decenter and devalue the individual self. Selflessness has long been regarded as one of the central virtues in traditional China, as one might expect, given the importance of the family as traditionally understood and practiced.[112] In the context of practicing *guanxi,* although each person is the initiator of his or her personal ties and networks, the self is not considered autonomous. The emphasis is placed not on the individual as an independent moral agent, but on the interconnectedness and interdependence of similar selves and on the reciprocity of personal obligations. The value of the individual, thus, is measured in terms of how successful he or she is in cultivating and maintaining *guanxi* or quasi-familistic networks, that is, how successful he or she is in fulfilling the requirement of mutual dependence and obligation.

All this having been said, it should be stressed that, although *guanxi* values may be responsible for many of the ills that are plaguing Chinese society and culture, it is not true that all network values and practices are necessarily detrimental to democratic development and the idea of individual rights. Some of these values, such as the prioritization of mutual obligation, can be valuable in cultivating citizen obligation and a sense of political community.[113] It should also be noted that Chinese political culture is undergoing fundamental changes and many of the values and practices underlying the traditional shared way of relating are losing their appeal among the younger and better educated generations. Chu and Ju have demonstrated that such core traditional values as submission to authority have been greatly weakened in the recent past and that concerns with individual interests and autonomy are on the rise.[114] What this forebodes for the reconstruction of Chinese political culture is not yet clear; for the time being, one has to concur with Chu and Ju that individualism takes at best a marginal place in the cultural configurations of contemporary China.[115]

Chapter Six

In Lieu of a Conclusion:
The Language of Rights and
Democratic Change in China

In a special issue of *Political Studies,* David Beetham laments that the subject of human rights occupies only "a marginal position" in the discipline of political science. By political science he means the entire field of political inquiry which in the main includes comparative politics, international relations, and of course political theory. Although acknowledging that the concept of rights is "an important theme" in political theory, he goes on to stress that it is the idea of *human* rights that has not been given adequate attention. This marginality, he adds, can be traced to a long held skepticism which treats the idea of human rights as "philosophically insecure, morally problematic and politically impractical."[1] Beetham's concern is understandable when we place it in the larger context of an ongoing debate over whether the traditional notion of rights, usually understood as civil and political rights, can and should be expanded to ground second- and third-generation rights. However, it appears that his concern has been overstated, even if we accept as valid his implicit assumption that there is a nontrivial distinction between what political scientists generally refer to as rights and the notion of human rights. It may be true that few or no special courses on *human* rights have been offered in the political science curriculum, but this does not entail the claim that the idea has been marginalized. The sheer quantity of books and articles devoted specifically to the topic of rights—to which the notion of human rights is a late addition—within the field of political theory alone is testimony to the contrary. In fact, some have argued that it is not the relative scarcity of rights or rights-related talk, but its uncritical and indiscriminate proliferation that has raised serious questions.[2]

Contrary to Beetham's view, the language of rights or human rights has in recent years become an increasingly indispensable conceptual tool for political scientists and actors alike to articulate a vision of political change *vis-a-vis* democratization in the developing world.[3] The broad appeal of this language is no doubt a cause for celebration, for the idea of human rights represents one of the highest moral aspirations in the evolution of the human race. It expresses a fundamentally important value that, though originated in the West, is bound to transcend national boundaries. Today few would seriously challenge this crucial value without incurring great political and moral costs for themselves; even the most authoritarian governments recognize, at least formally, a wide array of rights their citizens are expected to enjoy. Lately the so-called Asian value debate has caught a great deal of attention among academics and politicians alike worldwide.[4] But a close reading of the statements made by both sides of the dispute suggests that the focal point is, for the most part, not so much about the value of human rights *per se* as it is about the selective use of the rights language and the cultural limits of rights practice. Considering this, I believe we would be better served by shifting the discourse from desirability to applicability. Instead of dwelling on whether the human rights standard ought to be respected—an issue which seems to have in large measure been settled, we may refocus our attention on how and to what extent a language of rights can be used in a way that allows us to set and attain our moral and political goals. This shift may help shed light not only on some of the unresolved theoretical issues with respect to the subject, nature, ground and correlativity of rights, but also on the question of desirability itself.

All too often, those who employ the idea of rights or human rights as a conceptual tool to articulate a vision of political change *vis-à-vis* democratization tend to ignore or deemphasize social, economic and cultural contingencies in the country to which this concept is applied. It is frequently said that exposing the historical origins of the idea of rights does not negate its universal validity; and that culture is an evolving system and there is no absolute threshold for the idea of rights to be integrated into a culture. It is further cautioned that claims to cultural uniqueness must be taken with a grain of salt when they are advanced by political elites, for they often serve as an expedient excuse for suppressing dissenting voices and maintaining the status quo. These points are well taken. At the same time, however, one cannot help but notice a disconcerting phenomenon, that is, that while the idea of rights appears to be gaining momentum around the globe, a wide, if not widening, disparity exits between the attractiveness of this important value and the resistance or even hostility to it, between its rhetorical appeal and the failure to take it seriously.

How does one explain this state of affairs? What forces lie behind such resistance or failure? Why does this gap exist? Can it be closed or at least narrowed? If the answer is yes, how should we go about doing it? What are the conceptual tools available to us? These and other related questions, as mentioned in the introductory chapter, constitute the central concern of this study. While the preceding chapters can be read as an attempt to grapple with understanding and explanation, the final chapter seeks to answer the question of how and to what extent the idea of rights or human rights may be able to provide a viable language for articulating visions of democratic change in a non-Western and non-rights-based context. But before I take up this task, it is necessary to put major pieces of the puzzle together by rehearsing briefly what has been said so far.

In chapter two, I set out to retrieve the concept of political culture and for two reasons. The first is to provide justification for a culturally sensitive approach to political ideas and doctrines. Since classical antiquity, this approach has been an integral part of political and social discourse. As such, it should be assigned the kind of legitimacy and weight it justly deserves in the study of politics. The second is to try to bring a modest amount of order and clarity to the political culture concept. This effort is particularly needed given that there is so much ambiguity and confusion surrounding the use of the concept. Conceptual clarity serves the twin purpose of allowing for effective communication and guiding research and analysis.

After reviewing and rejecting three influential uses of the concept of political culture, I have defined political culture, following Chilton and Thompson (but not endorsing some of their arguments), *as a shared way of relating among a group or groups of people,* and added a qualifier "particularly pertaining to the management of collective affairs" to highlight the political nature of the concept. This definition has several conceptual advantages over the three approaches discussed. It views political culture as a socially constructed and commonly shared framework of values, expectations, and practices, and both embodied in ideas and beliefs and expressed through social action and interaction in real situations. It maintains a pluralist understanding of shared ways of relating and seeks such an understanding by placing cultural values and practices in institutional settings.

Political culture thus defined sets the stage for exploring the liberal concept of rights, its cultural grounding, and the possibility of applying it to a different politico-cultural context. In chapter three, a conceptual analysis of the notion of rights has been offered. This analysis has shown that a fruitful understanding of this notion requires more than conceptual clarity. There are different kinds of rights, different kinds of rights-holders, and different kinds of grounds on which rights are justified. Questions about these cannot be satisfactorily answered except by relating rights to the characteristics of the rights-holder, to the circumstances prior to his or her possession of such rights, and to the various moral, legal, political, and conventional relationships to which he or she belongs. I have argued that whatever definition, theory, or scheme of justification one advances, none in itself is capable of offering an understanding sophisticated enough to capture the complexity and subtlety of the notion. Only a pluralist approach that is sufficiently sensitive to such complexity and subtlety can provide the opportunity to fully appreciate the concept of rights.

Taking this approach, I have considered the liberal concept of rights by placing it in historical perspective. While liberal rights emerged under specifically modern conditions as a crucial part of the liberal doctrine, questions of rights arose much earlier in time. In both classical and medieval political thought, the idea of rights occupied a significant position. The preliberal or what I tend to call nonliberal conception of rights is characterized by its quest for the just, good and virtuous. It is oriented toward and consistent with a teleologically given end and signifies a disposition or determination to do the right thing in accordance with justice, reason and law. In contrast, the liberal conception of rights is undergirded by an entirely different set of ideas and assumptions. In both traditional and contemporary liberal theory, the idea of rights is predicated on the ontological primacy of the individual. Rather than grounded in an understanding of the just portion between persons which is a hallmark of the objective sense of rights found in classical and medieval theory, the liberal notion of rights rests on a subjective sense of rights as something privately owned by or naturally implanted in the individual *qua* moral agent.

Although concerns about the individual may be found in all societies and all ages, the discovery and valorization of the individual that has laid the groundwork for liberal theory is a relatively new phenomenon. As I have indicated in chapter four, the assigning of preponderant weight to the individual vis-à-vis society—to his/her mind as the arbiter of truth, to his/her value as the basis of morality, and to his/her interest as the justification for social and political arrangements—is generally referred to as individualism, and individualism is a shared way of relating that emerged only in the modern West. Among the historical forces that helped shape an individualistic culture, the Reformation and Cartesianism remained unparalleled both in the breadth of their reach and in the depth of their transforming power. If Luther and Calvin initiated an inward-turning process that defined the individual's unmediated relationship with God's grace, Descartes pioneered a metaphysical self who enjoyed a privileged, distinct, and autonomous existence in the universe.

If, as evidence has shown, an individualistic culture took shape only in the wake of the Reformation in the modern West and this culture furnished a comfortable bedding for the emergence and entrenchment of the liberal concept of rights, is it tenable to say that liberal rights cannot take hold where such a comfortable bedding is lacking? Take China for example. The idea of rights was introduced into the Chinese language more than one hundred years ago, yet it still has a tough time getting assimilated into the consciousness and practice of ordinary people. Is this an indication that an individualistic way of relating is absent? If this is, in what sense can we say that the Chinese political culture failed to provide an important grounding for the development of liberal rights? To these and other questions I have offered chapter five as an answer.

To talk about the Chinese political culture as if it were a unified and immutable whole is to invite criticism. However, there is strong reason to believe that Confucianism played a far greater role than Taoism or Legalism or Buddhism or the combination of them in shaping the mind and behavior of the average Chinese. The core features of Confucianism have been encapsulated into two crucial concepts, namely *Li* (ritual) and *Ren* (benevolence). While *Li* is a set of rules and standards ascribing duties and obligations in a hierarchically structured society, *Ren* signifies an internalization of these rules and standards. The mutually reinforcing relationship between them reduced the individual to a mere role player bound by a self-imposed sense of duty. One does not have to look very far to see such role playing in the traditional Chinese family where the value of individual members lay not in their moral capacity to formulate a rational plan of life, but in their fulfillment of a set of hierarchically structured and ascriptive duties and responsibilities.

The dismantling of the traditional family in contemporary China has not fundamentally changed the way Chinese individuals conduct themselves personally and politically. If Confucian familism provides a conceptual framework for understanding the Chinese politico-cultural tradition, quasi-familism or *guanxi* network that is characterized by the primacy of personal ties and the ethical imperative of reciprocal obligation holds the key to studying elite and popular culture in contemporary China. Despite a long standing Confucian tradition that emphasizes the individual's self-development, and despite the breakdown of the traditional family as a political and cultural institution, the basic structure of the Chinese political culture remains duty-based and nonindividualistic. It tends to de-center the individual by placing him/her in a complex web of social relations and mutual obligations, and by disallowing him/her an autonomous sphere of activity in which one may pursue an independently conceived end of one's own without interference or intrusion.

If the foregoing discussion carries any force, what sensible conclusions can be drawn from it? I have suggested that since the liberal concept of rights as a moral and political doctrine presupposes and is grounded in an individualistic way of relating, it would likely have difficulty getting entrenched in a political and cultural context where such a way of relating is radically lacking. Consequently, a rights-based argument as ordinarily understood would likely be of limited success in providing a viable language for articulating political change vis-à-vis democratization.

Sensible as it may be, however, this conclusion is essentially a negative one and serves a limited purpose. Now the important question facing us is what constructive steps should be taken to make the idea of rights or human rights a meaningful part of the Chinese democratizing experience. I have advanced the thesis that for liberal rights to bear on democratization in China, a re-description of this notion is required that is sensitive both to the particularities of liberalism and to the Chinese politico-cultural tradition. Following the footsteps of anthropology, cultural studies in conjunction with or for the purpose of promoting human rights typically take developing nations as the object of inquiry; rarely does one encounter a cultural perspective from which the issue of human rights in the industrialized West is investigated. This is to a large extent understandable, because violation of human rights occurs more frequently and on a larger scale in developing nations, particularly poverty-stricken and war-torn ones. But this should not be an excuse to ignore the fact that a cultural approach to rights discourse in the West may shed light on differences in value and the constraints they place on rights talk and practice. An account of the cultural groundings of liberal rights has been given precisely for the purpose of bringing the liberal cultural context back into the equation. In the pages that follow, an examination of how the liberal notion of rights fared in the Chinese context will be presented and a redescribed notion of rights delineated and defended. Emerging from this redescription is what I come to call the idea of embedded rights. Because it appeals to and incorporates some of the most enduring moral categories in the Chinese culture and tradition, this idea would likely resonate with a large audience, thus opening the door to a transformative dialogue between nonliberal China and the liberal West. Finally I will provide a sketch of what kind of democracy it would be likely for the idea of embedded rights to promote and how this idea can be used to articulate democratic development in China.

RIGHTS DISCOURSE IN THE CHINESE CONTEXT

Rights discourse in China was destined to be controversial from the very beginning, not only because circumstances surrounding its birth and early development were extraordinary, but also because translation of the term "rights" into *quanli*—a phrase that bands power and profit together—created potentially serious problems for an adequate appreciation of what it is that makes something a right and somebody a right-holder. To say this is of course not to endorse any sort of linguistic determinism. However contextually loaded they may be, words, terms, or concepts we use do not determine how we think and act. But to go to the other extreme and claim that language merely *re*presents and is separate from the *re*presented is also mistaken. As Wittgenstein and others have reminded us, language does not simply designate, but is constitutive of the reality we are experiencing and recreating. As such it regulates or influences the way we frame questions about and make sense of the social and political reality in which we live; it is a medium, so to speak, through which we view the world around us and act accordingly.[5] As we shall see, more than one hundred years later, rights discourse continues to be constrained by the problems and ambiguities to which the initial linguistic rendering of the term contributes, despite that the unique historical process which brought the issue to the fore no longer obtains.

Rights discourse in China emerged in the wake of the two Opium Wars and the subsequent colonization by Western powers certain parts of the country, especially regions along the coast and near major waterways in the mainland. Facing the dire situation of total conquest and subjugation, the Qing government scrambled to find strategies for national revitalization. As critical components of the self-strengthening program, manufacturing industries were established to make products for military and commercial use, students were sent abroad to Europe and the United States to acquire the technical know-how, and governmental agencies were set up to cope with foreign affairs. An unintended consequence of all this was that with the door gradually opening up and interactions with the world increasing, novel ideas and values began flooding in. In a relatively short time, many came to realize that the West was powerful not only because of its advanced weaponry; equally important, if not more so, was that it had a superior social and political system that went with indestructible gunboats and fierce cannons. Hence, along with a nascent industrial and military establishment, attempts were made at legal, political and educational reform.[6]

Under such trying circumstances, rights discourse came abruptly onto the national stage in response to the challenge posed by the West. Unlike their Western counterparts, the Chinese had no long period of intellectual gestation that would allow them to reflect on the idea, no repository of comparable words and concepts at their disposal, and no historical frame of reference to help them put arguments in perspective. All they had in their possession were a newly introduced value that sounded alien, a deeply flawed Confucian tradition that could not deliver and thus must be rejected, and a pressing national goal of rejuvenation that overshadowed all other important domestic concerns.

The term *quanli,* alien as it may sound, is not a borrowed expression; it has indigenous roots that can be traced back, if not earlier, to Sima Qian's *Records of History* and Huan Kuan's *On Salt and Iron* in the early Han Dynasty.[7] There it was produced by artificially combining two otherwise separate words in order to bring out and amplify a meaning that neither alone could convey. This meaning, however, is nowhere close to and in fact has little or nothing to do with what we denote as rights. In modern usage, as in classical one, the first character of the phrase *quan* essentially means "power," whereas the second *li* signifies "profit." There are certainly other connotations associated with either word, for example, "weighing" and "provisionally" for *quan* and "sharp" and "convenient" for *li,* but in the context of talking about a politically and morally charged concept, they were unintended and irrelevant.

That the word "power" often triggers a negative response among ordinary Chinese is no secret. One can attribute this negativity to a long history of power abuse in dynastic China and the concomitant presence of a power structure that discouraged power sharing and accountability. As Xun Zi put it, "Power in the hands of one man is strong, and in the hands of two men weak."[8] In popular minds, power is frequently equated with officialdom, and officialdom is virtually synonymous with license, privilege, wealth, insolence and corruption. In other words, power is the very opposite or absence of benevolence, righteousness, principle, trust, and integrity, all of which are the basic categories of Confucian morality.

What has been said about power can be applied to the word "profit" with only minor modifications. In premodern China there has been a distinct Confucian tradition that disparages profit makers, in particular merchants. Profit is believed to be intimately linked to and indeed entail the bending or abandoning of one's principles much the same way power is perceived to override established rules of conduct. Since Confucius and his disciples advanced the thesis that "A noble man appreciates righteousness and a base man profit," profit making has been relegated to the bottom of the moral ladder and merchants were viewed, consciously or unconsciously, as a morally dubious profession.[9] It is a deeply ingrained prejudice—one that lingers on in the hearts and minds of many even today—that if one is to pursue profit, one can do it only at the expense of truth, love, honesty and friendship.[10]

It is thus enigmatic that a combination of two words that enjoyed a morally unfavorable reputation in traditional China had been chosen to communicate a morally sanctified term, namely "rights." The enigma gets even harder to understand when one bears in mind the availability of other words and combinations with morally favorable undertones; for example, the word "power" could be joined together with the word "righteousness (*yi*)" or "way (*dao*)" or "reason (*li*)" to yield a combination entirely different in connotation. As mentioned earlier, committing "rights" to a matter of acquiring power plus profit is potentially problematic. The problem is created, however, not only by what it commits, but more significantly by what it omits. What has been omitted in the current translation is a built-in sense of justice, reason and law that underpins the English word "right," the French word "droit," and the German word "recht." This omission—a point which has been so far largely ignored by those who write about human rights in China[11]—has important ramifications for rights discourse in the Chinese context. Power in itself is neither just nor unjust, neither rational nor irrational, neither legitimate nor illegitimate. In other words, there is nothing inherently good or bad about power, and whether it is good or bad ordinarily depends on how the user uses it. The same applies to profit. But right is different. A right always is imbued with a strong sense of being just, rational and legitimate, whether it is a valid claim or entitlement or immunity or privilege. In this regard the idea of rights understood as *quanli* is impaired at birth and becomes vulnerable to all kinds of misinterpretation and abuse.

The lack of a built-in sense of justice, reason and law is, arguably, the most serious disability in the term *quanli*. For, without a sense of justice, reason and law, the idea of rights appears to have no moral anchoring. To find such anchoring, one must either reclaim existing moral sources or look elsewhere for enlightenment. In the years leading up to the nationalist revolution in 1911, efforts had been taken by rights advocates to expound and justify the concept by invoking traditional moral categories such as duty, self-cultivation and conscience. But under the circumstances, especially at the time of the May 4th Movement when dismantling the old cultural order was viewed as a priority, the first option was clearly against the current. Not surprisingly, thus, Western moral categories such as individual liberty were heavily drawn upon in defense of rights. As part of a gathering trend to address the human condition in China, defenders of rights employed a radically novel language to publish radical views in radical magazines. The result was a radicalization of rights discourse, which seems to have made the idea appear even more alien, more impractical, and more removed from the concern and reach of the larger society.

The centripetal force that drew the attention of an overwhelming majority of educated Chinese at that historical moment was national salvation. Whether this led some of the prominent figures in modern Chinese history such as Sun Yatsen to reject the idea of rights remains open to debate, but one thing is clear, that is, that national salvation was a goal that everyone could agree to regardless of ideological preference. Towering above all other domestic issues, this goal profoundly influenced and indeed defined the way rights discourse was carried out throughout the tumultuous years of revolution and civil strife. It is not accidental therefore that rights were frequently justified on the instrumentalist ground that they helped China regain power and prestige in the eyes of the world. This was the case even with those who espoused the intrinsic value of rights as a defining feature of man *qua* man as opposed to slave; they saw consistency rather than conflict between the individual's nature-endowed rights and subordination of these rights to an overpowering collective agenda.[12]

If we take a look, even a cursory one, at the early development of rights discourse in China, we can't help but notice several interesting characteristics. First, debate on rights arose largely if not exclusively as a reaction to the challenge posed by the West in the aftermath of war and conquest. That the debate was caught in the conflict between China and the West was really unfortunate. Whether one calls it bad timing or sheer accident, circumstances were such that the question of rights became inseparably entangled with international power relations. Now that international power relations entered into the equation, attention began to be diverted from focusing on the intrinsic value of the idea of rights to some externalities that had absolutely nothing to do with its justification. Second, rights discourse was also closely associated with radical politics. Obviously this connection is historical rather than logical, but radicalism fostered the view that power and prosperity demanded and could not be achieved without a complete overhaul of the traditional culture through imported ideas and values. Radicals from anarchists (*a la* Liu Shipei) to nationalists (*a la* Zou Rong) to communists (*a la* Chen Duxue) all converged on this point, that is, that Confucian morality and the social and cultural system it sustained were totally bankrupt and had neither the authority nor the conceptual tools to undertake the task of national revitalization. In other words, traditional moral categories were fundamentally incompatible with and indeed antithetical to modern and scientific Western concepts such as rights, individual liberty and democracy.

Third, an instrumentalist conception of rights was a preferred justificatory scheme. Endorsing a widely perceived need for national salvation, rights advocates tended to see rights as a useful program to liberate the populace and rebuild a Chinese nation that would stand tall among nations. They justified the idea on grounds of its utility to promote societal progress or allow individuals to fulfill their responsibilities as parts of the larger whole—a view that clearly shows the influence of Mill, Rousseau and Bentham among the most favored Western thinkers. In their understanding, human beings were not so much rights-bearing beings in the sense that rights help define who they are in the light of natural law, as they were persons bearing what nature has to offer so as to achieve life's ends. These ends included, but were not limited to, basic material conditions for survival or subsistence as well as the well-being of the entire community that was generally perceived to precede in importance any individual's interests.[13]

If we now turn to rights discourse in contemporary China, we can't help, either, but notice a remarkable continuity between then and now in terms of the way questions of rights are framed and tackled. To understand this historical continuity is important because it allows us to comprehend why some issues surface more frequently and seem to carry more weight than others in the rights debate. It also helps enlarge our understanding of what obstacles or advantages are involved in terms of improving rights discourse and ultimately building a human rights regime in the Chinese context. An enlarged understanding is certainly conducive to "representative thinking," to use Hanna Arendt's phrase,[14] and to facilitating a dialogical or consensual approach as many have come to adopt today.[15]

It is not uncommon that participants in the Chinese rights discourse join the debate often by asserting the universal standard of human rights and by denouncing the official position of the Chinese government as a pretext for maintaining authoritarian rule and resisting political change. With a few exceptions,[16] the official line of thinking is rejected *en bloc* without a careful analysis of its merits or demerits from both a historical and a theoretical standpoint. Whether the government's position represents the view of a majority of the Chinese citizenry is difficult to ascertain in a precise manner, but empirical studies to date seem to suggest that to a considerable extent it does.[17] It has been argued that indoctrination by the state plays a crucial role in making people see things the way they see and use language the way they use. It has also been maintained that accepted opinions can be changed or unpacked by telling a complete rather than truncated story about human rights. While these observations certainly contain some truth and caution needs to be taken with regard to official claims, it is nevertheless naive to say that people are embracing the government's position mindlessly or they can be easily deluded into accepting whatever the party proclaims. As critics have pointed out, things are much more complex now than a couple of decades ago; ordinary Chinese are very much capable of thinking for themselves, for example, by supporting the government's policies without identifying with the one-party regime, and are politically and legally savvy enough to identify and defend their own interests.[18] Thus, to say that they have been fooled or misled into sharing the government's view on human rights would be to seriously underestimate their critical ability. This point is particularly evident when we bear in mind that Chinese intellectuals writing today in and outside China endorse a number of key arguments made by their government while remaining critical of the latter's half-hearted political reform.[19]

It is worth noting, moreover, that the Chinese official position is not static but evolving. In recent decades, especially after the end of Mao's reign, the issue of human rights has undergone dramatic changes from nonexistence to a subject of debate, from its total denial to its partial acceptance, and from being ignored to being embraced in official commentaries. In addition to the establishment of various human rights centers and institutes within the academic setting and the publication of a large quantity of materials on the topic, the two human rights Covenants were signed in 1997 and 1998 respectively (but with only the Covenant on Economic, Social and Cultural Rights ratified in 2001). A national organization, China Society for Human Rights Studies, was founded in 1993, devoting its resources to the study of human rights.[20] Whether these developments signify an improvement of human rights conditions in China is not entirely clear, but it would be safe to say that authorities in Beijing are now taking the issue more seriously than they ever did at any given point in time since the founding of the republic.

Rights discourse in contemporary China bears striking resemblance to its predecessor one century earlier. Apart from a shared instrumentalist conception of rights that is heavily favored by both rights theorists and the party state, three additional features deserve our attention. The first is that the question of human rights is frequently relegated to and bound up with international relations and power struggle. The perception that the issue of human rights is a matter of foreign policy and, specifically, of resisting pressure imposed by the West is prevalent. It is true that the Chinese government has contributed substantially to this misrepresentation through officially controlled media, but the West, particularly the United States, also has played a role in its perpetuation by adopting a double standard in handling world affairs. For example, it is incomprehensible that the British, after nearly one hundred years of delay to put in place a democratically elected governing body in Hong Kong, suddenly began to worry about the colony's democratic future on the eve of its return to the Chinese control. It is equally puzzling that the United States provided strong support, both financially and militarily, for its democratic ally Israel while doing little or nothing to help the Palestinian refugees return to their homeland forcibly taken and occupied by the Israeli government. The upshot is a widely shared skepticism among ordinary Chinese about the West's intentions and motives in promoting human rights.[21]

Related to this artificial linkage between human rights and international power relations, secondly, is the selective use of the rights language. Rhetorically, the Chinese government subscribes to the entire gamut of human rights as enumerated in various United Nations instruments, but in practice certain rights, especially those that are perceived to be threatening to political stability, are given only a superficial nodding. Placed under the rubric of a right to subsistence that has the double connotation of a basic level of material living and national autonomy vis-à-vis the West, and subordinate to the national goal of modernization that is richly reminiscent of the 19th century self-strengthening movement, the idea of social and economic rights has been well received by the Chinese public. The protection and promotion of social and economic rights on which leaders in Beijing stake their legitimacy is an avowedly top priority, and until very recently has borne noticeable fruit in terms of providing food, shelter, work, education, and healthcare for Chinese citizens.[22] But as economic reform deepens, serious issues begin to surface in the last couple of decades. Notwithstanding the perilous "Three Agriculture Problems" which motivated the publication of a shocking report on real-life events in the Chinese countryside, efforts to make industries and bureaucracies lean without a proper construction of the social safety net for job retraining, education, healthcare, and retirement have considerably raised the poverty line in cities.[23]

The third feature takes the shape of a philosophical argument. The argument has been made in a series of responses to international criticisms through the 1990s and well articulated by Liu Huaqiu in a statement at a UN World Conference on Human Rights in 1993. It goes like this. The notion of rights is a product of history; as such, it is intimately connected with the cultural tradition, economic development and social system of a given country. There are no abstract and absolute rights, only historically informed and concrete ones. Rights practice, thus, cannot be judged merely by resorting to such an allegedly universally valid set of standards. As historical development differs in different countries, so do the requirements for interpreting and protecting human rights. In the Chinese context, attempts to meet these requirements need to be firmly grounded in social stability and economic growth. Consequently, to declare the human rights standard of a particular country as the only viable model for all to follow is untenable.[24]

It should be pointed out that this account does not exhaust the way the issue of (human) rights is raised and dealt with, but it does provide a glimpse of the central questions that, as some accurately put it, pose a challenge *for* (instead of *to*) human rights. This challenge has been counter-challenged by human rights advocates. The framework in which criticisms take place is often presented as a dichotomy between universalism and relativism. For all its conceptual parsimony, however, this way of framing the debate is in my view misleading, and for two broad reasons. One is that a purely relativist position is rarely if ever found in existing literature on human rights and may never have existed even in cultural anthropology in the sense in which the universalist has described it, namely one that allows no possibility of value communication and transfer. Cultural anthropologists such as Franz Boas and Ruth Benedict who have been frequently labeled as cultural relativists actually rested their case on the twin pillars of cultural configuration and dissemination.[25] Similarly, critics of universalism like Lee Kuan Yew and Bilahari Kausikan who are widely portrayed as opponents of human rights in fact do not reject human rights, if one judges by what they say, as they disagree with the way rights discourse is being carried out and with some of the assumptions and beliefs underlying the prevailing conception of human rights.[26]

The other reason is that the universalist claim itself is problematic. The most troubling aspect of such a claim is about the meaning of universality. A typical argument in its defense is to assert that human rights are universal by virtue of the fact that we are all human. Notwithstanding the question of who are and should be rights-bearers, the assumption that our common humanity entails universality is mistaken. True, we all share certain basic needs, material and nonmaterial, such as food, clothes, dignity and liberty, yet this does not in any way determine what we eat and wear and what it is that constitutes dignity and liberty. Nor does it determine the means by, and the extent to, which we satisfy them. The dilemma for the universalist is that we cannot talk about human rights meaningfully without addressing the substantive issue of what rights should be respected and the reason for doing so. However, once we begin to talk about substantive rights, we run into the difficulty of choosing among a plurality of criteria and standards for defining and respecting a right. The standards for respecting a right to healthcare (which, though not constitutionalized as such, can still be inferred from private law) in the United States, for example, are different from those in

France.[27] One can choose as many healthcare providers as one wishes in the former, with the proviso that one must have sufficient insurance coverage, whereas in the latter this right is honored by meeting the medical needs of each and every French citizen with no strings attached.

Sometimes "universal" is also taken to mean "international." This is equally unacceptable, mainly because something being international does not necessitate that it is universally valid. Neither is "cross-cultural," and for the same reason. Until we are clear about what universality means, therefore, a universalist argument for human rights is bound to be ambiguous and ineffective.[28]

Although an extreme universalist position, one that rejects all forms of cultural consideration, may still be found in rights discourse today, a growing number of theorists and advocates who insist on the universality of human rights do take culture into account in addressing human rights issues.[29] In a similar spirit of open-mindedness, those who are critical of universalist claims do not hesitate to admit the vast moral appeal of the idea of human rights. Adopting a culturally mediated approach, they conduct cross-cultural empirical studies and are convinced that such studies would allow us to go above the fray and see what it exactly means for a right to be universal and what role cultural traditions play in shaping the interpretation and practice of human rights.[30] This broad recognition of cultural relevance clearly shows that a universalism-versus- relativism paradigm needs to be replaced or fundamentally revised.

In the Chinese context, as we have seen, rights discourse was and still is constrained by cultural beliefs and practices. Take the rights-bearer for example. A preponderant emphasis on the human individual in the West has contributed immeasurably to the rise of rights thinking. In contemporary China, as in premodern one, deemphasizing the individual is the norm, not the exception. That this has a broad base of popular support has been suggested by various empirical studies in recent years. The Chinese government as party to a litigation, say, *Mr. Zhao, Qian, Sun, Li,* vs. *Politburo* is unthinkable to the average Chinese. It will take more than mere institutional overhaul—for example, establishing a truly independent judiciary—to haul members of the Politburo to answer charges before a court of law, because the perpetuation of certain institutions itself requires explanation. Of course this does not mean that things won't change in the future; it goes to illustrate the point that as much as we appreciate the broad moral appeal of (human) rights, we need to be "brutally honest" about the limits culture places on rights discourse and practice.[31] These limits may account, at least in part, for the gap between the rights-based argument and a widespread indifference or even resistance to it. The fact that authoritarian governments manipulate cultural questions does not change the reality, only aggravates it. The key question now is how to overcome such indifference or resistance, not by telling people that human rights are good *for* them, but by a carefully measured response to cultural concerns and a reconstructive effort to develop a rights discourse that is sufficiently sensitive to such concerns. This sensitivity, I believe, would have a salutary effect on value dialogue and a better chance to succeed in helping articulate a vision of democratic change in China.

THE IDEA OF EMBEDDED RIGHTS

Although the notion of rights has been slowly yet clearly gaining ground in recent years, the Chinese rights discourse as it stands now suffers from serious flaws. Linking human rights to international power relations, for example, sidetracks discussions on the true nature and purpose of rights, whereas prioritizing social and economic rights fosters a skewed vision, thereby hampering legal and political reform. Other deficiencies are less conspicuous but no less harmful. The lack of a sense of justice in the conception of rights is a case in point. As indicated earlier, translating "rights" into power plus profit fails to convey a built-in sense of justice, reason and law embedded in the English "right," the French "droit," and the German "recht." This failure is exacerbated by an unsymmetrical concern with the utility of rights, whether it is national salvation or the cultivation of self-responsibility, and by an exclusive emphasis on the historical and cultural circumstances in which rights discourse takes place. The result is a language of rights that has little or no moral grounding. The only grounding for justifying a rights claim is the Chinese constitution, a document that has been several times changed since the founding of the republic and seems to have stemmed from political necessity more than moral commitment.

In order to repair such deficiencies and reconstruct a rights discourse that would provide a viable tool for articulating democratic change, much needs to be done. While all may agree on this, there is no consensus over how we should go about doing it. Some suggest that pushing for a liberal democratic framework is *the* solution, because only in liberal democracy can human rights and cultural diversity flourish.[32] The problem with this view is that it ignores the issue of cultural mediation in any political engineering. Such omission time and again has proven ineffective and even counterproductive in instituting the democratic project, particularly in a nonliberal or illiberal setting. Others see things differently, arguing that a liberal conceptual framework such as the one espoused in the United States is incapable of providing a coherent moral vision, because the language of rights and the presumption of self-interested and autonomous individuals that undergirds it are the source of moral and political conflict, not the solution. Thus, rather than try to uncover the compatibility between Confucianism and human rights from which nothing is gained, one should focus on the Confucian moral vision as a genuine alternative.[33] This position also raises some questions. One is that it rests on an erroneous assumption. A rejection of the individualist claim does not automatically mean a rejection of rights altogether, any more than an endorsement of the Confucianism duty-based argument does not necessarily lead to an endorsement of authoritarianism. Still others delve into the Chinese political and cultural tradition to find sources of justification and support for the universalist language.[34] Attractive as the compatibility thesis may sound, however, it fails to reconcile important differences between two sets of cultural values and practices and makes rights discourse look redundant. If we have it and it is just as sound morally, one may ask, why do we need a language of rights after all?

This study offers an alternative approach to the rights-based argument for political reform in China. This alternative may be called a culturally sensitive engagement approach. It argues that to the extent that an individualistic way of relating is radically missing in China, it will help us accomplish little to impose a liberal agenda without fundamentally changing the way the Chinese think about and manage political affairs. To the extent, moreover, that the liberal doctrine itself is philosophically problematic, choosing a liberal seed such as political liberty as "the primary value," as one critic suggests, is unsatisfactory.[35] But this should not be interpreted as saying that one should let things take their own course. As the world is getting smaller, we cannot afford to entertain a bystander mentality and wait for a rights-friendly culture to ripen so that it would provide comfortable bedding for democracy. To do so would be to seriously discount the power of human agency in initiating change. In view of the social and cultural reality in today's China, the best possible course of action for reconstructing a healthy rights discourse and have it bear on political change *vis-à-vis* democratization is to take a positive engagement approach that combines political activism with cultural sensitivity. This means actively engaging a political regime in a continued process of democratic change through value dialogue and political innovation, while at the same time cultivating those conditions that are widely believed to be conducive to the institutionalization of a human rights regime.

The culturally sensitive engagement approach is predicated on two important assumptions. First, although culture is a relatively stable system, it is not an immutable and impenetrable whole. Rather, it is constantly changing and adapting to new ideas and situations. Oftentimes, behind the arguments about cultural particularity, there is an implicit view that culture is a closely knit way of relating impervious to spatial and temporal changes. This is a mistaken view. Secondly, any value can be transferred from one culture to another. The key question is not so much about its transferability as about how meaningfully and productively it can be accommodated in a different environment. In this regard, the liberal notion of rights as a time-tested human value is relevant to Chinese politics. Unfortunately, this notion is frequently couched in universal terms that give adequate attention neither to the context in which it originated nor to the context to which it is to be applied. As a consequence, it tends to lose much of its appeal when transferred to a different cultural setting. For liberal rights to take root and thrive, it is not enough simply to try to make a nonrights-based culture rights-friendly. Value exchange is acceptable insofar as it does not endanger or obliterate cultural identity. Compatibility is not necessarily required for value transfer to happen. It must be reminded, however, that we are often told that political culture needs to be transformed in order to sustain democratic ideas and institutions. Seldom do we hear that there is an equally important need for a redescription of democratic ideas and institutions in order to make them appeal broadly to local habits, beliefs and sentiments. This latter task is central to any discourse on the cultural applicability of human rights.

Viewed from this perspective, the culturally sensitive engagement approach may be read as an attempt to bring into contact two different sets of ideas and values through redescription and reconstruction. Analogous to what Charles Taylor and others view as the project of building "unforced consensus,"[36] it explores the possibility of a common discourse on the basis of which the idea of rights could become a meaningfully shared experience. This "exploring" has two parts. One is to look for ways to reform the dominant way of relating so that it would provide a firm grounding for an emerging value, and the other is to redescribe the idea of rights in a way that enables it to appeal to a broad audience and ultimately entrench itself in a different cultural context. The former task has been an important concern of a large number of thinkers both in and outside China, but the latter has drawn little scholarly attention, particularly less from defenders of liberal democracy and human rights. In the light of this, an attempt to redescribe liberal rights takes on an added significance.

It must be emphasized here that what is intended here is not a substantive, full-blown theory of rights. Rather it is better seen as a heuristic aimed at stimulating further discussions on the issue. Moreover, the idea of rights is a multi-dimensional and complex subject, and its redescription may proceed from several perspectives. Since a complete account is far beyond the scope of this study, I will be concerned only with the nature and ground of rights redescribed. What will be attempted in the pages that follow, specifically, is to make available a different conception of rights, and this conception would take into account of the constraints imposed by a nonindividualistic way of relating that is found in China today.

A proper place to begin a redescription of liberal rights may be to refresh our memory of what it is that needs to be redescribed. As we have seen in previous chapters, the liberal concept of rights presupposes and is grounded in an individualistic way of relating. It is founded on an assumption of the ontological primacy of the individual. It places the individual at the center of moral and political life and takes the individual—his or her dignity, autonomy, or interest—as the ultimate basis of justification for social, political, and legal arrangements. As a basic component of these arrangements, political and legal rights are instituted both as a protective shield against interference with freedom of action and as a positive requirement that others act in such ways as to facilitate that freedom. They are conceived as "valid claims," "trumps," or "side constraints" that empower the individual to pursue a course of life of his or her own choice and impose obligations on others to respect this choice. They are believed to be absolute in the sense that they are not subject to political bargaining or the calculus of social utility. As Rawls succinctly puts it, each individual *qua* moral person "possesses an inviolability founded on justice that even the welfare of society as a whole cannot override."[37]

Given that an essentially nonindividualistic way of relating obtains in the Chinese context, this conception of rights would be less likely to resonate with the cultural sensibility and understanding of the Chinese public. A plurality of reasons can be advanced to explain why a gap existed and still exists between the moral appeal of liberal rights and the failure to take them seriously. But, as has been shown, the cultural inability or unwillingness of a large majority of Chinese to identify with the concept may well be a contributing factor. Under the circumstance, one is naturally inclined to think that a nonindividualistic redescription of rights would perhaps have a better chance to succeed. The idea of embedded rights, I propose, would be a viable candidate to fulfill the task.

From an epistemological standpoint, embedded rights should be pluralistically and open-endedly construed. This claim is consistent with the developmental and pluralist character of the notion of rights which I have shown in chapter three. The historical path this notion has traveled makes it incumbent on us to treat it as an unfinished project that requires a pluralist and open-ended solution. Considered from this perspective, embedded rights should not be conceived merely as *individual* rights—rights which are assignable to, and secure goods for, individuals only, but also as nonindividual rights that are of a collective nature. Traditional liberal rights theorists tend to dismiss the idea of collective rights for fear of incapacitating the currency of rights.[38] This dismissal is untenable from both a practical and a theoretical standpoint. Collective rights can and should be defended, as some postliberal rights theorists argue.[39] But such defense has been founded typically on the same grounds on which individual rights are justified. This makes the argument for collective rights vulnerable to criticisms. Jeremy Waldron has advanced a view of collective rights not on the basis of the individual's autonomy or well-being, but on the basis of the conception of a community as a nonreducible entity and of the communal goods it secures for its members. Collective rights, he argues, are not the subject matter of individual rights; rather, they constitute a separate category and rest on a different justificatory ground. One must be cautious, however, about the difficulties that claims for collective or group rights present. For example, establishing or defining a collective identity is not always an easy thing to do, though analogies can be drawn from the rights of corporations and other collective entities. It is with respect to this ambiguity that the language of individual rights enjoys certain advantages over that of collective rights. But even given ambiguities like this, Waldron believes, there is no compelling reason for not framing collective goods such as a tolerant society and a shared language and cultural tradition in terms of human rights, particularly when such rights are claimed against other collectivities.[40]

By including the nonindividual category within the legitimate purview of rights talk, the idea of embedded rights opens up new possibilities for rights discourse. This, however, is not to say that its nonindividualistic nature consists merely in such inclusiveness. There is a more important sense in which it can be said to be nonindividualistic. Rights may be considered to be nonindividualistic in the deeper sense that they find their anchor not in a philosophical conception of the individual as a presocial and prepolitical being but rather in the understanding of him or her as a socially and culturally embedded being. Though assignable to and purporting to secure goods for individuals, rights are embedded in the social and cultural life of a people and in the process of social interactions between individual and society, and between individuals themselves. They are not something the individual *qua* subject possesses inherently and transcendentally. Rather they present themselves as social relations and as a way of adjusting social relations. Such adjusting is accomplished in accordance with a given conception of justice in a given society and at a given time. This is certainly not to deny that this conception or certain parts of it may be judged as unjust in different societies and at different times. Neither is it to say that it should not be improved or reformulated by every conceivable means as our moral ideal requires. It is merely to assert that the idea of rights can hardly transcend the constraints imposed by such a conception of justice.

The introduction of the concept of justice is intended to remedy a serious problem, namely the lack of a built-in sense of justice, in the Chinese rights thinking. Before I say more about this issue, it is helpful here to make a few preliminary remarks about the need for grounding the idea of rights in a conception of justice. In the first place, there is nothing new about grounding rights in a conception of justice. The deep connection between what is right and what is just has been a long-standing concern in Western political thought since the time of Plato and Aristotle. Whether it is conceived in the objective or subjective sense, a right is an integral part of giving what is due to someone. In fact, it is not only grounded in, but also in crucial ways synonymous with justice. In classical liberal thought, the most fundamental rights were rooted in the law of nature and endowed by our Creator, and by virtue of this rootedness and endowment, they were perceived to be just. In contemporary political discourse, Rawls has advanced the most influential argument for rights on the basis of an understanding of justice as fairness.

Secondly, in its early days, the notion of rights was defended typically by invoking imported concepts such as individual liberty due to the absence of a language of rights in the Chinese political and moral tradition. This defense is ineffective because the concepts invoked require justification themselves. During Mao's reign, no questions of rights arose under the condition of thought control when Marxism was declared the official ideology. When the issue of human rights is brought to the fore as a result of economic liberalization in recent decades, no moral language is readily available to ground rights discourse. That an instrumentalist view has played a significant role in shaping rights thinking, thus, should not come as a surprise. There are a number of problems with this view; perhaps the most troubling one is that it tends to tie public policy, especially the current economic reform, with the promotion of rights and justifies the notion merely by its perceived utility in the overarching national goal of modernization. This in turn may cause rights to be compromised, not only because rights are now subject to the review of public policy and can be sacrificed with few or no remedies if required by the latter, but also because the end of economic reform may signify the end of rights' useful life. It is imperative, therefore, that moral reasons that are independent of policy considerations and embodied in a conception of justice be formulated to ground rights talk and practice.

Thirdly, concern with justice has been an enduring theme in the Chinese moral and political tradition. In both Confucianism and other schools of thought, there are a rich variety of ideas and ideals about how a just relationship is to be constructed, say, between ruler and ruled, children and parents, and among members of a blood-based community. The paramount duty of the ruler to the ruled is a case in point. Mencius' oft-quoted comments on the prioritization of the interests and needs of the people over those of kings and emperors—along with his description of a commiserating rulership founded on a universally shared commiserating heart that cannot bear to see the sufferings of others—is only a most notable example.[41] Grounding rights in a conception of justice, therefore, would allow us to draw upon familiar moral and conceptual categories in the Chinese tradition, and in doing so broaden the appeal of the rights language.

The main features of embedded rights may be summarized as follows. The idea of embedded rights is a nonindividualistic way of understanding and construing rights. It views rights as embedded in the social interconnectedness of expectations and duties rather than as inhering in the individual presocially and prepolitically conceived. Recognizing rights as a way of ad-*justing* human relations on the basis of a conception of justice, not as things to be exclusively possessed, it places rights in relational terms. Rights are relational not merely in the sense that others are under a duty to perform, but more importantly in the sense that any right carries with it a generic duty to see justice done. Furthermore, the embedded view regards rights as a critical instrument for creating a more humane vision of collective life rather than as a mere protective shield for individual self-interests; in so doing, rights become intrinsically connected with and indeed go to define who we are and what we do.

Now, if a conception of justice is required to anchor the idea of embedded rights as I suggest it is, what would go into this conception? A culturally sensitive engagement approach recommends that the Chinese traditional moral and conceptual categories be tapped for use as sources of redescription. But, one may ask, can a duty-based (also referred to as virtue-based or role-based) Confucian tradition provide a theoretically sound grounding for the notion of rights? Rights theorists, particularly those who favor the choice theory, argue that a right expresses a choice by some individuals that others act or refrain from acting in a certain way. Whether or not an individual rights-bearer exercises that choice is entirely up to him or her to decide. In other words, a right is an affirmative power to control or release from control others in the fulfillment of duties. It is grounded in and embodies a conception of the individual as an autonomous, rational and sovereign being. According to this view, rights are primary and come first, whereas duties are derivative and come second. A right ordinarily implies a duty, but not vice versa.

The choice theory has had a wide influence over rights thinkers, and this influence is especially palpable when it comes to the issue of moral groundings for rights. Here, again, Joel Feinberg's fictitious Nowheresville where there are only duties but no rights springs to mind. Whether rights present themselves as "valid claims," "entitlements," "trumps," or "side constraints," it is clear that the notion typically denotes duties *solely* on the part of those against whom a valid claim is laid. Where there is no question of rights, duty does not surface ordinarily. In this regard, it seems intuitively impossible to advance a duty-based conception of rights, because a duty-based right is a contradiction in terms.

Taking issue with a proposed rights-based morality, Raz again brings the language of duty to bear on our conception of rights. According to Raz, rights are simply grounds of duties. To say that X has a right is to say that "an aspect of X's well-being (his interest) is a sufficient reason for holding some other person(s) to be under a duty."[42] It needs to be emphasized that Raz's formulation is not flawless; for example, it rests on a problematic notion of well-being/interest. If A's interest in securing X to B is a sufficient reason to hold C under a duty to provide or not to interfere, one may ask further, does this mean that B has a right that C perform or refrain from performing? It is also worth noting that Raz's view does not amount to a duty-based conception of rights. In fact, Raz accepts neither a rights-based nor a duty-based morality and opts for a pluralist understanding. Despite these qualifications, however, Raz's proposition suggests a plausible way to bring the language of duty to bear on rights thinking. As such, it may help shape the idea of embedded rights and a conception of justice that undergirds it in several aspects.

By bringing the notion of duty back into the equation, first of all, it would help us connect rights discourse with the Chinese moral and political tradition in a way that allows us to uncover a common language. In so doing, it would enable us to rethink and reuse that part of the duty-sensitive tradition, especially its deep concern with a just government, to furnish the underpinnings for a conception of rights. It must be stressed, however, that an argument for duties is no substitute for an argument for rights. The duty of the governing to promote and protect the well-being of the governed must be accompanied by the latter's willingness and assertiveness to hold the former accountable for acting or failing to act in certain ways. Passively waiting to benefit from the discharge of a duty without positively demanding what is due as a matter of justice is not to exercise a right. Such a positive or assertive self-consciousness, it seems to me, would be a big leap forward for a duty-sensitive people like the Chinese, and may take a long time to cultivate. But a partial emphasis on duty would provide a familiar frame of reference in which rights discourse may begin to have some meaningful resonance.

Invoking the language of duty in framing questions of rights may also lead to a reexamination of the concept of duty as traditionally understood in China. The traditional view holds that duties are hierarchically and as-criptively assigned. The two radical revolutions during the first half of this century largely dismantled this view. Though vestiges of it remain in vary-ing degrees in different parts of the country, it has perhaps run its course. A reconstruction of the notion of duty, one that is informed by the notion of rights, is thus not only possible, but also desirable. This reconstructed no-tion should and can be grounded in the widely accepted principle of egali-tarianism and reciprocity. To this end, Confucian ethical categories such as respect and trust could be revitalized to provide a much needed vocabulary by means of which ordinary people relate to one another, and to their gov-ernment. Such relating is to be built on the basis of an understanding that members of society owe to one another as a matter of duty equal respect and trust. This way, they would be able to reclaim a healthy form of social life that has until most recently been deprived of them by long periods of social disruption.

From a political point of view, the idea of duty should and can be re-constructed on the same egalitarian and reciprocal basis. Liberal theory em-phasizes the consent of the governed as the ground of political obligation. Traditionally the consent theory is predicated on the assumption that indi-viduals, prior to entering into political society, voluntarily act together to form a social compact and then use this compact to justify obedience to the wielding of political power necessary to the maintenance of organized life. The voluntary and contractual nature of consent-based obligation presup-poses an individualistic shared way of relating, and a shift from factual to responsive consent has not in any fundamental way changed this key fea-ture.[43] In China, where such a shared way of relating is radically absent, and where political obligation is in large measure based on such uncontested no-tions as membership, tradition, and the family, an unmodified consent the-ory would unlikely provide a viable alternative. This, however, does not mean that the consent theory is not a good one. Perhaps a semi-voluntary account of political obligation along the lines of a qualified benefit theory would fare better in Chinese society.[44] Political obligation is semi-voluntary in the following sense. Although one's choice not to obey political power is not a real choice and one's exit from political society not a real option, one does not have to acquiesce in the form of political rule which one does not approve of. Instead, one can participate actively and in good faith through all possible channels to let one's voice be heard, provided, of course, that such channels genuinely exist. In other words, each individual should understand that he or she has a share of responsibility in government. However, it should also be kept in mind that, as a matter of justice, obligations do not flow only upward from the governed to the governing, but more importantly downward from the governing to the governed. This emphasis on the downward flow of obligations is key to sowing the seeds from which responsive government would spring in the future.

Finally, giving equal weight to the notion of duty would enable us to couch the notion of rights in relational rather than possessive terms. Rights are not a one-way street that gives what Charles Taylor calls "option of waiver" without incurring any duty to the rights-holder. There is a kind of mutuality or reciprocity embedded in the notion of rights (and duties as well) which enables the rights-holder and the duty-performer to relate to each other in a way that benefits them both in particular and an organized life in general. A right, thus, should be construed in relational terms as a meeting of the rights-holder and the duty-performer. While rights are reasons for imposing duties on others, they express a moral desirability that human relations in society be adjusted in a particular way, one that is conducive to the advancement of human well-being individually and collectively. They are nothing but our legitimate expectations that others act or not act in certain ways. Whether an expectation is considered to be legitimate and thus should be met depends on the special conditions under which it emerges. The foundationalist account of the legitimacy of rights which rests ultimately on a presumed metaphysical ground, be it autonomy or human dignity, is inadequate. While an unforced consensus on what constitutes autonomy or human dignity is yet unavailable, taking these notions as grounds of rights tends to invite criticism. The relational character of rights as embedded in the interconnection of expectations and duties is particularly useful in lowering the possessive tone often associated with the liberal concept of rights.

Attractive as it is, however, Raz's is still a rights-centered approach to the relationship between rights and duties, and one can catch a lingering sense of imbalance that duties are there merely to enable rights. Some theorists go further than Raz in acknowledging the indispensable role that the language of duty plays in formulating questions of rights. Disputing the claim that rights often imply duties but duties cannot imply rights, Renteln argues that the relationship between the two is such that the existence of one may always imply that of the other. She raises two objections. "The first is that, in the cases where we would agree that there are such duties, there is also a corresponding right. If society recognizes duties to be kind to animals and babies, for instance, then, indeed, those entities could be said to have rights. The second is that, in those cases in which we are hesitant to assert the existence of a right, it is because the attribution of the duty seems dubious."[45] She adds that "just because a moral theory is couched in the language of duty does not imply that it cannot be a vehicle for the advancement of rights."[46]

Writing in a similar context that deals with the issue of culture and human rights, Chan contends that the Confucian duty-based morality would support many of the rights such as freedom of expression and the right to fair trial. However, it would endorse these rights on an instrumentalist basis and would accord them only a secondary place as something like "a fallback apparatus" in the overall scheme to realize the Confucian moral ideal "*Ren* (benevolence)." On some issues, Chan asserts, the Confucianist would disagree sharply with a postmodern liberal; for example, the Confucianist would have no problem sanctioning a right to choose and do what is morally commendable, but would have serious objections to a right to choose and do what is morally indecent, even with the proviso that the harm principle is firmly in place.[47]

If we accept Renteln's argument as valid, we would be justified in saying that duties are grounds of rights. Indeed, I would go even further in arguing that rights and duties are involved in a dialectical relationship and their correlativity is such that one always implies (instead of *may imply*) and depends on the other. My right to vote, for example, always implies a duty that is clearly assignable to both individuals and governments who may have an interest in interfering with my enjoyment of this right. It also implies a duty in a positive sense that individuals and governments as a matter of law provide real opportunities and necessary conditions (say, ballot box, transportation, registration, etc.) for its exercise. If, further, we accept Chan's argument as valid, we would be justified in saying that elements of the Confucian duty-based morality can be extracted and combined with elements from the liberal tradition to provide groundings for the idea of embedded rights. For example, the duty of the government to the people in terms of providing both moral leadership and material well-being was a central concern in Confucian thought on justice and political legitimacy.[48] This duty can be construed as the ground of a right that each citizen possesses that government perform and be responsive to the people to whom the said duty is owed.

Again, I must emphasize that it is by no means my intention to offer a substantive account of what would go into a conception of justice so that it would provide the basis for the idea of embedded rights. However, one general point about its structure is worth making. An adequate understanding of justice as it pertains to rights discourse in the Chinese context should be a hybrid one where traditional and modern, Chinese and Western ideas and values intersect. As far as tradition is concerned, two strands of thought may be utilized for the purpose of reconstruction. One is the notion of self-cultivation as the basis of a just society and the other the notion of public welfare as the basis of just political rule. That self-cultivation is a vitally important idea in Confucian thought has been widely noted.[49] The significance of this idea goes far beyond the transformation of the self into an object of the grand moral ideal *Ren;* it furnishes the moral foundation for the successful management of family, state and world affairs. With self-cultivation comes a society where people are virtuous, the family is prosperous and political rule is just. With self-cultivation, again, comes the expectation that members of society are accorded the same respect as they accord others.

The notion that public welfare takes precedence over the ruler's own interest also figures prominently in the Chinese tradition. Mencius' famous remarks on the importance of the people vis-à-vis the ruler are its most radical expression. "The people are the most important part of the state," says Mencius, "the community comes next, and the sovereign is the least important."[50] Xun Zi also holds that "Heaven created the people not for the sake of the sovereign; but it erected the sovereign for the sake of the people."[51] A similar line of thinking has been found in Confucian scholars and statesmen in successive generations.[52] It must be pointed out that despite the good intentions of the Confucian noble man, the admonition that the people be placed in the first did not get the attention it deserved in dynastic China. However, regardless of the fact that this may be attributable to the failure of the Confucian noble man, or the system, or both, to curb the abuse of political power, the belief that the government is under a duty to ensure public welfare by action or nonaction runs deep in the hearts and minds of the Chinese. It is precisely the fulfillment of this duty that provides the basis of political legitimacy and just rule. As mentioned previously, duties such as this can be construed as grounds of rights each and every citizen holds that government perform and be responsive to the people to whom the said duties are owed.

To be sure, incorporating traditional moral categories into a conception of justice is not sufficient, because many of the Confucian ideas and practices are either outmoded or simply wrong. There is a need for us to acquire an understanding of what ordinary people think about justice in contemporary China. This understanding would allow us not only to see cultural continuity, but more importantly to feel the pulse of the moment and furnish a blueprint for moral and political development in the foreseeable future. Under the conditions of a rapidly changing Chinese society, the latter seems all the more urgent. In recent years, a number of empirical studies have provided a glimpse if not a panoramic view of what the Chinese public is deeply concerned about. These studies focus on a wide variety of social, cultural, and political issues, not specifically on the question of justice and on what a just society ought to be, but the connection between the two is so close that knowledge of the former would almost certainly shed light on the latter.

Although surveys conducted in China sometimes reveal contradictory patterns, several trends seem unmistakable. One is that the majority of Chinese prefer social and economic stability to political freedom. While acknowledging that their living conditions have improved apparently as a result of economic reform in recent years (91.4%), according to one survey, only 1.8% and 0.9% of the people endorse 100% market economy and 100% private ownership respectively.[53] This risk aversion may have a great deal to do with political turmoil and social disruption in the recent past, but it may also have something to do with the perennial concern of the Chinese with substantive justice vis-à-vis material well-being rather than with procedural justice such as free choice. A second one is that, while individuals in today's China are increasingly aware and assertive of their rights, most are concerned more about their economic, especially property, rights than about social and political rights. As a recent study shows, the idea of sacrificing the individual for the common good has received 90.8% support.[54] Another survey has found that the level of political tolerance is considerably lower than that in democratic countries, which may portend serious limits on the protection of minority rights.[55] A third trend is that family ties and personal obligations remain a strong buttress of the social fabric. Chu and Ju suggest that as the cornerstone of Chinese life, "the force of close family ties" could provide "the inner strength of [cultural] reconstruction."[56] I could not disagree more with this assessment. On the contrary, I tend to argue, it is precisely close family or quasi-family ties and the concomitant division of inner and outer circles of *guanxi* network that pose a serious challenge to the "potential shift from obligations to rights as the guiding principle for social relations."[57]

What these and other related studies have revealed to us are elements of an emerging sense of justice. This sense of justice is fundamentally different from the liberal one ordinarily understood. It tends to value economic well-being more than political liberty; sanction government performance more than procedural fairness; uphold reciprocal obligations more than personal rights; and emphasize collective welfare more than individual interests. The implications it has for rights discourse in the Chinese context are profound. For example, if economic well-being is a priority vis-à-vis political liberty, there is no strong reason to believe that economic rights cannot be fully developed to lay the groundwork for the exercise of political and civil rights. In order for the language of rights to find its way successfully into the consciousness and practice of the Chinese public, a little detour may be needed. When formulating questions of rights, it would be beneficial for one to keep in mind a conception of justice that is broadly recognized in Chinese society today. This, however, by no means precludes any critique of beliefs and practices that may be viewed as wholly or partially unjust; neither should it restrict our efforts to remove the political, cultural, social and economic conditions under which injustice occurs.

A final cautionary note needs to be added. Although the idea of embedded rights is defendable, it is not immune to criticism. For example, one may argue that an asymmetrical emphasis on duty may undercut the notion of rights by making it a toothless weapon for individuals to protect their legitimate interests. It may, say, encourage conformity and subservience, reduce the already narrow range of free choice by the ordinary citizen, and leave the individual defenseless in face of the abuse of political power. Moreover, it is inadequate and even perilous to order collective life on the basis of the reciprocity of goodwill and a sense of duty, particularly the goodwill and sense of duty of those who wield political power. To the extent that conflict is an unfortunate yet inevitable consequence of human action, a similarly asymmetrical emphasis on the appropriateness and harmony of human relations tends to suppress it. Conflict suppression breeds close-mindedness and other social ills. These criticisms are important, but for reasons of space and time, I can offer only a general response, that is, that the idea of embedded rights has its limitations, but this does not mean that it is not a useful idea. As a transitional model of discourse, moreover, it may be made irrelevant by future developments in China.

EMBEDDED RIGHTS AND DEMOCRATIC CHANGE

In the wake of the fall of communist rule in Eastern Europe and the former Soviet Union, there has been a surge of optimism about liberal democracy.

It has been frequently said that liberal democracy is a time-tested and viable model of political rule which has a universal applicability beyond Europe and North America. Arguments against such universality in defense of cultural uniqueness are deficient from both a theoretical and a practical point of view. Theoretically, they misconceive or distort the issue by viewing cultural values as immutable and nontransferable and, ironically, by using Western concepts to justify cultural uniqueness. Practically, they fail to take full account of the empirical fact that liberal ideas and institutions have long become an integral part of democratic development in many non-Western nations. Liberal democracy, thus, is not only desirable but also practical as a model for political development. Indeed, as one critic contends, it provides the *only* viable model for political development *vis-à-vis* all other political ideologies; in this sense, it signifies "the end of history."[58]

This optimism may help us understand a widespread tendency among political thinkers and actors alike to equate liberal democracy with democracy in general. It is not uncommon that a general understanding of democracy is infused with liberal ideas and assumptions. Neither is it uncommon that democratization is conceived as liberalization and an argument for democracy is framed in terms of an argument for liberal values such as individual rights, individual liberty, and the free market.[59]

Does liberal democracy indeed signify the end of a long historical search for the best form of political life? Although liberal democracy presents itself as a vastly more attractive model of political development than communism, and although the idea of democracy is strongly influenced by liberal values and beliefs in the modern age, a claim like "the end of history" is in my view overstated. Not only are we confronted with different conceptions of democracy, all of which have useful things to say about what a democratic polity should be, but we also find actual democracies operating on principles and institutional arrangements which are considerably different from liberal ones. Even among the so-called liberal democracies, differences in value orientation and institutional operation abound. Thus, liberal democracy should not be understood in absolute and undifferentiated terms; it is but one among a number of possible models and the viability of each model depends to a considerable extent on the socio-economic and cultural context to which it is to be applied. As one critic writes, an uncritical endorsement of liberal democracy not only "leaves unanalysed the whole meaning of democracy and its possible variants," but also tends to ignore possible tensions "between the 'liberal' and 'democratic' components of liberal democracy."[60]

As this study has sought to show, the liberal concept of rights which serves as the keystone for liberal democracy presupposes and is grounded in an individualistic shared way of relating; as such, it would be unlikely to provide a viable language for articulating visions of political change in societies in which such an individualistic culture is radically lacking. To say this, however, is not to deny that liberal values are important human values, some of which may be utilized to facilitate democratic transition in a nonliberal cultural setting. Neither is it to imply that democratic ideas cannot be transferred to a nondemocratic or antidemocratic society. It merely calls attention to what Bhikhu Parekh calls "the cultural particularity of liberal democracy" and to the attendant view that cultural considerations should be a constitutive part of the democratic project.[61] The question, thus, is not whether or not a culture is suitable at all for democracy; this question, it seems to me, has been largely settled.[62] Rather, the questions are what kind of democracy is a most likely prospect for a culture and to what extent this kind of democracy can be successfully instituted given the limits set by social and cultural conditions on democratic development.

This is essentially the context in which the idea of embedded rights has been proposed. But granted that cultural constraints need to be taken into account, one may ask, how or in exactly what way can this idea provide a viable language for articulating China's democratic future? What kind of democracy would it be likely to promote or furnish a base for? Before taking up these questions, a brief account of the meaning of democracy is in order. This account can provide a useful frame of reference for discussing democratic change.

Democracy is generally defined as rule by the people. Over this general definition there seems little dispute. But what constitutes such rule has been a subject of intense debate. Joseph Schumpeter, in a classic statement, argues that democracy is an institutional mechanism through which political elites acquire the power to make decisions by competing for popular votes.[63] This understanding of democracy typically limits the role of the citizen to that of periodically selecting a representative body or a plurality of such bodies to rule *for* him or her. According to Schumpeter and others who follow him, representative democracy is the most ingenious form of popular rule created to meet the challenge posed by the large size of the modern nation-state. Participatory democrats, on the other hand, disagree with this interpretation. Carole Pateman, for one, believes that feasibility should not be the only criterion for defining democracy. Whether or not a polity is democratic should instead be assessed by the extent to which it maximizes fundamental democratic values such as freedom and equality. The Schumpeterian elitist-pluralist model is deficient, because it minimizes or narrows the range of freedom by handing over decision making power to political elites.

Participation maximizes individual freedom and political equality by directly involving the citizen in the decision-making process. Such involvement is vital because it helps cultivate democratic personality and fosters the development of democratic community.[64]

The Marxist offers another conception of democracy which is in important ways different from either the representative or the participatory model. The Marxist maintains that liberal representative democracy fails because it ignores the problem of social and economic inequality arising out of a class-based capitalist society. This failure makes liberal democracy and the value of individual freedom dubious at best. For without social and economic equality, there is no genuine political freedom and equality for the average individual. The most important task, thus, is to establish an egalitarian and classless society where the means of production is collectively owned and there would be no exploitation of one human being by another. Only in this kind of society, the Marxist believes, can equal citizenship and democratic participation become a reality.[65]

Each of these views examines the idea of democracy from a particular perspective, and each makes a distinct contribution to our understanding of this concept. Despite their differences, they all share an important concern about the tension between the actual and the ideal, between what a democracy is and what it should be. This concern, it seems to me, is key to unraveling some of the complex issues surrounding democratic development.

As suggested by democratic thinkers, democracy can be viewed as an unfinished yet potentially perfectible project.[66] It can be placed on a continuum, with the least democratic on one end and the most democratic on the other. Democratic change, thus, can be said to consist in a continued process in which movement from one end to the other (and sometimes back and forth) takes place. Two points need to be emphasized here. First, this conception of democracy has a teleological undertone. But if we view the end also as a constantly changing process in which new goals are set to meet the needs of new situations, problems associated with the teleological argument such as the plurality and indeterminacy of ends can be alleviated if not solved. Second, a working definition of democracy with a short list of basic criteria such as Dahl's seven institutional requirements is necessary for distinguishing between democratic and nondemocratic regimes, but it is not sufficient in the sense that it can tell us neither the possible undemocratic practices in existing democracies thus defined nor what a future democracy should be. In this regard, normative thinking is also required to provide a critical tool for evaluating and guiding the democratic project.[67]

Incorporating this normative dimension, this study offers a broad definition of democracy as self-government through participation in the management of collective affairs. How democratic a political regime is, thus, can be determined by the extent to which it maximizes equal and meaningful citizen participation at different levels and in different spheres of collective life.[68] Democracy is not merely a system of institutional arrangements through which political decisions are made, albeit responsively, for the ordinary citizen. It is more importantly a participatory process in which the average citizen takes an active part in making those decisions; only through active participation can democracy as self-rule be truly realized. It needs to be pointed out that a number of difficult issues are involved in this definition; for example, the institutional mechanisms for participation, the extent and frequency of participation, the role of expert knowledge in decision making, and decision rules must all be adequately addressed before participation can become a theoretically and practically viable solution to the problems resulting from the mere fact of living together. But, again, it is perhaps because these problems exist that participation becomes such an important idea, for participation is not only an act of casting votes, but also a valuable learning opportunity for citizens to explore and deliberate together the meaning of democratic autonomy and equality as well as possible ways of resolving conflict and building a commonly shared good life.

Bearing all this in mind, we can explore the questions raised earlier. The idea of embedded rights, in my view, can help provide a viable language for articulating visions of democratic change in China in a number of ways. First, as mentioned above, the idea of embedded rights seeks to incorporate and indeed grounds itself in the contemporary as well as the traditional Chinese concern with justice and reciprocal obligations. This kind of "incorporating" and "grounding" is important because it can help the Chinese find a familiar and effective conceptual tool for promoting a broader awareness of rights and framing and articulating their interests, expectations, and questions with regard to political affairs in terms of this notion. The historical fact that there is the lack of a language of rights in the Chinese political tradition, as critics correctly point out, poses certain difficult theoretical and practical issues for the establishment of a rights-based regime, but these issues are not insurmountable, and attempts have been made to construct a rights discourse based on the Chinese political and cultural tradition.[69]

It should be emphasized that though the language of rights has been through tough times in the past hundred years, it does now have resonance among the Chinese public, especially among intellectuals. In a survey study, for example, Chu and Ju have found that the Chinese do have an awareness of their political rights. When asked about whether one should have a right to know local government spendings, a majority of Shanghai residents answered in the affirmative.[70] The interviews I conducted on a field trip to China in 1997 have also confirmed this point.[71] As indicated earlier, moreover, there have been significant changes in the attitudes of the ruling elite toward human rights in recent decades. It appears that top-echelon officials have finally come to the realization that to ignore the issue of rights entirely is not a politically wise move and have begun to put the human rights dialogue openly on their political agenda. The publication by the Chinese government of the *White Paper* on human rights in 1991 and a follow-up report on the progress of human rights in 1995 is a case in point.[72] Whether or not this gesture is sincere remains open to debate, but from a practical standpoint, it does help the rights language to gain a wider currency in China.

In light of these facts, it seems to me that the question is no longer about whether or not a language of rights should be negotiated for importation from the West, because it already exists—though not firmly grounded—in the Chinese consciousness.[73] Rather, it is about how rights should be understood and utilized and what conception of rights should be promoted to provide an effective tool in facilitating democratic change in China.

This immediately leads to the second point about the utility of embedded rights. The idea of embedded rights can also provide an alternative view to the patriarchal conception of rights that has dominated the Chinese rights discourse since the introduction of this notion one hundred years earlier. According to this conception, rights are granted by a supreme authority, be it emperor, the state, or the party. As such, they can be infringed upon, taken away, or otherwise nullified by this authority as it sees fit. The idea that rights are natural in the sense of having originated in the individual by virtue of his or her inherent moral or human qualities is completely missing from modern Chinese rights thinking.[74] In a questionnaire survey I conducted on a field trip to northern China, for instance, the majority of local congressional representatives in one county were found to hold a similar view about the source of political rights. When asked about the sources of the right to vote, 64% said it was given by the party, while 12% said they were naturally born with this right. The rest answered "don't know."[75]

In order to make the notion of rights an integral part of China's democratizing experience, replacing the patriarchal conception of rights is among the fundamental tasks the Chinese are faced with. In the absence of such replacement, the language of rights would continue to produce limited impact on democratic development, because political patriarchalism is fundamentally antithetical to the idea of self-government. This does not mean, however, that a complete transformation of *rights as granted from the top down* into *rights as individually and inherently owned* must take place. Such transformation may not be possible any time soon, given social and cultural constraints. Neither is it necessary. Indeed, absent a well-entrenched civil society that is capable of regulating itself, it is not inconceivable that a highly individualistic conception of rights would adversely affect democratization by creating a fragmented and chaotic public life in China. The idea of embedded rights may be able to steer clear of this danger while creating a conceptual framework for meaningful discussions on rights. It could do so by rejecting both the liberal and the patriarchal conception of rights, and by advancing a hybrid understanding of rights as neither individually and naturally owned nor granted by a supreme authority, but as socially negotiated and constructed artifacts. As such, rights are an integral part of social and political experience and do not have a presocial and prepolitical objective existence. They should be seen as originated in the necessity to adjust human relations in society and founded upon a conception of justice that is informed by normative reflection as well as by tradition.

This understanding of the nature and grounds of rights is, in my view, superior to the patriarchal conception of rights. But it also raises some theoretical and practical difficulties. For example, basing rights on a conception of justice requires an answer not merely to the question of what standards of justice are to be applied, but equally importantly to the question of who sets the standards of justice and how to apply them. There are no clear-cut and nonproblematic answers to these questions. Economic solutions are potentially just as perilous as political ones. The above-quoted "Three Agriculture Problems" is a case in point. In today's China, there seems no lack of standards, and the problem is rather with institutional mechanisms and office holders who interpret and enforce them. Given the status quo, it seems to me, the best that one can suggest is to build rights practice on a trial-and-error basis and make adjustments along the way where and if necessary.

Third, embedded rights can further be used as a language of reconciliation and cooperation. This language is badly needed for alleviating the tension between the governing and the governed and for rebuilding public trust. During the past century, tremendous pains and sufferings have been inflicted upon the Chinese as a people by revolution, war, and other political misfortunes. Of all the governments instituted, none was able to deliver its promise about a stable and prosperous China. As a result, popular trust toward government has been severely damaged. The revival of popular trust in the early fifties after the communist takeover did not last long, and was followed by endless political campaigns and persecutions. Today, suspicion of and hostility toward the government on all levels run rampant.[76] Certainly there are culturally rooted reasons for such suspicion and hostility, but the ruling elite, whether nationalist or communist, had done too little to restore public confidence in government. The reconstruction of social and political trust, thus, should be a top priority for the Chinese democratic cause, for, as Putnam has shown in a seminal study of Italian democracy, such trust is an essential component of the "moral resources" that foster civic virtues such as public-spiritedness and cooperativeness and provide important underpinnings for democratic institutions.[77]

Political reconciliation and cooperation should begin by emphasizing that people have certain rights. These rights are socially embedded legitimate expectations, not metaphysically grounded individualistic demands, and they express, in general, a moral conviction that people have a legitimate interest in their well-being and government has, as a matter of justice, an obligation to promote and protect this interest. Since the well-being of the people may not be identical with what the ruling elite perceives it to be, this creates a burden on the ruling elite and the government it represents to consult the public about its interests and expectations. The shift of focus from the governing to the governed, from the will of the Party to the real interests of real people, and from forced consensus to public consultation is a first step toward building a responsible and responsive government and restoring popular trust.

The emphasis on the obligation of the governing to the governed, as indicated earlier, has been a long-standing concern in the Chinese traditional conception of justice. While it can still be used as a conceptual framework for promoting democratic development in China, at least at its initial phase, this concern increasingly shows its limitations in face of the impact of democratic ideas. One of the limitations is that it gives no attention to political participation and makes good government depend solely on the good intention of the ruling body to discharge its duty. The idea of embedded rights is designed to remedy this defect by incorporating participation as a central component of the Chinese democratic project. It does not operate on non-participation, on a passive citizenry that merely stands to benefit from the government's fulfillment of its obligations. Rather, it encourages the average citizen to participate in the political process by voicing and bringing his or her interests and expectations to bear on institutional and policy changes. It is predicated on the assumption that participation need not be conceived exclusively as an adversarial process of contestation and opposition; it can be understood as a cooperative opportunity to manage collective affairs and as an obligation of each citizen to share the burden of governing.[78]

Needless to say, to make the idea of embedded rights work in China requires more than answering theoretical questions. Concrete measures must be taken to create favorable conditions for applying this idea, to broaden and deepen the consciousness of rights, and to ensure effective political participation through the establishment of institutional mechanisms. To accomplish all this takes time, patience, and a bit of luck. Bearing in mind China's socio-economic, cultural, and other contingencies, one should be cautious about democratic prospects in the world's most populous nation. Using democratic developments in other parts of Asia, particularly Taiwan, as evidence that China is bound to walk the same path is plausible, but it also has potential pitfalls. Recent political developments at the grassroots level also offers hope for Chinese democracy, but, again, much needs to be done before village election can become an entrenched and meaningful democratic practice.

If the idea of embedded rights can indeed be applied to facilitate democratic development in China, the kind of democracy it supports is unlikely to be liberal democracy. Liberal democracy, as I have suggested, is consistent with and presupposes an individualistic conception of rights, and this conception would play a limited role in shaping the nature and direction of political change in China due to social and cultural constraints. What kind of democracy, then, would the idea of embedded rights promote? In recent years, various models have been proposed for the Chinese democratic project. Bell envisions a bicameral representative democracy in which members of the upper house are selected through examination. This approach reflects both the Confucian concern with rule by the virtuous and the Chinese traditional institution of official recruitment.[79] Womack argues that, given that "a pluralism of societal forces" and the "stability of political expectations" "simply do not exist in mainland China at the present time," chances for liberal democracy to succeed there are slim. He proposes instead a party-state model of democracy in which democratic reform such as increasing citizen control over official selection originates from within the monopolistic communist party and then spreads over a broad institutional spectrum.[80] In addition to these, there is also a home-grown neo-constitutionalist argument. The neo-constitutionalist emphasizes the restructuring and empowering of the existing electoral system, namely the National People's Congress, and the creation as well of a judicial system genuinely independent from the party's interference.[81]

The models each provide a different yet valuable perspective from which to examine the prospect for democracy in China. A common assumption they all seem to share is that changes in political institutions or structures beginning at the top are necessary to launching the Chinese democratic project. This assumption clearly reminds one of the idea of crafting pioneered by

Rustow and embraced by a number of political scientists.[82] While Rustow is correct in making the distinction between causes and correlates, genesis and function in the study of democratic transition, his three-phase model seriously overestimates the so-called "contingent choice" of the political elite to bring about democratic change. A top-down approach, in my opinion, is incomplete because it does not adequately address the equally important question of grassroots democratic development. Political reform that is designed to proceed from the top down has its limitations; one of these is that the political elite does not have a sufficiently strong incentive to go along with such reform. The crisis of legitimation is often cited as a powerful incentive, but as the Chinese case has shown, economic development without political democracy can also help achieve political legitimacy, although this may prove costly over the long run.

The idea of embedded rights supports an approach to democratic development which combines top-down reform with grassroots participation. It argues that while democratization from within the communist party is important, grassroots participation is needed to provide a training ground for the cultivation and entrenchment of democratic norms and values on the one hand and to nourish societal forces capable of pushing the political elite forward on the democratic path on the other. Only the combination of these two directions of change, it seems to me, can help get the Chinese democratic project out of the stagnant situation in which it is now entrapped.

The kind of democracy that the idea of embedded rights is likely to promote may be called a consultative (as in contrast to oppositional) model. The model is consultative primarily in the sense that the views, interests, and expectations of the people should be consulted and incorporated into the national decision-making process. Consultation can take place through various channels; a special consultative body may be established to meet this need, or the existing system of People's Congress may be restructured and strengthened to do this job. Several of the main requirements of the consultative model need to be fleshed out.

1) A strong central authority is to remain in place and still assumes direct control over local governments from province down to the county as well as over major national policies. This strong central authority is needed at present for ensuring not only social and political stability, but also coherent economic development plans, sound national education programs, and competent foreign policies. But, at the same time, some moderate structural changes at the top should be instituted, particularly with regard to the role of the party in government. For example, the position of party secretary can be eliminated or at least made subordinate to the institutional authority of

bureau and department chiefs in central government bureaucracies and to that of governors in local provinces; further, no bureau and department chief or provincial governor can simultaneously hold the position of party secretary.

2) Grassroots political participation *vis-à-vis* village election should be strengthened, and there should be a gradual extension of this electoral process to township- and county-level government. Village election as it is conducted now has serious problems. Some of these are directly linked to defective institutional designs; for example, party interference with electoral results is not uncommon. But some are due to socially and culturally constrained behaviors such as indifference, fraud, noncooperation, and fear. The only way to improve on the effectiveness of village election and make the grassroots democracy work, it seems to me, is by creating the conditions in which abuses are less likely to occur. These include but are not limited to township- and county-level elections, changes in the nominating process, and tax relief for peasants.

3) Related to grassroots political participation is another urgent need to develop a sound legal system. This system consists not merely of a comprehensive legal code, but more importantly of courts, judges, and lawyers who use this code. It is only through using the law that the rule of law acquires meaning. If it is impractical at the moment to have a wholly independent judiciary like that of the United States, it is possible to elect a quasi-judicial body separate from the election of village administrators which would handle civil disputes according to the law. This would provide average citizens with opportunities to learn to resolve interpersonal conflict through legal channels rather than through administrative means as they are accustomed to. It would help regularize, spread, and entrench rights practice.

4) The election of top governmental officials at the provincial, municipal, and perfectural level should also be conducted, but it should be restricted to a form of indirect election. This form of indirect election would differ from the current practice in that it would be relatively free from the party's control over nomination and outcome. Again, in order to accomplish this goal, some moderate structural changes with respect to the party's role in government should be made.

5) Finally, control over the media should be loosened to some degree in order to provide a forum for public debate. Public debate is needed for the dissemination of information as well as for the collection of popular views for public consultation. A market-driven and totally free press is neither feasible nor desirable at this stage mainly because of the adverse effects it is likely to produce on political development. This, however, should not be interpreted as saying that a press tightly controlled by the monopolistic communist party is

desirable. A relatively free press can only be had in synchronization with the development of a relatively mature democratic process.

It is worth noting that the consultative model of democracy which the idea of embedded rights is likely to promote may be questionable on several theoretical grounds. Some may argue, for example, that it is a pseudo-democracy in the sense that it lacks most of the basic institutional features, such as national competitive election and freedom of speech and assembly, which define a democratic regime as we know it in the West. Two responses to this objection are possible. First, while a set of basic requirements are theoretically useful for understanding and assessing democratic development, they should not be taken as absolute, particularly in the absence of consensus on what democracy really is. The three models mentioned above, which each emphasize a different set of criteria, should shed some light on this point. This study has suggested a definition of democracy as the maximization of equal and meaningful participation in self-government. It places democracy on a spectrum, with no participation on one end and maximum participation on the other, and sees democracy not as the presence of certain fixed institutional features but as a process in which the ideal of self-government through participation in all spheres of life is being realized. Viewed from this perspective, the consultative model clearly falls far short of the democratic ideal, but neither is it at the no-participation end.

Second, as the idea of embedded rights is designed as a transitional conceptual framework for fostering rights consciousness and practice, the consultative model of democracy which this idea is likely to promote should also be considered a transitional model. The goal this model sets out to accomplish is a limited one; it is circumscribed not only by social and cultural considerations, but also by the limits of theorizing. Theory can provide guidance for democratic change, but it also has limits. One of these is that they must adapt to changing needs and situations in order to have any bearing at all on the real world of politics. In this regard, it is helpful to adopt a piecemeal approach to the problem of democratization which works rather than have a grand perfect plan which does not.

All this having been said, one should still be clear about the limitations of the idea of embedded rights and the consultative model it may promote in facilitating democratic change in China. To make this idea work and cultivate a participatory ethos clearly involves more than theoretical exposition and model building. What we could do in our capacity as students of politics is to observe, think, and recommend. This study has done just that, namely to reflect upon some of the important issues involved in the process of democratic change and to recommend a course of action for bringing about such change.

Appendix

In early 1997, I took a field trip to China and spent three months in one of the Northern provinces. While there, I conducted a survey of local people's congress representatives in one county and interviewed more than thirty individuals working in a wide range of professions. The original plan was to conduct questionnaire surveys in three counties geographically located in the northern, central, and southern region of the same province. But for various reasons, I had to abandon the original plan and instead focus on one county. This severely limited my ability to generalize.

The empirical inquiry I conducted in China is not a conceptually and methodologically well designed project. It does not stand the rigorous test of a scientific model designed to have broad explanatory power. In short, it is biased. The best I can say on the basis of such evidence is that it reflects the value orientations and practices of a particular segment of the population at a particular locality. Looked at this way, the data I have collected should be considered nothing more than a reality check. They provide a narrow and restricted view of contemporary Chinese political culture, the validity of which must be checked against other more rigorous empirical studies.

Despite its obvious deficiencies, however, my empirical research is interesting in two respects. First, the region I have selected is widely recognized as one of the most culturally and politically conservative and economically underdeveloped areas in China. As such, it may serve as a baseline point of reference against which more culturally and economically advanced regions can be studied. Second, although the questionnaire survey may be statistically insignificant, the interviews I have conducted are useful. The interviewing method has been employed widely by anthropologists and sociologists alike and proven to be a reliable research tool.

The data have been collected during a period of three months. They consist of two parts. The first is a survey questionnaire with multiple-choice answers specifically designed for local people's congress representatives. The questionnaire has a total of thirty questions, and these questions have been framed with two main objectives in mind. One is to find out how the concept of rights is perceived, understood, and practiced and the other to gather information about how people relate to one another and how their way of relating reflects their perception and understanding of rights. Except for special terms, the language used to design the questionnaire is kept as simple and plain as possible in order to avoid misunderstanding. In certain cases, vernacular or idiomatic expressions are used. This reflects my understanding that the way questions are framed and the language is used affect survey results considerably. Even with these precautions taken, I realized in the process of conducting the survey that questionnaire is a simplistic way of obtaining information about the way of relating among ordinary people. For both questions asked and answers provided typically lack contexts, and these contexts, in my view, are an important part of an adequate understanding of culture. The problem of context skipping was brought to my attention at one point when I found that some of those surveyed tried to rephrase the questions asked or wrote comments on the margin to explain why a particular answer was given.

As mentioned earlier, the survey was conducted in one county. There are one hundred sixty local people's congress representatives in that county, seventy five of whom have been surveyed. These representatives were chosen according to their willingness to participate and through personal contact, that is, personal network. Mailing out questionnaires to all representatives was ruled out, because I was advised that I would never get them back if I chose to do so. The survey was completed within a period of six weeks. Townships and villages located in the mountain areas did not receive representation in the survey because it was difficult to travel to those places. Of the seventy five representatives surveyed, 28% are county government officials, 21.3% village cadres, 13.3% township cadres, 8% peasants, 8% managers of local industries, 6.7% workers in local industries, 5.3% individual entrepreneurs, and 9.3% a mixture of teachers, provincial employees working in the county, army personnel, and one scientist. The survey questionnaire begins with questions about their sex, age, marital status, education, family income, party membership, terms served in the local people's congress, and then moves to questions about political culture and rights. Interesting as they may be, some of the questions asked do not have direct bearing on this study. In the following, I will list those questions that I believe are most relevant to the study of contemporary Chinese political culture.

The second part of the data is personal interview. Personal interviews were also conducted in the central region of the province, but in a broader area. They also involve a wider range of people in various professions. There are township cadres, peasants, officials in provincial, city and county governments, businessmen, journalists, university professors, factory workers, and writers. The length of time for each interview was from one to three hours. The setting for interview varied from office, hotel, restaurant, to home. The atmosphere was for the most part casual. Conversation typically began with my request for information about the structural features of local people's congress and about the way it actually worked. This served as a springboard to other topics such as cultural, social and political conditions. Except for two occasions when the interview was conducted in group, all interviews were conducted on a person-to-person basis. But even in a group setting, interviewees talked as candidly as in a person-to-person setting, because they were called together by network friends.

The findings from interviews are equally rich in substance. But, again, some of the conversations had little or no bearing on this study. I have already used a small portion of these conversations in chapter four in support of my thesis. In the following, I will list the date, the interviewee's profession, the length of time, and the locality of the interview.

SURVEY QUESTIONS

Q# 12. How were you elected to the county people's congress?

Q# 13. Why did you want to be the county people's congress representative?

Q# 14. When you vote a given candidate, what is the most important factor that affects your vote?

Q# 16. If the candidate for a county deputy mayor were honest and talented, yet he sometimes did things that made people uncomfortable, would you vote him or her in this case?

Q# 20. The Constitution says that citizens have various rights (including the right to vote); how do you think the term "rights" should be understood?

Q# 21. If the state decides to eliminate these rights (including the right to vote) from the Constitution, how do you feel about it?

Q# 22. Where do you think the rights as specified in the Constitution come from?

Q# 23. If the state decides that one married couple can have two children, but some people insist on having three, four, five, and even six children, what do you think the state should do about these people?

Q# 24. Before you cast your vote in the last election, was there any county leader, friend, or network associate who asked or hinted that you should vote for a particular candidate?

Q# 25. If one of the candidates were one of your relatives, and this relative of yours was nice but lacked leadership qualities, whom would you vote in this situation?

Q# 26. If the county people's congress, under the instruction of the county party committee and government, decided not to count some votes in order for a particular candidate they liked to be elected, what action would you take to rectify this?

Q# 28. In your memory, have you ever criticized your parents face-to-face?

Q# 29. In your memory, have you ever criticized your superiors openly?

Q# 30. You quarreled with your neighbor, and your neighbor hit you. Later on, a mutual friend talked with both of you, and your neighbor apologized to you face-to-face for what he had done. Your mutual friend suggested that you settle the dispute in private. Under such circumstances, which do you think would be the best solution, settling this in private or suing your neighbor in court?

INTERVIEWS

April 3; division chief in a provincial bureau; one hour; his office.

April 5; general manager of a trading company; one hour; his home.

April 8; businessman; one hour; hotel.

April 8; division chief in a provincial bureau; two hours; his office.

April 9; journalist; one hour and half; his home.

April 11; journalist; two hours; his office.

April 12; group interview (six municipal people's congress representatives); three hours; restaurant.

April 14; municipal people's congress representative; one hour; his home.

April 15; group interview (party secretary, worker, two cadres in a factory); one hour and half; my home.

April 17; township deputy party secretary; two hours; his office.

April 17; township party secretary; one hour; her office.

April 17; township deputy mayor; one hour; his office.

April 18; township people's election committee chairman; one hour and half; his office.

April 20; municipal county people's congress chairman; two hours; friend's home.

April 22; freelance writer; two hours; his home.

April 23; county people's congress personnel; one hour; hotel.

April 24; county grain bureau chief; one hour; his office.

April 24; township deputy mayor; one hour and half; his office.

April 26; village party secretary; one hour; friend's home.

April 28; special assistant to a municipal bureau chief; two hours; restaurant.

May 10; national people's congress representative and scientist; two hours; his home.

May 25; journalist; one hour and half; his home.

May 25; university professor; one hour and half; his home.

Notes

NOTES TO CHAPTER ONE

1. For a most recent example, see Terence Ball, *Reappraising Political Theory* (Oxford: Clarendon Press, 1995).
2. See Jane Mansbridge, *Beyond Adversary Democracy* (NY: Basic Books, 1983) for an empirical inquiry of democratic theory; Jennifer L. Hochschild, *What's Fair?* (Cambridge, MA: Harvard University Press, 1981) for a survey study of the issue of justice; Susan Moller Okin, *Justice, Gender and the Family* (NY: Basic Books, 1989) for a feminist critique of liberalism; and more recently, Jack Crittenden, *Beyond Individualism* (NY: Oxford University Press, 1992) for a psychological rendering of liberal theory of the self.
3. The absence of moral argument in early political development literature and its adverse effect on developing nations should give political theorists reason to participate in model-building. For an example of the absence of moral argument, see Samuel P. Huntington, *Political Order in Changing Societies* (New Haven, CT: Yale University Press, 1968).
4. The path of contemporary rights discourse has been pioneered by the works of the following authors, among others. Leo Strauss, *Natural Right and History* (Chicago: University of Chicago Press, 1953); C. B. Macpherson, *The Political Theory of Possessive Individualism* (Oxford: Clarendon, 1962); D. D. Raphael, ed. *Political Theory and the Rights of Man* (Bloomington, IN: Indiana University Press, 1967); John Rawls, *A Theory of Justice* (Cambridge, MA: Harvard University Press, 1971); Robert Nozick, *Anarchy, State and Utopia* (NY: Basic Books, 1974); Ronald Dworkin, *Taking Rights Seriously* (Cambridge, MA: Harvard University Press, 1977); Michael J. Sandel, *Liberalism and the Limits of Justice* (Cambridge: Cambridge University Press, 1998); Joseph Raz, *The Morality of Freedom* (Oxford: Clarendon Press, 1986).
5. A.P. d'Entreves, *Natural Law* (NY: Harper Torchbook, 1965), 14.
6. See Jeremy Waldron, ed. *'Nonsense upon Stilts'* (London: Methuen, 1987).
7. Asbjorn Eide, "The Universal Declaration in Space and Time," in *Human Rights in a Pluralist World*, eds. Jan Berting, et al. (Westport, CT: Mechler, 1990),15–32.

8. Judith N. Shklar, "The Liberalism of Fear" and Benjamin R. Barber, "Liberal Democracy and the Costs of Consent," in *Liberalism and the Moral Life*, ed. Nancy L. Rosenblum (Cambridge, MA: Harvard University Press, 1989), 21–38 and 54–68.

9. For a treatment of a variety of liberalisms in contemporary political discourse, see David Johnston, *The Idea of a Liberal Theory* (NJ: Princeton University Press, 1994).

10. David Beetham, "Introduction: Human Rights in the Study of Politics," *Political Studies* 43 (Special Issue 1995):6.

11. Robert A. Dahl, *Democracy and Its Critics* (Hew Haven, CT: Yale University Press, 1989), 221.

12. For espousal of such a culturally sensitive approach, see John Rawls, "The Law of Peoples," in *On Human Rights,* eds. Stephen Shute and Susan Hurley (NY: Basic Books, 1993), 41–82; Daniel A. Bell, "A Communitarian Critique of Authoritarianism," *Political Theory* 25:1 (1997):6–32.

13. Richard E. Flathman, "Introduction," in *Concepts in Social and Political Philosophy*, ed. Richard E. Flathman (NY: Macmillan, 1973), 1–40; Michael Shapiro, ed. *Language and Politics* (NY: New York University Press, 1984).

14. Stephen Chilton, *Grounding Political Development* (Boulder, CO: Lynne Rienner, 1991).

15. Alan R. White, *Rights* (Oxford: Clarendon, 1984), 14.

16. Ibid, 112.

17. Ibid, 113–114.

18. Ian Shapiro, *The Evolution of Rights in Liberal Theory* (NY: Cambridge University Press, 1986), 5.

19. Jacob Burckhardt, *The Civilization of the Renaissance in Italy* (London: G. G. Harrap, 1960); Quentin Skinner, *The Foundations of Modern Political Thought* (NY: Cambridge University Press, 1978).

20. Max Weber, *The Methodology of the Social Sciences* (NY: The Free Press, 1949).

21. Steven Luke, *Individualism* (Oxford: Blackwell, 1973).

22. Ian Watt, *The Rise of the Novel* (Berkeley, CA: University of California Press, 1957), 60.

23. Daniel Shanahan, *Toward a Genealogy of Individualism* (Amherst, MA: University of Massachusetts Press, 1992), 20.

24. Louis Dumont, *Essays on Individualism* (Chicago: University of Chicago Press, 1986), 62.

25. Jacques Maritain, *Three Reformers* (London, Sheed & Ward, 1947), 16.

26. Ian Watt, *The Rise of the Novel* (Berkeley, CA: University of California Press, 1957), 13.

27. For a recent and controversial study of the collectivist culture with regard to the Holocaust, see Daniel Jonah Goldhagen, *Hitler's Willing Executioners* (NY: Alfred A. Knopf, 1996).

28. Robert N. Bellah, et al., *Habits of the Heart* (Berkeley, CA: University of California Press, 1985).

29. Tan Qixiang, "Temporal and Geographical Differences in Chinese Culture," in *Reevaluating Chinese Traditional Culture* (Beijing: Sanlian Shudian, 1987), Vol. 1, 27–55.

30. For such a comparison, see Li Zehou, *Essays on Ancient Chinese Thought* (Beijing: Renmin Chubanshe, 1985).

31. Yu Yingshi, *A Contemporary Interpretation of Chinese Intellectual Tradition* (Nanjing, Jiangsu: Jiangsu Renmin Chubanshe, 1995).

32. Qian Mu, *Political Dynamics and Failures in Dynastic China* (Taipei, Taiwan: Dadong Tushu Gongsi, 1977), 10–15.

33. Xu Yangjie, *A Historical Study of the System of the Kinship Family in Song and Ming Dynasties* (Beijing: Zhonghua Shuju, 1995).

34. Lucian W. Pye, *The Mandarin and the Cadre* (Ann Arbor, MI: University of Michigan Press, 1988); Carol Lee Hamrin and Suisheng Zhao, ed. *Decision-Making in Deng's China* (NY: M. E. Sharpe, 1995).

35. Mayfair Mei-hui Yang, *Gifts, Favors, and Banquets* (Ithaca, NY: Cornell University Press, 1994); Godwin C. Chu and Yanan Ju, *The Great Wall in Ruins* (Albany, NY: SUNY, 1993).

36. Inoue Tatsuo, "Liberal Democracy and Asian Orientalism," in *The East Asian Challenge for Human Rights*, ed. Joanne R. Bauer and Daniel A. Bell (NY: Cambridge University Press, 1999), 60–87.

37. Henry Rosemont, Jr., "Human Rights: A Bill of Worries," in *Confucianism and Human Rights*, ed. Wm. De Bary and Tu Wei-ming (NY: Columbia University Press, 1998), 54–66.

38. Sumner B. Twiss, "A Constructive Framework for Discussing Confucianism and Human Rights," in *Confucianism and Human Rights*, ed. Wm. De Bary and Tu Wei-ming (1998), 27–53; and Wm. De Bary, *Asian Values and Human Rights* (Cambridge, MA: Harvard University Press, 1998).

39. For most recent universalist arguments in the context of the Asian value debate, see Inoue Tatsuo, "Liberal Democracy and Asian Orientalism," and Jack Donnelly, "Human Rights and Asian Values: A Defense of 'Western' Universalism," in *The East Asian Challenge for Human Rights*, ed. Joanne R. Bauer and Daniel A. Bell (NY: Cambridge University Press, 1999), 27–59 and 60–87; Ann Kent, *Between Freedom and Subsistence* (Hong Kong: Oxford University Press, 1993); Marina Svensson, *Debating Human Rights in China* (Lanham, MD: Rowman & Littlefield, 2002).

40. Daniel A. Bell, "A Confucian Democracy for the Twenty-First Century," Conference Paper (1996). Quoted by Inoue Tatsuo, "Liberal Democracy and Asian Orientalism," in *The East Asian Challenge for Human Rights*, ed. Joanne R. Bauer and Daniel A. Bell (NY: Cambridge University Press, 1999), 28.

41. Brantly Womack, "Party-State Democracy: A Theoretical Exploration," in *Mainland China after the Thirteenth Party Congress*, ed. King-yuh Chang (1990), 11–29.

42. For a review of the neo-constitutionalist recommendations, see Andrew Nathan, *China's Transition* (NY: Columbia University Press, 1997), 231–245.

NOTES TO CHAPTER TWO

1. Larry Diamond, "Introduction," in *Political Culture and Democracy in Developing Countries,* ed. Larry Diamond (Boulder, CO: Lynne Rienner, 1993), 7.
2. Demosthenes, *Demosthenes against Timocrates* (Cambridge, MA: Harvard University Press, 1926), 375.
3. Xenophon, *The Constitution of Lacedaemonians* (London: George Bell and Sons, 1908), 204–230.
4. Plato, *The Laws* (NY: Basic Books, 1980), 64.
5. Plutarch, *Plutarch's Lives* (London: J. M. Dent and Sons, 1970), 136.
6. Ibid, 123, 135, 140.
7. Plato, *The Laws* (NY: Basic Books, 1980), 24 and *passim.*
8. Plato, *Plato's Republic* (Indianapolis, IN: Hackett, 1974), especially Books 3, 4, 8 and 9; *The Sophist and the Statesman* (London: Thomas Nelson and Sons, 1961), 273–283, 310–338.
9. Aristotle, *The Politics of Aristotle* (London: Oxford University Press, 1946), Book 7; *Nichomachean Ethics* (Indianapolis, IN: The Liberal Arts Press, 1962), Book 1 and 10.
10. Aristotle, *The Politics of Aristotle* (London: Oxford University Press, 1946), 332.
11. Ibid, 181.
12. Emile Durkheim, *Montesquieu and Rousseau: Forerunners of Sociology* (Ann Arbor, MI: University of Michigan Press, 1960).
13. Montesquieu, *The Spirit of the Laws* (London: Cambridge University Press, 1989), 314–317.
14. Ibid, 315.
15. Ibid, 187–210, 308–333.
16. Montesquieu's loose use of the term is notorious. This understanding of laws as a set of structural principles can be found throughout in *The Spirit of the Laws,* especially in Book 19, chapter 27.
17. Herbert Simon, "Human Nature in Politics," *American Political Science Review* 79 (1984): 293–304; William P. Kreml, *Psychology, Relativism and Politics* (NY: New York University Press, 1991).
18. Montesquieu, *The Spirit of the Laws* (London: Cambridge University Press, 1989), 236, 246–263.
19. Jean-Jacques Rousseau, *The Social Contract and Discourses* (London: J. M. Dent and Sons, 1973), 228.
20. Jean-Jacques Rousseau, *Emile* (NY: Basic Books, 1979), 458.
21. Jean-Jacques Rousseau, *The Government of Poland* (Indianapolis, IN: Hackett, 1985), 3.
22. Hannah Arendt, *Lectures on Kant's Political Philosophy* (Chicago: University of Chicago Press, 1982), 71.
23. Jean-Jacques Rousseau, *The Social Contract and Discourses* (London: J. M. Dent and Sons, 1973), 132–168.
24. Jean-Jacques Rousseau, *The Government of Poland* (Indianapolis, IN: Hackett, 1985), 29–30.

25. A similar observation is developed in David Cameron's comparative study *The Social Thought of Rousseau and Burke* (Toronto: University of Toronto Press, 1973).

26. Edmund Burke, *The Works of Edmund Burke* (London: G. Bell, 1900), Vol. 6, 146–147.

27. Edmund Burke and Thomas Paine, *Reflections on the Revolution in France* and *The Rights of Man* (NY: Anchor Books, 1973), 33.

28. Ibid, 33 and *passim*.

29. Ibid, 103–125, 149–168. A critical account of this argument is given by Michael Freeman, *Edmund Burke and the Critique of Political Radicalism* (Chicago: University of Chicago Press, 1980), esp. chapter 4, "The Sociology of Conservatism," 53–83.

30. Edmund Burke, *Selected Letters of Edmund Burke* (Chicago: University of Chicago Press, 1984), 299.

31. Peter A. Lawler, "The Human Condition: Tocqueville's Debt to Rousseau and Pascal," in *Liberty, Equality, Democracy*, ed. Eduardo Nolla (NY: New York University Press, 1992), 1–20.

32. Jack Lively, *The Social and Political Thought of Alexis de Tocqueville* (Oxford: Clarendon Press, 1962), 23–70.

33. Alexis de Tocqueville, *Democracy in America* (NY: Vintage Books, 1945), Vol. 1, 288–325; *The Old Regime and the French Revolution* (NY: Doubleday & Company, 1955), 210–211.

34. Alexis de Tocqueville, *Democracy in America* (NY: Vintage Books, 1945), Vol. 2, esp. 99–168.

35. Ibid, 202.

36. Edward B. Tylor, *Primitive Culture* (London: J. Murray, 1920), Vol. 1, 1.

37. A.L. Kroeber and Clyde Kluckhohn, *Culture: A Critical Review of Concepts and Definitions* (NY: Vintage Books, 1963), 85–87.

38. Franz Boas, *The Mind of Primitive Man* (NY: Collier Books, 1963), 149–179 and "Methods of Research," in *General Anthropology*, ed. Franz Boas (1938), 666–686; Ruth Benedict, *Patterns of Culture* (Boston, MA: Houghton Mifflin, 1934), 223–278.

39. Ruth Benedict, *Patterns of Culture* (Boston, MA: Houghton Mifflin, 1934), 48.

40. Elvin Hatch, *Theories of Man and Culture* (NY: Columbia University Press, 1973), 217–228, 314–335; David Kaplan and Robert A. Manners, *Culture Theory* (Eaglewood Cliffs, NJ: Prentice-Hall, 1972), 55–60.

41. A. R. Radcliffe-Brown, *Structure and Function in Primitive Society* (Glencoe, IL: The Free Press, 1965); Branislaw Malinowski, *A Scientific Theory of Culture and Other Essays* (Chapel Hill, NC: University of North Carolina Press, 1963).

42. Adam Kuper, ed. *The Social Anthropology of Radcliffe-Brown* (London: Routledge & Kegan Paul, 1977), 15.

43. Elvin Hatch, *Theories of Man and Culture* (NY: Columbia University Press, 1973), 229, 298.

44. Leslie A. White, "The Concept of Culture," *American Anthropologist*, 61:1 (1959):231.

45. Leslie A. White, *The Science of Culture* (NY: Farrar, Straws, 1949), 122.
46. Leslie A. White, "The Concept of Culture," *American Anthropologist,* 61:1(1959):231–236.
47. Clifford Geertz, *The Interpretation of Cultures* (NY: Basic Books, 1973), 89.
48. Roy Wagner, *The Invention of Culture* (Chicago: University of Chicago Press, 1975), esp. 35–70.
49. Ibid, 37.
50. Talcott Parsons, "Introduction," in *Theories of Society,* ed. Talcott Parsons, *et al.* (NY: Free Press, 1961), Vol. 2, Part Four, "Culture and the Social System," 963–993.
51. Emile Durkheim, *The Division of Labor in Society* (NY: Macmillan, 1984), esp. 31–87, 269–290.
52. Talcott Parsons, *The Structure of Social Action* (NY: Free Press, 1949), 309.
53. Paul Bohannan, "*Conscience Collective* and Culture," in *Emile Durkheim, 1858–1917: A Collection of Essays,* ed. Kurt H. Wolff (Columbus, OH: Ohio State University Press, 1960), 77–96.
54. Ibid, 81.
55. Emile Durkheim, *Sociology and Philosophy* (NY: The Free Press, 1974), 26.
56. Emile Durkheim, *The Elementary Forms of the Religious Life* (NY: The Free Press, 1965), 29, 56, 242–243, 253, 259, 465–466, 483.
57. Max Weber, *The Theory of Social and Economic Organization* (NY: The Free Press, 1947), 118–119.
58. Ralph Schroeder, *Max Weber and the Sociology of Culture* (London: Sage Publications, 1992), 1–32.
59. Max Weber, *The methodology of the Social Sciences* (NY: The Free Press, 1949), 72, 76, 81.
60. Max Weber, *The Theory of Social and Economic Organization* (NY: The Free Press, 1947), 89.
61. Max Weber, *The Methodology of the Social Sciences* (NY: The Free Press, 1949), 92.
62. Talcott Parsons, "Introduction to 'Culture and the Social System,'" in *Theories of Society,* ed. Talcott Parsons, *et al,* (NY: Free Press, 1961), 963–993; Talcott Parsons and Edward A. Shils, "Values, Motives, and Systems of Action," in *Toward a General Theory of Action,* ed. Talcott Parsons and Edward A. Shils (Cambridge, MA: Harvard University Press, 1952), esp. 159–189.
63. Max Weber, *The Protestant Ethic and the Spirit of Capitalism* (London: Routledge, 1930), esp. 155–183.
64. Gabriel A. Almond, "The Intellectual History of the Civic Culture Concept," in *The Civic Culture Revisited,* ed. Gabriel A. Almond and Sidney Verba (Newbury Park, CA: Sage Publications, 1989), 1–36.
65. Gabriel A. Almond, "Comparative Political Systems," *Journal of Politics,* 18 (1956):391–409; Gabriel A. Almond and Sidney Verba, *The Civic Culture* (Princeton, NJ: Princeton University Press, 1963), esp. Ch. 1, 3–42.
66. Gabriel A. Almond and Sidney Verba, *The Civic Culture* (Princeton, NJ: Princeton University Press, 1963), 14–26.

67. Ibid, 14.
68. For a critique of this liberal bias, particularly with regard to the impact of class structure and liberal ideology on political competence (or the perception of political competence), see Carole Pateman, "The Civic Culture: A Philosophic Critique," in *The Civic Culture Revisited,* ed. Gabriel A. Almond and Sidney Verba (Newbury Park, CA: Sage Publications, 1989), 57–102.
69. Gabriel A. Almond and G. Bingham Powell, Jr., *Comparative Politics: System, Process, and Policy* (Boston, MA: Little, Brown, and Company, 1978).
70. Edward W. Lehman, "On the Concept of Political Culture: A Theoretical Reassessment," *Social Forces* 50 (March 1972):362.
71. Dale Hoak, ed. *Tudor Political Culture* (London: Cambridge University Press, 1995).
72. Carole Pateman, "The Civic Culture: A Philosophic Critique," in *The Civic Culture Revisited,* ed. Gabriel A. Almond and Sidney Verba (Newbury Park, CA: Sage Publications, 1989), 80–86.
73. Lucian W. Pye, "Introduction," in *Political Culture and Political Development,* ed. Lucian W. Pye and Sidney Verba (Princeton, NJ: Princeton University Press, 1965), 3–26; Archie Brown, "Introduction," in *Political Culture and Political Change in Communist States,* ed. Archie Brown and Jack Gray (NY: Holmes and Meier, 1977), 1–24.
74. Ibid, 7 and ibid 16, respectively.
75. Lucian W. Pye, *The Spirit of Chinese Politics* (Cambridge, MA: MIT Press, 1968) and *The Mandarin and the Cadre: China's Political Cultures* (Ann Arbor, MI: University of Michigan Press, 1988).
76. Jack Gray, "China: Communism and Confucianism" and Stephen White, "The USSR: Patterns of Autocracy and Industrialism" in *Political Culture and Political Change in Communist States,* ed. Archie Brown and Jack Gray (NY: Holmes and Meier, 1977), 197–230, 25–65.
77. Stephen Chilton, *Grounding Political Development* (Boulder, CO: Lynne Rienner, 1991), 64.
78. Lowell, Dittmer, "Political Culture and Political Symbolism: Toward a Theoretical Synthesis," *World Politics* 29 (July 1977):566.
79. Ibid, 570–581.
80. Stephen Chilton, *Grounding Political Development* (Boulder, CO: Lynne Rienner, 1991), 65.
81. Dan Sperber, *Rethinking Symbolism* (London: Cambridge University Press, 1975), 48.
82. Young C. Kim, "The Concept of Political Culture in Comparative Politics," *Journal of Politics* 26 (1964):336.
83. Edward W. Lehman, "On the Concept of Political Culture: A Theoretical Reassessment," *Social Forces* 50 (March 1972):368.
84. Robert C. Tucker, "Culture, Political Culture, and Communist Society," *Political Science Quarterly* 88 (June 1973):173–190.
85. Stephen Chilton, *Grounding Political Development* (Boulder, CO: Lynne Rienner, 1991), 59–61.

86. Ibid, 68.
87. Ibid, 71–78.
88. Michael Thompson, et al., *Cultural Theory* (Boulder, CO: Westview Press, 1990).
89. Ibid, 104.
90. Emile Durkheim, *Sociology and Philosophy* (NY: The Free Press, 1974); Leslie A. White, "The Concept of Culture," *American Anthropologist* 61:1 (1959):231–236.
91. Michael Thompson, et al., *Cultural Theory* (Boulder, CO: Westview Press, 1990), 83–99.
92. Emile Durkheim, *The Elementary Forms of the Religious Life* (NY: The Free Press, 1965).
93. Michael Thompson, et al., *Cultural Theory* (Boulder, CO: Westview Press, 1990), 33.
94. Ibid, 23.
95. Stephen Chilton, *Grounding Political Development* (Boulder, CO: Lynne Rienner, 1991), 109.

NOTES TO CHAPTER THREE

1. Ronald Beiner, *What's the Matter with Liberalism* (Berkeley, CA: University of California Press, 1992), 81.
2. Joel Feinberg, "The Nature and Value of Rights," *The Journal of Value Inquiry* 4 (1970):243–257.
3. Adamantia Pollis and Peter Schwab, ed. *Human Rights* (NY: Praeger, 1979).
4. This is sometimes called the objective sense of a right following the usage of Continental scholars. See Richard Tuck, *Natural Rights Theories* (London: Cambridge University Press, 1979), 7–15.
5. F. H. Pollock and F. W. Maitland, *The History of English Law* (Cambridge, London: University Press, 1923), 124.
6. Annabel S. Brett, *Liberty, Right and Nature* (London: Cambridge University Press, 1997).
7. Hugo Grotius, *The Rights of War and Peace* (NY: M. W. Dunne, 1901), 3–6; quote from Richard Tuck, *Natural Rights Theories* (London: Cambridge University Press, 1979), 74.
8. Thomas Hobbes, *Leviathan* (London: J. M. Dent and Sons 1914), 66–74, 110–117.
9. John Locke, *Two Treatises of Government* (NY: Cambridge University Press, 1963), 309–318, 327–344, 446–453.
10. Jeremy Bentham, *An Introduction to the Principles of Morals and Legislation* (NY: Hafner Publishing Company, 1948), 224–225.
11. J. L. Austin, *Lectures on Jurisprudence* (London: J. Murray, 1881), 609–700; W.N. Hohfeld, *Fundamental Legal Conceptions* (New Haven, CT: Yale University Press, 1919), 27–31; H. L. A. Hart, "The Ascription of Responsibility and Rights," in *Logic and Language,* ed. Antony Flew (Oxford: Basil Blackwell, 1952), 145–166.
12. Alan R. White, *Rights* (Oxford: Clarendon, 1984), 7.

13. Ibid, 9–10.
14. For representative discussions on the subject and object of rights, see Douglas Husak, "Why There Are No Human Rights" and Alan Gewirth, "Why There Are Human Rights," *Social Theory and Practice* 11:2 (Summer 1984):125–141 and 235–248; Maurice Cranston, "Human Rights, Real and Supposed" and D. D. Raphael, "Human Rights, Old and New," in *Political Theory and the Rights of Man*, ed. D. D. Raphael (Bloomington, IN: Indiana University Press, 1967), p43–53 and 54–67.
15. J. P. Plamenatz, *Consent, Freedom and Political Obligation* (NY: Oxford University Press, 1968), 82.
16. H. J. McCloskey, "Rights," *Philosophical Quarterly* 15:59 (April 1965):117.
17. Ibid, 119.
18. Joel Feinberg, "The Nature and Value of Rights," *Journal of Value Inquiry* 4 (1970):256.
19. W. N. Hohfeld, *Fundamental Legal Conceptions* (New Haven, CT: Yale University Press, 1919), 36–40.
20. Ibid, 60.
21. H. L. A. Hart, *Essays in Jurisprudence and Philosophy* (Oxford: Clarendon Press, 1983), 35.
22. Ibid, 35–36.
23. H. L. A. Hart, "Are There Any Natural Rights?," *Philosophical Review* 64:2 (April 1955):175–191.
24. Mary Peter Mack, ed. *A Bentham Reader* (NY: Pegasus, 1969), 257.
25. H. L. A. Hart, *Essays on Bentham* (Oxford: Clarendon Press, 1982), 181–188.
26. David Lyons, "Rights, Claimants, and Beneficiaries," *American Philosophical Quarterly* 6:3 (July 1969):173–185.
27. Joseph Raz, "On the Nature of Rights," *Mind* 93 (1984):194.
28. Alan Gewirth, "The Basis and Content of Human Rights," in *Nomo XXIII: Human Rights,* ed. J. Roland Pennock and John W. Chapman (NY: New York University Press, 1981), 123–124.
29. Alan R. White, *Rights* (Oxford: Clarendon, 1984), 93–115.
30. H. L. A. Hart, "Are There Any Natural Rights?," *Philosophical Review* 64:2 (April 1955):175–191; Ronald Dworkin, *Taking Rights Seriously* (Cambridge, MA: Harvard University Press, 1977), esp. 266–278; Joel Feinberg, "The Nature and Value of Rights," *Journal of Value Inquiry* 4 (1970):243–257; Richard Wasserstrom, "Rights, Human Rights, and Racial Discrimination," *Journal of Philosophy* 61:20 (October 1964):628–641; and Alan Gewirth, "The Basis and Content of Human Rights," in *Nomo XXIII: Human Rights,* ed. J. Roland Pennock and John W. Chapman (NY: New York University Press, 1981), 119–147.
31. J. S. Mill, *Utilitarianism, On Liberty, and Considerations on Representative Government* (London: J. M. Dent and Sons, 1972); R. M. Hare, *Moral Thinking* (Oxford: Clarendon Press, 1982); and T. M. Scanlon, "Rights, Goals, and Fairness," in *Theories of Rights,* ed. Jeremy Waldron (London: Oxford University Press, 1984), 137–152.

32. Joseph Raz, "Rights-Based Moralities," in *Theories of Rights,* ed. Jeremy Waldron (London: Oxford University Press, 1984), 182–200; and John Finnis, *Natural Law and Natural Rights* (London: Oxford University Press, 1980).

33. Joseph Raz, "On the Nature of Rights," *Mind* 93 (1984):194–214; H. J. McCloskey, "Human Needs, Rights, and Political Values," *American Philosophical Quarterly* 13 (1976):1–18; and David Lyons, "Rights, Claimants, and Beneficiaries," *American Philosophical Quarterly* 6:3 (July 1969):173–185.

34. Rex Martin, *Rawls and Rights* (Lawrence, KS: University of Kansas Press, 1985).

35. John Rawls, *A Theory of Justice* (Cambridge, MA: Harvard University Press, 1971), esp. 3–194.

36. Ibid, 60, 302.

37. H. L. A. Hart, *Essays on Bentham* (Oxford: Clarendon Press, 1982), 166–167.

38. R. G. Frey, "Act-Utilitarianism, Consequentialism, and Moral Rights," in *Utility and Rights,* ed. R. G. Frey (Minneapolis, MN: University of Minnesota Press, 1984), 63.

39. Alan R. White, *Rights* (Oxford: Clarendon, 1984), 100–106.

40. Alan Gewirth, "The Basis and Content of Human Rights," in *Nomos XXIII: Human Rights,* ed. J. Roland Pennock and John W. Chapman (NY: New York University Press, 1981), 123.

41. Brian Barry, "On Social Justice," in *Concepts in Social and Political Philosophy,* ed. Richard Flathman (NY: Macmillan, 1973), 427–429.

42. Alan R. White, *Rights* (Oxford: Clarendon, 1984), 114.

43. Leo Strauss, *Natural Right and History* (Chicago: University of Chicago Press, 1953), 120–164. It is worth noting that this recapitulation ignores some of the controversies in the classical scholarship; it ignores, for instance, the debate over natural versus legal justice and the related issue of natural versus conventional law as well. For brevity I assume it is possible to construct an account of the naturalness of political society and its laws as being consistent with the natural right principle. Cf. also Plato, *The Republic* (Indianapolis, IN: Hackett, 1974), Book 1, 2, 4, 6, 7 and *The Laws* (NY: Basic Book, 1980), Book 1, 3, 5, 6, 12; Aristotle, *The Politics* (London: Oxford University Press, 1946), Book 2, 3, 4, 7 and *Nicomachean Ethics* (Indianapolis, IN: The Liberal Arts Press, 1962), Book 1, 2, and 5; Cicero, *On the Commonwealth* (Indianapolis, IN: The Bobbs-Merrill Company, 1929), Book 1, 3, 6 and *On the Law* (Cambridge, MA: Harvard University Press, 1928), Book 1 and 2.

44. Paul E. Sigmund, *Natural law in Political Thought* (Lanham, MD: University of America Press, 1971), 33–34; Thomas Aquinas, *The Political Ideas of St. Thomas Aquinas,* ed. Dino Bigongiari (NY: Hafner Press, 1953), 96–104.

45. Richard Tuck, *Natural Rights Theories* (London: Cambridge University Press, 1979); Brian Tierney, "Tuck on Rights: Some Medieval Problems" and "Origins of Natural Rights Language," *History of Political Thought*

4:3 (Winter 1983):429–441 and 10:4 (Winter 1989):615–646; Arthur Stephen McGrade, "Ockham and the Birth of Individual Rights," in *Authority and Power,* ed. Brian Tierney and Peter Lineham (London: Cambridge University Press, 1980), 149–165; Annabel S. Brett, *Liberty, Right and Nature* (London: Cambridge University Press, 1997); and Kenneth Pennington, *The Prince and the Law, 1200–1600* (Berkeley, CA: University of California Press, 1993).

46. Brian Tierney, "Origins of Natural Rights Language," *History of Political Thought* 10:4 (Winter 1989):632; Thomas Aquinas, *The Political Ideas of St. Thomas Aquinas,* ed. Dino Bigongiari (NY: Hafner Press, 1953), 212.

47. Walter Ullmann, *The Individual and Society in the Middle Ages* (Baltimore, MD: The Johns Hopkins University Press, 1966), 46.

48. Ibid, 48.

49. Olga Tellegen-Couperus, *A Short History of Roman Law* (NY: Routledge, 1993).

50. Kenneth Pennington, *The Prince and the Law, 1200–1600* (Berkeley, CA: University of California Press, 1993), 44.

51. Walter Ullmann, *The Individual and Society in the Middle Ages* (Baltimore, MD: The Johns Hopkins University Press, 1966), 19–20.

52. Ibid, 37.

53. Brian Tierney, "Origins of Natural Rights Language," *History of Political Thought* 10:4 (Winter 1989):639.

54. Brian Tierney, "Tuck on Rights," *History of Political Thought* 4:3 (Winter 1983):438.

55. Annabel S. Brett, *Liberty, Right and Nature* (London: Cambridge University Press, 1997), esp. 123–164. It may be of interest to note that this argument or elements of it did not end abruptly upon the arrival of the modern era but continued to hold sway in and around the time of the English Revolution when the neo-roman theories about the connection between free individuals and free state came to take a part in political discourse. See Quentin Skinner, *Liberty before Liberalism* (London: Cambridge University Press, 1998).

56. A. E. Taylor, "The Ethical Doctrine of Hobbes," in *Thomas Hobbes: Critical Assessments,* ed. Preston King (London: Routledge, 1993), Vol. 2, 22–39; Howard Warrender, *The Political Philosophy of Hobbes* (Oxford: Clarendon Press, 1957); C. B. Macpherson, *The Political Theory of Possessive Individualism* (Oxford: Clarendon, 1962).

57. For a recent example of this argument, see Pierre Manent, *An Intellectual History of Liberalism* (Princeton, NJ: Princeton University Press, 1994).

58. A natural law reading of Locke can be found in Richard Ashcraft, *Locke's Two Treatises of Government* (London: Allen and Unwin, 1987) and James Tully, *An Approach to Political Philosophy: Locke in Contexts* (London: Cambridge University Press, 1993). A traditional liberal reading is rendered critically by Ian Shapiro, *The Evolution of Rights in Liberal Theory* (NY: Cambridge University Press, 1986) and appreciatively by Ruth W. Grant, *John Locke's Liberalism* (Chicago: University of Chicago Press, 1987).

59. A. John Simmons, *The Lockean Theory of Rights* (Princeton, NJ: Princeton University Press, 1992).

60. Michael Oakeshott, *Rationalism in Politics and Others Essays* (Indianapolis, IN: Liberty Press, 1991), 221–294; Thomas Nagel, "Hobbes's Concept of Obligation," in *Thomas Hobbes: Critical Assessments,* ed. Preston King (London: Routledge, 1993), Vol. 2, 116–129.

61. A. E.Taylor, "The Ethical Doctrine of Hobbes" and Howard Warrender, "Hobbes's Conception of Morality," in *Thomas Hobbes: Critical Assessments,* ed. Preston King (London: Routledge, 1993), Vol. 2, 22–39 and 130–145.

62. G. S. Kavka, "Right Reason and Natural Law in Hobbes's Ethics," in *Thomas Hobbes: Critical Assessments,* ed. Preston King (London: Routledge, 1993), Vol. 2, 419–433.

63. Deborah Baumgold, *Hobbes' Political Theory* (NY: Cambridge University Press, 1988).

64. For a critique of attempts to impose unity on Hobbes, see Quentin Skinner, "Hobbes's 'Leviathan,'" in *Thomas Hobbes: Critical Assessment,* ed. Preston King (London: Routledge, 1993), Vol.1, 77–92.

65. Thomas Hobbes, *Leviathan* (London: J. M. Dent and Sons, 1914), 66; *De Cive* (Oxford: Clarendon Press, 1983), 47.

66. Annabel S. Brett, *Liberty, Right and Nature* (London: Cambridge University Press, 1997).

67. Thomas Hobbes, *Leviathan* (London: J. M. Dent and Sons, 1914), 66–67; *De Cive,* (Oxford: Clarendon Press, 1983), 52, 170.

68. Ibid, 68, 160, and ibid, 58–59, respectively.

69. Ibid, 112, 116; and ibid, 100–101, respectively.

70. W. von Leyden, "Introduction," in John Locke, *Essays on the Law of Nature* (Oxford: Clarendon, 1954), 25–26.

71. For a useful discussion of the intellectual relationship between Hobbes and Locke, see Peter Laslett, "Introduction," in John Locke, *Two Treatises of Government,* (London: Cambridge University Press, 1963), 80–105.

72. Leo Strauss, *Natural Right and History* (Chicago: University of Chicago Press, 1953), 202–251.

73. For an early critique of the Straussian position, see John W. Yolton, "Locke on the Law of Nature," in *John Locke: Critical Assessments,* ed. Richard Ashcraft (London: Routledge, 1991), Vol. 2, p16–33.

74. For example, Richard Ashcraft, *Locke's Two Treatises of Government* (London: Allen and Unwin, 1987).

75. James Tully, *An Approach to Political Philosophy: Locke in Contexts* (London: Cambridge University Press, 1993), 96–117. To do justice to Tully, it should be noted that he also uses the natural rights language in discussing Locke's theory of property; in fact the term "property" itself is understood in terms of "right." But, in his judgment, Locke sees this right not as a liberty, but as "resulting from, or entailed by" men's natural law duty to preserve mankind.

76. A. John Simmons, *The Lockean Theory of Rights* (Princeton, NJ: Princeton University Press, 1992), 97–99, 102.

77. Ibid, 100–101.

78. John Locke, *Essays on the Law of Nature* (Oxford: Clarendon, 1954), 111.

79. John Locke, *Two Treatises of Government* (NY: Cambridge University Press, 1963), *Second Treatise,* para. 6. Citation of this work will follow the convention of noting paragraph numbers in Locke scholarship.

80. Ibid, *Second Treatise,* para. 6, 17, 36.

81. Ibid, *Second Treatise,* para. 17, 23.

82. For the classical view that property is for Locke an exclusive right, see C. B. Macpherson, *The Political Theory of Possessive Individualism* (Oxford: Clarendon, 1962), esp. chapter 5, 194–262; for the opposite view that property is an inclusive right, see James Tully, *A Discourse on Property* (NY: Cambridge University Press, 1980).

83. "By property," Locke says emphatically, "I must be understood here, *as in other places,* to mean that Property which Men have in their Persons as well as Goods (emphasis added)." John Locke, *Two Treatises of Government* (NY: Cambridge University Press, 1963), *Second Treatise,* para. 173.

84. Ibid, *First Treatise,* para. 42, 86–98; *Second Treatise,* para. 7–13, 22, 27–38, 55–76, 119–122, 128.

85. Ibid, *Second Treatise,* para. 28.

86. Ibid, *Second Treatise,* para. 119–131.

87. Ibid, *Second Treatise,* para. 149, 154, 176, 180, 185, 190.

88. Ibid, *Second Treatise,* para. 130, 154, 158, 208, 212, 222, 225.

89. Ian Shapiro, *The Evolution of Rights in Liberal Theory* (NY: Cambridge University Press, 1986), 273.

90. Jeremy Waldron, ed. *'Nonsense upon Stilts'* (London: Methuen, 1987).

91. Friedrich A. Hayek, *The Constitution of Liberty* (Chicago: University of Chicago Press, 1960).

92. Ibid, 54.

93. Ibid, 22–53.

94. Ibid, 87.

95. J. S. Mill, *On Liberty and Other Writings,* ed. Stefan Collini (London: Cambridge University Press, 1989), 14.

96. For a critique of the idea of rights-based morality, see Joseph Raz, "Rights-Based Moralities," in *Theories of Rights,* ed. Jeremy Waldron (London: Oxford University Press, 1984), 182–200.

97. Rex Martin, *Rawls and Rights* (Lawrence, KS: Kansas University Press, 1985).

98. John Rawls, *A Theory of Justice* (Cambridge, MA: Harvard University Press, 1971), 3. A similar view has been expressed by H. L. A. Hart, "Are There Any Natural Rights?," *Philosophical Review* 64:2 (Apr. 1955):175; Robert Nozick, *Anarchy, State, and Utopia* (NY: Basic Books, 1974), ix; and Ronald Dworkin, *Taking Rights Seriously* (Cambridge, MA: Harvard University Press, 1977), xi.

99. John Rawls, *A Theory of Justice* (Cambridge, MA: Harvard University Press, 1971), 119.

100. Ibid, 255–256.

101. A similar description is found in Stephen Mulhall and Adam Swift, *Liberals and Communitarians* (London: Basil Blackwell, 1996), 2nd ed., xvi, where the authors treat Rawlsian liberalism as being situated between a libertarian

view represented by Nozick and a communitarian view as represented by Sandel, MacIntyre, and others.

102. Robert Nozick, *Anarchy, State, and Utopia* (NY: Basic Books, 1974); Michael Sandel, *Liberalism and the Limits of Justice* (Cambridge: Cambridge University Press, 1998), 2nd Ed.

103. John Rawls, *A Theory of Justice* (Cambridge, MA: Harvard University Press, 1971), 505–506.

104. Robert Nozick, *Anarchy, State, and Utopia* (NY: Basic Books, 1974), 28–33; Ronald Dworkin, "Rights as Trumps," in *Theories of Rights,* ed. Jeremy Waldron (London: Oxford University Press, 1984), 153–158.

105. H. L. A. Hart, "Are There Any Natural Rights?," *Philosophical Review* 64:2 (1955):182.

106. John Rawls, *A Theory of Justice* (Cambridge, MA: Harvard University Press, 1971), 4, 64, 205–221, 446–452. It may be of some interest to note that Raz has made a valid criticism with regard to the argument that rights can only be limited for the sake of rights. Raz suggests that this argument requires that one assign different weight to different kinds of rights and, in doing so, one is subject to the same difficulty a utilitarian solution is susceptible of. See Joseph Raz, "Liberalism, Autonomy, and Politics of Neutral Concern," in *Midwest Studies in Philosophy,* ed. Peter A. French, et al. (Minneapolis, MN: University of Minnesota Press, 1982), Vol. 7, 107.

107. Rex Martin, *Rawls and Rights* (Lawrence, KS: University of Kansas Press, 1985), 63–127.

108. For a defense of basic economic well-being as among the basic rights, see Henry Shue, *Basic Rights* (Princeton, NJ: Princeton University Press, 1980).

109. John Rawls, *A Theory of Justice* (Cambridge, MA: Harvard University Press, 1971), 116.

110. Chandran Kukathas and Philip Pettit, *Rawls* (Stanford, CA; Stanford University Press, 1990), 27.

111. Nagel points out that the Rawlsian original position with its presumption of neutrality with respect to the good is biased toward a liberal, individualistic conception of justice. Thomas Nagel, "Rawls on Justice," in *Reading Rawls,* ed. Norman Daniels (Stanford, CA: Stanford University Press, 1989), 2nd Ed., 1–15.

112. For the view that the hypothetical contract is not a contract at all and thus not binding in the sense in which Rawls uses it, see Ronald Dworkin, "The Original Position," in *Reading Rawls,* ed. Norman Daniels (Stanford, CA: Stanford University Press, 1989), 2nd Ed. 16–26.

113. John Rawls, *A Theory of Justice* (Cambridge, MA: Harvard University Press, 1971), 561. See also 251–256, 408–409, 505, 567.

114. Ian Shapiro, *The Evolution of Rights in Liberal Theory* (NY: Cambridge University Press, 1986), 274.

NOTES TO CHAPTER FOUR

1. Steven Lukes, *Individualism* (Oxford: Blackwell, 1973), esp. 125–145.

2. Max Weber, *The Methodology of the Social Sciences* (NY: The Free Press, 1949), 90.

3. Ernst Troeltsch, *The Social Teaching of the Christian Churches* (NY: Macmillan, 1931); Jacob Burckhardt, *The Civilization of the Renaissance in Italy* (London: G. G. Harrap, 1929).

4. Karl Marx, *Economic and Philosophic Manuscripts of 1844* (NY: International Publishers, 1964).

5. Alex de Tocqueville, *Democracy in America* (NY: Vintage Books, 1945).

6. Max Weber, *The Protestant Ethic and the Spirit of Capitalism* (London: Routledge, 1930), 222.

7. Elvin Hatch, *Theories of Man and Culture* (NY: Columbia University Press, 1973).

8. Lorenzo Infantino, *Individualism in Modern Thought* (NY: Routledge, 1998).

9. Will Kymlicka, *Liberalism, Community, and Culture* (NY: Oxford University Press, 1989).

10. Steven Lukes, *Individualism* (Oxford: Blackwell, 1973); Daniel Shanahan, *Toward a Genealogy of Individualism* (Amherst, MA: University of Massachusetts Press, 1992).

11. Koenraad W. Swart, "Individualism in the Mid-19th Century," *Journal of the History of Ideas* 23 (1963):79.

12. Ibid, 77–79.

13. Alexis de Tocqueville, *Democracy in America* (NY: Vintage Books, 1955), Vol. 2, 104.

14. Quoted in Steven Lukes, *Individualism* (Oxford: Blackwell, 1973), 11.

15. L.T. Hobhouse, *Liberalism* (NY: Oxford University Press, 1964), 66.

16. Lukes lists four such ideas: the dignity of man, autonomy, privacy, and self-development. But in the end, he believes that "the cardinal ideals of individualism" are liberty and equality. He does not explain, though, why self-development should not be included there, given the enormous role it comes to play in contemporary liberal thought. See Steven Lukes, *Individualism* (Oxford: Blackwell, 1973), 45–72, 158.

17. For examples, see Fred R. Dallmayr, *The Twilight of Subjectivity* (Amherst, MA: University of Massachusetts Press, 1981); George Kateb, *The Inner Ocean* (NY: Cornell University Press, 1992).

18. Daniel Shanahan, *Toward a Genealogy of Individualism* (Amherst, MA: University of Massachusetts Press, 1992), 13–34.

19. Ibid, p46.

20. Louis Dumont, *Essays on Individualism* (Chicago: University of Chicago Press, 1986), 55, 56.

21. Ian Watt, *The Rise of the Novel* (Berkeley, CA: University of California Press, 1957), 14.

22. Louis Dumont, *Essays on Individualism* (Chicago: University of Chicago Press, 1986), 234–268.

23. Ian Watt, *The Rise of the Novel* (Berkeley, CA: University of California Press, 1957), 60.

24. Colin Morris, *The Discovery of the Individual* (NY: Harper & Row, 1972), 3.

25. Louis Dumont, *Essays on Individualism* (Chicago: University of Chicago Press, 1986), 62.

26. Daniel Shanahan, *Toward a Genealogy of Individualism* (Amherst, MA: University of Massachusetts Press, 1992), 20.

27. Walter Ullmann, *The Individual and Society in the Middle Ages* (Baltimore, MD: The Johns Hopkins University Press, 1966), 32–42.

28. Alan Macfarlane, *The Origins of English Individualism* (NY: Cambridge University Press, 1979), 196.

29. Christopher Hill, *Reformation to Industrial Revolution* (London: Weidenfeld and Nicolson, 1967) and *The World Turned Upside Down* (Penguin Books, 1975).

30. David Weissman, "Introduction," in *Discourse on the Method and Meditations on First Philosophy*, ed. David Weissman (New Haven, CT: Yale University Press, 1996), 111.

31. William T. Bluhm, "Political Theory and Ethics," in *Discourse on the Method and Meditations on First Philosophy*, ed. David Weissman (New Haven, CT: Yale University Press, 1996), 306.

32. Charles Taylor, *Philosophical Arguments* (Cambridge, MA: Harvard University Press, 1995), 1–19.

33. Rene Descartes, *Philosophical Works* (London: Cambridge University Press, 1911), Vol. 1, 7–8.

34. Ibid, 16–17.

35. Ibid, 92.

36. Ibid, 82, 95, 106.

37. Ibid, 219–220.

38. Ibid, 140.

39. Ibid, 149.

40. Ibid, 150.

41. Ibid, 151.

42. David Weissman, "Metaphysics," in *Discourse on the Method and Meditations on First Philosophy*, ed. David Weissman (New Haven, CT: Yale University Press, 1996), 155.

43. Peter Markie, "The Cogito and Its Importance," in *Descartes*, ed. John Cottingham (Oxford: Clarendon, 1998), 50–78.

44. Ian Watt, *The Rise of the Novel* (Berkeley, CA: University of California Press, 1957), 13.

45. David Weissman, "Metaphysics," in *Discourse on the Method* and *Meditations on First Philosophy*, ed. David Weissman (New Haven, CT: Yale University Press, 1996), 189.

46. For example, Susan James takes issue with Taylor's use of the internal/external divide as a conceptual scheme to understand Descartes. See Susan James, "Internal and External in the Work of Descartes," in *Philosophy in an Age of Pluralism*, ed. James Tully (NY: Cambridge University Press, 1994), 7–19.

47. Charles Taylor, *Philosophical Arguments* (Cambridge, MA: Harvard University Press, 1995), 7.

48. Stephen Toulmin, "Descartes in His Time," in *Discourse on the Method* and *Meditations on First Philosophy*, ed. David Weissman (New Haven, CT: Yale University Press, 1996), 121–146.

49. Martin van Gelderen, "Liberty, Civic Rights, and Duties in Sixteenth-Century Europe and the Rise of the Dutch Republic," in *The Individual in Political Theory and Practice*, ed. Janet Coleman (London: Clarendon, 1996), 99–122.

50. Jacques Maritain, *Three Reformers* (London: Sheed & Ward, 1947).

51. Ernst Troeltsch, *The Social Teaching of the Christian Churches* (NY: Macmillan, 1931), 461.

52. Ibid, 468–469.

53. Ibid, 470.

54. Ibid, 472.

55. Jacques Maritain, *Three Reformers* (London: Sheed & Ward, 1947), 16.

56. Ernst Troeltsch, *The Social Teaching of the Christian Churches* (NY: Macmillan, 1931), 484.

57. Maritain notes that a feeling of freedom bordered on licence led Luther and his followers down on a path of debauchery and crime; they raped nuns and tore them from their cloisters to make them "wives." Jacques Maritain, *Three Reformers* (London: Sheed & Ward, 1947), 183–184.

58. Ernst Troeltsch, *The Social Teaching of the Christian Churches* (NY: Macmillan, 1931), 579–580.

59. Ibid, 582.

60. Ibid, 583.

61. Louis Dumont, *Essays on Individualism* (Chicago: University of Chicago Press, 1986), 55.

62. Ernst Troeltsch, *The Social Teaching of the Christian Churches* (NY: Macmillan, 1931), 589–590. It should be noted here that what Calvin means by the certainty of election may be seen as a general prescription, not an individually assigned promise. Only by viewing it this way will we be able to understand Calvin's idea of election and reprobation.

63. Louis Dumont, *Essays on Individualism* (Chicago: University of Chicago Press, 1986), 55.

64. Ernst Troeltsch, *The Social Teaching of the Christian Churches* (NY: Macmillan, 1931), 606.

65. Max Weber, *The Protestant Ethic and the Spirit of Capitalism* (London: Routledge, 1930).

66. Ibid, 103.

67. Christopher Hill, *Reformation to Industrial Revolution* (London: Weidenfeld and Nicolson, 1967).

68. Mervyn James, *Family, Lineage, and Civil Society* (Oxford: Clarendon Press, 1974), 97–98.

69. Ibid, 105–107.

70. Christopher Hill, *The World Turned Upside Down* (London: Penguin Books, 1972); Anthony Fletcher and John Stevenson, ed. *Order and Disorder in Early Modern England* (London: Cambridge University Press,

1985); David Underdown, *A Freeborn People* (Oxford: Clarendon Press, 1996).

71. Robert Tittler, "Political Culture and the Built Environment of the English Country Town," in *Tudor Political Culture,* ed. Dale Hoak (London: Cambridge University Press, 1995), 133–156.

72. Mervyn James, *Family, Lineage and Civil Society* (Oxford: Clarendon Press, 1974), 89, 191.

73. Robert Brenner, "Bourgeois Revolution and Transition to Capitalism," in *The First Modern Society,* ed. A. L. Beier, et al. (London: Cambridge University Press, 1989), 271–304.

74. Judith J. Hurwich, "Lineage and Kin in the Sixteenth-Century Aristocracy," in *The First Modern Society,* ed. A. L. Beier, et al. (London: Cambridge University Press, 1989), 33–64.

75. David Underdown, *A Freeborn People* (Oxford: Clarendon Press, 1996), 116–117; Susan Amussen, "Gender, Family and the Social Order, 1560–1725," in *Order and Disorder in Early Modern England,* ed. Anthony Fletcher and John Stevenson (London: Cambridge University Press, 1985), 196–217.

76. David Underdown, "The Taming of the Scold: the Enforcement of Patriarchal Authority in Early Modern England," in *Order and Disorder in Early Modern England,* ed. Anthony Fletcher and John Stevenson (London: Cambridge University Press, 1985), 116–136.

77. Mervyn James, *Family, Lineage and Civil Society* (Oxford: Clarendon Press, 1974), 96–107.

78. Christopher Hill, *Reformation to Industrial Revolution* (London: Weidenfeld and Nicolson, 1967), 51–52.

79. A. L. Beier, *Masterless Men* (London: Methuen, 1985); Christopher Hill, *The World Turned Upside Down* (London: Penguin Books, 1972), esp. 32–45.

80. Mervyn James, *Family, Lineage, and Civil Society* (Oxford: Clarendon Press, 1974), 94.

81. Paul Langford, *Public Life and the Propertied Englishman* (Oxford: Clarendon Press, 1991), 207–214;

82. David Underdown, *A Freeborn People* (Oxford: Clarendon Press, 1996), 89.

83. Alan Macfarlane, *The Origins of English Individualism* (NY: Cambridge University Press, 1978).

84. For a review of these criticisms and Macfarlane's response to them, see Alan Macfarlane, *The Culture of Capitalism* (London: Basil Blackwell, 1987), 191–222.

85. Ibid, 196. Also see Lawrence Stone, "Goodbye to Nearly All That," *New York Review of Books* April 19, 1979, 40–41.

86. Barrington Moore, Jr., *Social Origins of Dictatorship and Democracy* (Boston: Beacon Press, 1966), 8.

87. Ibid, 10.

88. Christopher Hill, *Reformation to Industrial Revolution* (London: Weidenfeld and Nicolson, 1967), 99–122.

89. Paul Langford, *Public Life and the Propertied Englishman* (Oxford: Clarendon Press, 1991), 25–27.

90. Ibid, 65.

91. Barrington Moore, Jr., *Social Origins of Dictatorship and Democracy* (Boston: Beacon Press, 1966), 8–9; Paul Langford, *Public Life and the Propertied Englishman* (Oxford: Clarendon Press, 1991), 118.

92. Paul Langford, *Public Life and the Propertied Englishman* (Oxford: Clarendon Press, 1991), 71.

93. Alexis de Tocqueville, *Democracy in America* (NY: Vintage Books, 1945) and Robert N. Bellah, et al. *Habits of the Heart* (Berkeley, CA: University of California Press, 1985).

94. Alexis de Tocqueville, *Democracy in America* (NY: Vintage Books, 1945), Vol. 2, 104.

95. Ibid, 3.

96. Ibid, 6.

97. Ibid, 134–135.

98. Ibid, 203.

99. Robert N. Bellah, et al. *Habits of the Heart* (Berkeley, CA: University of California Press, 1985), 142.

100. Ibid, 56–62.

101. Ibid, 62–65, 75–82.

102. Ibid, 65–71, 336.

103. Ibid, 174.

104. Ibid, 167–195.

105. Ibid, 127.

NOTES TO CHAPTER FIVE

1. Tan Qixiang, "Temporal and Geographical Differences in Chinese Culture," in *Reevaluating the Chinese Traditional Culture* (Beijing: Sanlian Shudian, 1987), Vol. 1, 35. Unless indicated otherwise, all translations of sources in Chinese language will be mine. The titles of these sources will be footnoted in English only, with their Pinyin romanization given in brackets in Bibliography. Where the name of a given author has been well established in literature, the Wade-Gile system of spelling will be kept. All other lesser known names will be spelled by using the Pinyin system, so will the names of locality and dynasty.

2. Li Qinde, *Regional Cultures in China* (Taiyuan, Shanxi: Shanxi Gaoxiao Lianhe Chubanshe, 1995).

3. Some recognize four schools of thought, namely Taoism, Legalism, Confucianism, and Mohism (associated with the philosophy of Mo Tzu), as the major influences on the formation of the Chinese cultural tradition. See Liang Qichao, *A History of the Pre-Qin Political Thought* (Beijing: The Oriental Press, 1996).

4. Liu Zehua, *A History of Chinese Political Thought* (Hangzhou, Zhejiang: Zhejiang Renmin Chubanshe, 1996), Vol. 1, 362–368.

5. Lao Tzu, *Tao Te Ching*, in *Sources of Chinese Tradition*, eds. Wm. T. de Bary, et al. (NY: Columbia University Press 1960), 54. This is a slightly revised passage of the original translation.

6. Liu Zehua, *A History of Chinese Political Thought* (Hangzhou, Zhejiang: Zhejiang Renmin Chubanshe, 1996), Vol. 1, 330–331; and Roger T. Ames, *The Art of Rulership* (Honolulu, HI: University of Hawaii Press, 1983), 232.

7. Han Fei, *Han Fei Zi* (Shanghai: Shanghai Guji Chubanshe, 1989), 18.

8. Zhao Jihui, et al. *The History of Confucianism in China* (Zhengzhou, Henan: Zhongzhou Guji Chubanshe, 1991), 48–70.

9. Confucius, *Analects*, trans. Yang Bojun (Beijing: Zhonghua Shuju, 1980), 113.

10. *Book of Poetry*, in *Sishu Wujing*, ed. Zhu Xi (Tianjin: Tianjin Guji Chubanshe, 1988), 102.

11. Zhao Jihui, et al. *The History of Confucianism in China* (Zhengzhou, Henan: Zhongzhou Guji Chubanshe, 1991), 4.

12. Xun Zi, *Xun Zi*, trans. Zhang Jue (Shanghai: Shanghai Guji Chubanshe, 1995), 397.

13. *Book of Rituals*, in *Sishu Wujing*, ed. Zhu Xi (Tianjin: Tianjin Guji Chubanshe, 1988), 191–192.

14. *Book of History*, trans. Gu Baotian (Changchun, Jilin: Jiliin Wenshi Chubanshe, 1995), 116–127.

15. Confucius, *Analects*, trans. Yang Bojun (Beijing: Zhonghua Shuju, 1980), 23.

16. Xun Zi, *Xun Zi*, trans. Zhang Jue (Shanghai: Shanghai Guji Chubanshe, 1995), 393.

17. Mencius, *Mencius*, in *Sishu*, Chinese trans. Yang Bojun and English trans. James Legge (Changsha, Hunan: Hunan Chubanshe, 1992), 320.

18. Confucius, *Analects*, trans. Yang Bojun (Beijing: Zhonghua Shuju, 1980), 211.

19. Xun Zi, *Xun Zi*, trans. Zhang Jue (Shanghai: Shanghai Guji Chubanshe, 1995), 589.

20. *Book of Rituals*, in *Sishu Wujing*, ed. Zhu Xi (Tianjin: Tianjin Guji Chubanshe, 1988), 1–2.

21. Zhao Jihui, et al. *The History of Confucianism in China* (Zhengzhou, Henan: Zhongzhou Guji Chubanshe, 1991), 88.

22. Confucius, *Analects*, trans. Yang Bojun (Beijing: Zhonghua Shuju, 1980), 123.

23. Xun Zi, *Xun Zi*, trans. Zhang Jue (Shanghai: Shanghai Guji Chubanshe, 1995), 585.

24. Qian Mu, *Political Dynamics and Failures in Dynastic China* (Taipei, Taiwan: Dongda Tushu Gongsi, 1977).

25. Guo Moruo, *Ten Critical Essays* (Beijing: The Oriental Press, 1996), 87–107; Li Zehou, *Essays on Ancient Chinese Thought* (Beijing: Renmin Chubanshe, 1985), 7–51; and Qian Xun, *Pre-Qin Confucianism* (Shengyang, Liaoning: Liaoning Jiaoyu Chubanshe, 1991), 11–130.

26. Li Zehou, *Essays on Ancient Chinese Thought* (Beijing: Renmin Chubanshe, 1985), 16–33.

27. Confucius, *Analects,* trans. Yang Bojun (Beijing: Zhonghua Shuju, 1980), 123.
28. Ibid, 2.
29. Ibid, 131.
30. Ibid, 163.
31. Zhao Jihui, et al. *The History of Confucianism in China* (Zhengzhou, Henan: Zhongzhou Guji Chubanshe, 1991), 60; Qian Xun, *Pre-Qin Confucianism* (Shengyang, Liaoning: Liaoning Jiaoyu Chubanshe, 1991), 21; Li Zehou, *Essays on Ancient Chinese Thought* (Beijing: Renmin Chubanshe, 1985), 22.
32. *Book of History,* trans. Gu Baotian (Changchu, Jilin: Jilin Wenshi Chubanshe, 1995), 117–127.
33. Confucius, *Analects,* trans. Yang Bojun (Beijing: Zhonghua Shuju, 1980), 11.
34. Ibid, 12, 129, 136; also Mencius, *Mencius,* in *Sishu,* Chinese trans. Yang Bojun and English trans. James Legge (Changsha, Hunan: Hunan Chubanshe, 1992), 316, 320, 392.
35. *The Great Learning,* in *Sishu,* Chinese trans. Yang Bojun and English trans. James Legge (Changsha, Hunan: Hunan Chubanshe, 1992), 2–10.
36. Confucius, *Analects,* trans. Yang Bojun (Beijing: Zhonghua Shuju, 1980), 128; Mencius, *Mencius,* in *Sishu,* Chinese trans. Yang Bojun and English trans. James Legge (Changsha, Hunan: Hunan Chubanshe, 1992), 272; *The Great Learning,* in *Sishu,* Chinese trans. Yang Bojun and English trans. James Legge (Changsha, Hunan: Hunan Chubanshe, 1992), 12.
37. Confucius, *Analects,* trans. Yang Bojun (Beijing: Zhonghua Shuju, 1980), 183.
38. Ibid, 78.
39. Ibid, 2; Mencius, *Mencius,* in *Sishu,* Chinese trans. Yang Bojun and English trans. James Legge (Changsha, Hunan: Hunan Chubanshe, 1992), 494.
40. Li Zehou, *Essays on Ancient Chinese Thought* (Beijing: Renmin Chubanshe, 1985), 25–28; Zhao Jihui, et al. *The History of Confucianism in China* (Zhengzhou, Henan: Zhongzhou Guji Chubanshe, 1991), 68–70.
41. Deng Xiaojun, *The Logical Link between Confucian and Democratic Thought* (Chengdu, Sichuan: Sichuan Renmin Chubanshe, 1995); Wm. Theodore de Bary, *The Liberal Tradition in China* (NY: Columbia University Press, 1983).
42. Wm. Theodore de Bary, *Asian Values and Human Rights* (Cambridge, MA: Harvard University Press, 1998).
43. Ibid, 63.
44. Gao Qicai, *Chinese Customary Laws* (Changsha, Hunan: Hunan Chubanshe, 1995); Joseph W. Esherick and Mary Backus Rankin, ed. *Chinese Local Elites and Patterns of Dominance* (Berkeley, CA: University of California Press, 1990).
45. Yu Yingshi, *A Contemporary Interpretation of the Chinese Intellectual Tradition* (Nanjing, Jiangsu: Jiangsu Renmin Chubanshe, 1995), 25–42.
46. Francis L. K. Hsu, *Under the Ancestors' Shadow* (Stanford, CA: Stanford University Press, 1971).

47. Hsiao Tung Fei, *Peasant Life in China* (London: K. Paul, Trench, Truber, 1939).

48. Yu Yingshi, *A Contemporary Interpretation of Chinese Intellectual Tradition* (Nanjing, Jiangsu: Jiangsu Renmin Chubanshe, 1995), 28.

49. Hui-chen Wang Liu, "An Analysis of Chinese Clan Rules," in *Confucianism and Chinese Civilization,* ed. Arthur F. Wright (NY: Atheneum, 1964), 25–30.

50. Qian Mu, *Political Dynamics and Failures in Dynastic China* (Taipei, Taiwan: Dongda Tushu Gongsi, 1977), 10–15.

51. Xu Yangjie, *A Historical Study of the System of the Kinship Family in Song and Ming Dynasties* (Beijing: Zhonghua Shuju, 1995), 3–4.

52. For a recent discussion of the disintegration of the clan family system, see He Huaihong, *The Hereditary Society and Its Disintegration* (Beijing: Sanlian Shudian, 1996).

53. Xu Yangjie, *A Historical Study of the System of the Kinship Family in Song and Ming Dynasties* (Beijing: Zhonghua Shuju, 1995), 7.

54. Ibid, 13–27.

55. Yu Dunkang, "The Confucianist Ethics and the Chinese Traditional Culture," in *Culture: China and the World,* ed. Gan Yang, et al. (Beijing: Sanlian Shudian, 1987), Vol. 3, 272–313.

56. Xu Yangjie, *A Historical Study of the System of the Kinship Family in Song and Ming Dynasties* (Beijing: Zhonghua Shuju, 1995), 472–481.

57. Ibid, 16–17.

58. Ibid, 22–23.

59. Francis L.K. Hsu, *Under the Ancestors' Shadow* (Stanford, CA: Stanford University Press, 1971), esp. 28–53, 107–130,167–199; Hsiao-Tung Fei, *Peasant Life in China* (London: K. Paul, Trench, Trubner, 1939), 27–55, 73–78; Wei Hongyun, ed. *An Investigative Study of Country Life in Eastern Hebei Province* (Tianjin: Tianjin Renmin Chubanshe, 1996), 437–439.

60. During a research trip to a northern Chinese village in early 1997, I was informed about the widespread practice of ancestor worship and witnessed in several households I visited small altars, burnt incense and the portraits of ancestors hanging above the altars.

61. Hui-chen Wang Liu, "An Analysis of Chinese Clan Rules," in *Confucianism and Chinese Civilization,* ed. Arthur F. Wright (NY: Atheneum, 1964), 21.

62. Francis L.K. Hsu, *Under the Ancestors' Shadow* (Stanford, CA: Standord University Press, 1971), 108.

63. Hui-chen Wang Liu, "An Analysis of Chinese Clan Rules," in *Confucianism and Chinese Civilization,* ed. Arthur F. Wright (NY: Atheneum, 1964), 21.

64. Ibid, 26–27.

65. Francis L.K. Hsu, *Under the Ancestors' Shadow* (Stanford, CA: Stanford University Press, 1971), 206–216; Wei Hongyun, ed. *An Investigative Study of Country Life in Eastern Hebei Province* (Tianjin: Tianjin Renmin Chubanshe, 1996), 415–422.

66. Hu Shi, *Basic Principles in Chinese Philosophy* (Beijing: The Oriental Press, 1996), 110–118.

67. Confucius, *Analects,* trans. Yang Bojun (Beijing: Zhonghua Shuju, 1980), 2.

68. Confucius, *Analects*, trans. Yang Bojun (Beijing: Zhonghua Shuju, 1980), 2, 7, 13, 14, 40, 111, 128 188; Mencius, *Mencius*, in *Sishu*, Chinese trans. Yang Bojun and English trans. James Legge (Changsha, Hunan: Hunan Chubanshe, 1992), 266, 278, 406, 424, 518, 544; *Book of Rituals*, in *Sishu Wujing*, ed. Zhu Xi (Tianjin: Tianjin Guji Chubanshe, 1988), 115, 155, 191–192, 256–265, 323; *The Great Learning*, in *Sishu*, Chinese trans. Yang Bojun and English trans. James Legge (Changsha, Hunan: Hunan Chubanshe, 1992), 6, 12; *The Doctrine of the Mean*, in *Sishu*, Chinese trans. Yang Bojun and English trans. James Legge (Changsha, Hunan: Hunan Chubanshe, 1992), 38, 40, 42; Xun Zi, *Xun Zi*, trans. Zhang Jue (Shanghai: Shanghai Guji Chubanshe, 1995), 397, 407, 585, 587, 620; *Zuo Zhuan*, trans. Guan Shuguang (Zhengzhou, Henan: Zhongzhou Guji Chubanshe, 1993), Vol. 1, 3, 13, 155, 373, 460.

69. Here I adopt a widely accepted interpretation of filial piety. In a recent article, Yue Qingping challenges this view, arguing that the idea of filial piety has a positive side and can be modified to provide a moral grounding for contemporary life. See Yue Qingping, "Filial Piety and Modernization," in *The Ideas and Behaviors of Chinese*, ed. Qiao Jian and Pan Naigu (Tianjin: Tianjin Chubanshe, 1995), 123–136.

70. Confucius, *Analects*, trans. Yang Bojun (Beijing: Zhonghua Shuju, 1980), 2.

71. Quoted from Xu Yangjie, *A Historical Study of the System of the Kinship Family in Song and Ming Dynasties* (Beijing: Zhonghua Shuju, 1995), 65.

72. Ibid, 65.

73. Francis L.K. Hsu, *Under the Ancestors' Shadow* (Stanford, CA: Stanford University Press, 1971), 224.

74. Ibid, 271–272.

75. For example, Lucian W. Pye, *The Spirit of Chinese Politics* (Cambridge, MA: MIT Press, 1968); Richard H. Solomon, *Mao's Revolution and the Chinese Political Culture* (Berkeley, CA: University of California Press, 1971); Jack Gray, "China: Communism and Confucianism," in *Political Culture and Political Change in Communist States*, ed. Archie Brown and Jack Gray (NY: Holmes and Meier, 1977), 197–230.

76. For example, Fei Xiaotong, *From the Soil* (Berkeley, CA: University of California Press, 1992); Liang Shumin, *The Essential Meanings of Chinese Culture* (Shanghai: Xuelin Chubanshe, 1986); Sun Longji, *The Underlying Structures of Chinese Culture* (Taipei, Taiwan: Tangshan Chubanshe, 1983).

77. Lucian W. Pye, *The Dynamics of Chinese Politics* (Cambridge, MA: Oelgeschlager, Gunn & Hain, 1981).

78. Li Yiyuan, "The Conception of the Universe in Traditional China and Modern Business Behavior," in *The Ideas and Behaviors of Chinese*, ed. Qiao Jian and Pan Naigu (Tianjin: Tianjin Renmin Chubanshe, 1995), 17–39.

79. Huang Guoguang, "*Renqing* and *Mianzi*: The Chinese Power Game," in *Modernization and the Chinese Culture*, ed. Qiao Jian (Tianjin: Tianjin Renmin Chubanshe, 1985), 167–180; Ambrose Yeo-chi King, "Kuan-hsi and Network Building," *Daedalus* 120:2 (Spring 1991):63–84.

80. Gary G. Hamilton and Wang Zheng, "Introduction," in *From the Soil*, Fei Xiaotong (Berkeley, CA: University of California Press, 1992), 20–24.

81. Hugh D.R. Baker, *Chinese Family and Kinship* (London: Macmillan, 1979); William L. Parish and Martin K. Whyte, *Village and Family in Contemporary China* (Chicago: University of Chicago Press, 1978).

82. For a detailed explanation of this field trip, see Appendix.

83. Lucian W. Pye, *The Mandarin and the Cadre* (Ann Arbor, MI: University of Michigan Press, 1988).

84. John K. Fairbank, *The Great Chinese Revolution* (Cambridge, MA: Harvard University Press, 1987), 271–342.

85. Li Zhishui, *The Private Life of Chairman Mao* (NY: Random House, 1994).

86. David Shambaugh, "Deng Xiaoping: The Politician," in *Deng Xiaoping: Portrait of a Chinese Statesman*, ed. David Shambaugh (Oxford: Clarendon Press, 1995), 49–82.

87. Ruan Ming, *Deng Xiaoping: Chronicle of an Empire* (Boulder, CO: Westview Press, 1994), 100.

88. Kenneth Lieberthal and David Lampton, eds. *Bureaucracy, Politics, and Decision Making in Post-Mao China* (Ann Arbor, MI: University of Michigan Press, 1992).

89. Suisheng Zhao, "The Structure of Authority and Decision-Making," in *Decision-Making in Deng's China*, ed. Carol Lee Hamrin and Suisheng Zhao (Armonk, NY: M. E. Sharpe, 1995), 233–245.

90. Lucian W. Pye, *The Dynamics of Chinese Politics* (Cambridge, MA: Oelgeschlager, Gunn & Hain, 1981).

91. Chen Yizi, "The Decision Process behind the 1986–1989 Political Reforms," in *Decision-Making in Deng's China*, ed. Carol Lee Hamrin and Suisheng Zhao (Armonk, NY: M. E. Sharpe, 1995), 133–152.

92. Carol Lee Hamrin and Suisheng Zhao, "Introduction," in *Decision-Making in Deng's China*, ed. Carol Lee Hamrin and Suisheng Zhao (Armonk, NY: M. E. Sharpe, 1995), xxx-xxxi.

93. Yan Jiaqi, "The Nature of Chinese Authoritarianism," in *Decision-Making in Deng's China*, ed. Carol Lee Hamrin and Suisheng Zhao (Armonk, NY: M. E. Sharpe, 1995), 3–14.

94. Personal interviews, April 12, 17, 18, and 20, 1997.

95. James R. Townsend, *Political Participation in Communist China* (Berkeley, CA: University of California Press, 1967).

96. Fei Xiaotong, *From the Soil* (Berkeley, CA: University of California Press, 1992).

97. Tianjian Shi, *Political Participation in Beijing* (Cambridge, MA: Harvard University Press, 1997), 34–88.

98. Mayfair Mei-hui Yang, *Gifts, Favors, and Banquets* (Ithaca, NY: Cornell University Press, 1994), 130.

99. Yeonsik Jeong, *Interest Representation in Socialist Market Economies* (Columbia, SC: University of South Carolina, Ph.D. dissertation, 1997).

100. Personal interview, April 11, 1997.

101. Personal interview, April 5, 1997.

102. Personal interview, April 12, 1997.

103. Personal interview, April 18, 1997.

104. Godwin C. Chu and Yanan Ju, *The Great Wall in Ruins* (Albany, NY: SUNY Press, 1993), 134, 151–153,

105. See Appendix for some of the survey questions.

106. Godwin C. Chu and Yanan Ju, *The Great Wall in Ruins* (Albany, NY: SUNY Press, 1993), 100. Chu and Ju attribute the cause of mutual suspicion to the Cultural Revolution during which social relationships, including even the family, completely broke down. But I believe the sources of distrust run deeper and can be traced to the kinship family culture.

107. Cf. Lucian W. Pye, *The Spirit of Chinese Politics* (Cambridge, MA: MIT Press, 1968).

108. Personal interview, April 17, 1997.

109. Lianjiang Li and Kevin O'Brien, "Chinese Villagers and Popular Resistance." Paper presented at the 24th Sino-American Conferences on Contemporary China, June 15–17, 1995.

110. Andrew J. Nathan and Tianjian Shi, "Cultural Requisites for Democracy in China," *Daedalus* 122:2 (Spring 1993):111–113.

111. Godwin C. Chu and Yanan Ju, *The Great Wall in Ruins* (Albany, NY: SUNY Press, 1993), 157.

112. Lucian W. Pye, "The State and the Individual," in *The Individual and the State in China,* ed. Brian Hook (Oxford: Clarendon, 1996), 16–42.

113. Mayfair Mei-hui Yang, *Gifts, Favors and Banquets* (Ithaca, NY: Cornell Univeristy Press, 1994).

114. Godwin C. Chu and Yanan Ju, *The Great Wall in Ruins* (Albany, NY: SUNY Press, 1993), 153–160; 233–236.

115. Ibid, 168.

NOTES TO CHAPTER SIX

1. David Beetham, "Introduction: Human Rights in the Study of Politics," *Political Studies* 43 (1995):3.

2. Mary Ann Glendon, *Rights Talk* (NY: The Free Press, 1991).

3. For example, Francisco Panizza, "Human Rights in the Process of Transition and Consolidation of Democracy in Latin America," Sidgi Kaballo, "Human Rights and Democratization in Africa," and Kenneth Christie, "Regime Security and Human Rights in Southeast Asia," *Political Studies* 43 (1995):168–188, 189–203, 204–218 respectively.

4. On the politician side, see Lee Kuan Yew (with Fareed Zakaria), "Culture is Destiny," *Foreign Affairs* 73:2 (March/April 1994):109–126; Kim Dae Jung, "Is Culture Destiny?," *Foreign Affairs* 73:6 (November/December):189–94; Bilahari Kausikan, "An East Asian Approach to Human Rights," *Buffalo Journal of International law* 2:2 (Winter 1993):263–283. On the academic side, see Joanne R. Bauer and Daniel A. Bell, ed. *The East Asian Challenge for Human Rights* (NY: Cambridge University Press, 1999); Lynda S. Bell, et al., ed. *Negotiating Culture and Human Rights* (NY: Columbia University Press, 2001); David P. Forsythe and Patrice C. McMahon, ed. *Human Rights and Diversity* (Lincoln, NE: University Nebraska Press, 2003).

5. Cf. Richard Flathman, "Introduction," in *Concepts in Social and Political Philosophy,* ed. Richard Flathman (NY: Macmillan, 1973), 1–40.

6. Jonathan Spence, *The Search for Modern China* (NY: W. W. Norton & Company, 1990), esp. 194–244; John K. Fairbank, *The Great Chinese Revolution 1800–1985* (Cambridge, MA: Harvard University Press, 1987), esp. 100–121.

7. *Ci Hai* (Shanghai: Shanghai Cishu Chubanshe, 1980), 1252.

8. Xun Zi, *Xun Zi,* trans. Zhang Jue (Shanghai: Shanghai Guji Chubanshe, 1995), 300.

9. Confucius, *Analects,* trans. Yang Bojun (Beijing: Zhonghua Shuju, 1980), 39.

10. For a contemporary depiction of power and profit as corroding forces of the social fabric, see Li Shidong et al., ed. *Another Kind of Beast* (Beijing: Wenhua Yishu Chubanshe, 2001).

11. For example, R. Randle Edwards, et al., *Human Rights in Contemporary China* (NY: Columbia University Press, 1986); Ann Kent, *Between Freedom and Subsistence* (Hong Kong: Oxford University Press, 1993); Marina Svensson, *Debating Human Rights in China* (Lanham, MD: Rowman & Littlefield, 2002); Stephen C. Angle, *Human Rights and Chinese Thought* (NY: Cambridge University Press, 2002).

12. Marina Svensson, *Debating Human Rights in China* (Lanham, MD: Rowman & Littlefield, 2002); Stephen C. Angle, *Human Rights and Chinese Thought* (NY: Cambridge University Press, 2002).

13. According to one account, Gao Yihan and Dai Jitao were among the first to advocate a right to subsistence in the 1920s. Marina Svensson, *Debating Human Rights in China* (Lanham, MD: Rowman & Littlefield, 2002), esp. 147–149.

14. Hannah Arendt, *Between Past and Future* (NY: Penguin Books, 1956), 241.

15. For example, Charles Taylor, "Conditions of an Unforced Consensus on Human Rights," in *The East Asian Challenge for Human Rights,* ed. Joanne R. Bauer and Daniel A. Bell (NY: Cambridge University Press, 1999), 124–144; Sumner B. Twiss, "A Constructive Framework for Discussing Confucianism and Human Rights," in *Confucianism and Human Rights,* ed. Wm. Theordore de Bary and Tu Weiming (Cambridge, MA: Harvard University Press, 1998), 27–53.

16. For example, Stephen C. Angle, *Human Rights and Chinese Thought* (NY: Cambridge University Press, 2002).

17. For a summary of empirical studies of this sort, see Ming Wan, *Human Rights in Chinese Foreign Relations* (Philadelphia, PA: University of Pennsylvania Press, 2001), esp. chapter 2.

18. Ibid, 31–37.

19. Xia Yong, *The Origins of the Concept of Human Rights* (Beijing: Zhongguo Zhengfa Daxue Chubanshe, 1992), esp. Part Four, "Human Rights and Harmony."

20. Marina Svensson, *Debating Human Rights in China* (Lanham, MD: Rowman & Littlefield, 2002), 261–290.

21. Ming Wan, *Human Rights in Chinese Foreign Relations* (Philadelphia, PA: University of Pennsylvania Press, 2001), 16. I reached much the same

conclusion on a field trip to China 1997. During a group interview of municipal People's Congress representatives, for instance, I was bombarded
with the question of what moral authority a country such as the United
States has to criticize China's human rights practice while it itself has a poor
record of respecting human rights overseas and what its real motives are for
doing so.

22. Ann Kent, *Between Freedom and Subsistence* (Hong Kong: Oxford
University Press, 1993).

23. The "Three Agriculture Problems" was initially stated by a Hubei Provincial
party official in a letter to the State Council. It summarizes the peasant problem in contemporary China as follows: "Peasants are really suffering, the
countryside is really poverty-stricken, and agriculture is really dangerous."
For a detailed account of the "Three Agriculture Problems," see Chen Guidi
and Chun Tao, *An Investigation on the Chinese Peasant* (Beijing: Renmin
Wenxue Chubanshe, 2004).

24. For Liu Huaqiu's statement, see James T. H. Tang, ed. *Human Rights and
International Relations in the Asia-Pacific Region* (London: Pinter, 1995),
213–217. For an example of official thinking on human rights, see Niu
Yong, et al. *The Protection and Development of Human Rights in China*
(Taiyuan, Shanxi: Shanxi Gaoxiao Lianhe Chubanshe, 1992).

25. See Chapter Two on "Integrationism."

26. Lee Kuan Yew (with Fareed Zakaria), "Culture is Destiny," *Foreign Affairs*
73:2 (March/April 1994):109–126; Bilahari Kausikan, "An East Approach
to Human Rights," *The Buffalo Journal of International Law* 2:2
(Winter):263–283.

27. For most recent arguments to constitutionalize social and economic rights,
see Cecile Fabre, *Social Rights under the Constitution* (Oxford: Clarendon
Press, 2000) and Ross Zucker, *Democratic Distributive Justice* (NY:
Cambridge University Press, 2001).

28. For a most recent universalist argument in the context of the Asian value de-
bate, see Jack Donnelly, "Human Rights and Asian Values: A Defense of
'Western' Universalism," and Inoue Tatsuo, "Liberal Democracy and Asian
Orientalism," in *The East Asian Challenge for Human Rights,* ed. Joanne R.
Bauer and Daniel A. Bell (NY: Cambridge University Press, 1999), 27–59
and 60–87; Ann Kent, *Between Freedom and Subsistence* (Hong Kong:
Oxford University Press, 1993); Marina Svensson, *Debating Human Rights
in China* (Lanham, MD: Rowman & Littlefield, 2002).

29. For an extreme universalist position, see Marina Svensson, *Debating
Human Rights in China* (Lanham, MD: Rowman & Littlefield, 2002).

30. For example, Alison Dundes Renteln, *International Human Rights*
(Newbury Park, CA: Sage, 1990); Abdullahi A. An-Na'im, "The Cultural
Mediation of Human Rights: The Al-Arqam Case in Malaysia," in *The East
Asian Challenge for Human Rights,* ed. Joanne R. Bauer and Daniel A. Bell
(NY: Cambridge University Press, 1999), 147–168; Marie-Benedicte
Dembour, "Following the Movement of a Pendulum," in *Culture and
Rights,* ed. Jane K. Cowan, et al. (London: Cambridge University Press,
2001), 56–79; Corinne Packer, "African Women, Traditions, and Human

Rights," in *Human Rights and Diversity*, ed. David P. Forsythe and Patrice C. McMahon (Lincoln, NE: University of Nebraska Press, 2003), 159–181.

31. Abdullahi A. An-Na'im, "Introduction: 'Area Expressions' and the Universality of Human Rights," in *Human Rights and Diversity*, eds. David P. Forsythe and Patrice C. McMahon (Lincoln, NE: University of Nebraska Press, 2003), 1–21.

32. Inoue Tatsuo, "Liberal Democracy and Asian Orientalism," in *The East Asian Challenge for Human Rights*, ed. Joanne R. Bauer and Daniel A. Bell (NY: Cambridge University Press, 1999), 60–87.

33. Henry Rosemont, Jr., "Human Rights: A Bill of Worries," in *Confucianism and Human Rights*, ed. Wm. De Bary and Tu Wei-ming (1998), 54–66.

34. Sumner B. Twiss, "A Constructive Framework for Discussing Confucianism and Human Rights," in *Confucianism and Human Rights*, ed. Wm. De Bary and Tu Wei-ming (Cambridge, MA: Harvard University Press, 1998), 27–53; and Wm. De Bary, *Asian Values and Human Rights* (Cambridge, MA: Harvard University Press, 1998).

35. Baogang He, *The Democratization of China* (NY: Routledge, 1996), 221.

36. Charles Taylor, "Conditions of an Unforced Consensus on Human Rights," in *The East Asian Challenge for Human Rights*, ed. Joanne R. Bauer and Daniel A. Bell (NY: Cambridge University Press, 1999), 124–144.

37. John Rawls, *A Theory of Justice* (Cambridge, MA: Harvard University Press, 1971), 3.

38. Maurice Cranston, "Human Rights: Real and Supposed," in *Political Theory and the Rights of Man*, ed. D. D. Raphael (Bloomington, IN: Indiana University Press, 1967), 43–53.

39. Will Kymlicka, *Liberalism, Community and Culture* (NY: Oxford University Press, 1989); and Michael Freeman, "Are There Collective Human Rights?," *Political Studies* 43 (1995 Special Issue):25–40.

40. Jeremy Waldron, "Can Communal Goods Be Human Rights?," *Archives Europeennes de Sociologie* 28 (1987):2:296–322. For a defense of group rights based on the disadvantaged group principle, see Owen Fiss, "Groups and the Equal Protection Clause," in *Equality and Preferential Treatment*, ed. Marshall Cohen, et al. (Princeton, NJ: Princeton University Press, 1977), 84–154.

41. Mencius, *Mencius*, in *Sishu*, Chinese trans. Yang Bojun and English trans. James Legge (Changsha, Hunan: Hunan Chubanshe, 1992), 320 and 540.

42. Joseph Raz, *The Morality of Freedom* (Oxford: Clarendon, 1986), esp. chapters 7 and 8, 165–216. See, also, "On the Nature of Rights," *Mind* 93 (1984):194–214 and "Rights-Based Moralities," in *Theories of Rights*, ed. Jeremy Waldron (London: Oxford University Press, 1984), 183–200.

43. For factual consent, see Joseph Tussman, *Obligation and the Body Politic* (NY: Oxford University Press, 1960), esp. 23–57; for responsive consent, see Hanna F. Pitkin, "Obligation and Consent II," *American Political Science Review* 60 (March 1966):39–52.

44. For such a qualified benefit theory, see George Klosko, *The Principle of Fairness and Political Obligation* (Lanham, MD: Rowman & Littlefield, 1992).

45. Alison Dundes Renteln, *International Human Rights* (Newbury Park, CA: Sage, 1990), 43.

46. Ibid, 44.

47. Joseph Chan, "A Confucian Perspective on Human Rights for Contemporary China," in *The East Asian Challenge for Human Rights,* ed. Joanne R. Bauer and Daniel A. Bell (NY: Cambridge University Press, 1999), 212–237. A similar view that Confucianism or certain parts of it are compatible with the concept of rights is found in Seung-Hwan Lee, "Was There a Concept of Rights in Confucian Virtue-Based Morality?," *Journal of Chinese Philosophy* 19 (Sept. 1992):3:241–262.

48. Confucius, *Analects,* trans. Yang Bojun (Beijing: Zhonghua Shuju, 1980), Book 7; Mencius, *Mencius,* in *Sishu,* Chinese trans. Yang Bojun and English trans. James Legge (Changsha, Hunan: Hunan Chubanshe, 1992), Book 1, Part One; and *Book of Rituals* (1988), esp. Book 8, 26, 27, 31 and 40.

49. Tu Wei-ming, *Centrality and Commonality* (Albany, NY: State University of New York Press, 1988); Wm. Theodore de Bary, *The Trouble with Confucianism* (Cambridge, MA: Harvard University Press, 1991).

50. Mencius, *Mencius,* in *Sishu,* Chinese trans. Yang Bojun and English trans. James Legge (Changsha, Hunan: Hunan Chubanshe, 1992), Book 14, 540.

51. Xun Zi, *Xun Zi,* trans. Zhang Jue (Shanghai: Shanghai Guji Chubanshe, 1995), 614.

52. Zhao Jihui, et al., *The History of Confucianism in China* (Zhengzhou, Henan: Zhongzhou Guji Chubanshe, 1991).

53. Yang Zhong, et al., "Political Views from Below," *PS: Political Science & Politics* 30:3 (September 1997):476–477.

54. Godwin C. Chu and Yanan Ju, *The Great Wall in Ruins* (Albany, NY: SUNY Press, 1993), 157, 168.

55. Andrew J. Nathan and Tianjian Shi, "Cultural Requisites for Democracy in China," *Daedalus* 122:2 (Spring 1993):111–113.

56. Godwin C. Chu and Yanan Ju, *The Great Wall in Ruins* (Albany, NY: SUNY Press, 1993), 277.

57. Ibid, 314.

58. Francis Fukuyama, *The End of History and the Last Man* (NY: Free Press, 1992).

59. Larry Diamond, *Developing Democracy* (Baltimore, MD: The Johns Hopkins University Press, 1999).

60. David Held, "Democracy: From City-States to a Cosmopolitan Order?," *Political Studies* 40 (1992 Special Issue):11.

61. Bhikhu Parekh, "The Cultural Particularity of Liberal Democracy," *Political Studies* 40 (1992 Special Issue):160–175.

62. The ongoing debate over Asian values, in a strict sense, is not about the applicability of democracy to non-Western countries, for even the most authoritarian governments in Asia endorse democracy explicitly; it is rather about the applicability of certain aspects of liberal democracy, the idea of individual rights in particular, in the Asian cultural context. Viewed from this perspective, arguments aimed at repudiating the view that China is culturally unsuited for democracy are in my opinion misplaced.

63. Joseph A. Schumpeter, *Capitalism, Socialism and Democracy* (NY: Harper & Row, 1942), 269.

64. Carole Pateman, *Participation and Democratic Theory* (NY: Cambridge University Press, 1970).

65. Cf. David Held, "Democracy: From City-States to a Cosmopolitan Order?," *Political Studies* 40: (Special Issue 1992):17–18.

66. Giovanni Sartori, *The Theory of Democracy Revisited* (Chatham, NJ: Chatham House, 1987); Robert A. Dahl, *Democracy and Its Critics* (New Haven, CT: Yale University Press, 1989); Sanford A. Lakoff, *Democracy* (Boulder, CO: Westview Press, 1996).

67. Giovanni Sartori, *The Theory of Democracy Revisited* (Chatham, NJ: Chatham House, 1987), 8, 165–167, 478.

68. John D. May has proposed a definition of democracy as the "necessary correspondence" between governmental acts and popular preferences. "A regime is democratic relative to another regime," he says, "insofar as its arrangements yield closer correspondence between its governmental acts and the preferences of the persons who are affected by those acts." This formulation is notable for its clarity and precision, but it is flawed in several respects. One is that it ignores the moral and intellectual development of democratic citizenship through participation in decision making and other areas of political life. See John D. May, "Defining Democracy: A Bid for Coherence and Consensus," *Political Studies* 26:1 (March 1978):1–14. A virtually identical formulation is voiced by Michael Saward, "Democratic Theory and Indices of Democratization," in *Defining and Measuring Democracy*, ed. David Beetham (London: Sage Publications, 1994), 6–24.

69. Joseph Chan, "The Asian Challenge to Universal Human Rights," in *Human Rights and International Relations in the Asian Pacific Region*, ed. James T. H. Tang (London: Pinter, 1995), 25–38; Du Gangjian and Song Gang, "Relating Human Rights to Chinese Culture," in *Human Rights and Chinese Values*, ed. Michael Davis (Hong Kong: Oxford University Press, 1995), 35–56.

70. Godwin C. Chu and Yanan Ju, *The Great Wall in Ruins* (Albany, NY: SUNY Press, 1993), 154.

71. See Appendix.

72. *Beijing Review* 34:44 (Nov. 1991) and 39 (Special Issue Jan. 1996).

73. For an account of rights thinking in modern China, see Andrew J. Nathan, "Sources of Chinese Rights Thinking," in R. Randle Edwards, et al. *Human Rights in Contemporary China* (NY: Columbia University Press, 1986), 125–164.

74. Andrew J. Nathan, "Political Rights in Chinese Constitutions," in R. Randle Edwards, et al. *Human Rights in Contemporary China* (NY: Columbia University Press, 1986), p7–124.

75. See Appendix.

76. Godwin C. Chu and Yanan Ju, *The Great Wall in Ruins* (Albany, NY: SUNY Press, 1993), 100.

77. Robert D. Putnam, *Making Democracy Work* (Princeton, NJ: Princeton University Press, 1993), 163–185.

78. The idea that political participation such as voting is a duty of the average citizen can also be found in other cultures. See Joseph Lapalombara, *Democracy, Italian Style* (New Haven, CT: Yale University Press, 1987).

79. Daniel A. Bell, "A Confucian Democracy for the Twenty-First Century," Conference Paper (1996). Quoted in Inoue Tatsuo, "Liberal Democracy and Asian Orientalism," in *The East Asian Challenge for Human Rights,* ed. Joanne R. Bauer and Daniel A. Bell (NY: Cambridge University Press, 1999), 28.

80. Brantly Womack, "Party-State Democracy: A Theoretical Exploration," in *Mainland China after the Thirteenth Party Congress,* ed. King-yuh Chang (Boulder, CO: Westview, 1990), 11–29.

81. For a review of the neo-constitutionalist recommendations, see Andrew Nathan, *China's Transition* (NY: Columbia University Press, 1997), 231–245.

82. Dankwart A. Rustow, "Transitions to Democracy," in *Transitions to Democracy,* ed. Lisa Anderson (NY: Columbia University Press, 1999), 14–41; Guiseppe DiPalma, *To Craft Democracies* (Berkeley, CA: University of California Press, 1990).

Bibliography

Almond, Gabriel A. "Comparative Political Systems." *Journal of Politics* 18 (1956):391–491.

———. "The Intellectual History of the Civic Culture Concept." In *The Civic Culture Revisited,* edited by Gabriel A. Almond and Sidney Verba. Newbury Park, Calif.: Sage Publications, 1989.

Almond, Gabriel A., and Sidney Verba. *The Civic Culture.* Princeton, NJ: Princeton University Press, 1966.

———, ed. *The Civic Culture Revisited.* Newbury Park, Calif.: Sage Publications, 1989.

Almond, Gabriel A., and G. Bingham Powell, Jr. *Comparative Politics.* Second Edition. Boston, MA: Little, Brown, and Company, 1978.

Ames, Roger T. *The Art of Rulership.* Honolulu, HI: University of Hawaii Press, 1983.

Amussen, Susan D. "Gender, Family and the Social Order, 1560–1725." In *Order and Disorder in Early Modern England,* edited by Anthony Fletcher and John Stevenson. London: Cambridge University Press, 1985.

Angle, Stephen C. *Human Rights and Chinese Thought.* NY: Cambridge University Press, 2002.

An-Na'im, Abdullahi A. "Introduction: 'Area Expressions' and the Universality of Human Rights." In *Human Rights and Diversity,* edited by David P. Forsythe and Patrice C. McMahon. Lincoln, NE: University of Nebraska Press, 2003.

———. "The Cultural Mediation of Human Rights: The Al-Arqam Case in Malaysia." In *The East Asian Challenge for Human Rights,* edited by Joanne R. Bauer and Daniel A. Bell. NY: Cambridge University Press, 1999.

Aquinas, Thomas. *The Political Ideas of St. Thomas Aquinas,* edited by Dino Bigongiari NY: Hafner Press, 1953.

Arendt, Hannah. *Lectures on Kant's Political Philosophy.* Edited by Ronald Beiner. Chicago: University of Chicago Press, 1982.

———. *Between Past and Future.* NY: Penguin Books, 1956.

Aristotle. *The Politics of Aristotle.* London: Oxford University Press, 1946.

———. *Nichomachean Ethics.* Indianapolis, IN: The Liberal Arts Press, 1962.

Ashcraft, Richard. *Locke's Two Treatises of Government.* London: Allen and Unwin, 1987.

———, ed. *John Locke: Critical Assessments,* Vol. 2. NY: Routledge, 1991.

Austin, John. *Lectures on Jurisprudence.* London: J. Murray, 1885.

Baker, Hugh D. R. *Chinese Family and Kinship*. London: Macmillan, 1979.

Ball, Terence, *Reappraising Political Theory*. Oxford: Clarendon Press, 1995.

Barber, Benjamin. "Liberal Democracy and the Cost of Consent." In *Liberalism and the Moral Life*, edited by Nancy L. Rosenblum. Cambridge, MA: Harvard University Press, 1989.

Barry, Brian. "On Social Justice." In *Concepts in Social and Political Philosophy*, edited by Richard Flathman. NY: Macmillan, 1973.

Bauer, Susan R., and Daniel A. Bell. "Introduction." In *The East Asian Challenge for Human Rights*, edited by Susan R. Bauer and Daniel A. Bell. NY: Cambridge University Press, 1999.

Baumgold, Deborah. *Hobbes' Political Theory*. NY: Cambridge University Press, 1988.

Beetham, David. "Introduction: Human Rights in the Study of Politics." *Political Studies* 43 (Special Issue 1995):1–9.

———, ed. *Defining and Measuring Democracy*. London: Sage Publications, 1994.

Beier, A. L. *Masterless Men*. London: Methuen, 1985.

Beier, A. L., et al., eds. *The First Modern Society*. London: Cambridge University Press, 1989.

Beijing Review 34 (November 1991) and 39 (Special Issue January 1996).

Beiner, Ronald. *What's Matter with Liberalism?* Berkeley, CA: University of California Press, 1992.

Bell, Daniel A. "A Communitarian Critique of Authoritarianism," *Political Theory* 25:1 (1997):6–32.

Bell, Lynda S., et al., eds. *Negotiating Culture and Human Rights*. NY: Columbia University Press, 2001.

Bellah, Robert N., et al. *Habits of the Heart*. Berkeley, CA: University of California Press, 1985.

Benedict, Ruth. *Patterns of Culture*. Boston, MA: Houghton Mifflin, 1934.

Bentham, Jeremy. *An Introduction to the Principles of Morals and Legislation*. NY: Hafner Publishing Company, 1948.

Berting, Jan, et al., ed. *Human Rights in a Pluralist World*. Westport, CT: Meckler, 1990.

Bluhm, William T. "Political Theory and Ethics." In *Discourse on the Method* and *Meditations on First Philosophy*, edited by David Weissman. New Haven, CT: Yale University Press, 1996.

Boas, Franz. *The Mind of Primitive Man*. NY: Collier Books, 1963.

———. "Methods of Research." In *General Anthropology*, edited by Franz Boas. NY: D.C. Heath, 1938.

———, ed. *General Anthropology*. NY: D.C. Heath, 1938.

Bohannan, Paul. "*Conscience Collective* and Culture." In *Emile Durkheim, 1858–1917: A Collection of Essays,* edited by Kurt H. Wolff. Columbus, OH: Ohio State University Press, 1960.

Brenner, Robert. "Bourgeois Revolution and Transition to Capitalism." In *The First Modern Society,* edited by A. L. Beier, et al. London: Cambridge University Press, 1989.

Brett, Annabel S. *Liberty, Right and Nature*. Cambridge, London: Cambridge University Press, 1997.

Brown, Archie. "Introduction." In *Political Culture and Political Change in Communist States,* edited by Archie Brown and Jack Gray. NY: Holmes and Meier, 1977.

Brown, Archie, and Jack Gray, ed. *Political Culture and Political Change in Communist States.* NY: Holmes and Meier, 1977.

Burckhardt, Jacob. *The Civilization of the Renaissance in Italy.* London: G.G. Harrap, 929.

Burke, Edmund. *Selected Letters of Edmund Burke.* Chicago: University of Chicago Press, 1984.

———. *The Works of Edmund Burke,* Vol. 6. London: G. Bell, 1887.

Burke, Edmund, and Thomas Paine. *Reflections on the Revolution in France* and *The Rights of Man.* NY: Anchor Books, 1973.

Cameron, David. *The Social Thought of Rousseau and Burke.* Toronto: University of Toronto Press, 1973.

Chan, Joseph. "The Asian Challenge to Universal Human Rights." In *Human Rights and International Relations in the Asian Pacific Region,* edited by James T. H. Tang. London: Pinter, 1995.

———. "A Confucian Perspective on Human Rights for Contemporary China." In *The East Asian Challenge for Human Rights,* edited by Joanne R. Bauer and Daniel A. Bell. NY: Cambridge University Press, 1999.

Chang, King-yuh, ed. *Mainland China after the Thirteenth Party Congress.* Boulder, CO: Westview Press, 1990.

Chen Guidi and Chun Tao. *Zhongguo Nongmin Diaocha (An Investigation on the Chinese Peasant).* Beijing: Renmin Wenxue Chubanshe, 2004.

Chen Yizi. "The Decision Process behind the 1986–1989 Political Reforms." In *Decision-Making in Deng's China,* edited by Carol Lee Hamrin and Suisheng Zhao. Armonk, NY: M.E. Sharpe, 1995.

Chilton, Stephen. *Grounding Political Development.* Boulder, CO: Lynne Rienner, 1991.

Christie, Kenneth. "Regime Security and Human Rights in Southeast Asia." *Political Studies* 43 (1995):204–218.

Chu, Godwin C., and Yanan Ju. *The Great Wall in Ruins.* Albany, NY: SUNY Press, 1993.

Ci Hai. Shanghai: Shanghai Cishu Chubanshe, 1980.

Cicero, Marcus Tullius. *On the Commonwealth.* Indianapolis, IN: The Bobbs-Merrill Company, 1929.

———. *On the Law.* Cambridge, MA: Harvard University Press, 1928.

Cohen, Marshall, et al., ed. *Equality and Preferential Treatment.* Princeton, NJ: Princeton University Press, 1977.

Confucius. *Analects,* translated by Yang Bojun. Beijing: Zhonghua Shuju, 1980.

Cottingham, John, ed. *Descartes.* Oxford: Clarendon, 1998.

Cowan, Jane K., et al., ed. *Culture and Rights.* London: Cambridge University Press, 2001.

Cranston, Maurice. "Human Rights: Real and Supposed." In *Political Theory and the Rights of Man,* edited by D. D. Raphael. Bloomington, IN: Indiana University Press, 1967.

Crittenden, Jack. *Beyond Individualism.* NY: Oxford University Press, 1992.

Dahl, Robert A. *Democracy and Its Critics*. New Haven, CT: Yale University Press, 1989.

Dallmayr, Fred R. *Twilight of Subjectivity*. Amherst, MA: University of Massachusetts Press, 1981.

Daniel, Norman, ed. *Reading Rawls*. Stanford, CA: Stanford University Press, 1975.

Davis, Michael, ed. *Human Rights and Chinese Values*. Hong Kong: Oxford University Press, 1995.

Daxue (The Great Learning). In *Sishu (Four Books)*, with Chinese translation by Yang Bojun and English translation by James Legge. Hunan: Hunan Chubanche, 1992.

De Bary, Wm. Theodore. *The Liberal Tradition in China*. NY: Columbia University Press, 1983.

———. *Asian Values and Human Rights*. Cambridge, MA: Harvard University Press, 1998.

———. *The Trouble with Confucianism*. Cambridge, MA: Harvard University Press, 1991.

De Bary, Wm. Theodore, and Tu Wei-ming, eds. *Confucianism and Human Rights*. NY: Columbia University Press, 1998.

Dembour, Marie-Benedicte. "Following the Movement of a Pendulum." In *Culture and Rights*, edited by Jane K. Cowan, et al. London: Cambridge University Press, 2001.

Demosthenes. *Demosthenes against Timocrates*. Cambridge, MA: Harvard University Press, 1926.

Deng Xiaojun. *Rujia Sixiang Yu Minzhu Sixiang De Luoji Jiehe* (The Logical Link between Confucian and Democratic Thought). Chengdu, Sichuan: Sichuan Renmin Chubanshe, 1995.

D'Entreves, A. P. *Natural Law*. NY: Harper Torchbook, 1965.

Descartes, Rene. *Philosophic Works*. London: Cambridge University Press, 1911.

Diamond, Larry. "Introduction." In *Political Culture and Democracy in Developing Countries*, edited by Larry Diamond. Boulder, CO: Lynne Rienner, 1993.

———. *Developing Democracy*. Baltimore, MD: The Johns Hopkins University Press, 1999.

———, ed. *Political Culture and Democracy in Developing Countries*. Boulder, CO: Lynne Rienner, 1993.

DiPalma, Guiseppe. *To Craft Democracies*. Berkeley, CA: University of California Press, 1990.

Dittmer, Lowell. "Political Culture and Political Symbolism," *World Politics* 29 (1977):552–582.

Donnelly, Jack. "Human Rights and Asian Values: A Defense of 'Western' Universalism." In *The East Asian Challenge for Human Rights*, edited by Joanne R. Bauer and Daniel A. Bell. NY: Cambridge University Press, 1999.

Du Gangjian and Song Gang. "Relating Human Rights to Chinese Culture." In *Human Rights and Chinese Values*, edited by Michael Davis. Hong Kong: Oxford University Press, 1995.

Dumont, Louis. *Essays on Individualism*. Chicago: University of Chicago Press, 1986.

Durkheim, Emile. *The Elementary Forms of the Religious Life*. NY: The Free Press, 1965.

———. *Montesquieu and Rousseau: Forerunners of Sociology*. Ann Arbor, MI: University of Michigan Press, 1960.

———. *Sociology and Philosophy*. NY: The Free Press, 1974.

———. *The Division of Labor in Society*. NY: Macmillan, 1984.

Dworkin, Ronald. *Taking Rights Seriously*. Cambridge, MA: Harvard University Press, 1977.

———. "The Original Position." In *Reading Rawls*, edited by Norman Daniel. Stanford, CA: Stanford University Press, 1975.

———. "Rights as Trumps." In *Theories of Rights*, edited by Jeremy Waldron. London: Oxford University Press, 1984.

Edwards, R. Randle, et al., *Human Rights in Contemporary China*. NY: Columbia University Press, 1986.

Eide, Asbjorn. "The Universal Declaration in Space and Time." In *Human Rights in a Pluralist World*, edited by Jan Berting, et al. Westport, CT: Meckler, 1990.

Esherick, Joseph W., and Mary Backus Rankin, ed. *Chinese Local Elites and Patterns of Dominance*. Berkeley, CA: University of California Press, 1990.

Fabre, Cecile. *Social Rights under the Constitution*. Oxford: Clarendon Press, 2000.

Fairbank, John K. *The Great Chinese Revolutions*. Cambridge, MA: Harvard University Press, 1987.

Fei, Hsiao-Tung. *Peasant Life in China*. London: K. Paul, Trench, Trubner, 1939.

———. *From the Soil*. Berkeley, CA: University of California Press, 1992.

Feinberg, Joel. "The Nature and Value of Rights." *Journal of Value Inquiry* 4 (1970) :243–257.

Finnis, John. *Natural Law and Natural Rights*. London: Oxford University Press, 1980.

Fiss, Owen. "Groups and the Equal Protection Clause." In *Equality and Preferential Treatment*, edited by Marshall Cohen , et al. Princeton, NJ: Princeton University Press, 1977.

Flathman, Richard. "Introduction." In *Concepts in Social and Political Philosophy*, edited by Richard Flathman. NY: Macmillan, 1973.

———, ed. *Concepts in Social and Political Philosophy*. NY: Macmillan, 1973.

Fletcher, Anthony, and John Stevenson, ed. *Order and Disorder in Early Modern England*. London: Cambridge University Press, 1985.

Flew, Antony, ed. *Logic and Language*. Oxford, London: Basil Blackwell, 1952.

Forsythe, David P., and Patrice C. McMahon, ed. *Human Rights and Diversity*. Lincoln, NE: University of Nebraska Press, 2003.

Freeman, Michael. *Edmund Burke and the Critique of Political Radicalism*. Chicago: University of Chicago Press, 1980.

———. "Are There Collective Rights?" *Political Studies* 43 (1995 Special Issue):25–40.

French, Peter A., et al., ed. *Midwest Studies in Philosophy*, Vol. 7. Minneapolis, MN: University of Minnesota Press, 1982.

Frey, R. G. "Act-Utilitarianism, Consequentialism, and Moral Rights." In *Utility and Rights*, edited by R.G. Frey. Minneapolis, MN: University of Minnesota Press, 1984.

———, ed. *Utility and Rights*. Minneapolis, MN: University of Minnesota Press, 1984.

Fukuyama, Francis. *The End of History and the Last Man*. NY: The Free Press, 1992.

Gan Yang, et al., ed. *Wenhua: Zhongguo yu Shijie (Culture: China and the World)*, Vol. 3. Beijing: Sanlian Shudian, 1987.

Gao Qicai. *Chinese Customary Laws*. Changsha, Hunan: Hunan Chubanshe, 1995.

Geertz, Clifford. *The Interpretation of Cultures*. NY: Basic Books, 1973.

Gelderen, Martin van. "Liberty, Civic Rights and Duties in Sixteenth-Century Europe and the Rise of the Dutch Republic." In *The Individual in Political Theory and Practice,* edited by Janet Coleman. London: Clarendon Press, 1996.

Gewirth, Alan. "Why There Are Human Rights," *Social Theory* 11:2 (Summer 1984):235–248.

———. "The Basis and Content of Human Rights." In *Nomo XXIII: Human Rights,* edited by J. Ronald and John W. Chapman. NY: New York University Press, 1981.

Glendon, Mary Ann. *Rights Talk*. NY: The Free Press, 1991.

Goldhagen, Daniel Jonah. *Hitler's Willing Executioners*. NY: Alfred A. Knopf, 1996.

Grant, Ruth W. *John Locke's Liberalism*. Chicago: University of Chicago Press, 1987.

Gray, Jack. "China: Communism and Confucianism." In *Political Culture and Political Change in Communist States,* edited by Archie Brown and Jack Gray. NY: Holmes and Meier, 1977.

Grotius, Hugo. *The Rights of War and Peace*. NY: M.W. Dunne, 1901.

Guo Moruo. *Ten Critical Essays*. Beijing: The Oriental Press, 1996.

Hamilton, Gary, and Wang Zheng. "Introduction." In Fei Xiaotong, *From the Soil*. Berkeley, CA: University of California Press, 1992.

Hamrin, Carol Lee, and Suisheng Zhao, eds. *Decision-Making in Deng's China*. Armonk, NY: M.E. Sharpe, 1995.

Han Fei. *Han Fei Zi*. Shanghai: Shanghai Guji Chubanshe, 1989.

Hare, R. M. *Moral Thinking*. Oxford: Clarendon Press, 1981.

Hart, H. L. A. "The Ascription of Responsibility and Rights." In *Logic and Language,* edited by Antony Flew. Oxford, London: Basil Blackwell, 1952.

———. "Are There Any Natural Rights?" *Philosophical Review* 64:2 (April 1955):175-191.

———. *Essays on Bentham*. Oxford: Clarendon Press, 1982.

———. *Essays in Jurisprudence and Philosophy*. Oxford: Clarendon Press, 1983.

Hatch, Elvin. *Theories of Man and Culture*. NY: Columbia University Press, 1973.

Hayek, Friedrich A. *The Constitution of Liberty*. Chicago: University of Chicago Press, 1960.

He, Baogang. *The Democratization of China*. NY: Routledge, 1996.

He Huaihong. *Shixi Shehui Jiqi Jieti (The Hereditary Society and Its Disintegration)*. Beijing: Sanlian Shudian, 1996.

Held, David. "Democracy: From City-State to a Cosmopolitan Order?" *Political Studies* 40: (Special Issue 1992):10–30.

Hill, Christopher. *Reformation to Industrial Revolution*. London: Weidenfeld and Nicolson, 1967.

————. *The World Turned Upside Down*. London: Penguin Books, 1975.

Hoak, Dale, ed. *Tudor Political Culture*. London: Cambridge University Press, 1995.

Hobhouse, L. T. *Liberalism*. NY: Oxford University Press, 1964.

Hobbes. *Leviathan*. London: J. M. Dent and Sons, 1914.

————. *De Cive*. Oxford: Clarendon Press, 1983.

Hochschild, Jennifer L. *What's Fair?* Cambridge, MA: Harvard University Press, 1981.

Hohfeld, W.N. *Fundamental Legal Conceptions*. New Haven, CT: Yale University Press, 1919.

Hook, Brian, ed. *The Individual and the State in China*. Oxford: Clarendon Press, 1996.

Hsu, Francis L. K. *Under the Ancestors' Shadow*. Stanford, Calif.: Stanford University Press, 1971.

Hu Shi. *Zhongguo Zhexueshi Dagang (Basic Principles in Chinese Philosophy)*. Beijing: The Oriental Press, 1996.

Huang Guoguang. "*Renqing* and *Mianzi*: The Chinese Power Game." In *Xiandaihua yu Zhongguo Wenhua (Modernization and the Chinese Culture)*, edited by Qiao Jian. Tianjin: Tianjin Renmin Chubanshe, 1985.

Huntington, Samuel P. *Political Order in Changing Societies*. New Haven, CT: Yale University Press, 1968.

Hurwich, Judith, "Lineage and Kin in the Sixteenth-Century Aristocracy." In *The First Modern Society*, edited by A.L. Beier. London: Cambridge University Press, 1989.

Husak, Douglas. "Why There Are No Human Rights." *Social Theory* 11:2 (Summer 1984):125–141.

Infantino, Lorenzo. *Individualism in Modern Thought*. NY: Routledge, 1998.

James, Mervyn. *Family, Lineage and Civil Society*. Oxford: Clarendon Press, 1974.

James, Susan. "Internal and External in the Works of Descartes." In *Philosophy in an Age of Pluralism*, edited by James Tully. NY: Cambridge University Press, 1994.

Jeong, Yeonsik. *Interest Representation in Socialist Market Economies*. Columbia, SC: University of South Carolina, Ph.D. dissertation, 1997.

Johnston, David. *The Idea of a Liberal Theory*. Princeton, NJ: Princeton University Press, 1994.

Kaballa, Sidgi. "Human Rights and Democratization in Africa." *Political Studies* 43 (Special Issue 1995):189–203.

Kaplan, David, and Robert A. Manners. *Culture Theory*. Eaglewood Cliffs, NJ: Prentice-Hall, 1972.

Kateb, George. *The Inner Ocean*. Ithaca, NY: Cornell University Press, 1992.

Kausikan, Bilahari. "An East Approach to Human Rights." *The Buffalo Journal of International Law* 2:2 (Winter):263–283.

Kavka, Gregory S. "Right Reason and Natural Law in Hobbes' Ethics." In *Thomas Hobbes: Critical Assessments*, Vol. 2, edited by Preston King. London: Routledge, 1993.

Kent, Ann. *Between Freedom and Subsistence*. Hong Kong: Oxford University Press, 1993.

Kim Dae Jung. "Is Culture Destiny?" *Foreign Affairs* 73:6 (Nov/Dec):189–94.

Kim, Young C. "The Concept of Political Culture in Comparative Politics." *Journal of Politics* 26 (1964):313–336.

King, Ambrose. "*Kuan-hsi* and Network Building." *Daedalus* 120:2 (Spring 1991):63–84.

King, Preston, ed. *Thomas Hobbes: Critical Assessments,* Vol. 2. London: Routledge, 1993.

Klosko, George. *The Principle of Fairness and Political Obligation.* Lanham, MD: Rowman & Littlefield, 1992.

Kreml, William P. *Psychology, Relativism and Politics.* NY: New York University Press, 1991.

Kroeber, A. L., and Clyde Kluckhohn. *Culture: A Critical Review of Concepts and Definitions.* NY: Vintage Books, 1963.

Kukathas, Chandran, and Philip Pettit. *Rawls.* Stanford, CA: Stanford University Press, 1990.

Kuper, Adam, ed. *The Social Anthropology of Radcliffe-Brown.* London: Routledge & Kegan Paul, 1977.

Kymlicka, Will. *Liberalism, Community and Culture.* NY: Oxford University Press, 1989.

Lakoff, Sanford. *Democracy.* Boulder, CO: Westview Press, 1996.

Langford, Paul. *Public Life and the Propertied Englishman.* London: Clarendon Press, 1991.

Lao Tzu. *Tao Te Ching.* In *Sources of Chinese Tradition,* edited by Wm. Theodore de Bary, et al. NY: Columbia University Press, 1960.

Lapalombara, Joseph. *Democracy, Italian Style.* New Haven, CT: Yale University Press, 1987.

Laslett, Peter. "Introduction." In John Locke, *Two Treatises of Government.* NY: Cambridge University Press, 1963.

Lawler, Peter A. "The Human Condition: Tocqueville's Debt to Rousseau and Pascal." In *Liberty, Equality and Democracy,* edited by Eduardo Nolla. NY: New York University Press, 1992.

Lee Kuan Yew (with Fareed Zakaria). "Culture is Destiny." *Foreign Affairs* 73:2 (March/April 1994):109–126.

Lee, Seung-Hwan. "Was There a Concept of Rights in Confucian Virtue-Based Morality?" *Journal of Chinese Philosophy* 19 (Sept. 1992):3:241–262.

Lehman, Edward W. "On the Concept of Political Culture." *Social Forces* 50 (March 1972):361–370.

Li, Liangjiang, and Kevin O'Brien. "Chinese Villagers and Popular Resistance" Paper presented at the 24th Sino-American Conference on Contemporary China, June 15–17, 1995.

Li Qinde. *Zhongguo Diyu Wenhua (Regional Cultures in China).* Taiyuan, Shanxi: Shanxi Gaoxiao Lianhe Chubanshe, 1995.

Li Shidong et al., eds. *Ling Yizhong Qinshou'(Another Kind of Beast).* Beijing: Wenhua Yishu Chubanshe, 2001.

Li Yiyuan. "Zhongguo Chuantong Yuzhouguan yu Xiandai Qiye Xingwei (The Conception of the Universe in Traditional China and Modern Business Behavior)." In *Zhongguoren de Guannian yu Xingwei (The Ideas and*

Behaviors of the Chinese), edited by Qian Jian and Pan Neigu. Tianjin: Tianjin Renmin Chubanshe, 1995.

Li Zehou. *Zhongguo Gudai Sixiang Shilun (Essays on Ancient Chinese Thought)*. Beijing: Renmin Chubanshe, 1985.

Li Zhishui. *The Private Life of Chairman Mao*. NY: Random House, 1994.

Liang Qichao. *Xianqin Zhengzhi Sixiangshi (A History of Pre-Qin Political Thought)*. Beijing: The Oriental Press, 1996.

Liang Shumin. *Zhongguo Wenhua Yaoyi (The Essentials of Chinese Culture)*. Shanghai: Xuelin Chubanshe, 1986.

Lieberthal, Kenneth, and David Lampton, eds. *Bureaucracy, Politics, and Decision-Making in Post-Mao China*. Ann Arbor, MI: University of Michigan Press, 1992.

Liji (Book of Rituals). In *Sishu Wujing (Four Books and Five Classics)*, edited by Zhu Xi. Tianjin, China: Tianjin Guji Shudian, 1988.

Liu, Hui-chen Wang. "An Analysis of Chinese Clan Rules." In *Confucianism and Chinese Civilization*, edited by Arthur F. Wright. NY: Atheneum, 1964.

Liu, Zehua. *Zhongguo Zhengzhi Sixiangshi (A History of Chinese Political Thought)*, Vol. 1. Hangzhou, Zhijiang: Zhijiang Renmin Chubanshe, 1996.

Lively, Jack. *The Social and Political Thought of Alexis de Tocqueville*. Oxford: Clarendon Press, 1962.

Locke, John. *Two Treatises of Government*. NY: Cambridge University Press, 1963.

———. *Essays on the Laws of Nature*. Oxford: Clarendon, 1954.

Lukes, Steven. *Individualism*. Oxford: Blackwell, 1973.

Lyons, David, "Rights, Claimants, and Beneficiaries." *American Philosophical Quarterly* 6:3 (July 1969):173–185.

Macfarlane, Alan. *The Origins of English Individualism*. NY: Cambridge University Press, 1979.

———. *The Culture of Capitalism*. London: Basil Blackwell, 1987.

Mack, Mary Peter, ed. *A Bentham Reader*. NY: Pegasus, 1969.

Macpherson, C. B. *The Political Theory of Possessive Individualism*. Oxford: Clarendon, 1962.

Malinowski, Bronislaw. *A Scientific Theory of Culture and Other Essays*. Chapel Hill, NC: University of North Carolina Press, 1944.

Manet, Pierre. *An Intellectual History of Liberalism*. Princeton, NJ: Princeton University Press, 1994.

Mansbridge, Jane. *Beyond Adversary Democracy*. NY: Basic Books, 1980.

Maritain, Jacques. *Three Reformers*. London: Sheed & Ward, 1947.

Markie, Peter. "The Cogito and Its Importance." In *Descartes,* edited by John Cottingham. Oxford: Clarendon, 1998.

Martin. Rex, *Rawls and Rights*. Lawrence, KS: University of Kansas Press, 1985.

Marx, Karl. *Economic and Philosophic Manuscript of 1844*. NY: International Publishers, 1964.

May, John. "Defining Democracy: A Bid for Coherence and Consensus." *Political Studies* 26:1 (March 1978):1–14.

McCloskey, H. J. "Rights." *Philosophical Quarterly* 15:59 (April 1965):115–127.

———. "Human Needs, Rights, and Political Values." *American Philosophical Quarterly* 13 (1976):1–18.

McGrade, Arthur Stephen. "Ockham and the Birth of Individual Rights." In *Authority and Power,* edited by Brian Tierney and Peter Lineham. London: Cambridge University Press, 1980.

Mencius. *Mencius.* In *Sishu (Four Books),* with Chinese translation by Yang Bojun and English translation by James Legge. Changsha, Hunan: Hunan Chubanshe, 1992.

Mill, J. S. *Utilitarianism, On Liberty, and Considerations on Representative Government.* London: J.M. Dent and Sons, 1972.

———. *On Liberty and Other Writings,* edited by Stefan Collini. London: Cambridge University Press, 1989.

Montesquieu, Charles de Secondat. *The Spirit of the Laws.* London: Cambridge University Press, 1989.

Moore, Barrington, Jr. *Social Origins of Dictatorship and Democracy.* Boston: Beacon Press, 1967.

Morris, Colin. *The Discovery of the Individual.* NY: Harper & Row, 1972.

Mulhall, Stephen, and Adam Swift. *Liberals and Communitarians.* London: Basil Blackwell, 1996.

Nagel, Thomas. "Hobbes' Concept of Obligation." In *Thomas Hobbes: Critical Assessments,* Vol. 2, edited by Preston King. London: Routledge, 1993.

———. "Rawls on Justice." In *Reading Rawls,* edited by Norman Daniel. Stanford, CA: Stanford University Press, 1975.

Nathan, Andrew. *China's Crisis.* NY: Columbia University Press, 1990.

———. *China's Transition.* NY: Columbia University Press, 1997.

———. "Sources of Chinese Rights Thinking." In R. Randle Edwards, et al. *Human Rights in Contemporary China.* NY: Columbia University Press, 1986.

———. "Political Rights in Chinese Constitutions." In R. Randle Edwards, et al. *Human Rights in Contemporary China.* NY: Columbia University Press, 1986.

Nathan, Andrew J., and Tianjian Shi. "Cultural Requisites for Democracy in China." *Daedalus* 122:2 (Spring 1993):95–124.

Niu Yong, et al., *Zhongguo Renquan de Baozhang yu Fazhan (The Protection and Development of Human Rights in China).* Taiyuan, Shanxi: Shanxi Gaoxiao Lianhe Chubanshe, 1992.

Nolla, Eduardo, ed. *Liberty, Equality and Democracy.* NY: New York University Press, 1992.

Nozick, Robert. *Anarchy, State and Utopia.* NY: Basic Books, 1974.

Oakeshott, Michael. "Introduction to *Leviathan.*" In Michael Oakeshott, *Rationalism in Politics and Other Essays.* Indianapolis, IN: Liberty Press, 1991.

Okin, Susan Moller. *Justice, Gender and the Family.* NY: Basic Books, 1989.

Panizza, Francisco. "Human Rights in the Process of Transition and Consolidation of Democracy in Latin America." *Political Studies* 43 (Special Issue 1995):168-188.

Parekh, Bhikhu. "The Cultural Particularity of Liberal Democracy." *Political Studies* 40: (Special Issue 1992):160–175.

Parish, William L., and Martin K. Whyte. *Village and Family in Contemporary China.* Chicago: University of Chicago Press, 1978.

Packer, Corinne. "African Women, Traditions, and Human Rights." In *Human Rights and Diversity,* edited by David P. Forsythe and Patrice C. McMahon. Lincoln, NE: University of Nebraska Press, 2003.

Parsons, Talcott. *The Structure of Social Action,* Vol. 1 and 2. NY: The Free Press, 1949.

———. "Introduction to 'Culture and the Social System.'" In *Theories of Society,* edited by Talcott Parsons, et al. NY: Free Press, 1961.

———, et al., ed. *Theories of Society.* NY: Free Press, 1961.

———. "Values, Motives and Systems of Action." In *Toward a General Theory of Action,* edited by Talcott Parsons and Edward A. Shils. Cambridge, MA: Harvard University Press, 1951.

Parsons, Talcott, and Edward A. Shils, ed. *Toward a General Theory of Action.* Cambridge, MA: Harvard University Press, 1951.

Pateman, Carole. "The Civic Culture: A Philosophic Critique." In *The Civic Culture Revisited,* edited by Gabried A. Almond and Sidney Verba. Newbury Park, CA: Sage Publications, 1989.

———. *Participation and Democratic Theory.* NY: Cambridge University Press, 1970.

Pennock, J. Ronald, and John W. Chapman, ed. *Nomo XXIII: Human Rights.* NY: New York University Press, 1981.

Pennington, Kenneth. *The Prince and the Law, 1200–1600.* Berkeley, CA: University of California Press, 1993.

Pitkin, Hanna F. "Obligation and Consent II." *American Political Science Review* 60 (March 1966):39–52.

Plamenatz, J. P. *Consent, Freedom and Political Obligation.* NY: Oxford University Press, 1968.

Plato. *The Republic.* Indianapolis, IN: Hackett Publishing Company, 1974.

———. *The Sophist and the Statesman.* London: Thomas Nelson and Sons, 1961.

———. *The Laws.* NY: Basic Books, 1980.

Plutarch. *Plutarch's Lives.* London: J.M. Dent and Sons, 1970.

Pollis, Adamantia, and Peter Schwab, ed. *Human Rights.* NY: Praeger, 1979.

Pollock, F.H., and F.W. Maitland. *The History of English Law.* Cambridge, London: University Press, 1911.

Putnam, Robert D. *Making Democracy Work.* Princeton, NJ: Princeton University Press, 1993.

Pye, Lucian W. "Introduction." In *Political Culture and Political Development,* edited by Lucian W. Pye and Sidney Verba. Princeton, NJ: Princeton University Press, 1965.

———. *The Spirit of Chinese Politics.* Cambridge, MA: MIT Press, 1968.

———. *The Dynamics of Chinese Politics.* Cambridge, MA: Oelgeschlager, Gunn & Hain, 1981.

———. *The Mandarin and the Cadre.* Ann Arbor, MI: University of Michigan Press, 1988.

———. "The State and the Individual." In *The Individual and the State in China,* edited by Brian Hook. Oxford: Clarendon Press, 1996.

Qian Mu. *Zhongguo Lidai Zhengzhi Deshi (Political Dynamics and Failures in Dynastic China).* Taipei, Taiwan: Dongda Tushu Gongsi, 1977.

Qian Xun, *Xianqin Ruxue (Pre-Qin Confucianism)*. Shenyang, Liaoning: Laoning Jiaoyu Chubanshe, 1991.

Qiao Jian, ed. *Xiandaihua yu Zhongguo Wenhua (Modernization and the Chinese Culture)*. Tianjin: Tianjin Renmin Chubanshe, 1985.

Qiao Jian and Pan Naigu, ed. *Zhongguoren de Guannian yu Xingwei (The Ideas and Behaviors of the Chinese)*. Tianjin: Tianjin Renmin Chubanshe, 1995.

Radcliffe-Brown, A. R. *Structure and Function in Primitive Society*. Glencoe, Ill: The Free Press, 1952.

Raphael, D. D. "Human Rights, Old and New." In *Political Theory and the Rights of Man*, edited by D. D. Raphael. Bloomington, IN: Indiana University Press, 1967.

———, ed. *Political Theory and the Rights of Man*. Bloomington, IN: Indiana University Press, 1967.

Rawls, John. *A Theory of Justice*. Cambridge, MA: Harvard University Press, 1971.

———. "The Law of Peoples." In *On Human Rights*, edited by Stephen Shute and Susan Hurley. NY: BasicBooks, 1993.

Raz, Joseph. *The Morality of Freedom*. Oxford: Clarendon Press, 1986.

———. "On the Nature of Rights," *Mind* 93 (1984) :194–214.

———. "Rights-Based Moralities." In *Theories of Rights*, edited by Jeremy Waldron. London: Oxford University Press, 1984.

———. "Liberalism, Autonomy, and Politics of Neutral Concern." In *Midwest Studies in Philosophy*, Vol. 7, edited by Peter A. French, et al. Minneapolis, MN: University of Minnesota Press, 1982.

Renteln, Alison Dundes. *International Human Rights*. Newbury Park, CA: Sage, 1990.

Rosemont, Henry, Jr. "Human Rights: A Bill of Worries." In *Confucianism and Human Rights*, edited by Wm. Theodore de Bary and Tu Wei-ming. NY: Columbia University Press, 1998.

Rosenblum, Nancy L., ed. *Liberalism and the Moral Life*. Cambridge, MA: Harvard University Press, 1989.

Rousseau, Jean-Jacques. *The Government of Poland*. Indianapolis, IN: Hackett Publishing, 1985.

———. *The Social Contract and Discourse*. London: J.M. Dent and Sons, 1973.

———. *Emile*. NY: Basic Books, 1979.

Ruan Ming. *Chronicle of an Empire*. Boulder, CO: Westview Press, 1994.

Rustow, Dankwart A. "Transitions to Democracy: Toward a Dynamic Model." In *Transitions to Democracy*, edited by Lisa Anderson. NY: Columbia University Press, 1999.

Sandel, Michael J. *Liberalism and the Limits of Justice*. Cambridge: Cambridge University Press, 1998.

Sartori, Giovanni. *The Theory of Democracy Revisited*. Chatham, NJ: Chatham House, 1987.

Saward, Michael. "Democratic Theory and Indices of Democratization." In *Defining and Measuring Democracy*, edited by David Beetham. London: Sage Publications, 1994.

Scanlon, T. M. "Rights, Goals, and Fairness." In *Theories of Rights*, edited by Jeremy Waldron. London: Oxford University Press, 1984.

Schroeder, Ralph. *Max Weber and the Sociology of Culture*. London: Sage Publications, 1992.

Schumpeter, Joseph A. *Capitalism, Socialism and Democracy*. NY: Harper & Row, 1942.

Shambaugh, David. "Deng Xiaoping: The Politician." In *Deng Xiaoping: Portrait of a Chinese Statesman*, edited by David Shambaugh. Oxford: Clarendon Press, 1995.

———, ed. *Deng Xiaoping: Portrait of a Chinese Statesman*. Oxford: Clarendon Press, 1995.

Shanahan, Daniel. *Toward a Genealogy of Individualism*. Amherst, MA: University of Massachusetts Press, 1992.

Shangshu (Book of History), translated by Gu Baotian. Changchun, Jilin: Jilin Wenshi Chubanshe, 1995.

Shapiro, Ian. *The Evolution of Rights in Liberal Theory*. NY: Cambridge University Press, 1986.

Shapiro, Michael, ed. *Language and Politics*. NY: New York University Press, 1984.

Shi, Tianjian. *Political Participation in Beijing*. Cambridge, MA: Harvard University Press, 1997.

Shijing (Book of Poetry). In *Sishu Wujing (Four Books and Five Classics)*, edited by Zhu Xi. Tianjin, China: Tianjin Guji Shudian, 1988.

Shklar, Judith. "The Liberalism of Fear." In *Liberalism and the Moral Life*, edited by Nancy L. Rosenblum. Cambridge, MA: Harvard University Press, 1989.

Shue, Henry. *Basic Rights*. Princeton, NJ: Princeton University Press, 1980.

Shute, Stephen, and Susan Hurley, ed. *On Human Rights*. NY: BasicBooks, 1993.

Sigmund, Paul. *Natural Law in Political Thought*. Lanham, MD: University of America Press, 1971.

Simmon, A. John. *The Lockean Theory of Rights*. Princeton, NJ: Princeton University Press, 1992.

Simon, Herbert. "Human Nature in Politics." *American Political Science Review* 79:2: (1984):293–304.

Skinner, Quentin. *The Foundations of Modern Political Thought*. NY: Cambridge University Press, 1978.

———. *Liberty before Liberalism*. London: Cambridge University Press, 1998.

———. "Hobbes' 'Leviathan.'" In *Thomas Hobbes: Critical Assessments*, Vol. 2, edited by Preston King. London: Routledge, 1993.

Solomon, Richard H. *Mao's Revolution and the Chinese Political Culture*. Berkeley, CA: University of California Press, 1971.

Spence, Jonathan. *The Search for Modern China*. NY: W. W. Norton & Company, 1990.

Sperber, Dan. *Rethinking Symbolism*. London: Cambridge University Press, 1975.

Stone, Lawrence. "Goodbye to Nearly All That." *New York Review of Books*, April 19, 1979, 40–41.

Strauss, Leo. *Natural Right and History*. Chicago: University of Chicago Press, 1953.

Sun Longji. *Zhongguo Wenhua de Shenceng Jiegou (The Underlying Structures of Chinese Culture)*. Taipei, Taiwan: Tangshan Chubanshe, 1983.

Svensson, Marina. *Debating Human Rights in China*. Lanham, MD: Rowman & Littlefield, 2002.

Swart, Koenraad. "Individualism in the Mid-19th Century." *Journal of the History of Ideas* 23: (1962):77–90.

Tan Qixiang. "Zhongguo Wenhua de Shijian Chayi he Diyu Chayi, (Temporal and Geographical Differences in Chinese Culture)." In *Zhongguo Chuantong Wenhua Zaijiantao* (Reevaluating Chinese Traditional Culture), Vol. 1. Beijing: Sanlian Shudian, 1987.

Tang, James T. H., ed. *Human Rights and International Relations in the Asian Pacific Region.* London: Pinter, 1995.

Tatsuo, Inoue. "Liberal Democracy and Asian Orientalism." In *The East Asian Challenge for Human Rights,* edited by Susan R. Bauer and Daniel A. Bell. NY: Cambridge University Press, 1999.

Taylor, A. E. "The Ethical Doctrine of Hobbes." In *Thomas Hobbes: Critical Assessments,* Vol. 2, edited by Preston King. London: Routledge, 1993.

Taylor, Charles. *Philosophical Argument.* Cambridge, MA: Harvard University Press, 1995.

———. "Conditions of an Unforced Consensus on Human Rights." In *The East Asian Challenge for Human Rights,* edited by Susan R. Bauer and Daniel A. Bell. NY: Cambridge University Press, 1999.

Tellegen-Couperus, Olga. *A Short History of Roman Law.* NY: Routledge, 1993.

Thompson, Michael, et al., *Cultural Theory.* Boulder, CO: Westview Press, 1990.

Tierney, Brian. "Tuck on Rights: Some Medieval Problems." *History of Political Thought* 4:3 (Winter 1983):429–441.

———. "Origins of Natural Rights Language." *History of Political Thought* 10:4 (Winter 1989):615–646.

Tierney, Brian, and Peter Lineham, ed. *Authority and Power.* London: Cambridge University Press, 1980.

Tittler, Robert. "Political Culture and the Built Environment of the English County Town, c. 1542–1620." In *Tudor Political Culture,* edited by Dale Hoak. London: Cambridge University Press, 1995.

Tocqueville, Alexis de. *Democracy in America,* Vol 1 and 2. NY: Vintage Books, 1945.

———. *The Old Regime and the French Revolution.* NY: Doubleday & Company, 1955.

Toulmin, Stephen. "Descartes in His Time." In *Discourse on the Method and Meditations on First Philosophy,* edited by David Weissman. New Haven, CT: Yale University Press, 1996.

Townsend, James R. *Political Participation in Communist China.* Berkeley, CA: University of California Press, 1967.

Troeltsch, Ernst. *The Social Teaching of the Christian Churches.* NY: Macmillan, 1931.

Tu, Wei-ming. *Centrality and Commonality.* Albany, NY: State University of New York Press, 1988.

Tuck, Richard. *Natural Rights Theories.* London: Cambridge University Press, 1979.

Tucker, Robert C. "Culture, Political Culture, and Communist Society." *Political Science Quarterly* 88 (June 1973):173–190.

Tully, James. *An Approach to Political Philosophy: Locke in Contexts.* London: Cambridge University Press, 1993.

————. *A Discourse on Property.* NY: Cambridge University Press, 1980.

————. *Philosophy in an Age of Pluralism.* NY: Cambridge University Press, 1994.

Tussman, Joseph. *Obligation and the Body Politic.* NY: Oxford University Press, 1960.

Twiss, Sumner B. "A Constructive Framework for Discussing Confucianism and Human Rights." In *Confucianism and Human Rights,* edited by Wm. Theodore de Bary and Tu Wei-ming. NY: Columbia University Press, 1998.

Tylor, Edward, *Primitive Culture,* Vol. 1. London: J. Murray, 1920.

Ullmann, Walter. *The Individual and Society in the Middle Ages.* Baltimore, MD: The Johns Hopkins University Press, 1966.

Underdown, David. *A Freeborn People.* Oxford: Clarendon Press, 1996.

————. "The Taming of the Scold: the Enforcement of Patriarchal Authority in Early Modern England." In *Order and Disorder in Early Modern England,* edited by Anthony Fletcher and John Stevenson. London: Cambridge University Press, 1985.

Von Leyden, Wolfgang. "Introduction." In John Locke, *Essays on the Laws of Nature.* Oxford: Clarendon, 1954.

Wagner, Roy. *The Invention of Culture.* Chicago: University of Chicago Press, 1975.

Waldron, Jeremy, ed. *'Nonsense upon Stilts.'* London: Methuen, 1987.

————. ed. *Theories of Rights.* London: Oxford University Press, 1984.

————. "Can Communal Goods Be Human Rights?" *Archives Europeennes de Sociologie* 28:2 (1987):296–322.

Wan, Ming. *Human Rights in Chinese Foreign Relations.* Philadelphia, PA: University of Pennsylvania Press, 2001.

Warrender, Howard. *The Political Philosophy of Hobbes.* Oxford: Clarendon Press, 1957.

————. "Hobbes' Conception of Morality." In *Thomas Hobbes: Critical Assessments,* Vol. 2, edited by Preston King. London: Routledge, 1993.

Wasserstrom, Richard. "Rights, Human Rights and Racial Discrimination." *Journal of Philosophy* 61:20 (October 1964):628–641.

Watt, Ian, *The Rise of the Novel.* Berkeley, CA: University of California Press, 1957.

Weber, Max. *The Methodology of the Social Sciences.* NY: The Free Press, 1949.

————. *The Protestant Ethic and the Spirit of Capitalism.* London: Routledge, 1930.

————. *The Theory of Social and Economic Organization.* NY: The Free Press, 1947.

Wei Hongyun, ed. *Jidong Nongcun Shehui Diaocha Yu Yanjiu (An Investigative Study of Country Life in Eastern Hebei Province).* Tianjin: Tianjin Renmin Chubanshe 1996.

Weissman, David. "Introduction" and "Metaphysics." In *Discourse on the Method and Meditations on First Philosophy,* edited by David Weissman. New Haven, CT: Yale University Press, 1996.

Weissman, David, ed. *Discourse on the Method and Meditations on First Philosophy.* New Haven, CT: Yale University Press, 1996.

White, Alan R. *Rights.* Oxford: Clarendon, 1984.

White, Leslie A. "The Concept of Culture." *American Anthropologist* 61:1 (1959):97–122.

————. *The Science of Culture.* NY: Farrar, Straws, 1949.

White, Stephen. "The USSR: Patterns of Autocracy and Industrialism." In *Political Culture and Political Change in Communist States,* edited by Archie Brown and Jack Gray (NY: Holmes and Meier, 1977.

Wolff, Kurt H., ed. *Emile Durkheim, 1858–1917: A Collection of Essays.* Columbus, OH: Ohio State University Press, 1960.

Womank, Brantly. "Party-State Democracy: A Theoretical Exploration." In *Mainland China after the Thirteenth Party Congress,* edited by King-yuh Chang. Boulder, CO: Westview Press, 1990.

Wright, Arthur F., ed. *Confucianism and Chinese Civilization.* NY: Atheneum, 1964.

Xenophon. *The Constitution of Lacedaemonians.* London: George Bell and Sons, 1908.

Xia Yong. *Renquan Gainian de Qiyuan (The Origins of the Concept of Human Rights).* Beijing: Zhongguo Zhengfa Daxue Chubanshe, 1992.

Xu Yangjie. *Song-Ming Jiazu Zhidu Shilun (A Historical Study of the System of the Kinship Family in the Song and Ming Dynasties).* Beijing: Zhonghua Shuju, 1995.

Xun Zi. *Xun Zi,* translated by Zhang Jue. Shanghai: Shanghai Guji Chubanshe, 1995.

Yan Jiaqi. "The Nature of Chinese Authoritarianism." In *Decision-Making in Deng's China,* edited by Carol Lee Hamrin and Suisheng Zhao. Armonk, NY: M. E. Sharpe, 1995.

Yang, Mayfair Mei-hui. *Gifts, Favors, and Banquets.* Ithaca, NY: Cornell University Press, 1994.

Yolton, John W. "Locke on the Law of Nature." In *John Locke: Critical Assessments,* Vol. 2, edited by Richard Ashcraft. NY: Routledge, 1991.

Yu, Dunkang. "Rujia Lunli Yu Zhongguo Chuantong Wenhua (The Confucianist Ethic and the Chinese Traditional Culture)." In *Wenhua: Zhongguo yu Shijie (Culture: China and the World),* Vol. 3, edited by Gan Yang, et al. Beijing: Sanlian Shudian, 1987.

Yu Yingshi. *Zhongguo Sixiang Chuantong de Xiandai Quanshi (A Contemporary Interpretation of Chinese Intellectual Tradition).* Nanjing, Jiangsu: Jiangsu Renmin Chubanshe, 1995.

Yue Qingping. "Xiao yu Xiandaihua (Filial Piety and Modernization)." In *Zhongguoren de Guannian yu Xingwei (The Ideas and Behaviors of the Chinese),* edited by Qiao Jian and Pan Naigu. Tianjin, China: Tianjin Chubanshe, 1995.

Zhao Jihui, et al., *Zhongguo Ruxueshi (The History of Confucianism in China).* Zhengzhou, Henan: Zhongzhou Guji Chubanshe, 1991.

Zhao, Suisheng. "The Structure of Authority and Decision-Making." In *Decision-Making in Deng's China,* edited by Carol Lee Hamrin and Suisheng Zhao. Armonk, NY: M. E. Sharpe, 1995.

Zhong, Yang, et al., "Political Views from Below." *PS: Political Science & Politics* 30:3 (September 1997):476–477.

Zhongyong (The Doctrine of the Mean). In *Sishu (Four Books),* with Chinese translated by Yang Bojun and English translation by James Legge. Changsha, Hunan: Hunan Chubanshe, 1992.

Zucker, Ross. *Democratic Distributive Justice.* NY: Cambridge University Press, 2001.

Zuo Zhuan (Zuo's Interpretation of the Spring and Autumn Annals), translated by Chen Xiangmin, et al. Zhengzhou, Henan: Zhongzhou Guji Chubanshe, 1993.

Index

Printed in the United States
by Baker & Taylor Publisher Services